CHRIST AMONG US

CHRIST AMONG US

A Modern Presentation
of the
Catholic Faith

(Second Revised Edition)

by

ANTHONY J. WILHELM

PAULIST PRESS
New York   Paramus

NIHIL OBSTAT:
Rev. Edward J. Ciuba
Censor Librorum

IMPRIMATUR:
Most Rev. Peter L. Gerety, D.D.
Archbishop of Newark

September 14, 1975

Library of Congress
Catalog Card Number: 72-86595

ISBN 0-8091-1746-0

Published by Paulist Press
Editorial Office: 1865 Broadway, N.Y., N.Y. 10023
Business Office: 400 Sette Drive, Paramus, New Jersey 07652

Printed and bound in the
United States of America

Contents

Contents

Preface

In the history of mankind there have been a few truly unique moments and special places—occasions when men of stature claimed an encounter with one who is beyond, a divine, transcendent reality.

On these occasions great movements have started that have affected billions of human lives and have changed our world. They have given men hope, courage, compassion, and led them to dream of life beyond.

This is the story of the farthest-reaching claim to contact with divinity in human history. It is a story of real men and actual events—some of the most striking men and most moving events of all time. It is particularly the story of the one who has been called history's outstanding personality, Jesus Christ.

We offer here that to which countless billions, like St. Paul, have dedicated their lives:

> To announce the secret hidden for long ages and through many generations, but now disclosed to God's people . . . to make known how rich and glorious it is among all nations. The secret is this: *Christ in you—among you the hope of glory to come* (Colossians 1, 26-27).

This story of Christ among us is a study of Catholic faith. Catholicism had a Council several years ago, as almost everyone knows, and the Church today is different. We hope that the image and personality of Christ will now begin to shine more clearly through us poor humans who are the Church.

Today while many feel that God is a dead issue in their lives, others believe that this story can—and has—changed their lives. Many of these feel that the Church is now in its most unsettling but promising period since the beginning of institutional Christianity. Perhaps the reader (particularly one who has heard the story before) will find in this contemporary presentation a new hope and a new purpose.

For one who comes to this book seeking something, only two

1

things are necessary: an open mind and a willingness to take a
risk. An open mind, because unless one is open and true to oneself, life is a waste. A willingness to take a risk because one may
come to believe. The believer becomes changed. Many things
may have to be renounced and life itself staked upon something
unseen. Friends, even loved ones, often do not understand. This
can be deeply upsetting. But unless it is tried, one will never
know the fulfillment it can bring.

The sensation of a swim in cool water cannot be explained to
someone who is unwilling to plunge in. A beautiful house cannot
be appreciated by looking at it only from a distance. The experience of love can never be had by one who is unwilling to risk
loving. So, too, the deep joys of belief and divine love come only
to one who is willing to try—to read, to persevere, to practice as
best he can.

Some Words about Using This Book....
    (especially for those who will use it as a guide in teaching
others)
We have tried to make this book...
    Useful for different types of people: The sentences in bold
print give a summary of the paragraph following. One who wants
merely to skim can read these. The paragraphs in small print are
for those who want to go more deeply into a particular subject;
these may be referred to later, for instance during a catechumenate, when more detailed information is desired. If this book is
used as the source for a class presentation, a good method would
be to combine two chapters as one lecture.
    Progressive: One thing builds on another, and important themes
are repeated so their meaning will be grasped more fully. The
DISCUSSION at the end of each chapter is meant not only to
help one grasp the point of the chapter, but to stimulate to further insights. The sections entitled FURTHER READING and
FURTHER VIEWING give suggestions for current books and
movies pertaining to the subject matter of the particular chapter;
the titles given are not meant to be an exhaustive list but only
representative ones that have come to the author's attention. The
asterisks marking book titles mean: * good general treatment for
anyone; ** for those who want to go a bit deeper.
    Relevant to daily life: Each chapter has a section called DAILY
LIVING. This contains practical applications of the preceding
teaching. The moral teaching of the Church is integrated into
these sections, instead of being left to the end of the book. The
PERSONAL REFLECTION which ends each chapter gives the
reader a chance to do something about what he has read.

Conciliar: This is a presentation of Catholicism in the light of Vatican Council II, the great event in the Church of our century. The teachings of the Council either form the basis of what is given here, or are incorporated into the presentation. Obviously only the highlights of most of the conciliar documents could be included.

Scriptural: The bible is the great legacy of all Christianity; there is no better way to learn Christ's teaching than through its words. Whenever possible, therefore, this book teaches from the bible. The use of a bible with this book is necessary. The Revised Standard Version, with the Apocrypha, has been used for most of the quotations herein.

Liturgical: The liturgy of the Church sums up its purpose on earth; it is the great way we make contact with God in the Church. Sections called IN THE LITURGY are incorporated throughout the book, so the reader can see how our worship expresses our belief.

Ecumenical: Among the greatest achievements of our time is that of Christian groups coming to appreciate one another, and a growing mutual respect among all men of good will. This book has tried whenever possible to present our common Christian teaching, and to give what is specifically Catholic as positively as possible while showing an appreciation of other viewpoints, non-Christian as well as Christian.

Transitional and Tentative: We ask those who use this book to bear in mind that this an interim effort. It might well be an overly audacious, even foolhardy attempt to speak about God and his revelation at a time when Christianity is undergoing a universal questioning and its theology a massive reconstruction.

Not long ago we could confidently set down volumes of precise information about God and his wishes for us. Today nothing is more apparent than that we know very little indeed. No one is more aware of this than the author. But many people have expressed the need for a book like this—a one-volume, adult-level presentation of our beliefs and practices at this moment in our post-conciliar, pilgrim Church. The author would be grateful for any comments and suggestions for improvement.

A work of many: In this age when we are again discovering ourselves as a Christian family, when cooperation, collegiality, and dialogue are flourishing, the author has had the help and guidance of many wonderful people. He is particularly indebted to Rev. Robert Quinn, C.S.P., with whom much of this was written, to his fellow priests and colleagues in the Christian ministry, especially those of the Paulist Major Seminary and the Archdiocese of St. Paul. A special and deep acknowledgment must also be given to the loyal and very patient lay group of Minneapolis, San Francisco, and Berkeley who contributed unstintingly to the preparation of this book.

1
Our Life and God

What is life all about? Is there a God? If there is a God, does he care about us? Can I make contact with God? To answer these questions, we begin with something all men seek . . .

SOMETHING TO LIVE FOR

If there is one thing that men seek from life, it is fulfillment. We need a purpose, something to live for, a goal that will truly fulfill us and bring us happiness.

Many live for a successful marriage and a good home; some want a pleasant job with financial security; some seek power, some a life of pleasure and leisure, or friends and social position.

Many today, including many younger people, find their purpose in the service of others. In this age of great social change and consequent confusion these highly motivated individuals are bringing about great good in our world.

Yet we must acknowledge that none of these things can completely satisfy our aspirations. No matter what we have, there is always something else we want. We also realize that these things cannot give us lasting and secure happiness, nor a lasting sense of accomplishment, for human weakness, tragedy or death can destroy what we have. "Man is like a breath; his days like a passing shadow" (Psalm 144, 4).

The conviction of the Christian believer is that two thousand years ago Jesus Christ revealed to us an ultimate purpose to our life: to live forever with God after death. We know that our greatest happiness in this life comes from love. From childhood everyone has an insatiable desire to love and be loved. Our happiness in human love, Christ tells us, is but a dim reflection

5

of the immense, unending joy of loving God and being loved
by him forever.

Jesus told us that this unending life of happiness after death is
such as we could not even begin to dream of. It is as if someone
lived his life in a closed room, never seeing or hearing anything
outside. Then one day someone opened the door to the outside
and showed him the world with its marvels. Christ did this for us,
but he revealed that our destiny is infinitely more wonderful—
so staggering that we can grasp it only bit by bit.

Jesus told us that we begin our life of love and happiness with
God while still here on earth. But this happiness is different from
what many people think. It does not come from satisfying our
desire for pleasure or material things or social achievement. It
comes from truly loving, and often involves suffering and sacrifice. It is realistic. It brings, not freedom from pain, but a deep
peace and sense of fulfillment even in the midst of pain.

Jesus showed us how to get along with others and how to bear
sufferings and frustration. He told us and showed us what we
can do about our loneliness and fears, our guilt and uneasiness,
and how to have true peace and security.

Jesus revealed that God has a plan by which we are to share in
his love and happiness, in other words, that there is a meaning to
human history. He told us not only that we have a place in God's
plan, but that (as is becoming more apparent today) the working out of this plan depends on us, on our free cooperation with
God as co-authors of history. Jesus' great follower, St. Paul, put
it this way:

> To me, though I am the very least of all the saints, this grace was
> given, to preach to the Gentiles the unsearchable riches of Christ,
> and to make all men see what is the plan of the mystery hidden
> for ages in God who created all things; that through the Church
> the manifold wisdom of God might now be made known . . . This
> was according to the eternal purpose which he has realized in
> Christ Jesus our Lord (Ephesians 3, 8-11).

The unique claim that Jesus made for his teaching was that he
has a special knowledge of God and his plan for us, and that he
alone can lead us to God. He said that he was sent by God, and

is, in fact, God's only Son: "I am the way, and the truth, and the
life. No one comes to the Father but through me" (John 14, 5).

Therefore the story of Jesus' teaching and of God's plan begins
with God himself . . .

HOW PEOPLE COME TO KNOW GOD

People come to a realization of God in countless ways. These
are some of them:

Some have grown from childhood with a knowledge of God,
are accustomed to pray and to make God a part of their thoughts
and decisions.

Some reflect on the course of their life, and have an unshakable
conviction of God's providence watching over them. Particularly in times of crisis, they realize, someone was there who
heard and understood.

Some find God's presence in nature—in hills and mountains, a
peaceful lake, an expanse of sky, there comes the conviction of
someone. A few might come closest while caught up in a moving
piece of music, in the contemplation of an art masterpiece, or
something similar.

Some are convinced that they have had an experience of God—
shattering, unforgettable, overwhelmingly joyous and unifying,
giving great peace and absolute certainty, profoundly affecting
their lives yet unexplainable to others. Many who testify to this—
and it is rarely and with great reluctance that they do so—are
balanced, successful, and credible people.

Some come to God through their desire for perfect love. We
know that everyone from childhood has a strong need of understanding affection, perhaps accentuated by suffering or continual
frustration. Yet we know that every human love has weaknesses
and will eventually disappoint us. We then look to someone,
beyond this life, who will never fail us, who can perfectly understand us and fulfill our aspirations and our desire for love.

Some are helped by demonstrations from reason for God's
reality. For example, an enormously complicated space satellite
cannot make itself and launch itself into orbit. It has to be
designed, built, and launched by intelligent human beings. Our

world and the countless stars act according to amazingly consistent laws in a universe that is far more complicated than any satellite. The vast universe must, therefore, have been planned and made by one of supreme intelligence and power. This one we call God.

Reasoning like this, "circumstantial evidence," might show some the need for a limitless, timeless force sustaining the universe. But God himself must give us an insight into himself if we are ever to know him as close, personal, interested, loving.

Some are helped by those they love who are lovers of God. The example of the deep faith of their friend or beloved, its effect on that one's life, and the generous love it seems to produce may gradually open the seeker to the divine lover.

Many cannot express why they believe in God or what he is to them. They are instinctively dumb before this unfathomable mystery. Even a master of language like Cardinal Newman said of this: ". . . words are such poor vehicles for what my mind holds and my heart believes." Perhaps the greatest obstacle a believer encounters in expressing his belief to an unbeliever—or even to himself—is the inability to communicate in understandable concepts.

Seeking God is for many like peering through a fog to see if there is a house at a particular spot; often all we catch is a glimpse, confused, uncertain. We never see God. But most of us reach certainty about him by a "cumulation of converging probabilities" which can give not just an opinion, but the deepest conviction. Some never attain this deepest conviction but seem permitted by God to remain in a state of constant quest. In the search for truth it is perhaps not important how many fragments of the staggering whole a man manages to perceive during his lifetime, but the courage and openness with which he continues his search.

As one moves toward truth he may come to realize that he is as much being sought as seeking, that the truth he seeks, the God he would love, is already deeply within him, soliciting his love. He comes to realize his conviction of this all along: one who becomes convinced of God could never recognize him unless he had somehow known him before.

WHAT IS NECESSARY TO KNOW GOD

As in any honest pursuit, we must be open to truth, not only the truth of absolute values but also the truth about ourselves, who we are and what we want ultimately from the experience of life. This requires courage, a willingness to be threatened by often unpleasant truth. The man who is self-assertive, self-satisfied, will have no reason to push out beyond himself in search of a higher good.

We must be willing to take time to question, observe, reflect. In our achievement-oriented society, particularly, it is hard for one to devote time to reflecting on ultimate values. Even when the satisfaction of achievement fails one and all one's striving seems useless, the consideration of a possible God behind it all is usually rejected as a demeaning crutch.

We must be open to our fellow men and treat them as our conscience demands, with dignity and justice. The mature person sees that in each man there is a spark, however dim, of enduring goodness. This spark is the divine within each man, and if one is ever to find God he must recognize and respect this spark in others. The one who is fundamentally turned in on himself, who seeks only his own good, will inevitably find only himself.

Christians believe that God has revealed—and is revealing—himself to men and that one must investigate this claim of revelation if one is to find God as he has shown himself to us. This seems logical to the Christian; if there is an infinite one, we who are finite cannot grasp him unless he reveals himself to us. Thus, although not all men will find God's revelation, it is the highest logic to search for it.

However, to meet God as he has revealed himself—to realize he is there—he must give us faith, the power to recognize him, the intuitive grasp of his reality. Ultimately whether one is a believer or an unbeliever depends on God. This explains why some find God, while others of equal intelligence and good will do not.

Today particularly many feel that God is missing from our world. Caught up by scientific advances and a technology by which man seems able to solve his own problems, a search for

God seems to many irrelevant and meaningless. Unbelief is for
many the accepted position today. Even some who consider
themselves Christians say that we must live as if "God is dead."

Unlike former days, the denial of God or of religion, or the
abandonment of them, is no longer an unusual and individual oc-
currence. Today it is not rare for such things to be presented as
requirements of scientific progress or of a certain new humanism
(*Pastoral Constitution on the Church in the Modern World*, no. 7).

**Why does not God make himself unmistakably known to all
men?** Today God is certainly not showing himself to us in any
tangible way; he is not at all apparent to the great majority of
men. One can only speculate about the meaning of this, but a
reason might lie in the true Christian view of God—that far from
being a Supreme One who demands that we acknowledge him
and give him our obeisance, God is one who is truly among us
loving us with great and intimate tenderness, soliciting our free
response of love.

Why are many people unable to find God? Some seem unable
to detach themselves from the pursuit of modern false gods:
money, social status, power, pleasure. As long as one primarily
seeks these, he will never find the living and true God.
Even the person of great good will who is continually occupied
with material things—for example, the world of science or business—must expect difficulty in coming to realize spiritual reality,
however noble his daily pursuits may be. To come to realize God
takes time and persevering effort.
Some reject a distorted image of God which pictures him as a
disinterested power, perhaps capricious, even vengeful. These
usually have not had the proper kind of love in their lives, may
have experienced much seemingly meaningless suffering, and so
cannot accept a loving God. They have never experienced the
love they have been told God is—and perhaps they have experienced the unlovingness of those who claim to be friends of God.

The Vatican Council says of this:

Some . . . seem more inclined to affirm man than to deny God.
Again, some form for themselves such a fallacious idea of God
that when they repudiate this figment, they are by no means
rejecting the God of the Gospel . . . Moreover, atheism results
not rarely from a violent protest against the evil in this world. . . .
Believers can have more than a little to do with the birth of

atheism. To the extent that they neglect their own training in the faith, or teach erroneous doctrine, or are deficient in their religious, moral or social life, they . . . conceal rather than reveal the authentic face of God and religion (Vatican Council II, *The Church in the Modern World*, no. 19).

One perceptive modern author writes:

One of the greatest obstacles to belief in God is the complacency of believers. It is not the adulterers, the takers of bribes, the licentious, whose conduct induces disbelief. It is the righteous, the solid citizens, the people of good reputation in the community. Such believers show few signs of ever having encountered the terrifying God; nor do they appear to live in that cold night of belief in which he is most truly found. Their god seems to be an idol, the idol of habit, routine, sentiment, and self-congratulation. By their words and actions, they treat God as a vague guarantor of the good order which makes them secure. He is the projection of that superego which keeps them conscientious when no one is looking. In his name, they dare to preach mere law and order, rather than also the freedom and inquiry through which the living God is found. Their god is the dead god of the middle classes (Novak, *Belief and Unbelief*, p. 182).

It seems that after a certain point in life one does not change one's basic position from belief to unbelief, or from unbelief to belief. This point seems to be the late teens or early twenties, or it may be even earlier, by the time of adolescence. Some believers may doubt after this, even consider themselves unbelievers, but this is usually a temporary state.

Many young people must go through a rejection—or better, a testing—of the authority structures of their life: their home, their religion, their belief in God, etc. This experience seems necessary for most thinking young people, and some older ones as well, that they might arrive at a more mature faith and one to which they are personally committed.

It is the believer's conviction that many seek God—and find him in the depths of their being—without realizing it: some through their unrelenting pursuit of truth, justice, the good of the community, or another humanitarian ideal—and many through their insatiable thirst for love. They are never satisfied. Through their total commitment to a transcendent ideal they are, to the believer, reaching the absolute we call God.

Some have a radical dissatisfaction with any human accomplishment, are unfulfilled by any human love. Nothing any longer impresses them. Even the wonderful interchange and intimacy of human love at its deepest level only elicits in them a further desire, one that cannot be satisfied.

Sometimes, perceiving no end to their quest, they lapse into a
seeming cynicism, take refuge in flippancy or strike out against
the believer—but to the discerning believer their reaction is only
the measure of their unknowing love, a love that might be far
greater than his. The believer must always pray, "O God, some
know and serve you as truth, honor, integrity, service . . . as well
as I, and perhaps better . . ."

*It seems, too, that the unbeliever has a providential role to-
ward the believer,* one of challenging him to consider aspects of
God that he might otherwise forget: God is truly inaccessible and
incomprehensible; we are totally dependent on his revelation of
himself and can never take for granted that we know much at all
about him and his will for us.

*The committed believer and unbeliever then have much in
common.* Both are dedicated seekers of truth. Both seek in darkness—to both God is an absence, one who is not there, for he is
not an object to be found. Yet he is there, for both believer and
unbeliever have an objective in their lifelong striving—though
called different names, conceptualized differently, by each. To
both, then, God is a presence and an absence, one who is there
and one who is not there.

**The constant temptation of the believer is to fabricate for him-
self a God with whom he will be comfortable,** who will not too
much upset his life, with whom he can come to terms once and
for all. When doubts come, or new and unsettling views about
God, this type of believer becomes confused, perhaps resentful
that his faith should be a struggle instead of a secure refuge.
Some of these who consider themselves believers, it is evident,
have simply never known the living God.

"We cannot believe in God once-for-all any more than we can
exist once-for-all. Faith must always realize itself, and yet must
always remain unrealized. If so, it must *beware* of seeking rest if
it should feel the fatigue of self-exertion, as must he who, tired of
existence, imagined he could find repose outside it." (Dewart,
The Future of Belief, p. 65).

**Doubts about God, then, must be expected even by believers
who try to know and love him faithfully.** Faith must grow, and
growth is often uncertain, painful. Those who tell us of overwhelming, rapturous experiences of God also testify to states of
"darkness" and terrible doubt during which God is no longer a

reality. God is utterly silent—and such a state may last for years.

The believer must try to deepen his faith, learn more, live his faith more fully—or else he might lose his ability to experience belief. He cannot consider himself superior to his unbelieving friend, as if his own faith could never slip away into obscurity. He must recognize that his faith is a free gift of God to which he must continually and freely commit himself. Humbly he must say daily, "Lord, I do believe—help my unbelief!"

WHAT CAN WE SAY ABOUT GOD?

We can learn something about God from examining the universe about us. As we learn of the skill of an artist or builder by examining his work, so we can learn about God through the universe he has made. We can come to grasp something of his power, vastness, beauty. "Ever since the creation of the world his invisible nature, namely, his eternal power and deity, has been clearly perceived in the things that have been made" (Romans 1, 20).

The Judaeo-Christian belief is that God has himself told us something about himself, revealed himself to us. He has done this in many ways, but particularly to the Israelites of the Old Testament. For example over three thousand years ago, he revealed himself to Moses as the living, all-pervading God: **Read Exodus 3, 2-6 and 13-14.**

God is "wholly other," transcendent, infinitely holy. Those to whom he has revealed himself have often testified to a feeling of utter awe, wonderment, profound abasement, a sort of "holy terror" in his presence. Thus the Jewish prophet Isaiah tried to describe his experience of God: **Read Isaiah 6, 1-7.** Moses' experience is also primitive but striking: **Read Exodus 33, 18-23.**

God has revealed that he is a loving, personal God, concerned with each of us. He loves each of us, believer and unbeliever, in a way that he loves nothing else in creation. We will see how he shows himself to be good, kind, patient and faithful. As the Jews of the Old Testament came to realize this, they compared God to a shepherd who carefully guides his helpless sheep, to a good king, a loving father, a mother: "Can a woman forget her sucking child, that she should have no compassion on the son of her womb? Even these may forget, yet I will not forget you" (Isaiah 49, 15).

God's ultimate revelation of himself was through his own Son, Jesus Christ. This is the uniquely Christian view of God—that he has a Son, Jesus Christ, and that this Son has come among us as a man. "In many and various ways God spoke of old to our fathers by the prophets, but in these last days he has spoken to us by a Son . . ." (Hebrews 1, 1-2).

Jesus teaches us what God is by calling him our Father. He is a Father who has not only given us life but who loves each of us with a limitless love, cares for us each day, and wants us to live happily, with him forever. He is a merciful Father, always ready with his forgiveness for us—as long as we are willing to forgive others. The Lord's Prayer, taught us by Jesus, beautifully expresses this:

> Our Father, who art in heaven, hallowed be thy name. Thy kingdom come, thy will be done on earth as it is in heaven. Give us this day our daily bread, and forgive us our trespasses as we forgive those who trespass against us. And lead us not into temptation, but deliver us from evil. Amen.

> *God reveals himself, we shall see later, as a loving "family" of three Persons* who draw us to themselves, to share their happiness. God is not just Father but also Son and Holy Spirit, to each of whom we have a special relationship of love. This paradox of one God who is yet three Persons is the mystery of the Trinity, discussed in chapter 7.

God respects each of us—our freedom, our dignity, our person —because he loves each of us. Though many are not yet aware of this, God enters into a most intimate "I-Thou" relationship with each of us. He calls each of us by our own name. Rather than absorbing us into himself, the God of our Judaeo-Christian revelation enables each of us to develop to our utmost as a person— even as he unites us most intimately with himself. To this paradox the greatest mystics testify.

God has revealed that even the sufferings of innocent people are somehow working out for the eventual happiness of us all. Though we cannot yet understand how, the wars, crimes, and terrible injustices of human history are somehow a part of his plan of sharing with us his love and happiness. Our vision is finite, it sees only the moment of this life—nothing, really, in comparison with an eternity of happiness (though we must be expected to cry out for an explanation while we are here below). We shall see, later, when we consider Jesus and his great work for us, more about the meaning of suffering.

A mind-boggling view of God is presented to us today by process theology which says, briefly, that God is so involved in our human situation that he actually suffers and rejoices with us, in other words, he experiences with us the daily working out of our destiny, with all its hopes and fears, joys and sorrows. God need not have done this, but he loves us so much that he wills to become this involved in the human process.

Ultimately, while we can know that God is—that we are in contact with him, that he is present to us—we cannot know what he is. We seek him, and try to apply to him our poor human categories, but he is "totally other," and all our speculations must ultimately end in awesome ignorance. He is always a hidden God.

Therefore we must expect to find mysteries in our study of God and religion—things about which we can know very little, or which make little sense to us. When we think that we understand him, or when we confidently predict his actions, then we are in trouble.

O, the depth of the riches and wisdom and knowledge of God! How unsearchable are his judgments and how inscrutable his ways! For who has known the mind of the Lord . . . (Romans 11, 33-34).

DAILY LIVING: PRAYER—OUR CONTACT WITH GOD

To come to know God as he really is, and to experience his love for us, it is absolutely necessary to try to contact him. This is prayer . . .

It is necessary for each person to try to pray. Others might testify about their knowledge of God, what he is like, but each person must form his own acquaintance with God. We might hear much about a wonderful person from those who have met him, but we will never really know that person until we have met him and communicated with him ourselves.

Just as every genuine human love relationship is unique and
can be fully experienced only by the lovers themselves, so each
person's love relationship with God is unique, can be achieved by
him alone, and cannot be communicated adequately to anyone
else. If one remains aloof, waiting for God to come to him without trying to reach God, he will never know God any more than
he could know another person whom he treated in this way.

The few whose persistent prayer has led them to experience a
love affair with the living God know that it can be a terrifying,
totally demanding, unbelievably fulfilling, fantastically wonderful
thing. Most of us will not—perhaps cannot—bring ourselves to
risk such an experience. But if we are wise we will not reject what
these lovers of the divine have to say. We will listen to their
insights, for they might be of immense help to us all as we
struggle enmeshed in our human condition. They are unanimous
in telling us that our moments of prayer are the most alive
moments of all, that when we pray we are on the threshold of life
and beauty and joy that are utterly unimaginable.

**Prayer is simply talking with God, trying to put ourselves in
touch with him,** contact him, become aware of him. By prayer,
"something out there" becomes someone personal, close, concerned. We can never be sure there is a God, nor come to know
what he is like, unless we pray. When one refuses to try to pray,
"the world becomes his jail."

God loves us and respects our freedom. He wants our mature
love. He will never force himself upon us. We must try to reach
out to him, freely, by prayer.

**The reason we pray is not to tell God something he does not
know, nor to change his mind. Rather, prayer makes us aware
of God, opens us to perceive his love and his desires for us.**
Prayer gradually makes us realize our complete dependence on
God, our radical need of him. It makes us appreciate, bit by
bit, how we are utterly bound to him by love. It also makes us
realize the great power we have to better our human condition.
When one prays the happenings of life, the joys as well as the
agonies, begin to take on a meaning.

**God always answers a sincere prayer, but not always in the
way we expect.** We tend to complain of unanswered prayers,

but we may have prayed for something that would ultimately be harmful, or we might be expecting God to do what is within our own power to bring about. God always responds, though, by giving his love in a far better way then we envisioned. Jesus said of this:

What father among you, if his son asks for a fish, will instead of a fish give him a serpent; or if he asks for an egg, will give him a scorpion? If you then who are evil, know how to give good gifts to your children, how much more will the heavenly Father give the Holy Spirit to those who ask him? (Luke 11, 11-13).

We should pray for ourselves and for others, including our enemies. Prayer for ourselves need not be selfish—on the contrary, it is usually an acknowledgment of our total human inadequacy. Prayer for others helps them to be open to God's love and our love and helps us to be open to them. We shall see more later about the power of prayer.

Some suggestions about how to pray: We can simply talk to God as to our best and most understanding friend, our loving Father. The best prayer is from our heart, in our own words. If we wish, we can use words someone else has composed, or we might say nothing, content just to be in God's presence, thinking about him, about ourselves, our loved ones, our life.

We can pray anywhere, anytime. But it is good to set aside a special time—perhaps in the morning and evening—and a special place, away from distractions. We read about Christ: "And in the morning, a great while before day, he rose and went out to a lonely place, and there he prayed . . . And after he had taken leave of them, he went into the hills to pray" (Mark 1, 35; 6, 46).

We need not say much. Christ warns us against imitating those who "think that by talking much they will be heard" (Matthew 6, 8). Reading, especially the bible, is food for prayer; people often cannot pray because they know so little about God, his actions and teachings.

Prayer can be difficult. But to try to pray, is to pray. One can feel utterly helpless when trying it for the first time, or returning to it as an adult. He wonders: How should I go about it? Will I be heard? Isn't there a danger of self-hypnosis? It can be like

talking into a phone with no one on the other end of the line.
One should expect these problems in trying to reach for an
Infinite One. But we must be willing to risk, to try.

If we persevere, gradually, perhaps very slowly and painfully,
the conviction grows that there is Someone. Things begin to fall
into place. We long for more contact, to know more, to have
more help, to give ourselves to him. Mysteriously, the bond of
love is growing.

SOME SUGGESTIONS FOR ...

DISCUSSION

If you are a believer, what do you personally conceive God
to be like?
What, for you, best makes God real in your life?
If you are an unbeliever—or a believer—can you appreciate the opposite point of view?

FURTHER READING

* *Your Religion: Neurotic or Healthy?*, Anderson (Doubleday,
1970)—An Episcopal priest shows incisively what happens
when churches preach wrong ideas about God.
** *The Estranged God*, Padovano (Sheed & Ward, 1966)—An
excellent and readable presentation of modern views on belief and unbelief, and the problem of God as seen by theology
today.
** *Do You Believe in God?*, Rahner (Newman, 1969)—Excellent
essays by an outstanding theologian on belief, unbelief, intellectual honesty, science and faith, etc.
** *God Within Process*, Baltazar (Newman, 1970)—An excellent
presentation of the new, evolutionary, process (& Teilhardian)
view of theism, together with questions of atheism, belief,
etc. An intriguing book for one who wants to broaden his
horizons.
** *The God Experience*, Whelan ed. (Newman Press, 1971)—
An excellent collection of essays on the various ways God is
experienced by man today, together with some insights into
faith and hope in the future.
** *God Is a New Language*, Moore (Paulist Press, 1968)—A
prodding plea for a new language to express our new in-

sights into Christian revelation; shows how inadequate language confuses and repels people.
** *The Problem of God,* Murray (Yale Press)—Treats the history of the problem of God, and the various forms of modern atheism.
** *Belief and Unbelief,* Novak (Macmillan, 1965)—A modern Catholic philosopher's way of arriving at God through a knowledge of oneself; includes a good appreciation of the position of the unbeliever.
** *From Anathema to Dialogue,* Garaudy (Herder & Herder, 1966)—A leading French Marxist details how a dialogue is possible with Christian believers, and a common striving to make the world more human.
** *The Future of Belief,* Dewart (Herder & Herder, 1966)—In this "breakthrough" book, one of the most influential of recent years, a practicing Catholic religious philosopher shatters all kinds of treasured china and attempts to completely recast traditional Christian doctrine; somewhat difficult reading, controversial, but most rewarding.

FURTHER VIEWING

The Top—8 minutes, color. Contemporary Films, Inc., 267 W. 25th St., New York, N.Y. 10001—Biting cartoon satire on man's pursuit of wealth.
The Late, Great God (Paulist Productions, 17575 Pacific Coast Hwy., Pacific Palisades, Calif. 90272)—27 minutes, in color—Probing analysis of the true and false understanding of the nature of God and the reasons for contemporary unbelief.
The Day God Died (Paulist Productions)—27 minutes, in color—Dramatic exploration of the effects of contemporary atheism.

PERSONAL REFLECTION

I am always in the presence of God, my loving Father. Each morning and evening I will offer this simple, expressive prayer:

"O God, help me to know what to do,
and give me the courage to do it."

2
God's Plan for Us Begins
with Creation

How did the human race begin? Is there a conflict between science and the bible? What is man's place in the universe? Will we survive after death? What of other worlds, angels, devils?

THE SOURCE OF OUR STORY

To answer the basic questions of our origin, we look to God's own record of his unfolding plan, history's all-time best-seller, the bible . . .

The bible is a collection of books inspired by God, revealing himself and his plan for our salvation. God is considered the principal author of the bible in that he influenced the men who wrote the books—even though they wrote freely and may not have been aware of his guidance—and so we say it was inspired by God. It expresses his revelation of himself to men and is therefore called his written "Word."

The bible is a religious book whose purpose is to tell of God and his plan for us, especially his great deeds on our behalf and his teaching about how to live and attain heaven. Since its authors were writing religious history, they related historical events only as a means of instructing and inspiring their readers. Sometimes they embellish their accounts with imaginative details, illustrate a point by a fictitious story, or omit things that would detract from their religious purpose.

The bible is a miniature library containing all sorts of writing. It contains poetry, prayers, hymns, love songs, riddles, fables, allegories, various kinds of historical narratives, folklore, biographies, prophecies, letters, etc. Each biblical author used the type of literature, or literary form, that best suited his purpose. Each literary form must be interpreted properly if the author is to be understood, as we today interpret poetry differently than we do a newspaper editorial, and a fairy tale still differently. These ancient oriental literary forms are often hard for us to understand, since they were the expression of the people of ancient times.

For example, a visitor to earth from another planet, understanding our language but nothing more about us, might read a newspaper and consider everything in it equally true—news columns, ads, comics, letters to the editor, etc.—whereas we know that each style of writing must be interpreted differently.

While the bible's purpose is religious, its basic story is an accurate historical record. Although the bible's religious revelation can be perceived only by faith, nevertheless archeology and other sciences are showing that it reports its historical setting with a good deal of accuracy. For example, modern archeologists using Old Testament stories have discovered some 2,000 ancient sites in the Middle East from their biblical descriptions.

We believe that God will somehow communicate with anyone who reads the bible story with an open, seeking mind. The deeds related in the bible were done for all men. They can have an effect upon us today just as much as they did upon the people to whom they originally happened. As we read the bible each of us should be open to the possibility of reliving, in his own life, these great happenings by which God brings us to himself. We shall see more of this later.

The bible is divided into the Old Testament, the story of God's revelation of himself and his plan up to the coming of Christ; and the New Testament, an outline of Christ's life and teachings. We begin our story with the Old Testament, usually classified as forty-five books, written by many authors over three millennia. The Middle Eastern traditions found in the first five books go back to the time of Moses (13th century B.C.) and beyond, and were first woven together on a major scale about the 10th century B.C. The last book of the Old Testament, Wisdom, was written about 50 B.C.

The first book of the Old Testament, Genesis, begins with the story of the origin of the world and of man. . . .

HUMAN BEGINNINGS

The story came to us in this way: Over 3,000 years ago, a band of ex-slaves found themselves wandering in the Sinai desert after a dramatic escape from pagan Egypt. In this remote place, God spoke to Moses, their leader, and made these tribes his chosen people, promising them great blessings. But the people, conscious of their vague past and uncertain future and aware of their weaknesses, began to ask Moses questions: How did it all start?—what was this God of theirs like?—was he really an all-powerful God?—if so, why did he choose them?—where did they come from, who were their ancestors?

The answer Moses and others gave—the story of the beginning of God's plan for our world—was elaborated over the centuries. Eventually it was written down as Genesis, the first book of the bible: **Read Genesis, 1, 1–2, 24.**

This story of creation is meant to teach us that God made everything that exists and that everything he has made is good. Genesis speaks of creation in six days to help its primitive audience better understand that God made everything, even the things worshipped by other peoples; the picture of God creating for six days and resting on the seventh is meant to teach a Jewish audience that they should rest on the sabbath.

Man is at the peak of creation, in some way like God himself, and is given everything in the world for his use. ". . . what is man that you are mindful of him, or the son of man that you care for him? Yet you have made him little less than God, and crown him with glory and honor" (Psalm, 8, 4-5).

The bible's account of creation can fit in perfectly with science's teaching on the evolution of the universe, even though, as we said, the bible is not meant to be a scientific text. God brings the world to realization, not by continual interventions—stepping in to "make" this or that—but in such a way that the higher emerges from the lower, by evolution. He is continually creating as he activates the whole, gigantic, unfolding process.

By his description of the creation of woman, the biblical author is emphasizing woman's dignity, that she too is a human being. This stands in sharp contrast to the common ancient view of woman as merely something to be used by man. This description also tells us of the origin of marriage—a wonderfully intimate union begun by God himself as a part of his unfolding plan for man.

The biblical story of human origins has been interpreted until relatively recently as meaning one original couple (monogenism). Many current biblical scholars take a broader view and point out that monogenism is not necessarily part of God's revelation. One says, ". . . the question about a monogenetic or polgenetic origin of man remains as obscure for the philosopher as for the paleontologist" (Schoonenberg, *God's World in the Making*, p. 50). Another says, "Studies in exegesis and conciliar history lead us to ask whether the intention of the author of Genesis, of St. Paul, and of the Fathers of the Council of Trent was really directed at the strict unity of origin of the human race and not rather at the universality of 'sin' " (Dubarle, *The Biblical Doctrine of Original Sin*, p. 228).

WHAT ARE WE?

"What is man? About himself he has expressed and continues to express many divergent and even contradictory opinions. In these he often exalts himself to the point of despair. The result is doubt and anxiety." (Vatican Council II, **The Church in the Modern World**, no. 12). Christianity, building on God's revelation to us, has reached certain conclusions about man:

Each of us is composed of soul, or spirit, and materiality. With the help of God's further revelation we can see this in the story of man made "in the image of God" and of "the dust of the earth." These are the two "aspects" of man, two "powers," two ways in which we can act.

By our soul, or spiritual aspect, we are "like God," persons, free, immortal, able to reflect on ourselves and realize ourselves. "By his interior qualities man outstrips the whole sum of mere things . . . surpasses the material universe . . . and shares in the light of the divine mind" (**Church in the Modern World**, no. 14).

By our materiality, or material aspect, we are connected with and dependent upon other things, limited, mortal, but capable of perfecting our universe. "Through his bodily composition man gathers to himself the elements of the material world . . . they

reach their crown through him, and through him raise their
voice in free praise of the Creator" (Church in the Modern
World, no. 14).

Each of us is a single, unified person. Our soul and materiality
are not two "parts," but rather two aspects of the one person
who does everything. Our spirit depends upon our materiality—
upon our brain, senses, etc.—that we might think and act.
Whether we have the loftiest "spiritual" thoughts or engage in
the most basic "animal" actions, it is ourselves, single persons,
who do these things.

Our soul, or spiritual power, is just as real as our materiality
which we can see and feel. It is the core of our being, our
conscious self, our innermost "me." It infuses every part of us
that is alive. It enables us to think and make free choices and
love. When we think, we call this power our intellect or mind;
when we make free choices and love, we call it our free will.

We can be sure that we have this spiritual aspect, or soul, even
aside from God's teaching about it. We have non-material or
spiritual ideas such as truth, love, etc. We can conceive and
carry out plans for the future, and can reflect on our past actions.
We make abstract judgments; we produce culture, art and
poetry, study philosophy and religion—all having little or nothing to do with our material survival.

> The existence of the human spirit is often best shown by man's
> triumphs over inhumanity, suffering and death. The diary of
> Anne Frank, a Jewish teenager's writings discovered in her Am-
> sterdam hideout after her cruel death at the hands of the Nazis,
> is a striking modern testimony to the power of the spirit.

> *Each person's soul, or spiritual power, comes specially from
> God,* but not by God's intervening and putting something in us
> from the outside. Our soul does not exist before we do as a
> person. Each person's soul is a special "aspect" of God's continu-
> ing creation of the universe—an individual spiritual power that
> comes about by the evolutionary process which God began, work-
> ing itself out in each of us. In the thinking of the great priest-
> paleontologist, Teilhard de Chardin, and others, the human soul
> first came about at the critical point of evolution when a primate
> became able to reflect on himself—and hence became human, a
> man, free and immortal, able to think and choose, however primi-
> tively, and to relate to others and to God.

By our soul each of us is specially related to God in a unique way. We might sometimes wonder, "How can the infinite God be concerned about me?" And yet he is, in a relationship with each one of us that is most intimate and will never be duplicated. The mystics say that God calls each of us by a secret name, lovingly, constantly, intimately.

Christ's great teaching is that, because of our soul, we will go on living forever after death. Before Christ came, men could not be certain of this immortality. He stated emphatically, "Truly, truly, I say to you, if anyone keeps my word he will never see death" (John 8, 51).

Mankind generally has believed in some sort of survival after death. Man's instincts and desires lead him to yearn for this perfection of happiness. "Unless man is immortal the universe is a stairway leading nowhere." If death completely destroys the human personality, then the peak of creation is left unfinished. God would be like a half-witted artist, amusing himself with things that have no ultimate meaning, creating men and wiping them out. But his whole revelation of himself is that he is good, just, and loving.

Historian Arnold Toynbee sums up human belief in a personal immortality in the face of modern unbelievers: "For human beings who have once tasted the hope of personal immortality, the loss of this hope takes much of the light out of life, and the post-Christian racial survival ideologies offer no satisfactory substitute. If I have lost a dearly beloved wife or husband or child or parent, what consolation is it to me that the sacred rights of the community have been vindicated, or that a spaceman has landed on the moon? . . . Collective human triumphs are very fine, but they do not bring the dead back to life, and do not console me for my human losses . . ."

Each of us is responsible for what happens to us after death. We are free, in God's image, and God will never interfere with our freedom. At the end of our life we will have to give an account of it—of the good we have done and the evil as well— in perfect honesty, before God, without any deception or delusion. Christ reminds us pointedly, "What does it profit a man to gain the whole world and forfeit his life?" (Mark 8, 36).

Each year on Ash Wednesday it is a Catholic custom to have our foreheads marked with ashes by a priest who says, "Remem-

ber, man, that you are dust and to dust you shall return." It is a
striking reminder at the beginning of the forty days' Lenten
penance that our material body is perishable and we should
live for immortality.

**In God's plan all men are brothers, one human family, working
and sharing together.** The story of our common first parents
makes clear that we are all essentially the same and all have a
right to share in the world's goods. Discrimination and prejudice
among races insert themselves into mankind later, as a result of
sin.

God is continually creating. Rather than considering creation
as something over and done with, we should think of it as a
process that is continually developing, something like a magnificent painting that is gradually taking form and will be complete
only at the end of time.

**God's plan is for us to be "co-creators" with him, to develop
our world** in partnership with him. Thus God said, ". . . let them
have dominion over the fish of the sea . . . Be fruitful and
multiply and fill the earth and subdue it . . ." It is becoming
more and more apparent today that God loves us so much that
he associates us most intimately and powerfully with himself
and his works. We, by our achievements in making a better
world, work "in the presence of God" to carry out the plan for
the perfection of all things that he has left us to develop.

> This is developed further in Chapter 24 and in Vatican Council
> II's *Pastoral Constitution on the Church in the Modern World,*
> nos. 36, 57, 67. Some today (following particularly the thought
> of Teilhard de Chardin) believe that man is made to conquer and
> perfect the whole universe, that he is truly the center of God's
> creation.

**Love is the whole reason for creation, for us and for every-
thing that exists.** God is so loving that he wants to share his
happiness, the happiness of loving, at a fantastic, unimaginable
level with us, his creatures.

God need not have created anything. He is infinitely happy
within himself and needed nothing outside himself—he need
not have involved himself with us. But he loves—limitlessly.
The universe gives us a tiny glimpse of his beauty, and the

heights of human love a mere taste of the divine love he wishes to share with us.

OTHER WORLDS, ANGELS AND DEVILS

In our space age, man has become aware that he is only a part of a vast universe. Other creatures, angels, are mentioned numerous times in scripture.

Angels have traditionally been considered good spirits who worship God, act as his messengers, and guard and pray for us. Intermediaries or messengers between God and us, they were conceived of as moving with the swiftness of thought and are therefore often pictured as winged (cf. Rev. 12, 11-12; Ps. 103, 20).

The story of the angels, as traditionally conceived, is that God created them and gave them great happiness; he offered them an opportunity to show their gratitude to him, and in return he would give them even greater happiness in heaven. But some of them, led by Lucifer, or the devil, ungratefully refused to love God, and in fact wanted to take over God's position in heaven. Fixed forever on evil, they were relegated to hell, the state of eternal suffering and separation from God. (Cf. Revelation 12, 7-9; Isaiah 14, 12ff).

Today, theology is restudying the whole question of angels and devils. Perhaps scripture simply presupposes angels and devils as part of the biblical milieu, rather than directly affirming their actual existence as part of God's revelation. Nor does the existence of angels and devils seem to be a part of the strictly dogmatic teaching of the Church. The numbers and varieties which are mentioned may well be mythological exaggerations. And yet it is hard to dismiss the reality itself, so firmly rooted is it in the long tradition and liturgy of the Church.

"Possession" is the supposed taking over of a person's body by the devil or evil spirits, "obsession" the inhabiting of a place or objects by them. Many such cases can be explained naturally, as parapsychology particularly is showing us more and more today. For many theologians today, possession can be simply the coalescing of the very real evil that proceeds from men, concentrated in a certain person or place, and the ritual of exorcism ("driving out the evil spirit[s]") opposes this with the power of God's all-powerful love.

In any event, the portrayal of angelic creatures has served to bridge the gap between God and man, and remind man of unseen spiritual realities, of the dangers of sin and God's ever-present help. Today, when we face the almost limitless possibilities of life in space, references to angels should remind us how little we really know of God's creation.

Obviously then, there could be other rational creatures in the universe. They, too, would have been created by God and are loved and cared for by him. They would show forth other aspects of his infinite wisdom and love, perhaps some that man cannot. It is surely good for us to reach out lovingly toward them, for the same loving God would have made us all in some sense "brothers."

Contemplating the possibility of man one day standing face to face with other rational creatures should make us realize how ridiculous are our petty human divisions, our wars and other conflicts. Much of the science fiction of our time attempts to tell us this. At any rate, our concern in this book is with what we know of God's revelation to us in this world, staggering and limitless in itself.

DAILY LIVING: WORSHIPPING OUR CREATOR

When we realize that God is our Creator and that we are completely dependent on him, our most natural feeling is one of awe and reverence, and awareness of our nothingness before him. From ancient times man has always felt this way before the vast mystery of God. We want to know more about God, to pay him homage, and yet we know how very limited we are.

Worship is the way we honor God and try to be united with him. Just as a child naturally expresses his dependence on his human father, and desires to be with him, so it is natural for us to do this toward our almighty Father. Worship comes from "worthship"—showing what God is worth to us, how we revere and need him.

God has no need of our worship. But as it is unnatural for a son to ignore a good parent, so it is unnatural for us to ignore God who gives us all we have. Such ultimate selfishness brings only deep unhappiness.

We have the great privilege of being able to respond to God's love. The rest of creation—to the extent we know it—is irrational and cannot experience this love with the almighty. We are free to accept his love and to love in return.

God loves each of us infinitely, intimately, personally, with all-powerful love and he wants our personal love in return. He has an intimate, loving interest in each of us. Christ says, "Why even the hairs of your head are all numbered" (Luke 12, 7).

Instead of an infinite number of possible people, God created you and me, and guides us through life to an endless eternity with himself. Each of us is loved uniquely and each of us has a unique contribution: we can love God and we can give love to the universe in a way no one else can. Worship gradually makes us aware of God's incredible, tender, personal love.

We can worship God by ourselves, silently honoring him in our thoughts. Worship must be interior and sincere, or else it is a mockery: ". . . they who worship must worship in spirit and truth," says Christ.

It is also natural to express our worship with others, as anyone in love will show openly how he feels about his beloved. We are members of one human family, and it is as natural to join with others in worship as in any meaningful experience.

We worship, then, as full human beings when we read, speak, sing, stand, sit, kneel in reverence, etc. And we join with all God's creation in worship, and so we use things such as water, oil, fire, stone, bread and wine, branches of trees, ashes, etc. "And God saw everything that he had made and behold, it was very good" (Genesis 1, 31).

Ceremonies of worship are "signs" that express our spiritual feelings. A handshake is a simple ceremony; a person seeing it knows from this sign that two men are friends. A kiss between husband and wife is a sign of their love. So, too, religious ceremonies are the Church's "sign language" expressing our beliefs in a living way. Each time we take part in them we deepen our beliefs.

Some will feel closer to God while alone, perhaps when out amid nature's wonders, when listening to music, etc. God is infinite beauty, and when we enter into things of beauty we are being drawn to him. Some feel God's presence more in these moments than in church, in man's organized religious assembly. They may find formal worship difficult, meaningless. These should then seek God where they can find him—but they should also try to appreciate the meaning of religious worship, because one's personal contacts with God can remain vague and meaningless unless he seeks God in union with others. Conversely, a formal worship might become a delusion unless it is interior and sincere.

We must remember that if we are to approach the infinite God (even if we are not sure an infinite one is there) we must do so in a reverent setting. We would certainly prepare well for an interview with a president or other important person. Yet we often casually, sporadically approach the infinite God—and then are surprised when nothing comes of it. Worship must be something regular, consistent, given a special time and place in our life.

Christians believe that God has shown us a way to join together and worship him. As people in love want to show their love in the best possible way, so men have always wanted to worship God adequately. Our conviction is that God has come to our aid and told us how. Catholics believe that the Mass, given us by Christ himself, is a special way God has given us to worship him.

Worship, then, is an integral part of the study of Catholic Christianity. The official public worship of the Catholic Church is called the sacred liturgy. To aid this presentation from now on, appropriate ceremonies of the liturgy will be noted in sections called IN THE LITURGY.

SOME SUGGESTIONS FOR . . .

DISCUSSION

What is the most meaningful thing for you in the bible's account of creation?
What do you think of the Christian notion of man's exalted, eternal place in the universe?
Can you understand why worship is natural and necessary for the believer?

FURTHER READING

* *Understanding the Bible*, Hunt (Sheed & Ward, 1962)—A brief, fairly easy-to-read yet thorough commentary on the story of the Old and New Testaments.
** *The Two-Edged Sword*, McKenzie (Bruce, 1956)—A well-written, incisive, somewhat detailed interpretation of the Old Testament, showing its relevance for us today.
** *The Making of Man*, Mooney (Paulist/Newman, 1971)—Some ways in which God enters into man's self-creation, theology, education, etc.
** *Christianity and Evolution*, Teilhard de Chardin (Harcourt Brace, 1971)—A scientific world picture for believers, and a religious vision for scientists.
** *The Third Peacock*, Capon (Doubleday, 1971)—A stimulating book about God and the problem of evil, creation, and the role of man.
** *Teilhard Explained*, DeLubac (Paulist Press)—An excellent, brief introduction to the thought of the great priest-paleontologist.
** *The Future of Man*, Teilhard de Chardin—Essays by the above on man and his universe. The book might be followed by one on his spiritual thought, *The Divine Milieu*, or *The Hymn of the Universe*.

FURTHER VIEWING

Sky—10 minutes, color. Contemporary Films, Inc., 267 W. 25th St., New York, N.Y. 10001—A portrayal of the heavens from dawn to dusk and their effect on the world.

PERSONAL REFLECTION

I might make some private, sincere act of worship each day. This Sunday, the Lord's day, I might join with others in worshipping God.

Each Sunday Catholics worship by taking part in the Mass, and everyone is welcome to come and take part. When one first attends, it is natural to be somewhat confused by the ceremonies, the priest's clothing, etc. These will be explained later.

Since the Mass is so central to Catholicism, and since it takes time to familiarize oneself with it, we recommend that those seriously studying Catholicism begin to attend Mass.

If you wish to attend, ask a Catholic friend to accompany you. A good rule is to stand, sit, or kneel when everyone else does.

3
God's Gift of Himself and
Our Rejection of Him

What is God's plan for us? How do we usually respond to God? Why are we drawn to sinful things and actions of which we are ashamed? How does God help us overcome our weaknesses?

GOD'S GREAT GIFT AND HIS DESIRE FOR MAN

A person in love wants to share his happiness with the one he loves. A boy in love with a girl wants to be with her to make her happy. God loves us. He made us to be happy with him in heaven forever.

But we could not exist for a moment in God's presence, much less speak with him and love him. We would be annihilated by even a glimpse of him. So God does something for us, to enable us to live with and love him forever. He gives us a great gift: Read Matthew 13, 44-46.

Christ was trying to describe something wonderful when he spoke of this "hidden treasure," the "pearl of great value" for which a man sells all he has. It is the greatest gift which God can give us, sanctifying grace.

Sanctifying grace is God's life and love within us, God's presence loving each of us. It is the way God lives within us and possesses us—the intimate, personal relationship of God to me. It is God himself giving me his friendship, his love, his very life —so we call it God's grace-presence within us.

"Sanctifying" means to make holy or like God. This new life truly makes us like God. "Grace" means a gift—we have no right whatever to it.

To understand this, consider the various personal relationships we have with others: Some we know slightly, as mere acquaintances; with others our mutual appreciation is growing, and with yet others we have a deep love, perhaps the love of friendship, or that of a man and woman, sharing love, strength, and inspiration on a profound level. There is also the relationship of parents to their children—a mother, for instance, communicating life to the child within her. Writers today speak of relationships as "I-it," and "I-thou," according to their meaningfulness. By grace we are most profoundly a "thou" in the eyes of the infinite God.

Sanctifying grace is the closest possible relationship between God and his human creatures. It is God's gift of himself in love to us—the closest possible love. It is also a love that gives us life itself, not just human life but the fullest possible sharing in the limitless life of God.

An orphan's adoption by a millionaire happens only rarely in our world; but by sanctifying grace the infinite God "adopts" us to live with him and share his wealth and his very life forever. "See what love the Father has given us, that we should be called children of God; and so we are" (1 John 3, 1; cf. Galatians 4, 7). We are "born again" into this new life (John 3, 5), and have a completely new relationship with God, that of a son to his Father (Romans 8, 14-17); we are a "new creation" (2 Corinthians 5, 17).

This presence has been called "supernatural" life, i.e., greater than our ordinary natural life, a sharing in God's own life, beyond this life in heaven. Through sanctifying grace we actually begin the life of heaven here on earth; we can begin to know and love God person-to-person and be loved by him.

This is a living love, a relationship that grows and develops as any love must—or else it dies. God's love continually presses us. We either grow in it, or we fall back. We shall see that this love, constantly increasing, never ceases but grows for eternity.

We cannot normally "feel" grace within us. But we shall see that Christ gave us ways to be sure of having this life-presence.

This most personal love of God for each of us has many wonderful aspects: His condescension, continually open to me, and indeed desirous of my constant communication with him; his mercy, continually forgiving me; his protection, unceasingly doing good things, somehow arranging the plan of the universe for me; his unending faithfulness to me, no matter how I treat him—unless I reject him entirely, and even then he wants to return to me.

We know how even a human love relationship can transform a person. Often a person's life is made or broken by whether or not he has someone who truly loves him. As love develops, one is raised beyond himself, taking on more and more the characteristics of his friend or beloved.

If human love can so change one, we can imagine what God's continual look of love must be doing to us. Unfortunately we are hardly ever aware of this, because it is so staggering, so beyond human comprehension. An unshielded look into an atomic pile could blind or kill, such is its power of radiation; one in grace has such interior beauty that if God ever permitted a glimpse of him as he really is, the beholder would be torn apart in ecstacy.

God's grace-presence gives us the power to transform everything we do into eternal happiness for ourselves and others. It expands us, giving us the possibility of life beyond our wildest dreams, and enabling us to share this with others. It is as if everything we touched turned into gold—except that by grace we can turn our every contact into unending, unimaginable happiness for all.

God's plan was that man would develop so that he could have his grace-presence, grow in it, and be with him forever in heaven. He would send his Son, Jesus Christ, to earth when men were ready, to fill us with a superabundance of his grace-presence. But man is weak, and God's plan now had to take account of man's hesitancy, his inability to trust himself to this infinite love.

MAN'S REJECTION OF GOD'S LOVE

Everyone who honestly faces himself is aware of his failings. We are all drawn to do things we later regret. We hurt ourselves and others, even those we love. This is sin, a dreary and inevitable fact over which men have puzzled for centuries.

The ancient Hebrews also pondered the fact that all men are

sinners. But unlike their pagan contemporaries—who often
thought of the gods as cruel, arbitrary, jealous of man—they
could not believe that God had originally formed man in such a
state of wretchedness and sin. It would be unreconcilable with
God's whole revelation of himself as good and loving.

The biblical author looked back to the beginning of the human race and set down the story of how man has sinned from
his origin. The background of the story we recall from chapter 2
of Genesis. The first humans are pictured in a luxurious garden,
with power over the rest of creation; man and woman are
intimately united, of "one flesh." "The man and his wife were
both naked and were not ashamed," i.e., they had complete
confidence, openness, esteem for one another. Above all man
is the intimate friend of God who speaks to him with love and
concern. Then comes tragedy: Read Genesis, chapter 3.

The first man chose his own way over God's. He had to make
a choice like everyone who was to follow him: to give himself
to God, or to rely on his own human power. He chose his own
way and rejected God's proffered love. "In one man all have
sinned," says St. Paul. We all sin as this first man did.

This story is symbolic, so its precise details are unimportant.
We do not know what the precise sinful action of the first humans actually was. The serpent is a symbol of evil, some male-
volent power outside of man; eating the forbidden fruit signifies
man choosing his own way over God's. The effects of their sin
are attested by the experience of anyone who has ever done
serious wrong.

Is God revealing that Adam and Eve were perfect specimens of
mankind? No, we need only believe that they had true human
liberty. Is God saying that they were created in a state of sublime
happiness and grace from which they fell? This has been the
traditional view, but the biblical imagery probably refers to the
ideal to be sought after, rather than describing something that
actually once existed.

The worst effect of their sin is that man and woman no longer
have confident access to God's friendship. They are pictured as
hiding from him and are finally put out of the garden. They also
notice they are naked. Man has lost confidence and trust in his

fellow humans, has difficulty communicating with them, is subject to social conventions and shame. Man's labor and woman's motherhood—their typical roles—are made difficult and full of anxieties. Woman's help to man becomes servitude. Man no longer has access to the tree of life, i.e., death now becomes a brutal and painful experience. Man's struggle against the serpent, against evil, becomes continual, difficult.

Work has become more burdensome because of this sin; but work itself is natural, necessary, and our privilege, fashioning the universe as "co-creators" with God himself. After the first sin we read, ". . . cursed is the ground because of you; in toil shall you eat of it all the days of your life . . . in the sweat of your face you shall eat bread." But from the beginning man was to work with God, to ". . . fill the earth and subdue it . . ." It is our attitude toward work that sin changes.

The whole physical world has somehow become involved in man's original sin. Man's work to subdue it is now burdensome and painful. But the universe is still good and, as we shall see, redeemed man can work powerfully with God's grace to bring it to perfection.

This description of sin is a masterful presentation of the way in which we all encounter evil: the temptation, first rejected, then dallied with—then the fall. Our sin, too, is basically one of pride, trying to "be like God," putting our judgment over his. Afterwards we are ashamed, but God seeks us out through our unrelenting conscience. We must face the consequences of our sin. Yet God is always willing to give us a fresh start, promising that we can overcome the serpent of evil with his help.

Why did God let man sin? Why did he not make us so we could not sin? We have no complete answer but perhaps, analogously to human love, we could not enjoy the reward of God's love unless we knew that we had done our part to freely earn it. This means there must be the possibility of not earning it, of not loving, of sinning, and this is what man used his freedom to do.

Further, consider what sin costs God. What is more incredible than that God should subject himself to continual refusals, possibly an eternal refusal, by his creatures? To tolerate such a rebuff God must infinitely love and desire man just as he is. Sin thus proves God's great love, respect and solicitude for each of us.

This is the heart of the matter: God's incredible love wishes to exalt us to himself. But we must freely respond to his love and cooperate in his plan for us. He allows our disobedience because it proves how he respects our freedom, our dignity as a person, our true lovableness. No matter how we strike out at him he still respects us. Even when we do not respect ourselves, the infinite God does.

The evil of sin must also be seen in perspective. God puts us on earth so we can freely choose his love, and this is such a brief moment of choice when compared to eternity! It is like asking a child to spend a few minutes alone in a dark room, and in return giving him a lifetime of tremendous joy—except that for our brief trust God gives us eternal joy.

As mankind developed, men continued to sin, and each generation was affected by the faults of its predecessors. The story of Cain and Abel ("sons" of Adam and Eve in the sense that any of us are) shows how evil men could become: Read Genesis 4, 1-81. In this story we see the basic sin in all human relationships: selfish individualism. "Am I my brother's keeper?" should sound familiar to all of us.

The story of the flood and Noah's Ark (Genesis, chapters 6-9) is another symbolic story showing the widespread evil of man, and how God continued to bless the few who served him. After the flood, the ages of men decrease, an ancient literary device to show man's gradual moral deterioration. Then comes the incident of the tower of Babel (Genesis 11, 1-9), another symbolic story showing how men tried to defy God, ended in confusion, and brought disastrous effects upon future generations. As time passed, Adam's sin went on snowballing.

This, then, is original sin: the effect of the sin of the first humans plus the accumulated sin of mankind. We all inherit this accumulation of mankind's defects, its lack of love, its ignorance and corruption. Each of us adds to this common burden of sin by his own sinful acts. Because of it we have a proneness to sin ("concupiscence") passed on from parents to children.

Just as physical heredity and environment transmit certain defects to an infant, so everyone from the womb grows in a sinful moral environment. We experience not only love but what it is to be unloved and therefore we will be unloving in return. We unconsciously adopt the unloving attitudes and values of our society—for example, the pervading notion that money and material success are the important goals of one's life.

This "sin" is "original," then, because it afflicts all of us at our origin, as well as having its inception at the origin of the human race. It is "sin" for us only in an analogous sense, because we have not willed it. But it is real: by it we are alienated from God and others and are prone to willful sins of our own.

From the sin begun by Adam and Eve we should learn particularly the necessity of humility—to know ourselves as we really are, to acknowledge our weakness and limitations. Pride is its opposite, an unrealistic love of ourselves. The first sin and every sin is basically pride, succumbing to the temptation, "You will be like God . . ." It is, for all of us, the greatest obstacle to God's love.

FACING OUR SINS

From this story of sin we see that our sins are rejections of God's love and of our fellow man. They are refusals to respond, to let ourselves be loved by God. Adam's sin is typical: God's love surrounds us in countless ways, and to sin we must hide from him, turn away from his loving care. In doing this we also turn away from our fellow man. We turn in on ourselves, choosing our way over God's and our neighbor's.

Everyone has a conscience which he must follow, by which he knows right and wrong. His mind judges that some actions are good, and therefore should be done, and other things are wrong and must be avoided. If one is not true to these judgments, he is untrue to himself, and can never expect real happiness.

Our conscience must be guided by God, because only he is infinitely wise and sees what is truly right and wrong. Just as we make mistakes in other things, so we sometimes form a mistaken sense of morality. We must investigate, to make sure that our conscience agrees with God's loving plan for us. We shall see that he has given us concrete moral guides, particularly through Christ's teaching. Reflection on Christ's teaching through the centuries has shown us certain things about this.

Love is the great rule of morality. Sin, we saw, is at least a partial rejection of God's love, a refusal to love our fellow man as we should. All the rules are simply ways to love, and a proof of our love.

Some sins are worse than others, because they deliberately reject love and cut us off from God's grace-presence and our fellow man. In a serious matter we might fully and deliberately choose to reject God and our fellow man, to follow our own selfish way. Obviously we should avoid all sin, but particularly serious sins of this sort. Everything we do in serious sin is vitiated, empty, ultimately useless. Only when we are truly sorry and are forgiven can we enjoy God's love and grace-presence once more. Later we shall consider this further.

These normally are serious sins against love: Deliberately refusing to acknowledge God or to pray; seriously injuring another or his reputation; refusing to help another in serious need; serious offenses of sexual immorality, scandal, stealing, drunkenness, refusing to use our talents, prejudice or discrimination against others.

Each sin of ours, and especially serious sin, makes it harder for us to know God's truth and follow it. Obviously the grossly immoral person—one seeking primarily his own pleasure, power, wealth—will never be able to accept God's teachings. Most people, of course, are not such deliberate sinners. But even their occasional sins make it harder for them to accept God's teachings and follow them.

Each sin of ours adds to the burden of sin in the world, and blocks the spread of God's love to our fellow man. Each sin causes us to draw away from others; we fail to do our part to spread love and happiness.

GOD'S PLAN OF GREATER LOVE

Though man went on sinning seriously against God, God did not destroy man nor abandon him. We might have expected God to reject our race, considering the accumulated sin of mankind—the continual wars, crimes, cruelty, and terrible injustices that we have inflicted upon one another. But God is infinite love and compassion.

Let us suppose that we had new neighbors who rejected our

offer of friendship, and then continually insulted us, while their children destroyed our property and abused us at almost every opportunity. How long would we tolerate them?

God used man's sins to show even greater love. He promised that he would save us from our sins. His promise to save us is described as the curse which he put on the serpent; there will be a constant battle with evil, and it can hurt us, but eventually it will be overcome by the offspring of the woman: "I will put enmity between you and the woman, and between your seed and her seed; he shall bruise your head, and you shall bruise his heel" (Genesis 3, 15).

Then God gradually unfolded his plan: Despite man's sin, and in fact because of it, God sent his own Son into the world to give us his grace-presence and love beyond measure. Christ, the offspring of the woman, would crush the power of evil and bring us overwhelming grace. This is why each year during the Easter vigil service the Church says of Adam's sin: "O happy fault, that merited such a redeemer!" Out of the great evil of sin God has brought far greater good.

IN THE LITURGY

The texts of the Mass are filled with allusions to our sinfulness and our need of grace: "I confess to almighty God . . . ," "Lord, have mercy, Christ, have mercy . . . ," ". . . forgive us our trespasses," "Lamb of God, you take away the sins of the world, have mercy on us," etc.

DAILY LIVING: GOD'S CONSTANT HELPS

Because we are weak and prone to sin we need God's constant help. By his grace-presence God continually gives us many promptings to know what to do and strength to do it. These constant helps are called his actual graces.

Actual graces are the continuous ways in which God's grace-presence prompts us to do good or avoid evil. They come for particular "acts." They are the innumerable little ways in which God within us makes his presence known. If we are sensitive to them, we will recognize them many times a day: a prompting comes to do some good act, to pray, to help someone, to avoid a sinful situation, or to realize more clearly a truth about God or ourselves, to see another with greater appreciation, etc.

Our every good thought or action is initiated and supported by God's actual graces. We cannot do a thing to reach heaven without his help. "For it is God who of his good pleasure works in you both the will and the performance" (Philippians 2, 13).

God continually gives these promptings, makes these overtures, even to those not yet related to him by sanctifying grace. He constantly and lovingly "prods" even the worst sinners. He invites them in all sorts of ways to make their free commitment of love to him, to let him possess them and love them by his grace-presence.

God gives us these helps particularly if we ask for them, and even more so if we are determined to follow them when he gives them. We need much prompting from God's actual graces especially as we study religion, to know and follow his truth sincerely and courageously.

SOME SUGGESTIONS FOR...

DISCUSSION

Can you understand how sin is a refusal to accept God's love—and how it affects all of us?

Can you see how mankind would need a savior?

What do you find most effective in dealing with our proneness to sin?

FURTHER READING

°° *Man and Sin*, Schoonenberg (University of Notre Dame Press, 1965)—An outstanding Dutch theologian's new, challenging view of sin as a continuing state of mind that rejects God, with reflections on the nature of original sin.

°° *The Biblical Doctrine of Original Sin*, Dubarle (Herder & Herder, 1964)—A thorough, penetrating study of how the newer views on original sin are quite compatible with scripture; the author's thesis is summarized in chapter 7.

** *Christ and Original Sin,* DeRosa (Bruce, 1967)—An excellent
and clearly-written summary of current theological thinking
about original sin, and also about Christ's divinity and true
humanity.

PERSONAL REFLECTION

Sin from the start began "snowballing," cut our whole race off
from God, and brought the horrors of death, wars, crime, cruelty,
and untold suffering into our world. This is the terrible, cumula-
tive effect of sin. My personal sins can also cut me off from God,
and can affect many others, causing unhappiness and pain of
which I may not even be aware.

My sins also make it more difficult, and sometimes impossible
to know and believe in Christ's teachings. Christ said, "If anyone shall do the will of my Father, he shall know my teaching,
whether it be from God." I should honestly and sincerely think
over my sins, especially my serious sins—perhaps during my
evening prayer. I will determine to do all in my power to avoid
them especially the one that does the most harm to others.

4

God's Plan Unfolds in the Old Testament

Has God ever shown his concern with human affairs? Can we see God's plan at work anywhere in history? What is the unique importance of the Jewish people?

THE GREAT PEOPLE OF THE COVENANT

The story of mankind after the first sin is a dreary one of continuing infidelity to God. Sin seems to dominate everywhere. But God is silently at work, and when men are ready, he steps into human history. He selects a tiny group of people and with them begins his new plan for the salvation of the world.

The Old Testament tells the story of God's preparation of his people for the coming of Christ. It is concerned with only one people, the Jews. Other nations are mentioned only incidentally. It does not even give a complete history of the Jews, but only of the events that directly concern God's plan.

We should note especially that the main themes of the Old Testament look forward to completion in the New Testament. God's people of the Old Testament are the forerunners and basis of his people of the New Testament, Christ's Church. Vatican Council II said this clearly and gratefully:

The Church of Christ acknowledges that . . . the beginnings of her faith and her election are found already among the patriarchs, Moses and the prophets . . . that all who believe in Christ are included in Abraham's call, and that the salvation of the Church is mysteriously foreshadowed by the chosen people's exodus. . . . The Church, therefore, cannot forget that she re-

43

ceived the revelation of the Old Testament through the people
with whom God in his inexpressible mercy concluded the ancient
covenant. Nor can she forget that she draws sustenance from the
root of that well-cultivated olive tree onto which have been
grafted the wild shoots, the Gentiles (*Declaration on the Relationship of the Church to Non-Christian Religions*, no. 4).

We should try to "enter into" the events of this story, since it
was written as much for us as for the people of two or three
thousand years ago. It is the Christian conviction that this story
is meant for everyone, that it is the high point of man's relationship with God. It tells of the great events that have profoundly influenced our human situation and particularly our
Western civilization. If we read of these events sympathetically
and openly, trying to understand their meaning, they can tell
us much about the meaning of our life and our relationship
with God and other people. Countless millions have become
deeper, better human beings through this story—and so can we.

God stepped into human history by making himself known to
Abraham, the first of the patriarchs, about 1900 B.C. Abraham
was a donkey caravanier, the leader of his tribe, living at Ur (in
modern Iran). God changed his name from Abram, and made
him great promises: Read Genesis 12, 1-3.

God then made a covenant—an agreement or testament—with
Abraham. A covenant is the ancient way by which two parties
solemnly bound themselves together. It was a contract, a promise, or pledge, and those making it called down punishment on
themselves if they should break it.

A covenant was made by some visible sign or ceremony signifying the internal union of the parties concerned. When Abraham
asked for a sign of the covenant, God told him to cut in half
several animals and lay the pieces opposite each other. Then,
"as the sun was setting, Abram fell into a deep sleep; and terror
came upon him, a great darkness. The Lord said to Abram,
'Know for certain . . .' (and) when the sun had set and it was
dark, a smoking fire pot and a flaming torch passed between
the pieces. On that day the Lord made a covenant with Abram
. . ." (Genesis 15, 8ff.)

The ceremony or ritual was sometimes, as in Abraham's case,
for both parties to pass between the divided parts of an animal;

sometimes there was a shedding of blood, considered the sacred principle of life by the ancients; sometimes it was an exchange of gifts, or eating and drinking together the "covenant meal."

Today we often make agreements in this way: a treaty signed by representatives of two nations; a business contract concluded at a meal and then signed by the parties; a bet made with a handshake; particularly one based on love, as an exchange of wedding vows symbolized by an exchange of rings.

The covenant with Abraham is described in Genesis: Read Genesis 17, 1-12. By this covenant God promised Abraham great posterity, a fruitful land, and extraordinary blessings on his descendants and through them on all mankind. Abraham and his descendants for their part were to serve God and have faith in his promises. Circumcision was to be the sign of the covenant.

This is the first great and extraordinary sign of God's love: he binds himself by a covenant with man—and, further, he is faithful to it even when man is not. Now a new relationship of intimacy, a truly personal union, begins between God and man. We see how great is our worth and dignity to God—a unique concept when compared to other beliefs in which the soul often loses its identity, and where the individual means little.

Abraham was outstanding for his faith in God, so much so that he was ready to obey God's command to sacrifice his only son, Isaac. His obedience began to reverse the trend begun by Adam's disobedience:

Take your son, your only son Isaac, whom you love, and go to the land of Moriah, and offer him there as a burnt offering upon one of the mountains of which I shall tell you. . . . Abraham built an altar there, and laid the wood in order, and bound his son Isaac, and laid him on the altar, upon the wood. Then Abraham put forth his hand, and took the knife to slay his son. But the angel of the Lord called to him from heaven, and said, "Abraham, Abraham." And he said, "Here am I." He said, "Do not lay your hand on the lad or do anything to him; for now I know that you fear God, seeing you have not withheld your son, your only son, from me" (Genesis 22, 2. 9-12).

God's covenant with Abraham was renewed with his son, Isaac, and with his grandson, Jacob or Israel, from whose twelve sons came the twelve tribes of the Jewish nation. The family had now settled in the land to which God had directed them, present-day Israel. Like Abraham, Jacob's name was changed to fit his new role in God's plan:

And God said to him, "Your name is Jacob; no longer shall your name be called Jacob, but Israel shall be your name." So his name was called Israel. And God said to him, "I am God Almighty: be fruitful and multiply; a nation and a company of nations shall come from you, and kings shall spring from you. The land which I gave to Abraham and Isaac I will give to you, and I will give the land to your descendants after you" (Genesis 35, 10-12).

The scriptures tell how Joseph, Israel's son, went to Egypt and became a leader of that country. Some Hebrews followed, and increased in numbers and wealth. But then the Egyptians began to enslave them. God, however, was watching over his people and raised up their greatest leader, Moses, to lead them out of bondage.

Moses was the great Israelite leader chosen by God to deliver his people out of Egypt. We saw earlier his great experience of God, how the Lord came to him in a burning bush and revealed that he was the living God of the patriarchs:

"Do not come near; put off your shoes from your feet, for the place on which you are standing is holy ground." And he said, "I am the God of your father, the God of Abraham, the God of Isaac, and the God of Jacob." And Moses hid his face, for he was afraid to look at God (Exodus 3, 5-6).

Then God gave Moses his mission:

"Say this to the people of Israel. 'The Lord, the God of your fathers, the God of Abraham, the God of Isaac, the God of Jacob, has sent me to you . . . I have observed you and what has been done to you in Egypt; and I promise that I will bring you up out of the affliction of Egypt, to the land of the Canaanites . . . a land flowing with milk and honey' " (Exodus 3, 15-17).

Moses went to Pharaoh and demanded that he let the Israelites leave Egypt, but was refused. This Pharaoh is thought to be the famous and egotistical Rameses II, whose images cover Egypt and whose mummy can be seen today in the Egyptian Archeological Museum in Cairo. In the records of his reign we find nothing about the Israelites, but we know that Semite slaves worked on his great store cities, and the Israelites at this time were a small, unorganized group, probably scarcely noticed in the continual migrations across Egypt's borders.

After a series of plagues—natural yearly occurrences that could be interpreted as divine interventions—Pharaoh still would not let them go. Finally, God told Moses that on a particular night each Israelite family was to slaughter a lamb, put some of its blood on the doorposts of their houses, and eat it with unleavened bread and bitter herbs: Read Exodus 12, 1-14.

This was the Passover or Pasch, begun by the paschal meal. It began the events leading up to the old covenant. Later Christ will eat this meal to begin his new covenant. The story continues, telling in figurative, hyperbolic language of what was probably the death of Pharaoh's firstborn son: Read Exodus 12, 29-32.

Saved by the blood of the lamb, the Israelites fled from Egypt and with God's help passed through the waters of the Red Sea—most probably a passage through the marshy "Sea of Reeds," aided by favorable winds which later brought high waters in which Pharaoh's pursuing soldiers were drowned. By this natural event, God again aided his people—and gave a prophetic sign of what his new people would do in Christian baptism, passing through water to salvation and freedom.

This is the great event of the Exodus, the deliverance of the Israelites from Egypt. It happened about 1270 B.C. It is the central event of Jewish history, the striking proof of God's intervention on behalf of his people, and the foundation of their hope that he would one day do so again. Strikingly unlike their pagan neighbors, the Jews retold this greatest event of their history year after year, century after century—and still recount it—as proof of God's intervention in their behalf.

THE MAKING OF THE OLD COVENANT

Free of their enemies, the Israelites now journeyed some three hundred miles through the harsh, debilitating Sinai desert. Fi-

nally they came to the Sinai mountains near the tip of the penin-
sula, a desolate, silent, awesome place even today.

At Mount Sinai, God made his great covenant with the Israelites: Read Exodus 19, 1-6.

This was the old covenant, or Old Testament. Moses is the
mediator of this old covenant, a figure of Christ who will mediate
the new and perfect covenant. Moses alone can enter God's
awesome presence: Read Exodus 19, 16-25.

By this covenant the promises made to Abraham and his descendants are extended to all the Israelites who are now made
God's own people. Here the straggling, motley and probably terrified band of ex-slaves are formed into a great people. Circumcision continues to be a sign of their unique destiny.

In return for making the Israelites his own people, God asked
them to keep their part of the covenant, summarized in the ten
commandments. This simple moral code was known throughout
the Middle East at that period, particularly in the famous Code
of Hammurabi—except that Israel's concept of God, as we shall
see, was totally unique: Read Exodus 20, 1-17.

The ten commandments were supplemented by a whole set of
other laws organizing and administering the life of the people in
an orderly way. Thus much of the first five books of the Old
Testament (the Pentateuch) is concerned with property and
criminal laws, rules of worship and sacrifice, regulations about
health and marriage, etc.

Then Moses "sealed" or accepted the covenant on behalf of the
people by a sacrifice culminating in the sprinkling of animal's
blood: Read Exodus 24, 3-8. We saw that important covenants
were often made by some such sign or ceremony. Later Christ
will inaugurate the new, perfect covenant by shedding his blood
for us in sacrifice.

This is the "church" of the Old Testament, God's people, the
Israelites gathered together. This is what "church" originally
meant—God's people called together by him, under the authority of their leaders, his representatives, to receive his teaching
and show their acceptance of it by sacrifice.

Israel's whole future was to be judged by whether or not she
kept this covenant, but almost immediately the people broke it,
idolatrously worshipping a golden calf. God pardoned and

spared his people through Moses' intercession, after he had
fasted for forty days in reparation—here again we see Moses as
the savior of his people, a forerunner of Christ. These violations
of the covenant were to happen repeatedly. After the first
enthusiastic acceptance of the covenant the people grew restless, dissatisfied. So God kept them in the desert for a whole
generation, toughening and disciplining them until they forgot
the fleshpots of Egypt. Discipline is always necessary for one to
be faithful to God and resist the lure of merely material things.

The Israelites wandered for forty years through the desert, but
God gave them many signs of his presence and protection: a
cloud during the day, and the fire of lightning by night, a
discovery of water when they most needed it, and the food of
the desert manna tree to sustain them.

By these events, God reveals but also conceals himself, since
they can always admit of a natural explanation. As with the signs
of the Exodus—the plagues, passing over the Sea of Reeds, the
thunder and lightning and earthquake of Sinai—it takes faith to
realize God is acting. God is always a hidden God. "No man can
see my face and live," he told Moses. And so it is with all his
actions through history, and with us today.

But the story of the forming of Israel, and particularly Israel's
concept of God, is strikingly unique in history. Everything in
Israel's culture came from surrounding cultures, but her religion,
the heart of her national life, was opposed in every way to that
of her neighbors. The surrounding gods were very human, fight-
ing, lustful, often cruel, capricious and unpredictable, needing
to be placated by magic or human sacrifice, whose cults often
glorified war, pillage, the degradation of women, incest, etc.

Israel's God is wholly different from man, always takes the
initiative, fills him with awe, can neither be controlled by magic
nor manipulated by sacrifice; he demands man's total submission.
He is the Lord of all history, but yet is loving, good, always
faithful to his people. Israel's unique concept of Yahweh, their
God, can be summed up in two poignant passages: **Read Exodus
15, 11-16; and Deuteronomy 7, 6-12.**

If man were to form his idea of God from his desert experience,
the God so conceived would be created in the image and likeness

of the desert. He would be an unforgiving enemy, harsh and
cruel. He would . . . be not unlike the Mesopotamian Nergal who
seems to exhibit the character of the murderous burning sun, or
of the Syrian Hadad, a stormy warrior who flings his thunder-
bolts with awesome abandon. The God of Israel was not a reflection of the desert; yet the desert was the scene where man in the
Old Testament encountered God. No one who is at all familiar
with the Old Testament can think that the God whom Israel
encountered in the desert derived his character from the desert; if
he had, no Israelite poet could ever have said that his covenant
of love is above all his works. Such a God could have claimed
only that terrified submission which man must pay to superior
irrational force ("Into the Desert" by John L. McKenzie, in *The
Way*, London, Vol. 1, No. 1).

**Moses died within sight of the Promised Land, and Joshua was
selected by God to lead the people across the Jordan and into
Canaan.** They "passed over" the Jordan into the Promised Land.
This was the land to which Abraham had been led by God centuries before; today, it is, roughly, the State of Israel. Eventually,
with God's consistent help, they conquered the land and divided it among the twelve tribes. Judges were placed as rulers
over the tribes.

The Exodus was over. God had kept his promise. He had given
the Israelites a home of their own. But they were still unfaithful
to him.

**The Israelites broke the covenant again and again, but God
was always faithful.** His people worshipped pagan gods and
adopted immoral pagan customs. The Old Testament then portrays God as allowing disasters to come upon them—war, famine,
plague, conquest, exile—in order to bring them back to repentance. He continually forgave them and allowed them to renew
the covenant.

A touching description of God's love for his unfaithful people
is Hosea's tragic story of his marriage with the prostitute, Gomer.
After the birth of their three children, Gomer takes up with other
men, leaves Hosea, and again becomes a prostitute. Because he
still loves her, Hosea seeks her out and takes her back. Thus God
loves his unfaithful people and takes them back—including us
today:

She decked herself with her rings and jewelry, and went after her lovers, and forgot me, says the Lord. Therefore, behold, I will allure her, and bring her into the wilderness, and speak tenderly to her . . . And in that day, says the Lord, you will call me "My husband," and no longer will you call me "My Baal" (false god) (Cf. Hosea, chapters 1-3).

IN THE LITURGY

At Mass the first scripture reading is normally a passage from the Old Testament, recounting some part of this great story for our benefit today.

During the first official eucharistic prayer, the priest asks God to accept our offerings "as once you accepted the gifts of your servant Abel, the sacrifice of Abraham, our father in faith, and the bread and wine offered by your priest Melchisedech."

In the Litany for the Dying, the Church asks Abel, Abraham, and the patriarchs and prophets to pray for us, and then petitions: "Deliver, O Lord, the soul of your servant, as you delivered Abraham from Ur of the Chaldees . . . as you delivered Isaac from becoming a sacrifice at the hand of his father, Abraham . . . as you delivered Moses from the power of Pharaoh, King of Egypt . . ."

And in the burial service the Church prays: "May the angels lead you to the bosom of Abraham (heaven)."

During the Easter Vigil Service, the high point of the Church's year, the great Easter hymn is chanted, pointing out the connection between Christ and Moses, and Christ and the paschal lamb:

Jesus Christ, our Lord, paid to the eternal Father the whole debt of Adam, blotting out the bond that still held us forfeit, with his dear blood. The paschal feast is this! Here the lamb is slain, with whose blood the doors of his faithful people are made holy. This night long ago thou didst rescue the sons of Israel, our fathers, out of Egypt.

DAILY LIVING: MEETING GOD

In human history men have met God in a decision of conscience and have been led by him to an "exodus" in search of freedom and dignity. Often, as with the Israelites, the journey was painful and confusing. The early Christians who gave up everything were an example, as were the countless peoples who sought a human identity, the waves of immigrants who peopled America, those today who risk death escaping Iron Curtain repression, and those who struggle for civil liberties.

Currently many who struggle for human rights echo this great human tradition. Aware of their weaknesses but driven by conscience, they ask: "Let my people go . . . to be able to vote freely. . . to advance themselves and live decently in their own land!"

God communicates with us today through the events of our life as he did to the great men of the Old Testament. But he is always the hidden God who will never overwhelm us. We must be alert to the signs he gives us, to his overtures of love. In the things that happen to us we should try to perceive what lesson he is trying to teach, what bit of love he is trying to communicate to us. Everyone and everything that is part of our life can have a meaning for us.

If we do not recognize God acting in our life, perhaps it is because we are not yet ready to take the risk of opening ourselves to his love. One who is unwilling to risk, to give of himself in love, will never perceive the love that is being offered him. To the one who is willing to love, on the other hand, life is full of wonderful meanings.

Abraham had to be willing to give up what was most dear to him, and Moses had to risk his life and the lives of many others. God may not ask this of us, but he does ask that we try to live up to our conscience, be true to ourself, and avoid any serious sin that might alienate us from him and our fellow man.

SOME SUGGESTIONS FOR . . .

DISCUSSION

Can you see the value of covenants, particularly one between God and man?

Is there an "exodus" of current or past history that has particularly impressed you?

Do you find meaningful the notion of God communicating with us through the events of life?

PERSONAL REFLECTION

A "passing over" from slavery and suffering, through the desert to freedom and happiness was necessary for the Israelites. Later Christ will accomplish his great work by passing over from suffering and death to life. So anyone who would find God today must undergo suffering in order to enter eternal joy.

In the desert Israel was alone before God: there were no distractions, no place to run and hide. Their decision was whether to live or die. If they wanted to survive, there was only one way: total submission to God's will. Realizing that God alone could save them, Israel enthusiastically accepted his covenant.

Sometimes God must bring us "into the desert," make us realize our total inadequacy, so that we will give ourselves to him. I should ask for the faith to recognize him in my sufferings and inadequacies.

5

Priests, Kings and Prophets
Prepare the Way

SACRIFICES, PRIESTS AND KINGS

After Mount Sinai, God dwelt among his people with an extraordinary familiarity. He was present especially above the Ark of the Covenant, a small gold-covered chest containing the commandments, which was placed in the tabernacle, a portable temple-tent (Exodus, chapters 25-27). From here God communicated with Moses and his other representatives among the people. In this, we have a prelude to our practice of reserving the eucharist, Christ's special presence among us, in the tabernacles of our churches.

As God's people came to know him they worshipped him, to show their feelings toward him, to give themselves to him, and be united with him. They wanted to show their recognition that he was their God, and to express their obligations to him. As with any growing love, they also wished to be transformed, united with him.

They worshipped God particularly by sacrifice—by publicly offering gifts to him. Just as men have always expressed their feelings toward one another by giving gifts, so they offered gifts to the deity.

The great events of life are celebrated by giving gifts, expressing many things, particularly a desire to be united with one we love. We give birthday presents and wedding gifts, we exchange gifts at Christmas, etc. Gifts express love, praise, thanks, repentance, and they often implicitly ask for something. A gift stands for the giver—accepting the gift means acceptance of the one who gave it, as when a girl accepts a young man's ring. Above

54

all, then, a gift expresses our desire to be united in love with the one to whom we give it.

Sacrifice meant offering a gift, by a priest, changing it in some way, and eating of it. People would take some gift that represented themselves, and offer it to God by means of their representative, a priest. He would change or transform the gift to signify that they were giving it to God, that it no longer belonged to them—often he would kill a living gift, or victim—and then he would burn it to further show God's acceptance and possession of it. Sometimes there would be a meal or banquet, a communion, to further signify union with God by eating of what was now divine.

Abel had offered sacrifice to God, as had Noah, and Abraham had been ready to sacrifice his only son. After one of Abraham's victories, the mysterious figure of Melchisedech offered bread and wine to God in thanksgiving, a foreshadowing of what Christ and the Christian priesthood would do.

And Melchisedech, king of Salem, brought out bread and wine; he was priest of God most high and he blessed him and said, "Blessed be Abram by God most high, maker of heaven and earth ..." (Genesis 12, 18-20).

A sacrifice had sealed the old covenant, and the Israelites were guided by God to lay down definite norms for sacrifices. These were offered by the priests at an altar set aside for this in the tabernacle (Leviticus, chapters 1-7). As when any group offers a gift, one person, the priest, made the offering.

The priests were men specially chosen to offer sacrifice, and to bring God's blessings to the people. They were essentially mediators, "go-betweens." God chose Aaron, Moses' brother, as his first priest and his descendants were to carry on the work of the priesthood. They were made priests at a special ceremony during which they were anointed with oil and clothed in special garb:

"Then bring near to you Aaron your brother, and his sons with him, from among the people of Israel, to serve me as priests ... And you shall make holy garments for Aaron your brother, for glory and for beauty ... and you shall take the anointing oil, and pour it on his head and anoint him" (Exodus 28, 1-2; 29, 7).

Later Christ will offer his life as the perfect sacrifice to begin the new covenant and the elements of sacrifice will then be brought to perfection. All the sacrifices before Christ prepared the way for his perfect sacrifice which would attain the perfect union of man with God.

In the most solemn and significant Hebrew ritual, the Sacrifice of Atonement, the high priest once a year sacrificed a bull and goat outside the sanctuary, then took their blood into the Holy of Holies, and sprinkled it over the covering of the Ark where Yahweh dwelt. Since their life was considered to be in their blood, these victims representing the people were united with God as far as it was possible to do so. Later the New Testament writers will show how Christ shed his blood, as he sacrificed his life to bring all mankind "once for all" into God's presence in heaven.

The Israelites also wanted a king and God inspired Samuel to anoint Saul. When he was killed, David was anointed king (c. 1000 B.C.). The job was evidently too much for Saul and he went slowly mad. The shepherd boy, David, was brought in to soothe Saul with his music, became a popular hero after he killed the giant Goliath, and then had to flee the paranoid ruler. Upon Saul's tragic death, David was chosen king by popular acclaim and made Jerusalem the capital city, bringing there the Ark of the Covenant. The biblical books 1 and 2 Samuel tell of this period.

David sinned but repented, and God promised that someday a king would come from his descendents whose kingdom would last forever. When the prophet Nathan excoriated David for his adultery with Bathsheba and his murder of her husband, he became a great figure of true repentence; then through Nathan God made him his great promise: Read 2 Samuel 7, 12-16.

Solomon, David's son, succeeded him and built the magnificent temple in Jerusalem in which he placed the Ark of the Covenant. There sacrifices to God took place daily. Solomon had a reign of great splendor, the high point of Israelite power and influence. But like many of his people he sinned by greed and idolatry, and eventually rebellion arose, in the midst of which Solomon died. The two biblical books of Kings tell of this and the following periods.

Because of their sinfulness, Israel was now split into the northern kingdom, Israel, and the southern kingdom, Judah, whose people came to be called "Jews." The latter, the two tribes of Judah and Benjamin, would contain the tiny "remnant" which would eventually fulfill God's promises. It is more than coincidental that as God's people of the Old Testament were split because of their sinfulness, so it was to be with his people of the New Testament: when Christendom became widely corrupted, its unity was also destroyed.

However, God did not abandon his people, but sent them in their degeneration another group of outstanding men, the prophets.

THE PROPHETS

The prophets were men especially called by God to speak in his name, his spokesmen to his people for several hundred years. They were one of the most amazing groups in history. Herdsmen, priests, noblemen, migrant workers, they shared one thing: a burning desire to return their people to faithfulness to the covenant and to deepen their understanding of it. They were the conscience of Israel. Through them Israel's religion was gradually purified and developed.

By their lives of total dedication and their outstanding deeds, the prophets gained acceptance in Israel—though, like forthright people, they were usually unpopular, and not infrequently were murdered by the people.

The great Elijah, for instance, whose cave can be seen today on Mount Carmel above the modern city of Haifa, had to contend with the weak and degenerate king Ahab and his infamous queen, Jezebel, and with the attraction of Baal-worship and its human sacrifice and other gross immoralities. The first book of Kings tells how Elijah pitted his sacrifice-offering against that of the prophets of Baal: God sent down lightning, "the fire of the Lord," to set fire dramatically to his offering, and the prophets of Baal were disgraced and slain. Jezebel then promised she would kill Elijah. He fled into the Sinai desert, weak and weary, wanting to die where God had first revealed himself to Israel. There God came to him and reassured him: **Read 1 Kings 19, 1-18.**

Then there is Amos, probably a migratory worker, a forceful man who castigated the wealthy for their oppression of the poor: ". . . they sell the righteous for silver, and the needy for a pair of shoes—they that trample the head of the poor into the dust of the earth, and turn aside the way of the afflicted . . ." (Amos 2, 6-7).

Amos particularly condemned their smug pride over their status which would eventually destroy them: **Read Amos 3, 1-2; 4, 1-5.**

In predicting the coming disaster, he spoke of the "remnant" which would be preserved faithful to the Lord:

Thus says the Lord, "As the shepherd rescues from the mouth of the lion two legs, or a piece of an ear, so shall the people of Israel who dwell in Samaria be rescued, with the corner of a couch and part of a bed" (Amos 3, 12).

Isaiah was the longest-lived of the prophets, and even as he foretold the destruction to come, he touchingly reminded the people of God's love:

But Sion said, The Lord has forsaken me, my Lord has forgotten me. Can a woman forget her sucking child, that she should have no compassion of the son of her womb? Even these may forget, yet I will not forget you (Isaiah 49, 14-15).

The prophets' predictions of destruction were largely ignored by the sinful people. Then the blow fell: first the northern kingdom was destroyed by the Assyrians who swept over the country and deported many of the people. Then the kingdom of Judah fell in 587 B.C. and the people were deported to Babylon. But the prophets consoled them, and many of the most beautiful psalms (religious hymns) are from this period. From this time on many of the Jews would be scattered "among the nations," in the diaspora, eventually providing bases for the spread of Christ's teachings.

At this critical time God promised a new, more perfect covenant. Jeremiah gives this great promise (cf. also Ezechiel 36, 24ff.): **Read Jeremiah 31, 31-34.**

The prophets' teaching now gradually converged toward the Messiah who was to come. These prophecies were given at different times and are scattered throughout the Old Testament. Many are obscure and seemingly contradictory, and evidently the prophets themselves did not understand exactly how they would be fulfilled; only when we study the life of Christ do we see how he fulfilled them.

Many of the prophecies concerned a new age, "the day of the Lord." Joel, for instance, saw it first of all as a time of judgment upon Israel:

> Let all the inhabitants of the land tremble for the day of the Lord is coming, it is near, a day of darkness and gloom, a day of clouds and thick darkness! (Joel 2, 1-2).

But it will also be a time of great blessings, when God's spirit is "poured out on all flesh." Peter's Pentecost sermon, the first announcement of the Christian message, will quote this: Read Joel 2, 28-29.

The "Messiah" or "Christ" means the one anointed with holy oil, as were the priests, kings, and prophets. The word "Messiah" meant particularly the king who would fulfill Israel's destiny. While the prophecies are often obscure, one looking at them with the help of faith can discern many characteristics of the Messiah who would begin this new age: Read Isaiah 35, 3-6.

The Messiah would be a great king of David's lineage whose rule would never end. This, we saw, was predicted by Nathan. We should note that the ideal king in those days was Yahweh's instrument, the one through whom he saved his people, who protected them from external enemies and from oppression by the powerful. A few centuries later the prophet Isaiah also told of the kingly Messiah who would be a descendant of David; his best-known prophecies concern Emmanuel, "God-with-us" (chapters 7-11). We shall see that Christ is this kingly descendant of David: Read Isaiah 9, 2-7.

A mysterious "Son of Man" also appears in connection with the messianic hopes of God's people. Christ will often use this title to refer to himself:

> I saw in the night visions, and behold, with the clouds of heaven there came one like the son of man, and he came to the Ancient of Days and was presented before him. And to him was given dominion and glory and kingdom, that all peoples, nations, and languages should serve him. . . . (Daniel 7, 13-14; cf. Psalm 110).

The "suffering servant" is perhaps the best-known figure of the Messiah, given by the prophet known as Second Isaiah. He stressed two ideas difficult for the Jews to grasp, but of deep importance to God's plan: all nations would be called to know and love God, and redemption would come about through the suffering of the innocent Servant of Yahweh—a figure of Christ: Read Isaiah 53, 3-7.

After the exile, a remnant of Jews returned to Jerusalem and began to rebuild. They were chastened and strongly attached to the Law—the five books of Moses (or Torah) elaborated and explained by tradition—and convinced more than ever of their destiny as the chosen people. A total theocracy, with Yahweh as their sole ruler, they considered the high priest his representative and their leader.

In the 4th century B.C. they were conquered by the Greeks, persecuted, and became somewhat hellenized. The Hebrew scriptures were translated into the Greek Septuagint about 250 B.C. Then the Assyrians swept over Palestine, and finally in the century before Christ the Romans conquered the land and installed a puppet king, Herod.

The Old Testament ends with God's people longing for the messianic age to come, but there is confusion about it. Many looked for a new time of great material prosperity. Others expected a great king, like David or Solomon, who would lead them to freedom and glory and establish once more the united kingdom of Israel.

Conscious of God's great deeds on their behalf over the centuries, they looked to his promises for the future. They were a small, almost obscure country on the fringe of a great empire. But they were a monotheistic stronghold in a world of polytheism, superstition, and rationalism; and their moral life was far above that of the rest of the Hellenistic world of the time.

We should note at this time the influential groups in Palestine who were to play a role in Christ's life: Besides the powerful priestly class, there were the Scribes or lawyers, the official interpreters of the Law, the most honored and influential group in the land. The Pharisees, originally concerned to keep the people free of foreign domination, had become narrowly nationalistic; they had added many minute traditions to the Law and exaggerated its literal fulfillment, rather than keeping its spirit.

The **Sadducees** were a proud aristocracy, more liberal in their interpretation of the Law and more open to the Gentiles, but as narrowly opposed as the Pharisees to any messianic changes. Both groups were more than content with the "status quo," and would be Christ's strongest opponents. The **Essenes**, the community of Qumran and the famous Dead Sea Scrolls, withdrew into the desert and lived a strict, celibate, community life to prepare for the coming of the Lord.

Lastly, there was the "remnant," the small number of people loyal to the Lord who were to be the start of the new Israel and the new covenant, the new people of God. Of no particular class or status, they tried to practice a purer, more perfect religion, in their hearts as well as externally. Mary, the mother of Christ, is their outstanding example. They are the "poor" of Israel, the "little ones" whose longing for the Savior is epitomized in this longing cry:

> But I am poor and needy; hasten to help me, O God! Thou art my help and my deliverer; O Lord, do not tarry! (Psalm 70, 5).

We can now sum up the main ideas of the Old Testament: God chooses the Israelites . . . makes a covenant with them, forming them into his people . . . speaking through human representatives who have his authority . . . and who guide the people in living the covenant and worshipping God by sacrifice . . . looking forward to the Messiah . . . who will establish a new and perfect covenant.

IN THE LITURGY

The **Psalms** are the inspired religious hymns or poems of the Old Testament. The Church uses many of them in her liturgy, and priests recite many of them each day as the Church's official prayer. They make excellent and inspiring reading for anyone.

At Mass, immediately before reading the Gospel, the priest asks God to cleanse his heart and lips as he did Isaiah's, so that he may be prepared to announce his Word. In one of the official eucharistic prayers, at the heart of the Mass, we ask God to accept our sacrifice ". . . as you accepted the offerings of your servant Abel, the just, the sacrifice of Abraham, our father, and that of your high priest, Melchisedech."

During the Advent season—which begins with the fourth Sunday before Christmas—we relive again each year the preparation for the coming of the Messiah. Passages from the prophet Isaiah are particularly set before us during this time.

DAILY LIVING: OUR FAITH EXPRESSED BY REVERENCE AND WORSHIP

Faith is the dominant role of God's people of the Old Testament from Abraham on. They are given very little to rely on, not even the assurance of a life after death, but are simply asked to have faith that God will bless them. And he did: far beyond their desire for lands and crops and offspring, he brought them to eternal happiness with himself.

When their faith would seem to be at its breaking point, God would intervene with some sign of his presence and love. Some miraculous event would take place, or a prophet would appear to encourage them. So, if we look closely, we can discern his action when we most need it in our lives.

Reverence for God was great among his people, so much so that they would not even pronounce his name. They had a great sense of awe in his presence. Abraham was seized with terror and felt himself dust and ashes before God; Moses and Elijah hid their faces in dread at his approach; Isaiah almost despaired; Daniel fell to the ground before God, his face pressed to the earth. Perhaps if we had a greater sense of reverence for God, we would be more aware of his presence in our lives.

God's people expressed their faith and gratitude for his help by worshipping him. They did this especially at the great moments in their history, by coming together as his people to worship him by sacrifice. So also today it is natural to show our gratitude for his action in our lives, and to do this not only as individuals but by worshipping together as his people.

The Mass, we saw, is the way Catholics come together each Sunday to worship God. It, too, is a sacrifice, the prolongation of the perfect sacrifice of Christ. When we take part we try to give ourselves to God, in his special presence, to be united with him.

Finally, God's special regard for the Jewish people, so shabbily treated throughout history—and in recent years with unbelievable cruelty—should lead us all to examine our consciences. Vatican Council II forcefully went on record against anti-Semitism:

> . . . the Church, mindful of the patrimony she shares with the Jews and moved not by political reasons but by the Gospel's spiritual love, deplores hatred, persecutions, displays of anti-Semitism directed against Jews at any time and by anyone . . . We cannot truly call on God, the Father of all, if we refuse to treat in a brotherly way any man. (*Declaration on the Relationship of the Church to Non-Christian Religions*, no. 4).

SOME SUGGESTIONS FOR . . .

DISCUSSION

Can you understand the role of prophets—and see how such men are needed throughout history, including today? What action of God in the Old Testament is particularly striking to you?

FURTHER READING

* *Understanding the Old Testament*, Anderson (Prentice-Hall, 1966, 2d Edition)—A good, general comprehensive text concerning the entire Old Testament.

FURTHER VIEWING

The Hate Syndrome—Paulist Productions, 17575 Pacific Coast Hwy., Pacific Palisades, Calif. 90272—A gripping, half-hour movie showing the collision of love and hate as an elderly Jewish teacher confronts a former pupil who now heads the American Nazi Party.

Christ Among Us

PERSONAL REFLECTION

God speaks to me today through the story of the Old Testament, as well as to the people of history. I cannot appreciate the Christian faith unless I appreciate this fact. I should read some of the Old Testament regularly, perhaps daily. For example: one of the psalms, the book of Job, parts of Proverbs, Wisdom, or Ecclesiasticus.

6
Christ Comes Among Us

How do we know about Jesus Christ? What was so unique about his life? Who did he claim to be? Why was he not accepted more widely? What relevance has his teaching for me today?

THE COMING OF JESUS CHRIST

We saw that the Jewish world of the first century was looking for the coming of the Messianic Age—a king, a kingdom that would fulfill the prophecies and bring God's blessings once again to his people. The New Testament tells of the coming of the Messiah and his fulfillment of these hopes.

An incident that took place during the first days of the Christian Church is recorded in the Acts of the Apostles: **Read Acts 3, 1-10.** This story of a man cured instantly "in the name of Jesus Christ of Nazareth" is typical of Christianity from the beginning. Jesus Christ of Nazareth was the inspiration and power of Christianity from its inception. He is probably the best-known person in the history of the world. Who was he, and what do we really know about him?

The New Testament is the principal source for the life and teachings of Jesus Christ, although he is mentioned briefly in a number of ancient writings. The New Testament, the second part of the bible, consists of 27 books: the four gospels, outlines of part of Christ's life and teachings; the Acts of the Apostles, some incidents in the life of the early Christian Church; the epistles, letters written by Christ's apostles to early Christian communities; and Revelation or the Apocalypse, a highly symbolic writing about the early Church and the final events of history.

The New Testament gives a substantially accurate outline of

Christ's life and teachings, but not a scientific, detailed biography. There is as much evidence for the authenticity of the main events and sayings contained in the New Testament story of Jesus as there is, for example, of Julius Caesar, or any other ancient historical figure. But the authors give only a framework, the substance of what Christ said and did. They were not writing biographies of Christ as people write biographies today.

The New Testament is the record of the early Church's growth in faith and understanding of who and what Jesus Christ is. The authors tell the story of Christ's saving deeds as seen through the eyes of believers writing for believers. Their concern is to show not only an event but its inner religious meaning. They are not greatly concerned about when or where a thing happened, the details of what happened, the exact words Christ used, etc. They show a gradual growth in understanding of who Christ was and of his revelation. To bring out the inner religious meaning of the events of Christ's life, they sometimes arrange details according to Old Testament concepts, and often express themselves in the imaginative language of their Semitic background.

To guide us in our interpretation of the New Testament, then, we use tradition, his Church's understanding of Christ's teachings. Since the New Testament came from the early Christian community, it is best interpreted in the light of the community's beliefs. This is found particularly in the other writings of Christ's early followers that have come down to us.

Since the New Testament is a record of faith, the reader must have faith—or at least be open to the possibility of faith—if he is to derive full benefit from it. The skeptic, the one whose mind is closed against the possibility of a divine intervention in Christ, well get little profit from it.

The four gospels, particularly, tell of Christ's life and teachings They are attributed to Matthew, Mark, Luke, and John. They are really four different accounts of the single "gospel," that is, the "good news" that God has come and saved mankind, climaxing his mighty deeds of the Old Testament. This good news was first announced by the preaching of the apostles and then gradually took on written form in the Christian Church.

The gospel authors take excerpts from Christ's life and teachings, and arrange and interpret them for the particular needs of

their audience. Matthew writes particularly to show that Christ is the promised Messiah; Mark's is the oldest and shortest gospel and is the basis for much of Matthew and Luke; Luke's is the most complete gospel, and shows particularly a very human and universal Christ; John's is the most symbolic of the gospels and was written to show that Jesus is the eternal Son of God who revealed himself through many "signs."

There is practically nothing known about the early life of Jesus, until he begins to preach publicly. The gospel writers are concerned primarily with his public teachings, his message through them to the world. But since the whole of the gospels was written to tell us something, we will consider briefly the story of Jesus' early years.

The life of Jesus begins with the story of the angel coming to Mary which brings out the divine origin of Jesus. Read Luke 26-38. Luke tells us in this account that God somehow communicated to Mary that she was to be the mother of the Savior, and she consented. She then miraculously conceived Jesus Christ. We celebrate this event as the feast of the Annunciation, March 25th.

These initial chapters of Luke and Matthew are the Jewish style of writing, in which the sacred Christian mysteries are illustrated by prophetic Old Testament situations. Here the angel's greeting alludes to the prophecy of Zephaniah (3, 14-20) in which God expresses his love for the virgin "Daughter of Sion." Thus Mary symbolizes all that God loves in Israel. Mary is the new Ark of the Covenant, the place where God dwells, for she too is "overshadowed by the power of the Most High" (Cf. Exodus 40, 35).

Mary, the mother of Jesus Christ, remained a virgin all her life. Joseph was the husband of Mary and the foster-father of Jesus. This is traditional Christian teaching. Luke emphasizes the virginal conception of Jesus by the question to the angel: "How can this be, since I have no husband?" (1, 34), and the angel's response. Matthew tells how Joseph's doubts upon seeing Mary pregnant were settled by a revelation that the conception was miraculous (Matthew 1, 18-25).

A modern Protestant theologian writes perceptively of this:

Her unique relation with the Spirit sets her in such close prox-

imity to God that she must remain alone in order to point out to
our eyes this unique choice of her Lord . . . Her virginity appears
at one and the same time as a sign of consecration and a sign of
solitary powerlessness which gives glory to the fullness and power
of God . . . a sign of poverty, of humility, and of waiting upon
God . . . a sign of emptiness and total trust in God who makes
rich such poor creatures as we are (Max Thurian, *Mary, Mother
of All Christians:* Herder & Herder, 1964, p. 31).

Regarding the "brothers" of Jesus mentioned in the gospels,
the word "brother" was commonly used among the Jews for any
blood relation (another woman, incidentally, is mentioned as the
mother of two of these). Matthew says of Joseph, "And he did
not know her (Mary) till she brought forth her firstborn son"
(Matthew 1, 25), but the word "till" as used here need not mean
any change in Mary's virginity after Christ's birth (Cf. Isaiah 46;
Matthew 12, 20). Nor does calling Jesus the "firstborn" son
imply Mary had other children; this title was always given to the
firstborn male, even if an only child (Cf. Exodus 13, 2).

Early Christian writings widely attest to Mary's perpetual
virginity: St. Basil sums up the early Christian teaching, "The
friends of Christ do not tolerate hearing that the Mother of God
ever ceased to be a virgin" (*Hom. in S. Christi Generationem,*
n. 5). The Reformers also held strongly to this belief, echoing
the Christian view through the centuries.

However, Mary's virginity should be seen as more than mere
physical inviolability. For many today whether Mary is or is
not physically a virgin is of small consequence; they see her
virginity as symbolizing something far greater, her profound
attitude of total openness to God alone, her total consecration of
herself to him before anyone and anything else—and in this each
of us, virginal or not, has the power to imitate her.

As we shall see (chapter 23), Mary is a figure of the Church,
and her virginity is a prophetic sign of the Church's ideal purity
and total dedication to Christ. She is the ideal Christian, totally
given only to God.

St. Luke continues the story by telling us that Mary went to
visit her cousin, Elizabeth, the mother of John the Baptist: "And
when Elizabeth heard the greeting of Mary, the babe leaped in
her womb. And Elizabeth was filled with the Holy Spirit, and she
exclaimed with a loud cry, 'Blessed are you among women and
blessed is the fruit of your womb! And why is this granted me,
that the mother of my Lord should come to me?'" (Luke 1,
41-43).

This greeting of Elizabeth concludes the first part of the prayer, the "Hail Mary." Mary is the last and noblest of the long line of Israel's "poor," the humble ones who will be the start of the new Israel. Mary's answer to Elizabeth, as Luke presents it, is a mosaic of Old Testament texts expressing joy at what God has done through her. The Church uses these verses in its blessing of a mother and her newborn child:

> "My soul magnifies the Lord, and my spirit rejoices in God my Savior; for he has regarded the low state of his handmaid . . ." (Cf. Luke 1, 46-55).

Luke continues with the oft-told story of the birth of Jesus: Read Luke 2, 1-7.

Christmas Day, December 25th, is the day on which we celebrate the birth of Jesus. It is a holyday on which all Catholics attend Mass to rejoice at this great event. The date was chosen by the early Christians to counteract a pagan feast on the same day. Jesus was actually born about 7 B.C.—our present calendar, which dates years from the birth of Christ, took the wrong year as a starting point.

Jesus' birth in poor circumstances is a lesson to us in humility and detachment from riches. The first to greet him were God's faithful poor, Mary, Joseph and the shepherds from the neighboring hills. Luke tells how an angel announced Christ's birth to the shepherds and invited them to be his first worshippers; he concludes with the song that has been immortalized in Christian worship:

> And suddenly there was with the angel a multitude of the heavenly host praising God and saying, "Glory to God in the highest, and on earth peace among men with whom he is pleased" (Luke 2, 13-14).

The gospels tell of other early events of Christ's life. These stories are meant to show that Jesus is the expected Messiah-king, and that he is more than human.

His circumcision is celebrated on January 1st, when he was given the name of Jesus, which means "Savior" (Luke 2, 21). This is celebrated each year as the Octave Day of the Nativity, and is a holyday in the United States on which all Catholics attend Mass.

His presentation in the temple forty days after his birth (Cf. Luke 2, 22-39) is celebrated each year on February 2nd, and is also called the feast of the Purification of Mary. Since Christ was hailed in this incident as the "light of revelation to the Gentiles," on this day in all Catholic churches the candles used in divine services are blessed—hence the popular name "Candlemas Day."

The coming of the Magi is told to portray the coming of the first Gentiles to worship Christ—celebrated as the Epiphany, January 6th—and the flight of the Holy Family into Egypt to escape Herod's persecution (Matthew, chapter 2).

> Matthew, to show that Christ is the new Moses, the new leader of God's people, parallels the coming of each in the first two chapters: Rulers and their courts tremble at the announcement of their births; Herod consults his scribes as Pharaoh did his astrologers; both tyrants decree the murder of children, from which both heroes escape; and both saviors, persecuted and away from their people, receive a heavenly message to return.

Christ's early years are summed up by Luke: He tells us how the child Jesus had been lost by his parents in Jerusalem when he was twelve. They found him in the temple in deep discussion with the teachers of the Law who ". . . were amazed at his understanding and his answers." When Mary reprimanded him, his response shows an awareness of his mission: "Did you not know that I must be in my Father's house?" Then he grew up, obediently, in simple, humble surroundings:

> And he went down with them and came to Nazareth, and was obedient to them: and his mother kept all these things in her heart. And Jesus advanced in wisdom and in stature, and in favor with God and man (Luke 2, 51-52).

Years pass, and then comes John the Baptist, the last of the prophets, preaching repentance and conversion to prepare the way for Christ. John developed as a strict ascetic in the desert, and one day appeared, a striking figure, proclaiming, "Repent, for the kingdom of heaven is at hand" (Matthew 3, 2).

John the Baptist asked people to be changed interiorly, to repent of their sins and be converted, to turn fully toward God. His "baptism" was a sign of this, a primitive forerunner of the Christian sacrament of baptism. When the people wanted to acclaim him the Messiah, he told them he was only preparing the way: "After me comes he who is mightier than I, the thong of whose sandals I am not worthy to stoop down and untie" (Mark 1, 7).

Jesus comes to John and asks to be baptized, and then prepares for his public life by a forty-day fast in the desert. Jesus asked for baptism to connect John's mission with what he would soon begin himself. His desert ordeal, climaxed by severe temptations from the devil, parallels the forty years the Israelites wandered in the desert, and is the model of our practice of penance during the forty days of Lent (Cf. Mark 1, 9-14; Matthew, 3, 13—4, 11).

Christ starts his mission in the harsh desert, as Israel had, to show that he is the beginning of God's new people. He is to be the "new Israel," the one who takes on himself all the aspirations and inadequacies of God's people, and begins a new, transformed people. In the desert he also faces God in stark loneliness, emptiness, fear, and the temptation to discouragement and rebellion—and thus purified he begins his mission or public life.

Christ's public life is the two or three years that he spent preaching, teaching, and working miracles, leading up to his suffering and death. He became known as a great preacher, a reader of hearts, and a wonder-worker:

And he went about all Galilee, teaching in their synagogues and preaching the gospel of the kingdom and healing every disease and every infirmity among the people. So his fame spread throughout all Syria, and they brought him all the sick, those afflicted with various diseases and pains, demoniacs, epileptics, and paralytics, and he healed them. And great crowds followed him from Galilee and the Decapolis and Jerusalem and Judea and from beyond the Jordan (Matthew 4, 23-25).

THE KINGDOM OF GOD IS HERE!

The central theme of Christ's preaching is the good news of the kingdom of God: ". . . Jesus came into Galilee, preaching the gospel of the kingdom of God, and saying, 'The time is fulfilled,

and the kingdom of God is at hand. Repent and believe in the
gospel' " (Mark 1, 14-15).

Jesus' announcement of the kingdom was what the Jewish people had been anticipating for hundreds of years. We saw how
they were awaiting this new, wonderful messianic age of great
blessings. Christ now revealed that it was coming about. This
was the best possible news they could hear—and thus it is called
the gospel, the good news.

But when Christ revealed that his kingdom was an interior,
spiritual one, only a comparative few accepted him. These were
the small remnant, the poor ones whose hearts were truly open
to God's teaching and rule. We saw how most people expected
a great political king, or one who would bring many material
blessings, or who would perfectly observe the Law—but Christ
asked an interior change in oneself to belong to his kingdom.

The kingdom of God is his loving rule, his reign over us, and
our submission to him. When we believe in him and do his will,
we belong to his kingdom. God's reign or kingdom is his guiding
presence, his grace-presence, within us; to submit to his loving
guidance is to belong to the kingdom.

To be a part of God's kingdom, Christ said, we must undergo
an interior conversion. We must have a change of heart, repenting of our sins, determined to begin a new life: "Repent and
believe in the gospel"—here Christ was fulfilling what John the
Baptist had announced. Then in the beautiful and famous "Sermon on the Mount" Christ tells us how to live this conversion in
order to be a part of his kingdom (Cf. Matthew, chapters 5-7).
He begins with the eight beatitudes, the way to true happiness
(the word "blessed" means "happy"): Read Matthew 3, 3-12.

In this kingdom the poor, the humble, the oppressed, the "little
people" are the happy ones—a complete reversal of the world's
usual standards whereby the rich and powerful are the favored
ones. Everyone who has experienced injustice and looked to God
for a better life knows what Jesus was talking about.

A new commandment, love, is the one important rule in this
kingdom. The Jews, we saw, lived by the Law, particularly the
commandments. Now Jesus summed up the whole law of his
kingdom: "A new commandment I give to you, that you love one

another; even as I have loved you, that you also love one another" (John 13, 34).

We will live in this new kingdom forever. Those who follow Christ and become part of his kingdom will be raised up from death: ". . . whoever sees the Son and believes in him, shall have everlasting life, and I will raise him up on the last day" (John 6, 40). This was indeed tremendous news to the Jews who, we saw, had only begun shortly before the time of Christ to think of the notion of a personal life after death, and were not at all clear about it. It has also been tremendous news to those who have grasped it down through the centuries.

Now on earth, those who follow Christ pray and work to extend God's kingdom of love more and more to all men. One day in heaven the kingdom will be completed—God's love will rule over us all—and we will see creation in all its glory and understand the "why" of suffering and injustice. During our present life we pray as Christ taught us: ". . . thy kingdom come, they will be done on earth as it is in heaven."

Christ chose apostles to help spread his kingdom. They were the beginning of his Church: "And he appointed twelve that they might be with him and that he might send them forth to preach" (Mark 3, 14). Inspired by Christ, they would try to make themselves and all men submissive to God's love. He gave them "the keys of the kingdom," the power to guide men to his truth and love.

THE PROMISED MESSIAH—AND HIS REJECTION

"I am the way and the truth and the life. No one comes to the Father but by me" (John 14, 6).

Jesus thus proclaimed that he was the one sent by God as the perfect king, priest, and prophet. This summed up his earthly mission. As the "way" Jesus is our king, the perfect king predicted in the Old Testament, now come to begin an eternal spiritual kingdom. As the "truth" Jesus is the perfect prophet or teacher looked for in the Old Testament, come to give us the fullness of God's truth. As the "life" Jesus is, as we shall see, the perfect priest who sacrificed himself for us.

There is the very human story of Jesus' encounter with the
Samaritan woman who had five husbands and was then living
with another man. Jesus revealed her past to her, and she typi-
cally tried to distract him by launching a defense of her Samaritan worship. Then she referred to the coming Messiah whom the
Samaritans thought of as a great prophet to come. Jesus told her
simply, "I who speak with you am he" (John 4, 5-42).

Christ proclaimed that he was sent by God—the Messiah, but
in a new, fuller, spiritual sense. We saw that the Jewish people
expected the Messiah to be a great worldly leader, the inaugu-
rator of a new age of political power and material blessings.
Christ, however, did not accept the title of Messiah in this sense;
while he never denied it, he seemed always uncomfortable with
it. His ministry was to establish a spiritual kingdom among men,
not just a material one. He was bringing messianic blessings that
were eternal, beyond his people's fondest dreams. But only those
who are willing to hear the truth can know of this: **Read
John 18, 33-37.**

Jesus continually spoke of himself as the "Son of Man," who
would one day come on the clouds of heaven (Daniel 7, 13-14).
(In Ezechiel this term simply means "man.") As he was on trial
for his life ". . . the high priest began to ask him, and said to him,
'Art thou the Christ, the Son of the Blessed One?" And Jesus said
to him, 'I am. And you shall see the Son of Man sitting at the
right hand of the Power and coming with the clouds of heaven' "
(Mark 14, 61-62).

He shocked his followers by speaking of himself as a humiliated and suffering Son of Man, the "suffering servant" who had
been predicted. (Isaiah 52, 13-53, 12.)

And he began to teach them that the Son of Man must suffer
many things, and be rejected by the elders and chief priests and
scribes, and be killed, and after three days rise again. And he said
this plainly. And Peter, taking him aside, began to rebuke him
(Mark 8, 31-32).

Many who had heard him were skeptical, but he offered proof
of his divine mission by working miracles, fulfilling the messianic
prophecies, and making prophecies of his own. In particular, he

predicted that he would return alive after his death; so astounding was this that only a chosen few later grasped it: Read John 2, 18-22.

In his teaching Jesus purged the old Law of its formalism and legalism, and completed it by his more perfect law of love. "Do not think that I have come to destroy the Law or the Prophets," he said, "I have not come to destroy but to fulfill" (Matthew 5, 17). He "spoke with authority" about the Law, and declared that what God wants is love, mercy, justice, honesty. He rebuked the Pharisees for their hypocrisy, their elaborate system of observances, mistaking the means for the end. Chapter 23 of Matthew is one of the most scathing condemnations in all literature. Finally, Jesus told them, because of their blindness "the kingdom of God will be taken away" from them, and given "to a people yielding its fruits" (Matthew 21, 43).

Most of the people did not accept Jesus, but a small number did. They were to be the beginning of his Church. The crowds who had been drawn to him by his miracles largely deserted him when he refused the role of the long-awaited political Messiah. Because he loved all men without exception, most men rejected him; Matthew quotes him as wryly commenting:

> For John came neither eating nor drinking, and they say, "He has a demon"; the Son of Man came eating and drinking, and they say, "Behold, a glutton and a drunkard, a friend of tax collectors and sinners!" (Matthew 11, 18-19).

Stung by his fearless preaching, the hypocritical leaders of the people decided that he would have to die. As his influence over the people grew, they saw him as a threat to their autocratic authority. Despite his holiness and miracles they rationalized that he was an incorrigible troublemaker and for the good of the people he would have to be eliminated. Like many who try to suppress freedom movements today, they became very much concerned with the public safety and order. They then approached Judas, Christ's traitorous apostle, and made a deal to seize his master for what a cheap suit of clothes would cost today.

After a triumphal entry into Jerusalem on Sunday, Jesus began the last week of his life, called by Christians "Holy Week." On Holy Thursday he ate his last supper with his apostles. That night, with Judas' help, he was seized by his enemies.

A farcical trial was held, Christ's enemies convicted him of blasphemy, and he was condemned to death. Like many bigots of our own day, they wanted everything to be legal. Pilate, the Roman governor who alone had the power of life. and death, seems to have been convinced that Jesus was innocent. But when the Jewish authorities threatened to report him to the emperor for tolerating a rival to Caesar, he gave Christ to them.

Mocked and beaten and scourged, Jesus carried his cross to Calvary, and there he was crucified. After three hours on the cross, he died. It was the first "Good Friday." To his followers, this looked like the end of all their hopes.

But on Easter Sunday morning Jesus came back alive again as he had predicted he would. For forty days he appeared to his followers, and then finally disappeared from the earth on Ascension Thursday. His followers returned to Jerusalem, somewhat encouraged, to await the coming of the Holy Spirit, as he had told them.

IN THE LITURGY

The "liturgical year" is the way in which we relive each year the great events of Christ's life by a series of feasts. It is centered around the two great Christian feasts of Christmas and Easter.

The Mass, our great act of worship, is centered on Christ. We learn his words and teachings especially in the scripture readings. We should remind ourselves that Christ is speaking to us as they are read.

The Rosary is a devotion meaningful to some Catholics, centered around the life of Christ. It is a series of prayers said on certain beads together with meditations on the important events in the life of Jesus, and Mary's connection with him.

DAILY LIVING: THE LIFE OF HIS KINGDOM IS LOVE

Jesus taught us above all to love God and our neighbor: Love is the cornerstone of his teaching. It was so important in his eyes that he exhorted us to love even our enemies—a teaching that was nothing short of revolutionary: Read Matthew, 5, 43-48.

He lived all his teachings, but particularly that of love. He proved his love by dying for us, and as he was dying he prayed for his enemies: "Father, forgive them, for they do not know what they are doing" (Luke 23, 34).

Each one of us, in some small way, can imitate Christ's love. Christ showed his love in many ways during his life. In our life there is usually some one aspect of love, some virtue, that we particularly need. We might consider what one characteristic—or more—we need especially.

Jesus loved God humbly, perfectly submissive to his will. This desire to do the Father's will was so outstanding that he could say, ". . . I always do the things that are pleasing to him" (John 8, 29). Even in terrible anguish, contemplating his coming sufferings and death, he prayed: "Father if it is possible, let this cup pass away from me; yet, not as I will but as you will" (Matthew 26, 39).

Jesus taught us that we learn how to love by prayer. He taught us to pray by his constant example. He frequently spent the whole night in prayer; he began all his important actions with prayer; he prayed especially in suffering and crisis (Cf. Luke 6, 12; John, chapter 17; Matthew 26, 36-44; Luke 23, 34 and 46). He particularly taught us humble prayer in the parable of the Pharisee and the publican (Cf. Luke 18, 9-14).

Jesus had courage in doing the Father's will, and in speaking the truth, no matter what people thought or what it cost him. (Cf. Matthew 15, 12-14).

Jesus showed a special love for the sick, the poor, sinners, and those despised by others. (Cf. Luke 7, 1-7; John 9, 1-38; Luke 7, 36-50).

He taught us to love our neighbor, regardless of his race or social status, particularly in the parable of the good Samaritan (Cf. Luke 10, 30-37).

He taught us pointedly to forgive those who injure us, or else God will not forgive our misdeeds, in the parable of the unmerciful servant (Cf. Matthew, 8, 21-35).

Jesus' whole life exemplified a detachment from wealth and

human possessions. We saw his humble birth and background. During his public life he showed a special love for the poor, and had no home and few possessions of his own. One day he remarked, "The foxes have dens, and the birds of the air have nests; but the Son of Man has nowhere to lay his head" (Matthew 8, 20). The ultimate foolishness of greed is shown in the parable of the rich man and Lazarus (Cf. Luke 16, 19-31).

Jesus continually taught us that God will always forgive us, no matter what we have done, as long as we are truly sorry. The wonderful parable of the prodigal son illustrates God's love and mercy (Cf. Luke 15, 11-32).

SOME SUGGESTIONS FOR . . .

DISCUSSION

What, to you, is the most meaningful thing about Christ's life and preaching?
What particular characteristic of Jesus Christ do you think you need most?
Can you see modern parallels to the action of Christ's enemies, particularly in their trying to legally dispose of him?

FURTHER READING

* *The New Testament in Modern English,* Phillips (Macmillan, 1965)—This is considered by some to be the most meaningful version of the New Testament in English, thoroughly up-to-date with only a few Anglicizations.
* *The New English Bible, New Testament* (Oxford University Press and Cambridge University Press, 1961)—Another superb version of the New Testament in modern English, a bit more "restrained" than the Phillips version.
* *The New American Bible*—Excellent new translation by American Catholic scholars.
* *Good News for Modern Man*—Widest-selling book in print; a "pop" version of the New Testament.
* *Mastering the Meaning of the Bible,* McKenzie (Dimension Books)—Brief essays on the patterns by which to appreciate the Old and New Testaments; includes some fine insights into the personality of Christ.

** *The Power and the Wisdom,* McKenzie (Bruce, 1965)—A well-written, highly relevant exposition of the life of Christ and the development of the early Christian Church by one of America's best scripture scholars.

** *The Virginal Conception and Bodily Resurrection of Jesus,* Brown (Paulist Press, 1973)—An outstanding Scripture scholar's assessment of these two vital teachings in the light of the latest Scripture scholarship.

FURTHER VIEWING

The Gospel According to Matthew (Brandon Films, 221 W. 57th St., New York, N.Y. 10019)—A feature-length, widely acclaimed, powerful and moving portrayal of Christ's life.

Ecce Homo (Paulist Productions, 17575 Pacific Coast Hwy., Pacific Palisades, Calif. 90272)—Half-hour color life of Christ, excellently put together from art masterpieces.

PERSONAL REFLECTION

Christ asked for a change of heart, a conversion, a rejection of one's sins and a turning more fully toward him. I should get the inspiration and strength to do this if I meditate on his life each day, perhaps by reading at least a page of the New Testament, and then trying to apply to it my own life.

We suggest reading Luke's gospel since it is the most complete. A good book on the life of Christ can give a background to enrich this reading.

The great way Catholics believe they come into special contact with Christ is at Mass. By the power of God Christ becomes present among us, particularly under the appearance of bread and wine, and prolongs or re-presents his death and resurrection. He does this so we can all take part and offer ourselves to the Father with him. At holy communion especially we are united in a most intimate way with Christ under the appearance of bread, and with one another. This, then, is our great expression of worship and love.

In order to see and experience the Mass for yourself, we suggest that you attend Mass if you are not already doing so, each Sunday if possible. Later we shall discuss the Mass in detail.

7

Christ Reveals to Us the Father, the Spirit, and Himself

What did Jesus tell us God is like? How can we have a meaningful contact with God? Can we be sure that Jesus Christ is divine and that his teaching is God's own?

It is natural to want to reveal ourselves to someone we truly love. We want that person to know as much as possible about us—to come to know our family, our friends, our daily life, our hopes and fears—and to accept us as we really are.

Jesus Christ gradually revealed to us his origin and background, his innermost life and those with whom he shared it. He did this because he loves us and wants us to know about it.

"I am from him (God), and he has sent me" (John 7, 29). Jesus said this, and meant it in its fullest, deepest sense. To understand Jesus Christ, we must try to penetrate the mystery of God's inner life. This he has opened to us. But this is not all.

Jesus Christ told us how we can ourselves share in God's own inner life, in the life of heaven itself, while here on earth. This, he said, is God's plan: that we should even now begin to share most intimately in his very life. To understand ourselves, then, our yearnings and fantastic capabilities, we study God's own life as Jesus revealed it.

OUR FATHER

In the Old Testament, God had revealed himself as one God, the Father of his people. Amid pagan polytheism many Jews had died for this truth. They came to think of God as a Father, from whom all things come, whose love was poured out on them, even when they turned from him: "Israel, says the Lord, is my firstborn son . . . Israel in his boyhood, what love I bore him! It was I, none other, that guided those first steps of theirs, and took them in my arms, and healed, all unobserved, their injuries" (Hosea 11, 103).

Then gradually God came to be seen as the Father, in a special way, of the future king-Messiah: "I shall be to him a father, and he shall be to me a son" (Samuel 7, 14).

When Jesus came he spoke many times of God as a loving Father, his Father and ours. When he was twelve years old he was missing for three days; Mary and Joseph found him in the Temple and asked why he had left them. "Did you not know that I must be in my Father's house?" he replied. Like many a young man today, he had become aware of what his vocation in life was to be. He went to Nazareth, then, and was subject to Mary and Joseph, but his heart was more and more with his heavenly Father.

When he began preaching, Jesus continually spoke of God as our Father. He told us how to pray: "Our Father who art in heaven, hallowed by thy name . . ." To any who might see God as a righteous or distant figure, Jesus made clear that he is a loving Father who cares for all our needs: **Read Luke 12, 24-31.**

Jesus was completely caught up in doing his Father's will. One day when his apostles realized that he needed food and begged him to eat, he said, "I have food to eat of which you do not know." They wondered at this and he explained, "My food is to do the will of him who sent me, to accomplish his work" (John 4, 31-34). When his enemies badgered him, he told them, ". . . I preach only what the Father has taught me. I do always the things that are pleasing to him."

This total, selfless dedication to goodness has made Jesus history's most attractive figure.

THE HUMAN SON, ONE OF US

In Leningrad, Soviet Russia, the Museum of the History of Religion (the "Museum of Atheism") has large displays devoted to the abuses of organized religion and its supposed incompatability with the modern, scientific world. But in the whole build-

ing there is nothing about Christ, no deriding of him, no attack
on him.

In the larger art museums of the city there are many paintings
of Christ by various masters—usually of the compassionate, very
human Christ healing the sick or preaching to the poor—before
which thousands of men, women and children quietly pass. Even
in this professedly atheistic state, Christ is a unique and re-
spected figure.

Even for many today who say one can have no real contact
with God—who proclaim that "God is dead"—the figure of
Christ, the "man for others" is at the center of their life and
thought. They are attracted by him, and even as they debate
who he was, they live to imitate him.

In the first three gospels particularly, we see how very human
Jesus Christ was. For the first thirty years of his life he led the
uneventful life of a small town carpenter. He gradually became
more aware of his mission in life and when he began to preach
he suffered antagonism, insults, and the misunderstanding of his
own friends and neighbors. On one occasion they even tried to
kill him (Luke 4, 16-28). He was often hungry, thirsty, tired,
with no home to call his own (Luke 4, 2; John 4, 6; Matthew
8, 20).

He was sometimes sad, and cried over the death of his friend
Lazarus (John 11, 33-35). He could enjoy himself, too, and liked
to see others enjoy themselves. His first recorded miracle was
changing water into wine at a young couple's wedding reception
(John 2, 1ff.); he often accepted dinner invitations from his
friends (Luke 7, 36ff.); and he liked to be with little children,
despite his followers' attempts to chase them away (Matthew
19, 13ff.).

He was acutely conscious of the difficulties, frustrations, uncertainties and fears that any of us experience. Throughout his life
he "increased in wisdom . . ." (Luke 2, 52). As his preaching
continued he was constantly frustrated by the growing opposition
of his enemies, the powerful leaders of the people. He realized
that his preaching of conversion to the kingdom had failed, and
that now he would have to suffer and die to bring salvation to
his people. He saw that he was to be the suffering servant of

God predicted by Isaiah (chapters 50-53) who was to die to bring others to God.

He was strongly tempted from the outset, drawn to sin as if he could fall—though he never did (Matthew 4, 1-11). His lifelong struggle to do his Father's will reached its climax in his agony before his death: "Father, if thou art willing, remove this cup from me; yet not my will but thine be done" (Luke 22, 42). And as he was dying, he cried out in anguish and darkness of soul, "My God, my God, why have you forsaken me?" (Matthew 27, 46).

But to his closest followers, Jesus was a paradox, a mystery. He was close to them, spent many hours instructing them to the point where they argued with him and almost took him for granted. But there was always something of a mystery about him. His personality was powerful, he spoke with a unique authority, but yet he was open, asked questions to learn what people thought of him (Matthew 16, 13), and was shaken by the death of a close friend (John 11, 33-36).

He worked wonders unlike anyone before: " 'Girl, I say to thee, arise.' And the (dead) girl rose up immediately" (Mark 5, 41-42). But yet he confessed that there were some things he did not know: ". . . of that day or hour (the Judgment) no one knows, neither the angels in heaven, nor the Son, but the Father only" (Mark 13, 32). He said, "All things that the Father has are mine" (John 16, 15), but one another occasion he said, "The Father is greater than I" (John 14, 28).

Gradually he was unfolding his innermost self . . .

THE DIVINE SON

Jesus' great revelation is that the God who is our Father has an only Son, also God, and that he is this divine Son of God. Others are sons and daughters of the loving Father—but Jesus is the Son. Gradually this unfolds in the gospels. He calls the Father by the intimate term, "Abba" (Mark 14, 36.) He says that he is so close to his Father that he alone knows and reveals him:

"All things have been delivered to me by my Father; and no one

knows the Son except the Father; nor does anyone know the
Father except the Son, and to whom the Son chooses to reveal
him" (Matthew 11, 27).

The infancy stories of Matthew and Luke show the Church's
belief that Jesus' origin was with God. At the start of his public
preaching, after he was baptized, ". . . heaven was opened, and
the Holy Spirit descended upon him in bodily form as a dove,
and a voice came from heaven, 'Thou art my beloved Son, in
thee I am well pleased'" (Luke 3, 21-22). And in his last
prayer, before his death, Jesus summed up his work as the Son
of the Father: Read John 17, 1-5.

**Jesus showed that he was more than human, by his evident
holiness, his knowledge and superhuman insights, and his miracles.** People began saying, "Never has man spoken as this man"
(John 7, 46), and "Who, then, is this, that even the wind and the
sea obey him?" (Mark 4, 40). Then one day he made the bold
claim:

> "Abraham your father rejoiced that he was to see my day. He
> saw it and was glad." The Jews therefore said to him, "Thou art
> not yet fifty years old, and hast thou seen Abraham?" Jesus said
> to them, "Amen, amen, I say to you, before Abraham came to be,
> I am." They therefore took up stones to cast at him; but Jesus hid
> himself, and went out from the temple (John 8, 56-59).

John here tells us that Jesus is claiming the sacred name of
God, "I am." His hearers understand his claim, since they
would have stoned him to death as punishment for blasphemy.
He claimed to forgive sins, and his hearers concluded, "Who is
this man who speaks blasphemies? Who can forgive sins but God
only?" (Luke 5, 21). On another occasion he said openly, "My
Father and I are one." His hearers again took up stones to cast
at him, saying, "Thou, being a man, makest thyself God" (John
10, 33).

**The gospels tell us that Jesus was a wonder-worker, who per-
formed many miracles.** They mention some forty miracles of all
kinds, including three occasions on which he brought dead persons back to life. We do not know the details of his miracles,
or how many he really performed—the gospels, we saw, are

records of faith and are not greatly concerned about historical details. But even the 1st-century Jewish historian, Josephus, and the anti-Christian pagan writers conceded that Christ was a wonder-worker. In John's gospel especially, Christ's miracles are called his "works," performed to prove his divine power:

"... do you say of him whom the Father has made holy and sent into the world, 'Thou blasphemest,' because I said, 'I am the Son of God'? If I do not perform the works of my Father, do not believe me. But if I do perform them, and if you are not willing to believe the works, that you may know and believe that the Father is in me and I in the Father" (John 10, 36-38).

Only gradually, however, did it become clear who Jesus really was. The Jews for centuries had abhorred idolatry, the giving of divine honor to anyone or anything created. God had gradually become remote to them—even his name was too holy to be pronounced. So, though the people were awaiting a Messiah, they were totally unprepared for him to be divine. Then, too, Christ's mission on earth was to establish the kingdom of his Father among men, not to claim anything for himself. He shows his divinity more by his actions than by direct claims.

It is evident from the New Testament that there was a development in his followers' grasp of Jesus' divinity, that his apostles had no real understanding of this during his ministry. After the resurrection and the coming of the Holy Spirit they gradually came to understand—gradually, because they were not so much concerned with the abstract question of precisely who or what Jesus was, as with the great things God had done for us through him. They were caught up in preaching the tremendous good news of our salvation by Jesus to eternal life, and with trying to convert all mankind to share in this. But by the time of John's gospel and the epistle to the Hebrews, for instance, the realization of his divinity is expressed clearly (Cf. John 1, 1; 20, 28; Hebrews 1, 8-9).

We should not be surprised that Jesus' full identity took a while to penetrate the understanding of his followers. We who so glibly call Jesus divine should try to realize how difficult it must have been for his first followers to come to understand this—that the man with whom they had so intimately associated had within himself the fullness of the infinite God. Their every instinct as monotheists was to reject as utterly blasphemous any implication

that a man could in any way be divine. Only with the light of
the Holy Spirit through the years after Pentecost did they begin
to realize that this was so.

*Then, too, there is a sense in which Jesus developed in the
knowledge of himself and his mission.* He "increased in wisdom,
and in stature and in favor with God and man" (Luke 2, 52).
What he always was and what he basically knew in the depths
of his consciousness, that he was divine, he only gradually came
to grasp in the context of his life situation. This is an extraordinarily difficult thing for us who are only human to understand—
and ultimately it is a mystery—how a human intellect could come
to grasp the fact that one is a divine person.

Perhaps as we know that we are spiritual beings, that we have
a soul, but cannot directly conceive of or reflect on this aspect of
ourselves, and as we only gradually come to realize through the
experience of living what it means to be a human person—so Jesus
only gradually became reflexively conscious of his divine personality, gradually came to know himself more and more deeply.

How much Christ's divinity "broke through" or was communicated to his human consciousness is currently the subject of much
discussion. Many scholars today look at the Scriptural evidence
and think that Jesus fully realized his divinity at his resurrection,
when he was filled with the Spirit and glorified.

In any event, one thing is becoming clearer today: Jesus is a
more "human" figure, much more one of us, than many Christians,
accustomed to thinking of him primarily as divine, had previously
supposed.

**The resurrection of Jesus, his return to life after his death, is
the great testimony to his divinity.** He is the only person in
human history to have such striking testimony of his return to
life. Not only the early Christians, but billions of people through
history have staked their belief on this.

**The gospels go into detail to show that Jesus really died and
came back alive again:**

> And as Jesus was going up to Jerusalem, he took the twelve dis-
> ciples aside by themselves, and said to them, "Behold, we are
> going up to Jerusalem, and the Son of Man will be betrayed to
> the chief priests and the scribes; and they will condemn him to
> death, and will deliver him to the Gentiles to be mocked and
> scourged and crucified; and on the third day he will rise again"
> (Matthew 20, 17-19).

After a merciless scourging, Jesus had to carry his heavy cross through the city to the place of execution; the soldiers, fearing that he would die on the way, got help in carrying the cross (Matthew 27, 32).

After hanging on the cross for three hours, Jesus died. Soldiers examined Christ, saw that he was already dead and pierced his heart with a spear. His body was placed in a new tomb, and a heavy stone was rolled across the opening to seal the tomb; Christ's enemies, remembering his prediction that he would rise on the third day, placed a guard of soldiers around the tomb (John 19, 31-37; Matthew 27, 62-66).

On Easter Sunday morning, several women followers of Christ arrived at the tomb and were amazed to find it empty; an angel told them that Christ had risen. Then, Peter and John, hearing the news, ran to the tomb, and they too found it empty. Mary·Magdalen, seeing the empty tomb, concluded his body had been stolen; when Christ appeared to her, she thought he was the gardener (Luke 24, 1-3; John 20, 1-18).

On Easter Sunday evening, Christ appeared to the apostles in a closed room. That same evening, Christ appeared to two of his followers on a road outside Jerusalem (Luke 24, 13-35). St. Paul says that at another time Christ appeared to more than 500 people (1 Corinthians 15, 6). Apparitions of Christ are mentioned eleven times in all.

Christ's resurrection transformed his followers once they realized its meaning. Demoralized by Christ's death, they were not all disposed to believe that he had risen from the grave. They tell us that when Christ did appear, they thought he was a ghost, and he had to eat something to convince them that he was truly alive (Luke 24, 36-43)—that the apostle Thomas would not believe until he could examine the wounds in Christ's body—then he exclaimed, "My Lord and my God!" (John 20, 24-29).

After Christ's several appearances, he ascended into heaven, and his followers awaited the coming of the Holy Spirit as he had instructed them. They had begun to believe, but were still confused. Then the Spirit came and the staggering fact now began to penetrate—it would take some years yet, but gradually they came to realize: God had come among them in Jesus Christ. The wonderful person with whom they had talked and eaten and toiled, who had led them and inspired them and who now was gone from them—this man had had within himself the full power of the divinity.

They went forth to proclaim his resurrection and his message throughout the world. They called Christ "Lord" in the same way that the Old Testament had spoken of God; he is God's power and wisdom (1 Corinthians 1, 24), the perfect reflection of his glory (Hebrews 1, 3). They worked miracles in his name, and they willingly went to their deaths for him.

Belief in Christ's resurrection was, and is, the impetus behind the spread of Christianity. The early Christians never spoke of Christ as a dead hero, but as one living in their midst. As the early Christian Church developed, this was its key teaching, and it has been so through the centuries. The belief of billions of Christians through history is summed up by St. Paul:

> . . . and if Christ has not risen, vain is your faith, for you are still in your sins. Hence they also who have fallen asleep in Christ, have perished. If with this life only in view we have had hope in Christ, we are of all men the most to be pitied. But as it is, Christ has risen from the dead, the first-fruits of those who have fallen asleep (1 Corinthians 15, 17-20).

> *It is important to remember what we assert, as Christians, when we say that Christ is risen.* We are saying that his complete manhood is glorified, that it is perfect, unrestricted, unlimited, endowed with the fullness of divine power. We cannot imagine a risen humanity, and we should be careful of picturing the glorified Christ as being "here" or "there." When he wished his followers to realize that he was truly alive, he "appeared" to them, was "seen" by them, i.e., they realized that he was alive and glorified. We, too, by faith, "meet" the glorified Christ when we realize that he is alive and acting among us.

> *In the history of the ancient Christian Church at Antioch there is recorded the story of St. Marina,* a 3rd-century girl of pagan parents who became a Christian and was eventually beheaded for her beliefs. At her trial, the pagan governor exclaimed, "How stupid to worship a man as if he were a god—above all a man who came to such a disgraceful end as crucifixion!" Marina answered, "Why do you always bring up his crucifixion and never

speak of his resurrection? His death shows that he was a man, yes—but his resurrection shows him to be God!"

John's gospel particularly gives the reflection of the late first century Christian Church about Christ when it calls him the Word of God who became a man. This gospel shows a maturing reflection about Christ's divinity-in-humanity. It continually points to his "works," his miracles, as signs that he is divine. It begins: "In the beginning was the Word, and the Word was with God, and the Word was God . . . and the Word was made flesh, and lived among us" (John 1, 1-14). The prophets had proclaimed God's Word, his message, as best they could—now the living Word, the perfect expression of God the Father, has come among us.

To believe in Christ's divinity one must have an open mind and a willingness to live his teachings—and the power of faith. Skeptics, those whose minds are closed to his teachings or to moral improvement like Herod, Pontius Pilate, and the Pharisees, probably would have seen nothing had they been with the apostles when Christ appeared after his resurrection. Others' minds may be open but they lack the power of faith. (We shall consider this more fully in chapter 14 when we discuss faith.) St. Peter says,

God raised him on the third day and caused him to be plainly seen, not by all the people, but by witnesses designated beforehand by God, that is, by us . . . (Acts 10, 40-41).

One should consider Christ's whole teaching before accepting or rejecting his divinity. Christ gradually reveals himself, usually, through his messsage. As with Christ's first followers, it takes time to grasp the reality of who he is. If one is open to the truth and tries to live by what one discovers to be true, faith in Christ often comes as one ponders his teachings. The rest of this book concerns these teachings.

Jesus Christ is the perfect man, the "new Adam," the new head of the human race, the perfect lover of God and of us. He never sinned, nor did he ever turn aside from his Father's will. He is the only one in history who responded perfectly to God's outpouring love, and who never faltered in his constant, all-embracing love for his fellow man. St. Paul stumblingly grasps the reality of Jesus when he says that he is ". . . the image of the invisible God, the firstborn of every creature. For in him were created all things in the heavens and on the earth, things visible and things invisible. . . ." (Colossians 1, 15.)

Divine and perfect man though he is, Jesus Christ yet experienced all our human weaknesses and emotions, our joys and sorrows, our hopes and pain. St. Paul says that he "emptied himself" of his divinity, that he is ". . . one tempted as we are, like us in all things except sin." He struggled, as we must, to know the Father's will and to do it. As we saw previously, he underwent all of our difficulties, frustrations, uncertainties and fears—and because of his perfect sensitivity he experienced these things even more acutely than we ever could.

Jesus Christ, then, is both God and man. This is the mystery of the incarnation, the fullness of God in human flesh. ". . . the Word was made flesh and dwelt among us" (John 1, 14). Other cultures in their mythologies have had savior gods who came among men, but no one dreamed that the infinite, unique, "totally Other" God would become one of us.

By his incarnation, the Son of God has united himself in some fashion with every man. He worked with human hands, he thought with a human mind, acted by human choice and loved with a human heart. Born of the Virgin Mary, he has truly been made one of us, like us in all things except sin (*The Pastoral Constitution on the Church in the Modern World*, no. 22).

God the Son became a man through Mary, his human mother, whom we call the Mother of God. We call her this because her son, Jesus, is God. Mary is a human being, infinitely below the Almighty. She was chosen to give Christ his human body, but obviously not his divinity nor his human soul. But Mary is truly a mother—she is to Jesus all that any mother is to her son. Jesus is God the Son; the "I" or "ego" of Jesus is divine. Therefore, anything that Jesus has, he has as God. We can say that God had relatives, that God has a mother. The title "Mother of God" came to be used in early Christianity as a test of one's orthodox belief in Christ.

The "Hail Mary" is one of the most ancient prayers of the Church. The first part is Luke's portrayal of the angel's words to Mary at the moment of the incarnation, and also Elizabeth's greeting to her. The second is an ancient, popular petition.

Hail Mary, full of grace, the Lord is with thee; blessed art thou among women, and blessed is the fruit of thy womb, Jesus. Holy Mary, Mother of God, pray for us sinners, now and at the hour of our death. Amen.

Another ancient Christian belief is that Mary was conceived free from sin. This is Mary's immaculate conception, celebrated on December 8th, a holy day in the United States on which Catholics take part in Mass to rejoice in this privilege Christ has given Mary, the model Christian.

St. Augustine expressed the early Christian belief about Mary when he said that all men are sinners ". . . except the Holy Virgin Mary, whom I desire, for the sake of the honor of the Lord, to leave entirely out of the question when the talk is of sin" (*De nat. et grat.* 36, 42).

Mary's freedom from sin is something we should expect since she was chosen for the unique dignity of being God's human mother. Since Christ came to conquer evil, it is fitting that he should take his human body from a woman who was untainted with sin. Luke describes Mary's awe-filled realization: "He who is mighty has done great things for me, and holy is his name . . ." (Luke 1, 49).

By these privileges which God gave to Mary, we see that he always prepares people for their roles in his plan. As Mary was given great graces for her great role, so God gives us all the graces necessary to carry out his plan in our life.

The meaning of all this is that God loves us so much that he became one of us, to share his happiness with us. In our world, when a man loves a woman he wants to be with her, to share experiences, to make her happy. God loves us and comes among us, to share our experiences, to give us happiness beyond anything we can imagine. Perhaps this is why he became one of us, to convince us of this love and happiness. Otherwise we would never have believed our destiny.

THE HOLY SPIRIT

Christ spoke about the Holy Spirit who would be sent by the Father and himself to complete his work. Sometimes called the Holy Ghost, Christ calls him the Paraclete or Advocate, that is, a Helper or Comforter. The Spirit is to help the apostles to at last understand Christ and his teachings:

> But the Advocate, the Holy Spirit, whom the Father will send in my name, he will teach you all things, and bring to your mind whatever I have said to you . . . But when the Advocate has come whom I will send you from the Father, the Spirit of Truth who proceeds from the Father, he will bear witness concerning me (John 14, 26; 15, 26).

> In the Old Testament the Spirit of God was thought of as a manifestation of the Father, his life-giving "breath" which takes possession of a man, renewing him from within, making him responsive to God's Word. Thus the prophet Isaiah proclaims his mission: "The Lord has anointed me, on me his spirit has fallen" (61, 1). And Ezechiel beautifully proclaims the Lord's promise to his people: "I will give you a new heart, and breathe a new spirit into you; I will take away from your breasts those hearts that are hard as stone, and give you human hearts instead. I will make my spirit penetrate you, so that you will follow in the path of my law, and remember and carry out my decrees" (11, 19-20).

The Spirit worked within Jesus, a personal reality, guiding and inspiring him. At his baptism, ". . . the Holy Spirit descended upon him in bodily form as a dove . . ." (Luke 3, 22). "Then Jesus was led by the Spirit about the desert" (Luke 4, 1), before beginning his mission. As he starts his mission, the Spirit gives him power: **Read Luke 4, 14-19.**

Near the end of his life Jesus told his followers that the Spirit would make his teachings clear to them: ". . . it is expedient for you that I depart. For if I do not go, the Advocate will not come to you; but if I go, I will send him to you" (John 16, 7). After the Spirit came on Pentecost, Christ's disciples began to understand his teachings, among them the fact that the Father, Son and Holy Spirit are one God.

The Holy Spirit is the successor of Jesus, who continues his work among us and within us. He continually moved the early

Christian Church, and today he is the source of God's life in the Church and in each Christian. He is the power that enables us to believe in Christ and live his teachings: "No man can say Jesus is Lord except in the Holy Spirit," says Paul (1 Corinthians 12, 3). He is also our invincible power in the battle with sin and ignorance—though often we never suspect his presence, or suspecting it, we are afraid to open ourselves to him.

Reflecting on Christ's revelation, the Church has slowly penetrated into the mystery of the Father, Son, and Holy Spirit. As Christianity developed, scholars and people alike tried to understand Christ better, and his relationship to the Father and the Spirit. Guided by the Spirit, some facets of this mystery began to emerge, and were proclaimed by the Church in several councils.

There is but one God, but in God there are three divine, completely equal Persons. This is the mystery of the Blessed Trinity. Each of the Three Persons is really distinct from the other Two. Each is wholly God, equal to the other Two. One did not come before the others. Yet there is only one God.

Traditional Catholic theology puts it this way: the three divine Persons, distinct as Persons, possess the same one nature of God. This is based on the difference between the idea of "person" and that of "nature," taken originally from Greek philosophy and expanded by Christian thinkers: *person* tells *who* we are; *nature* tells *what* we are. Each of us, for example, is aware that he is a distinct person, different from everyone else. But each of us is also aware that he is human, has a human nature, and in this we are similar to everyone else. Each of us, then, is one person with one nature. It is quite possible—and this is the case with God—to have One who is Three Persons with one nature.

The Second Person of the Blessed Trinity, God the Son, took on a human nature, became a real man, and lived and died among us as Jesus Christ. St. Paul tells us, "Christ Jesus, who though he was by nature God, did not consider being equal to God a thing to be clung to, but emptied himself, taking the nature of a slave and being like unto men" (Philippians 2, 5-7). This is the mystery of the incarnation.

Jesus Christ, then, has two natures—a divine nature and a human nature. Jesus has his divine nature as God from eternity, together with the Father and the Holy Spirit. He took on a distinct human nature 2,000 years ago.

But Jesus is only one Person, God, the Son, who "uses" these two natures. With the power of his divine nature he acts as God; with the power of his human nature he acts as man. But whenever Jesus did anything it was the one Person of God the Son who did it.

It is good to remember that the Blessed Trinity is a mystery. We can know something about the Trinity, but in the final analysis very, very little. Life is full of mysteries—the ultimate composition of an atom, what life itself is, etc.—and so we should not be surprised that the inner life of God is the deepest of all mysteries. Whether or not one can accept our belief in the Trinity depends on God's gift of faith.

Through history men continue to achieve new insights into God's existence and nature. He is ever leading us to a truer, more profound knowledge of himself and our relationship to him. What is proof of God for one man is not for another; what is widely accepted in one period of history may not be later. We believe the Church's insights are true. But they are only a few stumbling words about One who is immense, immeasurable, impenetrable love.

The work of any man's lifetime should be an endless quest for the infinite—to try to know, to understand a bit more, to make some sort of contact with God. The tragedy is that men who give their lifetime to penetrating nature or organizing society never stop to study or reflect on the infinite God. If persevered in, no quest can be as rewarding. To this some of the greatest men of our civilization have testified.

The names of the Three Persons tell us something about them and their personal relationship to us. What one Person does for us the other Persons also do; yet each has a distinct role in God's plan. By grace we are joined to each in a distinct way:

The First Person is called the Father because he produces a Second Person, the Son. He is spoken of as our creator; the word "God" usually refers to him. He is the source from whom everything comes to us, and to whom our worship is ultimately directed. We address him personally when we pray the "Our Father"—the Lord's Prayer—and all the great prayers of Christian worship.

The Second Person is called the Son because he has his origin from the Father, and receives the same divine nature from the

Father. Similarly, a boy is called "son" because he has the same human nature as his father, received from his father. We saw that this Second Person is also called the "Word," the perfect expression of the Father.

Jesus Christ is the Son become man, our brother, through whom every grace comes to us, and through whom we worship the Father. By being joined to Jesus Christ, we share in the very life of the Trinity—we somehow become sons in the Son. Our whole life is to be a gradual reproducing of his life of sonship in ourselves. There is truly no limit to what we can do when united with him.

Though we pray *to* Christ, this prayer should lead us to pray *through* Christ and *with* Christ to the Father. We then share in Christ's perfect prayer to the Father. Our stumbling prayer becomes the prayer of Christ. This is the way the Church usually prays.

The Third Person is called the Holy Spirit because he is produced by the love of the Father and Son for one another. So great is their love that it produces another Person, Love himself, the Holy Spirit; our word "spirit" is taken from a word meaning breath or sigh, a universal sign of life and love.

The Holy Spirit is the gift, the love, of the Father and Son to us. He is the one through whom we enter the life of the Trinity. He comes from Christ into us; within us, he unites us to Christ and the Father.

The Spirit is the one who is the source within us of our Christian prayer and worship. Our ability to pray is from him. When we pray he prays within us. He gives form, meaning, power to our prayers. Thus we pray "in the Spirit."

The Spirit comes to the aid of our weakness; when we do not know what prayer to offer, to pray as we ought, the Spirit himself intercedes for us, with groans beyond all utterance. And God, who can read our hearts, knows well what the Spirit's intent is (Romans 8, 26).

One of the great lessons we derive from Christ's teaching about the Blessed Trinity is that God is not unlike us. Rather, God is Three Persons, a "family" who love one another with a joy and happiness that we can hardly begin to imagine.

To summarize our relationship to the Three Persons:

Everything comes to us from the Father, through the Son-made-man, Jesus Christ, and we receive it by means of the Holy Spirit within us.

We, in turn, return our love to the Father, through and with his Son, Jesus Christ, and we do this by the power of the Holy Spirit within us.

"... be filled with the Spirit, speaking to one another in psalms and hymns and spiritual songs, singing and making melody in your hearts to the Lord, giving thanks always for all things in the name of our Lord Jesus Christ to God the Father" (Ephesians 5, 18-20).

IN THE LITURGY

Almost every prayer and ceremony of the Church is done in the name of the Blessed Trinity. The Sign of the Cross and the Doxology are ancient prayers in their honor. We celebrate Trinity Sunday on the first Sunday after Pentecost each year.

At Mass, the Sign of the Cross is used several times from the beginning to the last blessing. The "Lord, have mercy on us . . ." asks their mercy; the "Glory to God in the highest," which follows, praises them. The Creed summarizes our belief in the Trinity.

Most other Mass prayers are addressed in the Church's ordinary way: to God the Father through the Son, in union with the Holy Spirit—for example, the conclusion of the collects. The climax of the offering of our gift in every Mass is when we silently pray: "Through him (Christ), with him, and in him all honor and glory is given to you, God, Almighty Father, in the unity of the Holy Spirit.'"

At Mass, we also affirm our belief in the incarnation. In the Creed, for instance, we profess that God the Son, the Word of God, "was made flesh . . . and became man." In the eucharistic prayer, at the heart of the Mass, we recount the fact that God the Son has become man in Jesus Christ.

DAILY LIVING: OUR DIGNITY AS BEARERS OF THE TRINITY AND BROTHERS OF CHRIST

In revealing the Blessed Trinity to us, Christ showed us something of God's inner life, and his amazing desire to be known to his creatures.

But this is not all. Christ said, "If anyone loves me, he will keep my word, and my Father will love him, and we will come to him and make our abode with him . . ." (John 14, 25). And speaking of the Holy Spirit, he said, ". . . you shall know him, because he will dwell with you and be in you" (John 14, 17).

The Blessed Trinity dwells intimately within us. This is God's grace-presence. As long as we have grace, what we really have with us is this presence of God, united to us in the most intimate way possible. This is the "indwelling" of the Blessed Trinity.

This indwelling presence means that even now we are beginning the life of heaven. Anywhere, anytime—as long as we are not isolated by serious sin—we can communicate with the Trinity within us, and be confident of their help.

By this indwelling presence we can come to know and experience the divine Persons. The Father, we realize, is our Father who loves us and shares his life with us. The Son is our brother, Jesus Christ, who is like us and communicates the Father's love to us and leads us to the Father. The Holy Spirit is most intimately within us, uniting us to Jesus, joining us to the Father— and to one another—through and with Jesus.

This indwelling presence means that we must respect our body and the bodies of others. St. Paul's words to his Corinthian converts who had been abusing their bodies might also be reminders to any of us:

> Or do you not know that your members are the temple of the Holy Spirit, who is in you, whom you have from God, and that you are not your own? For you have been bought at a great price. Glorify God and bear him in your body (1 Corinthians 6, 19-20).

We respect the dignity of our body by developing our talents, and by avoiding overindulgence—in alcohol, drugs, smoking, or sex. Young people especially must be careful of abusing their bodies or those of others, particularly by lustful "heavy petting" or intercourse outside of marriage. Sex should be sacred and beautiful, and only when there is a marriage commitment should we give another person rights over our body or receive such rights.

Many people today are systematically and tragically destroying their health by over-indulgence in smoking or drinking—and particularly by the rash use of drugs. It would seem that the moderate use of alcohol or tobacco (or perhaps even marijuana, as a Presidential Commission recently declared) are not harmful—but some people have addictive tendencies and must stay away from the use of these things; we should be honest and courageous enough to recognize our own weaknesses in this regard. We are given only one body, one liver, one set of lungs, one brain, to take care of and develop and not to destroy.

We respect the dignity of others by treating them with true love and consideration. We should desire for all men everything that we seek for ourselves. We fail in this if we take advantage of anyone or abuse anyone, for example, by unjustly overworking them, showing prejudice against them, by unjust anger, bearing a grudge, etc.

Another reason for respecting ourselves and others is because God the Son became one of us, thereby teaching us that a human being is something wonderful indeed in God's eyes. He is the "firstborn among many brethren" (Romans 8, 29). In what better way could God bring home to us our tremendous dignity?

Because of the incarnation our earth is now especially sacred and worthy of our best efforts to develop it, to make it a better place for us all. While we are interested in space and the possibility of rational beings on other planets, yet we know that we have had God the Son among us, on our planet. He thought enough of us to become one of us—this should be a constant spur to our efforts.

God's Word . . . entered the world's history as a perfect man, taking that history up into himself and summarizing it. He . . . taught us that the new command of love was the basic law of human perfection, and hence of the world's transformation . . . that the effort to establish a universal brotherhood is not a hopeless one (*The Pastoral Constitution on the Church in the Modern World* no. 38).

A perceptive modern writer puts it this way:

"In the Christian experience . . . God does not dip his finger into history; he totally immerses himself in it. When he visits the world he does not come slumming. He comes to stay." (Dewart, *The Future of Belief,* Herder & Herder, 1966, p. 194).

SOME SUGGESTIONS FOR . . .

DISCUSSION

If you are a Christian, how do you think of the Persons of the Trinity?
What does the Christian belief that God became a man mean to you?
Is the presence of God real to you, at least sometimes?

FURTHER READING

* *The Jesus Myth,* Greeley (Doubleday, 1971)—Essays regarding the person and teachings of Jesus, and the challenge he offers to men of every era.
* *Gospels Without Myth,* Evely (Doubleday, 1971)— A somewhat radical reappraisal of various concepts in the gospels, including a stimulating discussion of miracles.
** *The Christ,* Schoonenberg (Herder, 1971)—A penetrating and fresh look at God and his relationship to us, and particularly at the problem of God-in-man, Jesus Christ, by an outstanding Dutch theologian—deep but rewarding reading.
** *The Creative Advance,* Peters (Bethany Press, 1966)—An easy-to-read, excellent introduction to process thought and its implications for our view of God and ourselves; this can be "mind-blowing" in its breadth and implications.

FURTHER VIEWING

Nothing But a Man (Brandon Films, 221 W. 57th St., New York, N.Y. 10019)—92-minute film, superbly done, on the struggle of a lone Negro in the South to maintain his human dignity in the face of discrimination.
Hey Janitor, (Paulist Productions, 17575 Pacific Coast Highway, Pacific Palisades, Calif. 90272)—A contemporary story of spiritual death and rebirth. 28 minutes.

PERSONAL REFLECTION

The Blessed Trinity lives within us as long as we do not deliberately cut ourselves off from this grace-presence. The more I try to be aware of this presence during the day, the greater is my power of love, the easier it is to do good, and the greater will be my happiness and that of everyone with whom I come in contact.

The Blessed Trinity also lives within the bodies of others; an awareness of this will lead me to respect them.

I should set aside time, even just a few minutes each day, to communicate with the Trinity within, asking help to know what to do and to have the courage to do it.

8
Christ Saves Us by His Death and Resurrection

What is the ultimate reason why God came among us? What is the high point of human history? Why did Christ suffer and die? Is there any meaning to the suffering, humiliation, frustration in our lives? Why are joy and hope natural to a good Christian?

IN CHRIST WE DIED AND ROSE AGAIN

We have seen how God himself came among us in Jesus Christ. He told us of God's own innermost life, the Blessed Trinity, and how the divine Persons dwell intimately within us. He shared our human joys and afflictions, and gave us a whole new way of life. He showed us by his own example how to live totally for God.

Jesus Christ, however, not only taught us how to attain heaven. More fundamentally, he made it possible for us. From Adam on, man had been cutting himself off from God by sin. Pride and selfishness had become imbedded in human nature. Men were divided within themselves, from one another, and from God.

God's plan was to share his own life with us forever—and God's love is unwavering. He would save man from the predicament into which his sins had put him. We call God's actions toward man a "history of salvation." Its high point is the coming of the Savior.

God prepared our race for many years, from the first humans through the whole Old Testament period. He tried to attract men by being generous with them, giving his love in the measure that men could respond to it. Even when his chosen people violated their covenant with him again and again, he continued to reach out with his love and forgiveness. He worked slowly, by our standards, because he will never force men to come to him. Our love must always be given freely.

Men had become so sinful that it seemed that God's plan had failed, that the living God was dead—or at least missing. Widespread slavery, degradation of women, religious prostitution, human sacrifice, cruelty to the weak, average citizens taking their recreation watching other humans being torn apart—this was the world of 2,000 years ago. But it was the "fullness of time" for which God had been preparing. Men had experienced the depths of sin. A faithful remnant acutely realized their need of a savior and longed for his coming. The Father then responded in an undreamed of way.

God sent his own Son, Jesus Christ, to overcome the power of sin and fill us with his grace-presence. In his plan we are to grow in this gift of himself, this new life, until we are with him face to face forever in heaven. Jesus summed up his mission: "I came that they may have life, and have it abundantly" (John 10, 10). Those who knew that mankind needed a savior, never dreamed it would be God's own Son.

Jesus could save us because he opened himself totally to the Father. He alone perfectly responded to the Father's will. "I seek not my own will, but the will of him who sent me" (John 5, 30). He was the perfect man, truly human, but untouched by the pride and selfishness around him. He is the "new Adam," the fresh starting-point, the new and perfect head of our race. His obedience made up for the disobedience of Adam and all of us. He showed us how to respond to love. He "emptied" himself, and the Father could then fill him with life and love for all mankind. Read Philippians 2, 5-11.

We must remember that each of us is in need of Christ as our Savior, because each of us is a sinner. We are all born into the situation and environment of sin that we call original sin. We all need to be freed, raised up from our own prideful disobedience. We fall again and again into sin. We need to be opened to God's love. We need someone to pick us up, to carry us beyond our sins to God.

What we could never do because of our sins, God did for us by becoming a man in Jesus Christ. As a loving parent stoops to a helplessly crippled child and carries it along, so God accomplished for us what we could not do for ourselves.

Jesus Christ saved us by his death and resurrection. While every action of Christ's life helped to save us, his great central act of love was his death and resurrection. St. Paul says succinctly, "Jesus our Lord . . . was put to death for our trespasses and raised for our justification" (Romans 4, 25).

Christ's death and resurrection were able to help us because he united us to himself, so that we could share in what he did. In a mysterious and wonderful way we died and rose again with him. We know how love causes one to suffer with his beloved: parents suffer anguish at seeing their children in pain, a wife's sufferings cause her husband mental torments. Some people love enough to give up life itself for the one they love.

In Viet Nam some time ago a young American officer risked sniper fire by crawling out to save a poor, dying peasant, and was killed by a bullet through the head. Some years ago a California mother offered, quite sincerely, to die in place of her criminal son who had been sentenced to the gas chamber for murder.

So Christ identified us with himself, and died for our sins. Totally innocent himself, he yet gave himself totally for us. He is completely, unreservedly the "man for others." He said, "Greater love has no man than this, that a man lay down his life for his friends."

But Christ did even more. We were his enemies, because of our sins, and yet he laid down his life for us and made us his friends. St. Paul exclaims,

"Why, one will hardly die for a righteous man—though perhaps for a good man one will dare even to die. But God shows his love for us in that while we were yet sinners Christ died for us" (Romans 5, 7-9).

By dying for us Christ made up for our sins. When he was killed, he killed sin's power over us; when he was buried, the power of sin was buried with him. **Read Romans 6, 4-11.**

Theology expresses in several ways what Christ did: He "redeemed" us, bought us back from our subjection to sin; "satisfied" for our sins, made "reparation" for them, i.e., repaired the damage they had done; he brought about our "justification"; he "merited" grace for us; he "atoned" for our sins, made us "at one" again with God.

By rising to new life Christ obtained for us the new life of God's grace-presence. Christ is now the head of a revitalized human race, the "firstborn of many brethren." He offers us this new life, a sharing in God's own life, God himself within us. If we accept it, it is the beginning of an unimaginable intimacy with him that will never end.

After his death Jesus "descended into hell"—he went, not to the hell of the damned, but through the "underworld," the state of being cut off from God, abandoned, powerless—the consequence of his decision to die the death of a sin-laden man. Then "he preached to the spirits in prison" (1 Peter 3, 19)—those who had lived since Adam and were awaiting salvation. He freed them and brought them with him when he ascended into heaven.

Christ's death and resurrection is the great turning-point in human history. An old world ended, and a whole new way of life, a new vision of reality began. Now we can have a life of unimaginable love and intimacy with God himself.

THROUGH CHRIST'S PERFECT WORSHIP WE CAN NOW REACH GOD

Through Christ's death and resurrection we can be sure of reaching God. Men have always sought to contact God, to know if he is there, if he is interested. We wonder how we can reach him. As with men from primitive times, we want to be united with him, transformed, "taken up" into a new life with him. So it is that men have always worshipped God, attempting to reach him particularly by offering him gifts in sacrifice. But men were only too aware of the inadequacy of their offerings.

Christ's death and resurrection was the one, perfect sacrifice by which man reached God. We saw how God's people had worshipped him by sacrifices of animals and crops, offered by their priests. These sacrifices prepared the way for Christ's perfect sacrifice in which he offered his life as our gift to the Father.

For if the sprinkling of defiled persons with the blood of goats and bulls and with the ashes of a heifer sanctified for the purification of the flesh, how much more shall the blood of Christ, who through the eternal Spirit offered himself without blemish to God, purify your conscience from dead works to serve the living God (Hebrews 9, 13-14).

Christ is our mediator, our perfect yet understanding priest. His obedience and love made his death the perfect sacrifice. He was the perfect "go-between." The Old Testament priests had offered sacrifices to God in the name of his people, and brought blessings from God. Christ offered his life to his Father and brought us the gift of eternal happiness. The priests of the old law were imperfect men. Christ is the perfect man, yet one like us who understands our weaknesses. He is the greatest priest of all, our one perfect mediator. **Read Hebrews 5, 1-10.**

As Melchisedech had offered bread and wine in thanksgiving for one of Abraham's victories, so Christ offered bread and wine—and transformed it, as we shall see—as a prelude to his sacrifice.

Christ's ascension into heaven completed his resurrection. His mission on earth was now totally fulfilled. He has returned to the Father and is glorified at his "right hand" in heaven.

Christ's glorification dramatically showed that the Father accepted his sacrifice and that we could now be united with God forever. To have meaning, a gift must be accepted by the one to whom it is given. In the Old Testament the death and burning of the sacrificial victim was meant to show God's acceptance of the gift, its transformation into something divine. Christ's resurrection and ascension strikingly showed that his gift of himself on our behalf was accepted by his Father.

THE NEW AND UNENDING COVENANT OF LOVE

Christ fulfilled beyond all expectation the passover of the Old Testament: he passed from death to life and from this world to the Father, bringing us all with him. God had passed over Egypt, saving his people from death and slavery, and the Israelites had passed over the waters of the Red Sea and the Jordan, to become united with God in the Sinai covenant and the Promised Land. Whenever the Jews ate the annual paschal meal, they looked forward to a new passover, a new exodus to a new freedom and happiness.

Christ fulfilled this longing by making it possible for us to pass with him to eternal happiness. He is the "Lamb of God" (John 1, 29) sacrificed to save us all. "Christ, our paschal lamb, has been sacrificed," says St. Paul (1 Corinthians 5, 7). Read John 8, 32-36.

By dying and rising Jesus Christ brought us from slavery under sin to the perfect freedom of God's redeemed people. This is the new exodus and Christ is the new Moses leading us all to freedom and eternal happiness. If we join ourselves with him, our sins can no longer enslave us or prevent us from attaining true happiness.

> Christ timed his passover to coincide with the annual com- memoration of the first passover. He began his passage from death to life by eating the Jewish paschal meal, his last supper. As Moses had done, Christ gave his followers a ritual by which his passover would be commemorated for future generations. He said over the bread, "This is my body which is being given for you. Do this in remembrance of me"—and as he passed the last cup of wine, "This cup is the new covenant in my blood, which shall be shed for you" (Cf. Matthew 26, 17-29).
> Christ's ritual meal, however, would enable his followers through the centuries to rise above time and actually share in his very death and resurrection. This is the Mass, the great sacrifice and family meal of his Church.

By dying and rising for us Jesus Christ began the new, perfect, eternal covenant. The ancient covenants of God with his people culminated in the old testament of Mount Sinai. Moses had sealed this covenant by sprinkling the people with the blood of sacrificed animals; so now Christ shed his own blood in sacrifice to begin the new and unending covenant, the new testament. At the last supper before he died, he said, "This cup is the new covenant in my blood, which shall be shed for you" (Luke 22, 20; Cf. Hebrews, chapters 8-10).

> In the Old Testament the blood of sacrificed animals was brought by the high priest into the Holy of Holies, the part of the tabernacle where God dwelt among his people. Now Christ offered his blood and entered God's dwelling place in heaven, bringing us with him, fulfilling man's yearning for union with God which could only be hinted at before. "Christ . . . by a great

and more perfect tabernacle, not made with hands, that is, not of this creation, neither by the blood of goats or of calves, but by his own blood, entered once for all into the Holies" (Hebrews, 9, 11-12).

By this new covenant God promises us a life after death of unending, unimaginable happiness, sharing his own life, living as he does. By the old testament God gave his people land and temporal prosperity if they lived up to their agreement; they did not even suspect an unending life after death, much less know how to attain it. Now God is offering us himself forever. This is the most perfect gift of love possible, the closest personal relationship that we could have with him.

Our part of this covenant of love is simply to accept Jesus Christ and live by his teaching of love. So close, so personal is this relationship of love which God offers us, that his own Son, Jesus Christ, is the living, walking, flesh-and-blood sign of it. Jesus Christ, in fact, is the new covenant. He unites in himself God and us. By believing in him we enter into this covenant. He, personally, is the great proof, the great sign that such a love relationship is for real. By accepting him we begin eternal life, God's grace-presence within us, here and now.

When we accept Christ and this new covenant we pledge ourselves to love. He showed us that this was a covenant of love in the best way he could, by dying for love of his Father and us, to unite us in love. If we make this new covenant we must determine to love. As marriage is the covenant which seals the deep love relationship of a man and woman, so our covenant with God supposes that we have fallen in love, that we want to commit ourselves to a life of love with God and our fellow man.

WHAT THIS COST AND WHY

We should pause and meditate on the gospel story of Christ's sufferings and death, in order to appreciate God's great love in saving us. As we do this, we should remember that our sins contributed to his sufferings.

As Jesus went about preaching and teaching, his death seemed more and more imminent, constantly present before his eyes. He said he ". . . must suffer many things and be rejected by this generation" (Luke 17, 25). His disciples were shocked and scandalized by these predictions; when they went up to Jerusalem for the last time ". . . they were in dismay, and those who followed were afraid" (Mark 10, 32).

After the last supper with his apostles, Jesus went to pray in the garden of Gethsemani where he came to realize vividly the sins he was taking upon himself and the death that awaited him. This caused a mental agony so terrible that ". . . his sweat became as drops of blood running down upon the ground" (Luke 22, 44).

He shrank from the ordeal ahead, but clung to his Father's will: "Father, if it is possible, let this cup pass away from me; yet not as I will, but as you will" (Matthew 26, 39). Meanwhile, his apostles slept.

Judas, one of his chosen twelve apostles, betrayed him with an embrace of friendship, and he was seized by his enemies (Matthew 26, 47-49).

His followers deserted him. As he had predicted, Peter, their leader, crumbled before a maidservant's mockery and denied him with an oath: "I do not know him!" (Luke 22, 57).

He was taken before the Jewish high priests where he unequivocally declared his divine mission. For this he was slapped, humiliated, and found guilty of death (Matthew 26, 63-67).

During the night and next morning he was mocked, beaten, spat upon, and made the butt of a condemned fool's game. He was then taken before Pontius Pilate, the Roman governor. Pilate found him innocent of any offense, but the mob, undoubtedly including many he had helped, were aroused by his enemies and demanded his death: "Crucify him! Crucify him!" (Luke 23, 21).

Then Pilate, to appease them ". . . took Jesus and had him scourged"—a flaying with spikes, leaden balls, and razor-like metal—from which men not infrequently died.

> And they stripped him and put on him a scarlet cloak; and plaiting a crown of thorns, they put it upon his head, and a reed into his right hand; and bending the knee before him they mocked him . . . and they spat on him, and took the reed and kept striking him on the head (Matthew 27, 28-30).

At last Pilate ". . . handed him over to them to be crucified."

Crucifixion was the death reserved for the lowest criminals. "And so they took Jesus and led him away" (John 19, 16). As he carried his cross to the hill of Calvary outside Jerusalem, he had to be helped lest he die along the way. Arriving at Calvary, ". . . they crucified him there, and the robbers, one on his right hand and the other on his left. And Jesus said, 'Father, forgive them, for they do not know what they are doing'" (Luke 23, 33-34).

He hung dying for three hours—a death since analyzed as a kind of asphyxiation. After forgiving his enemies, he promised heaven to a repentant thief and murderer. He saw his mother standing humiliated and desolate beneath the cross, and he commended her to his one still-faithful disciple. Later his Church would take her as its own.

Then he felt depths of desolation, cut off from his Father, estranged, abandoned, and he cried, "My God, my God, why hast thou forsaken me?" (Matthew 27, 46).

This is the way Jesus showed his love for the Father and for us. The cost never mattered. He always put God first, living and dying in total, trusting obedience to his Father's will.

In doing this he gave himself totally for others—for us. God "made Christ to be sin" for us—thus Paul tries to describe Christ's fearful experience of taking on our sins as if they were his own, of being totally abandoned by his Father for us.

God willed that Jesus should redeem us in this way so that his love would be unmistakably plain to us. When we see his own Son humiliated and killed, we can begin to realize what it is for a God to love. In no other way could he have made so clear his unfailing love. In no other way would we have been convinced that we are lovable in the eyes of the infinite God.

In this is love, not that we loved God, but that he loved us and sent his Son to be the expiation for our sins . . . that those who believe in him may not perish, but may have life everlasting (John 3, 16; 1 John 4, 10).

This is how God establishes his kingdom, his rule of love over our hearts. Jesus came as a humble, loving prophet rather than as a powerful king. Where people might have expected a great display, Jesus made clear that he wanted to convert our hearts through love. This is always God's way: instead of compelling submission or awed adoration, he wants our freely-given love.

Christ's death on the Cross shows strikingly the "powerlessness of God" in this world, that is, that he does not save us by means that seem effective to us, but rather overcomes evil by his apparent defeat at its hands. This is the paradox of the Cross and this is freshly evident in today's world. It is becoming more and more apparent that God cannot be expected to intervene in our affairs with displays of power—that his followers are decreasing in worldly and institutional importance—but by this apparent absence from the world he is prodding us to use our human resources to work with him to bring it to perfection. Though God is truly present, close, acting in our lives—and some are especially aware of this—yet he is there to show us how to help ourselves. Too often in the past we have depended on his intervention instead of becoming truly involved ourselves in the mundane struggles of the "terrible everyday." And too often we have tended to judge our success as Christians by worldly standards.

Thus the false image of a God who continually intervenes at our behest, who can be coaxed and cajoled, is dead. This is perhaps expressed best by the influential German Lutheran theologian who was hanged by the Nazis in 1945, Dietrich Bonhoeffer:

> God is teaching us that we must live as men who can get along very well without him. The God who is with us is the God who forsakes us (Cf. Mark 15, 34). The God who makes us live in this world without using him as a working hypothesis is the God before whom we are ever standing. Before God and with him we live without God. God allows himself to be edged out of the world and onto the cross. God is weak and powerless in the world, and that is exactly the way, the only way, in which he can be with us and help us. Matthew 8, 17 makes it crystal clear that it is not by his omnipotence that Christ helps us, but by his weakness and suffering.

> *Christ died for the sins of all of us, not merely because his fellow Jews wanted him killed.* Though many of his countrymen rejected him, some accepted him, the men who began his Church. After the destruction of Jerusalem (which was taken as a sign of God's rejection of the Jews), a tragic hatred developed between Christians and Jews. The beginnings of this are evident even in the New Testament: Pilate is gradually exculpated and the Jews are held increasingly guilty. The Fathers of the Church, the leaders of the developing Christian world, often expressed bitter sen-

timents against the "Christ-killers," and the Jews reacted by vilifying Christ. From the ghettos of the Middle Ages to the savagery of the Nazi "final solution" (all too frequently tolerated by Christians) we see how man can even use religion in a strange and distorted way. Spurred by the memory of the Nazi horrors, a new era may be opening today in Jewish-Christian relations. Vatican Council II says emphatically:

. . . what happened in his passion cannot be charged against all the Jews without distinction, those then alive, nor against the Jews of today . . . The Jews should not be presented as rejected or accursed by God . . . The Church . . . decries hatred, persecutions, displays of anti-Semitism, directed against Jews at any time and by anyone (*Declaration on the Relationship of the Church to Non-Christian Religions,* no. 5).

Catholics are asked to perform some act of penance each Friday as a gesture of grateful love. Until recently American Catholics abstained from eating meat each Friday, but now may do this or some other act of penance of their own choosing (except for Ash Wednesday and the Fridays of Lent which are still days of abstinence from meat). On Friday, the day Christ sacrificed his life for us, we make this small sacrifice to discipline ourselves and to overcome our sinful tendencies, that we might be more fully joined to him.

The American Catholic bishops have made some practical suggestions for Friday penance: "It would bring great glory to God and good to souls if Fridays found our people doing volunteer work in hospitals, visiting the sick, serving the needs of the aged and the lonely, instructing the young in the Faith, participating as Christians in community affairs, and meeting our obligations to our families, our friends, our neighbors and our community, including our parishes, with a special zeal born of the desire to add the merit of penance to the other virtues exercised in good works born of living faith."

CHRIST IS IN GLORY AMONG US

Christ's resurrection is the key truth of our Christian faith. The first proclamation of the "good news," the pattern of the message that was to convert billions and change the world's history, stressed Christianity's basic and unique fact: Jesus Christ, who had been murdered, came alive from the grave by God's power and entered a perfect, glorified state. Read Acts 2, 22-36.

Christ's resurrection is the divine "seal of approval" on himself and his message, and tells us that, joined to him, we too shall live on forever as he said. He delivered us from the fear of death, and brought joy and hope to our lives: "I am the resurrection and the life; he who believes in me, even if he die, shall live; and whoever lives and believes in me, shall never die" (John 11, 25-26).

The New Testament says that Christ appeared on earth for forty days after his resurrection to complete the training of his apostles, and so that they could be absolutely sure that he was truly living among them. Forty is a Jewish "perfect number," one that recurs again and again in the scriptures.

After his resurrection Jesus could exercise his lordship in a way he had not done before. By overcoming death, the ultimate frustration of all human efforts, he began the full exercise of his superhuman, divine power among us. His mission will be fulfilled only at the end of the world, when all evil powers have been overcome.

Jesus shares his victory with us, for now we too have the power to rise and be glorified forever. Christ has a glorified body, impervious to space, time, pain, etc., perfect in every way. He promises that we, too, shall have a body when we rise. "If the Spirit of him who raised Jesus from the dead dwells in you, then he who raised Jesus Christ from the dead will also bring to life your mortal bodies, because of his Spirit who dwells in you" (Romans 8, 11).

We must join ourselves to Christ and take part in his death and glorification to attain eternal life with God. Everyone who is saved is somehow joined to him, whether they realize it or not. He is the one mediator for all. But some are called to join themselves to him more consciously, more fully.

We first join ourselves to Christ's death and glorification by faith and baptism. Baptism, we shall see, is the sacrament by whose ceremony we first take part in these great events. Sin dies. within us and we rise from its waters with the new life of God's grace-presence.

The Mass is the great way Christ himself prolongs for us his death and resurrection, so we can take part in it and thereby conquer our sins and receive his grace-presence. In each Mass Christ becomes present among us, and through a human priest presents for us his death and resurrection by means of signs or ceremonies. Taking part in the Mass is, we believe, the greatest way of sharing in Christ's love.

We call Jesus Christ the King of the universe, of angels and of men, because all things belong to him as God, and because as man he redeemed us. The Church celebrates the Feast of Christ the King on the last Sunday of October. To the extent that he was humbled for us, now he is exalted: **Read Philippians 2, 8-11.**

What if there are rational "people" on other planets, in other star systems—are they saved, able to attain heaven? There are many possibilities: they might be in an original innocence; they might be as yet unredeemed; they might also have been redeemed by Christ—God could have taken on other created natures besides our own. The possibilities are limitless. God can bring his creatures to happiness with himself in an infinite number of ways. What we do know is that he himself has come and brought us to himself forever.

Alice Meynell pictures what may be the scene when all creation is gathered in eternity:

O, be prepared, my soul!
To read the inconceivable, to scan
The million forms of God those stars unroll
When, in our turn, we show to them a Man.
("Christ in the Universe")

We are to be God's instruments for restoring harmony to material creation, to bring it to perfection by our work and love. The material universe is also God's good creation, but it became tainted by the sin of Adam and all of us. Now it "cries out to redeemed man" to become perfect, to share fully in Christ's redemption. Every advance in perfecting the universe in which we live carries out God's plan for this.

Jesus Christ is among us here and now, more fully than when he was visibly among men 2,000 years ago. "I am with you always, to the close of the age" (Matthew 28, 20). Though invisible, he is closely united to us. He is not in some place beyond outer space. He is as much around us, beneath us, within us, as above our heads. He is personally giving us all the graces by which we attain heaven and by which we bring others and the universe itself to perfection. He is especially united to us in his Church.

At the end of the world he will appear visibly once more to judge the whole human race. Then his work among us will be done. He will deliver all men in this kingdom of love to his Father forever.

Christ's work among us was to be completed by the Holy Spirit whom he would send. At his resurrection Christ was filled with the Spirit. He could now release the full influence of this Spirit of love upon men. The Spirit would enable us to understand Christ's teachings and give us the courage to follow them: **Read The Acts of the Apostles 1, 4-8.**

IN THE LITURGY

In each Mass Christ is present, prolonging his sacrifice, his own death and resurrection, so we can make it our own. Each time we take part, we can offer perfect worship to God. We renew our covenant of love. We take a gigantic step, the greatest possible on this earth, toward our transformation into the divine, our union with God.

The prayers of the Mass emphasize that it is a re-presentation or prolonging for us of Christ's death and glorification.

At the consecration of each Mass we are particularly reminded of Christ's death, as the priest says separately over the bread and wine, "This is my body . . . this is the chalice of my blood." And immediately after the consecration, we are "calling to mind the blessed passion of the same Christ, your Son, our Lord, and also his resurrection from the grave and glorious ascension into heaven . . ." Immediately before communion we call on Christ, the "Lamb of God," to have mercy on us.

The communion of each Mass particularly brings to mind Christ's resurrection: a meal gives life, and at communion we are united to the living Christ to share in his life of grace.

The Church offers all the great prayers of her liturgy to the Father through Christ, our mediator. The formula ". . . through Christ our Lord" occurs again and again.

We relive annually the event of our salvation by the ceremonies of Holy Week, the most sacred time of the year:

On Palm Sunday palm branches are blessed and distributed to the people and there is a procession as on the first Palm Sunday. During the Mass following, the gospel story of Christ's passion is read.

On Holy Thursday evening we celebrate the anniversary of the last supper by a Mass which expresses our gratitude for the great gift of the eucharist and our sorrow at the sufferings of Christ which began on that night.

The service on Good Friday commemorates the death of Christ by means of readings, prayers, and the singing of the passion, along with veneration of the cross and holy communion. After the service of Good Friday, the tabernacle is empty and the altar bare. From now until Holy Saturday we relive the time when the dead body of Christ was in the tomb.

On Good Friday also in many churches there are special services to commemorate the Three Hours during which Christ hung on the cross.

Easter Sunday, on which we commemorate Christ's resurrection, is the greatest feast of the Christian Church. Our Easter service begins with the Easter Vigil on Holy Saturday night: a new fire is lighted and blessed, to represent Christ the "light of the world." From the fire we light the paschal candle, also representing Christ, and then the candles of the congregation. A hymn of triumph is chanted, and then the several instructions telling the story of God's care for his people over the centuries. Baptismal water is blessed and Christ's resurrection is symbolized by drawing the paschal candle from the "tomb" of the water.

At this time, there may be the baptism of new converts, the heart of this service. In the ancient Christian Church, the Easter Vigil was the great occasion for baptizing converts—they were united to Christ's resurrection and received his new life of grace during this celebration of his resurrection. Then all present renew their baptismal vows, once more committing themselves to Christ. The first Mass of Easter is celebrated, preferably about midnight. Christ reenacts in person his death and resurrection for us.

Each Sunday is a "little Easter." The reason Christians worship and Catholics take part in Mass on Sunday is to celebrate this great day of Christ's victory over sin and death. Sunday is the center of the Christian week.

From Easter to Ascension Thursday, the Masses have a joyous theme. The paschal candle, representing Christ, is lighted at the main Masses.

Ascension Thursday, 40 days after Easter, is a holyday in the United States on which Catholics attend Mass to celebrate Christ's triumphant ascent into heaven.

In popular devotion, the Stations of the Cross are a series of fourteen pictures or crosses on the walls of Catholic churches. They commemorate the journey of Christ to Calvary, his death and his burial. Their purpose is to help us realize God's love and mercy in saving us, and incite sorrow for our sins which have caused Christ such suffering. Many churches now have a 15th Station commemorating the resurrection. There are booklets available with suggested meditations for the Stations.

Devotion to the Sacred Heart of Jesus is for some, particularly older Catholics, a way of showing their love for Jesus Christ. The heart of Jesus, pierced for us, has become the symbol of his love for us and his mercy toward sinners.

Some people take part in Mass and Holy Communion on the first Friday of every month, to show their love of Christ and to atone for his rejection by men.

The five sorrowful mysteries of the Rosary commemorate Christ's sufferings, and the first two glorious mysteries, his resurrection and ascension.

Every Catholic church not only has many crosses throughout, but also has a crucifix, or image of Christ on the cross, as a constant reminder of his death for us. It is a common Catholic custom to have a crucifix in one's home, on one's person, one's Rosary, etc.

The "Sign of the Cross" is a way of outwardly professing one's belief, not only in the Blessed Trinity, but also in the suffering and death of Christ for us on the cross.

DAILY LIVING: OUR ATTITUDE TOWARD SIN AND SUFFERING

Christ chose his suffering and death freely to show us the seriousness of sin. He did not have to suffer and die, but he—God himself—went through this humiliation and anguish to free us from our sins, to make it possible for us to attain heaven. He thereby tried to convince us to do all in our power to avoid sin, since serious sin is the one thing that disrupts the universe and that might cut us off forever from God.

A genuine awareness of what Christ suffered should also make us keenly anxious to help others avoid sin—and perhaps eternal alienation from God.

We can have some insights into the often agonizing mystery of why God allows us to suffer. We cannot understand fully the "why" of pain, but we can see something of its necessity; if we were perfectly happy, possessing everything we want in this world, we might become smug, complacent, proud, and cease reaching out longingly for God and the life beyond, which is our true destiny.

Also, God alone sees the whole picture. He asks us to trust him, much as a father might tell his child who must undergo a painful operation: "This is going to hurt, and you won't understand why—but trust me when I tell you that it will help you."

To say that God is not good because the innocent suffer, or to cease believing in him because of this, is shortsighted and childish. It is to want a God who will conform to our notion of what is ultimately good for us. Our good is not necessarily whatever we happen to desire, approve, or even greatly need, and we cannot expect the universe to be shaped according to our needs and desires. The Christian revelation is sure above all of one thing: that God draws the suffering ones to himself forever and engulfs them eternally in his love.

The cause of evil and suffering is not God, but rather our own clinging to the passing things that we must grow beyond if we are to attain our destiny, the total perfection in love that God wants us to have for eternity. So much of our human misery is brought about by our clinging to passing things, to status, to other persons, to material things, to spiritual feelings, etc. Our will, instead of aligning itself willingly with God's, struggles, holds itself aloof, clutches at these passing goods. Only slowly and painfully do we submit to Love, and let God take us over.

Then, too, for one who believes in an eternity of happiness, the sufferings of this life are only a brief instant by comparison—like

a painful injection that takes but a moment, in return for which
we have unending health.

Why innocent people so often suffer will be fully answered
only at judgment after death. Meanwhile, Christ's example shows
us strikingly how suffering can bring about great good.

Christ showed us that suffering has great power to spread love
in the world, to bring ourselves and others to heaven. God could
have saved the world from its sin in any way that he chose. The
suffering and death of his only Son was the way he used. He
thereby taught us that if we accept our sufferings, frustrations,
humiliations, they too can have great power for good—how much
we will realize only in eternity.

The follower of Christ, then, must suffer with Christ. Jesus said,
". . . he who does not carry his cross and follow me, cannot be my
disciple" (Luke 14, 27). And Peter says, "Unto this, indeed, you
have been called, because Christ has suffered for you, leaving you
an example, that you may follow in his steps" (1 Peter 2, 21).
There is simply no other road for a Christian.

When suffering comes, we should unite it with Christ's sufferings, asking him to help us bear it and profit from it. Besides
spreading love in the world, suffering can teach us humility, patience, tolerance, and our utter dependence on God. Many of us
learn in no other way. St. Paul put it: "I die daily . . . with Christ
I am nailed to the cross" (1 Corinthians 15, 31; Galatians 2, 20).

The Christian must continually die with Christ to rise with
him—disciplining himself, controlling his sinful instincts, that the
new life of grace might grow in him. "And they who belong to
Christ have crucified their flesh with its passions and desires"
(Galatians 5, 24). This is mortification—we die in order to live.
Read Matthew 16, 24-26.

As Christ's sufferings led to his triumphant glorification, so our
sufferings will someday end in the eternal joy of heaven. A transi-
tion from death to life—a passing through suffering to attain
joy—is the way God's plan is carried out in history. The Israelites
underwent the slavery of Egypt and then passed on to freedom.
Christ's suffering and death had to precede his resurrection and
glory: did not Christ have to suffer these things before entering
the eternal happiness of heaven? Our daily life often consists of

innumerable "dyings" and "risings" by which we become like Christ. Vatican Council II sums up our human situation:

"On earth, as yet pilgrims in a strange land, tracing in trial and oppression the paths he trod, we are made one with his sufferings, as the body is one with the head—suffering with him, that we may be glorified with him (Romans 8, 17)." (*Constitution on the Church.*)

Joy and hope are natural, then, to true followers of Christ. We know that whatever we suffer now will someday end in the joy of heaven with our glorified Savior.

SOME SUGGESTIONS FOR . . .

DISCUSSION

What does Christ's death and resurrection mean to you personally?
Does our human pain, the suffering of the innocent, frustration, etc. make more sense in view of the Cross?
Can you agree that a Christian must be basically an optimist?

FURTHER READING

* *The Jesus Myth*, Greeley (Doubleday, 1971)—Reflections by a popular priest/sociologist/writer on the person and message of Christ.
** *The Christ*, Schoonenberg (Herder, 1971)—A contemporary, existential, somewhat radical look at Jesus of Nazareth, his being and personhood, by an outstanding Dutch theologian.
** *Teilhard de Chardin on Love and Suffering*, Chauchard (Paulist Press Deus Book, 1966)—An excellent little book, taken from the thoughts of this great man, concluding to the optimism of the Cross.

FURTHER VIEWING

Parable (Protestant Council of the City of New York, 475 Riverside Drive, New York, N.Y. 10027)—A half-hour, color, very popular allegorical presentation of Christ's passion and its relationship to different types of people today; an excellent film to use as a basis of stimulating discussion.

New Born Again (The Grail, Loveland, Ohio)—A half-hour, unusual, imaginatively artistic portrayal in song and dance of
salvation history from creation to redemption.

Watts Made Out of Thread (Paulist Productions, 17575 Pacific
Coast Hwy., Pacific Palisades, Calif. 90272)—27 minutes, in
color—This American Film Festival winner explores the redemptive work of Christ and his presence in every man in a
humorous yet dramatically compelling way.

The Poker Game (Paulist Productions)—27 minutes, in color—Six
men discover that Christ has joined them as an uninvited
guest at their poker game.

PERSONAL REFLECTION

**Each time I look at a cross or crucifix, I realize that God loved
me enough to die for me.** That God should become a man, should
suffer and die—that he should put himself in a position where the
selfishness and cruelty of men could touch him—that he should
ever bother with man at all is a mystery—and the only possible
answer is his love. "By this we know his love, that he laid down
his life for us . . ." (1 John 3, 16).

**To be united with God by love, to have his grace-presence
growing within me, is the most important thing in life.** At this
moment I am either united with him, or separated from him by
unforgiven sin. It would be the ultimate tragedy to go through
life cut off from God's great love by an attitude of unrepentance.

An act of kindness or self-discipline on Friday can show my
love for Christ on the day he died, and help free me from the self-
enslavement of my sins. This Sunday I might worship God with
Christ at Mass, thanking him for his death and resurrection on
our behalf, and seeking to be more a part of it.

9
Christ Sends the Holy Spirit to Form His Church

THE SPIRIT FORMS GOD'S NEW PEOPLE

Read Acts 2, 1-4. **Christ sent the Spirit, as he had promised, to complete his work.** Christ had told his followers to await the coming of the Holy Spirit who would give them power to carry his teachings ". . . even to the very ends of the earth" (Acts 1, 8). He also had promised ". . . when the Spirit of truth comes, he will guide you into all the truth" (John 16, 13). Now on Pentecost the time of the Holy Spirit began.

With the coming of the Spirit Christ's followers went forth as God's new people. As God had chosen the twelve tribes of Israel in the Old Testament, so Christ chose the twelve apostles. As God had come down upon Mount Sinai to make Israel his people amid a storm, lightning, and earthquake, so now on Pentecost the Spirit comes amid fire and a roaring wind, to send Christ's followers forth as God's new people.

As God had begun his people of the Old Testament by making a covenant with them at Sinai, so Christ had begun the new People of God, his Church, by the covenant made in his death and resurrection. He had shed his blood on Calvary to establish the new covenant, as the old had once been sealed by the blood of animals on Sinai. The Church of the New Testament, then, "came forth from the side of the dying Christ." But only with the coming of the Spirit were Christ's followers aware of what he had done and of who they were.

Christ's followers are the new People of God, the Church of the

New Testament. God had chosen the Israelites and made them his church: he gathered them together, gave them his teaching, made a covenant with them, and lived in their midst. When God became man and dwelt among us in Jesus Christ, he also chose for himself a people, a Church.

The twelve apostles were its first and leading members, the remnant which would grow mightily. As God had dwelt among the Israelites, so Christ now lives among us in his Church. Christ said, "I have come not to abolish . . . but to fulfill (Matthew 5, 17). God's plan is consistent. The early Christians were reminded:

> . . . you are a chosen race, a royal priesthood, a holy nation, God's own people, that you may declare the wonderful deeds of him who called you out of darkness into his marvelous light. Once you were no people, but now you are God's people; once you had not received mercy, but now you have received mercy (1 Peter 2, 9-10).

The Spirit, symbolized by the unbridled, mighty wind, means power and freedom for Christ's followers. As ancient Israel had been freed from Egyptian slavery and made God's free people, so the Spirit now guarantees the freedom of Christ's followers. In the baptismal ceremony the priest breathes over those who are becoming Christians to symbolize the coming of the Spirit with power and freedom. No longer need we be slaves to sin, held back from happiness by sin. The Spirit brings us the power to be truly free, to attain unending happiness.

THE COMMUNITY OF THE SPIRIT

The Spirit enabled the apostles finally to understand Christ's teachings and courageously to go and spread them. Before the Spirit came they had been huddled together, weak, fearful, and confused. Now they began to realize that Christ, who had chosen them, was truly divine. They grasped the meaning of his teachings, and became eloquent and courageous witnesses.

They were led by Peter whose Pentecost sermon proclaimed Christ as the divine Messiah (Cf. Acts 2, 12-36). He assured his hearers that the apostles were not drunk, but filled with the fervor of the Spirit as the prophet Joel had foretold, "I will pour out my Spirit upon all flesh . . ." He told them that they had killed their Messiah, and then boldly concluded:

> This Jesus God raised up, and of that we are all witnesses. Being therefore exalted at the right hand of God, and having received from the Father the promise of the Holy Spirit, he has poured out this which you see and hear . . . Let all the house of Israel therefore know assuredly that God has made both Lord and Christ this Jesus whom you crucified. (Acts 2, 32-36).

The Spirit constantly guided Christ's first followers. The Acts of the Apostles, a sort of brief history of the first Christians, shows the Spirit acting again and again, and Paul's epistles mention the Spirit several hundred times. He is present at their meetings, guiding their decisions: "It has seemed good to the Holy Spirit and to us . . ." (Acts 15, 28). He guides the activities of the apostles: "And while Peter was pondering the vision, the Spirit said to him . . ." (Acts 10, 19). On some occasions his presence deeply stirs them:

> And when they had prayed, the place where they had gathered together was shaken, and they were all filled with the Holy Spirit, and spoke the word of God with boldness . . . And with great power the apostles gave their testimony to the resurrection of the Lord Jesus, and great grace was upon them all (Acts 4, 31-33).

This community formed by the Spirit had several very noticeable characteristics. These are given in the Acts of the Apostles, in its picture of the Jerusalem community of Christians.
—**the community was above all united in love.** Christ made clear that this was to be the outstanding characteristic of his followers:

> A new commandment I give to you, that you love one another. By this all men will know that you are my disciples, if you have love for one another (John 13, 34-35).

They practiced love to the extent of sharing all things in common (Acts 2, 44-45; 4, 32-35). As the Church grew this was

replaced by a more practical but equally generous spirit of help-
fulness to one another—such a spirit that a pagan contemporary
said of them, "See how they love one another."

—under the authority of the Twelve, with Peter as their leader
(Acts 1, 13; 6, 1ff). We shall see this more fully in the next
chapter.

—preaching constantly the good news that God had come and
saved us in Christ (Acts 2, 14ff; 3, 12ff).

—admitting new members to their community by baptism,
which had to be preceded by an interior conversion, a true
change of heart:

> Now when they heard this (Peter's Pentecost sermon) they were
> cut to the heart, and said to Peter and the rest of the apostles,
> "Brethren, what shall we do?" And Peter said to them, "Repent,
> and be baptized everyone of you in the name of Jesus Christ for
> the forgiveness of your sins; and you shall receive the gift of the
> Holy Spirit" (Acts 2, 37-38).

—celebrating together the eucharistic "breaking of the bread,"
the primitive Mass, as Christ had told them to. It was by this
particularly that they felt united with Christ and one another
(Acts 2, 42; 20, 11).

The Spirit fills and guides Christ's Church today so that it has
these same characteristics. He is in the Church as a whole, and in
each member, giving understanding, power, love, and freedom.
He will be with Christ's Church "forever . . . the Spirit of truth"
(John 14, 16-17).

A UNIFIED, UNIVERSAL COMMUNITY

Christ's followers were to be particularly united, as God's
people had always been. One of the great concerns of the Old
Testament was that God's people should always be united. When
Israel was split, it was regarded as an intolerable situation which
would someday be healed by God. Christ refers constantly to the
unity his Church should have. "There shall be one flock and one
shepherd" John 10, 16). It is the one vineyard, one tree, one
building, the bride, the one vine. Christ stressed this unity par-

ticularly the night before he died, when he prayed several times
that his followers would be one, so that men would believe his
teachings: Read John 17, 20-23.

We would expect Christ's Church to be united, in order to
avoid confusion and needless disputes, to better spread his teachings and love throughout the world, to give a confused world
some certainty about eternal happiness.

The unity of the first Christians was an evident, visible thing.
They were united in love, under the authority of the apostles,
sharing the same basic doctrines and the same worship that made
them one. St. Paul rebuked some who began dividing into factions: "Has Christ been divided up?" (1 Corinthians 1, 13; 12,
25). Speaking of their common worship, he said:

> The bread which we break, is it not a participation in the body of
> Christ? Because there is one loaf, we who are many are one body,
> for we all partake of the same loaf (1 Corinthians 10, 16-17).

On another occasion St. Paul gave his converts the ideal for
Christians: Read Ephesians 4, 1-6.

Perfect unity is the ideal, never quite achieved but always to be
striven for. Christ's apostles argued among themselves. The first
Christians at Jerusalem tended to form two factions, the "Hel-
lenists" and the "Hebrews." Soon, as the Church's mission became clearer, a better unity was achieved; but disputes still
arose, so that St. Paul wrote from trying experience (words that
could be repeated in any period since):

> "I appeal to you, brethren, by the name of our Lord Jesus Christ,
> that all of you agree and that there be no dissensions among you,
> but that you be united in the same mind and the same judgment"
> (1 Corinthians 1, 10).

Catholics consider their Church to be particularly united. Everywhere among every social group, it has the same basic teachings, the same basic moral code, the same authority to which all
submit, and the same ritual of Mass and sacraments. It has always had a basic, visible unity of structure throughout its history.
This unity was especially evident in Vatican Council II: 2,700
bishops representing over half a billion Catholics, meeting to-

gether, often disagreeing, but all concerned for unity in essential doctrines and morality.

Catholics also must work to heal the disunity of Christians for which they are partly to blame. The unity for which Christ prayed, the Christian ideal, is closer today than for centuries. But it is still a long way from reality. The weakness and sinfulness of Christians has caused our divisions. Striving to love more will bring us together.

Christ expanded the old law by making his Church catholic or universal. He would give all men the opportunity to become members of his new people, whatever their race or social position: "Go into all the world and preach the gospel to the whole creation" (Mark 16, 15). "Go therefore and make disciples of all nations . . . " (Matthew 28, 19).

Peter on Pentecost announced that anyone, Jew or Gentile, could now be saved through Christ. Inspired by the Spirit, he quotes the prophet Joel:

And it shall come to pass on the last days, says the Lord, that I will pour forth my Spirit upon all flesh. . . . And it shall come to pass that whoever calls upon the name of the Lord shall be saved (Acts 2, 17. 21; Joel 2, 28).

But it took some years for this idea of catholicity to penetrate the thinking of the early Christians. Imbued as they had been with the notion that God's people was restricted to the Jews, they made no attempt to convert the Gentiles. Then Peter was given a special vision which prompted him to baptize the first Gentile convert, Cornelius. He explained his action by saying, " 'God has shown me that I should not call any man common or unclean . . .' While Peter was still speaking these words, the Holy Spirit came upon all who were listening to his message. And the faithful of the circumcision . . . were amazed because on the Gentiles also the grace of the Holy Spirit had been poured forth . . ." (Cf. Acts, chapters 10 and 11).

St. Paul, the great "apostle of the Gentiles," was personally chosen by Christ to spread his teaching to all mankind. He had been Saul, a fanatical Pharisee, hater of Christians, and was one day on his way to Damascus to take as prisoners the Christians there. The story of his conversion is one of the most striking of all literature. **Read Acts 9, 3-22.**

He then took his Roman name, Paul, and directed his restless zeal to preaching Christ throughout the Roman empire, to Gentiles as well as Jews. Harried, misunderstood, driven by the Spirit, he travelled unceasingly spreading the gospel until his death in Rome as a martyr. Most of his epistles (letters written to young Christian communities) have come down to us; they comprise about half of the New Testament. Paul's own description of what he endured makes it easy to understand why he is the model of all Christian missionaries: **Read 2 Corinthians 11, 23 to 12, 9.**

This missionary aspect of Christ's Church—that it is to be preached to all mankind, as a way of love for everyone—came to be one of its distinguishing characteristics. This was in contrast to other sects of the ancient world. The label "catholic" became as well known as, and synonymous with the title "Christian." Paul could say, finally, "I thank my God through Jesus Christ for all of you, because your faith is proclaimed in all the world" (Romans 1, 8). Very soon the Church came to include all types of people, from every level of society, to the astonishment of the pagan world.

Throughout history Christians have tried to spread Christ's teachings to all mankind, at the cost of much suffering and a great sacrifice of human lives. Sometimes nationalism, forced conversions, or narrowness have weakened their witness. But in the great majority of cases they have been impelled by love and preached love above all else. Along with Christianity they spread civilization, peace and progress.

The Church . . . in establishing (Christ's) kingdom takes nothing away from the temporal welfare of any people. Rather does it foster and adopt, insofar as they are good, the ability, riches and customs of each people. Taking them to itself it purifies, strengthens, elevates and consecrates them. (*Constitution on the Church, no. 13*).

Catholics find their Church to be particularly catholic. It is for them a universal home, a place for anyone. It has often been remarked that every type of person, whatever his intelligence, background, race, or social position, can find satisfaction in Ca-

tholicism. Sometimes its very catholicity, its multiplicity of ways
to God, confuses those looking at it from without. But of its
many practices, a few are essential, many more are optional.
There is a basic unity and certitude and yet "something for
everybody."

> . . . each individual part contributes through its special gifts to
> the good of the other parts and of the whole Church. Through the
> common sharing of gifts and through the common effort to attain
> fullness in unity, the whole and each of the parts receive increase.
> *(Constitution on the Church, no. 13).*

True catholicity, however, is an ideal, as yet unrealized, toward
which we strive. The Church continually seeks to be more
"whole," to learn from all, so that it can more truly be "all things
to all men" (1 Corinthians 9, 22). "The Church must somehow
find expression in all languages, all historical situations, in all the
personalities who will ever come into human history." (Const. on
the Church in the Modern World).

UNION WITH CHRIST AMONG US

People in love want to be with each other. United with one
another they give each other love, strength, encouragement.
Sometimes they can be united only by thought, at a distance, and
then they long to be physically united.

Christ remains invisibly but really among us, in order to be
united with us in the closest possible intimacy. Though he saved
us 2,000 years ago, his love impels him to remain with us now,
personally drawing us to the Father and eternal happiness.

It is by being united with Christ that we learn his teachings
and receive his grace. Glorified, invisible among us, he is the
source of all the helps by which we attain heaven.

> St. Paul calls Christ's risen body a "spiritual body" which is
> "life-giving" (1 Corinthians 15, 44-45). By Christ's "body" St.
> Paul means the person of Christ himself, body, soul and divinity.
> He gives us from himself the new life of grace. This new life with
> Christ is invisible but real: ". . . your life is hidden with Christ in
> God" (Colossians 3, 3). Our life is truly a life in Christ—we are

"incorporated" into him. We can say with St. Paul, "I live, now not I, but Christ lives in me" (Galatians 2, 20).

This is what the Church really is: Christ among us, working through his Spirit, uniting us to himself and to one another in order to bring us to his Father. Christ is more involved now in human affairs, in our lives, than he was during his visible life on earth. Now glorified and all-powerful, he works among us through the Spirit. The Church is simply Christ reaching us through his Spirit with his teachings and grace-presence—and the way we return with him to the Father.

The Church, then, is Christ and all those who are united with him in the Spirit. It is Christ extended through space and time, joining us to himself, the "fullness of him'" (Ephesians 1, 23). "By communicating his Spirit, Christ made his brothers, called together from all nations, mystically the components of his own body" (Vatican Council II).

Christ gave many descriptions of the way we are united to him in his Church. The New Testament gives some ninety different images of the Church—all attempting to describe the mysterious and wonderful reality of Christ among us and one with us. Here are some of them:

The Church is *the bride*, and Christ is its loving bridegroom (Matthew 9, 15; Ephesians 5, 26ff). For many this is a particularly striking image.

It is a *"little flock"* of which he is the shepherd; "I am the good shepherd, and I know my own and my own know me, as the Father knows me and I know the Father; and I lay down my life for the sheep" (John 10, 14-15).

It is the field, the *vineyard* cultivated by God. Christ says, "I am the vine, you are the branches . . . apart from me you can do nothing" (John 15, 1ff).

It is *God's building*. Christ is the rejected stone that became the cornerstone (Matthew 21, 42). It is built on the foundation of the apostles (1 Corinthians 3, 11) and of Peter (Matthew 16, 18). We are to be "living stones" built into it (1 Peter 2, 5).

It is *our mother* meant to give us understanding, tender love and guidance (Galatians 4, 26).

It is *an exile* journeying on earth as in a foreign land (2 Corinthians 5, 6; Colossians 3, 1-4).

It is the place where the kingdom of God is particularly found, "the germ and beginning of that kingdom on earth . . . (which) strains toward the completed kingdom" (Vatican Council II).

It is *God's family* (Ephesians 2, 19). Our Father gives us his own life, and brings us into the loving life of the Trinity. The members of this family love one another and are dependent on one another. Each is important, each has something to contribute to the others; the weak members are given more honor, as a handicapped child might be the center of his family.

It is made up of sinners as well as good people, a "field" with weeds and wheat growing together (Matthew 13).

To express the union of Christ with his Church, St. Paul often called it Christ's body, of which Christ is the head. "Christ is the head of his body, the Church" (Colossians 1, 18). The head was considered by the ancients the dominant part, controlling and giving life to the rest of the body. Christ the head leads us and gives us his life of grace. The Holy Spirit can be called its soul. The soul gives unity to a body, and so the Holy Spirit is the invisible unifier of the Church; he joins the members to one another and to Christ the head; he inspires every good action in the members of the body.

All the members, as parts of the body, are united with one another as well as with Christ the head. Each member is important and what one does affects the others: Read 1 Corinthians 12, 12-27. As our physical body has millions of tiny cells, all working together and contributing to the life of the whole body, so the Church has millions of members helping one another spiritually. If one part of our physical body is sick or in pain, other parts often feel poorly; so if a member of the Church is "sick" in sin, he hurts not only himself but others as well. As the healthy parts of our body come to the assistance of a sick part, so the members of the Church by their prayers and good works can aid those who are in sin.

As each part of our physical body has a particular function, so each member of the Church has a particular role in bringing grace and holiness to the rest. "For just as in one body we have many members, yet all the members have not the same function, so we, the many, are one body in Christ" (Romans 12, 4-5). Some humble, "hidden" member may be helping the others far more effectively than those in positions of prominence.

Our physical body grows and adds new cells; so the Church strives to grow in love and add new members. "(We) grow up in all things in him who is the head, Christ. For from him the whole body . . . derives its increases to the building up of itself in love" (Ephesians 4, 16).

Through the members of his Church particularly Christ teaches us how to attain heaven and gives us his grace. He teaches us by using certain members to whom he has given the power to teach. He enables us to work with him in spreading his grace-presence to ourselves and others. "And the eye cannot say to the hand, 'I do not need thy help'; nor again the head to the feet, 'I have no need of you . . .'" (1 Corinthians 12, 21). God's plan, therefore, is that we "gain" Christ's grace for one another, helping others attain heaven, and others helping us. Paul deeply realized this:

> I rejoice now in the sufferings I bear for your sake; and what is lacking of the sufferings of Christ I fill up in my flesh for his body, which is the Church . . . (Colossians 1, 24).

We work with Christ by praying for others, offering our work and sufferings for them, and as we shall see, by taking part in his sacraments. There are people whom Christ's love will not help as it might have, people who will suffer needlessly unless we help them.

Because we are all joined together, the power of our love knows no bounds. We saw how each child is born into a situation of sin—an environment of selfishness, pride, dishonesty, hatred, etc. which we call original sin, and which has been snowballing since the first sin. Each child, in turn, will influence others as he grows by the evil which he does, adding to the accumulating sin of the world. But good also snowballs. Whenever we do an act of kindness, or act justly, patiently, honestly when tempted to do otherwise, this adds to the accumulating good and love in the world—and since our redemption by Christ this has a new power to affect men eternally. Often we can see this in practice: we do a kindness to someone, that person is moved by our consideration to be kind to another, etc.

We are never alone or without help in Christ's body. Even if it seems that we haven't a friend in the world, Christ is always

helping us and countless other members—including people we
will not know until the next life—are working with him to help
us. At this very moment someone on the other side of the world
may be praying or suffering, and Christ may be using their love
to help us attain heaven.

IN THE LITURGY

At Mass during the eucharistic prayer we pray for the Church,
for its guidance, peace, and unity throughout the world.

In the Prayer of the Faithful and particularly during the
eucharistic prayer, we pray for all the types of people within the
Church: the clergy and laity, the living and dead, and "us sinners" that we might be united with the saints.

Before communion we pray that Christ will give his Church
peace and unity. At the handshake or embrace of peace we show
our desire to be united with one another. Communion, which is
the body of Christ, as we shall see, both symbolizes and brings
about the unity of Christ's Church.

DAILY LIVING: LOVING OUR FELLOW MEMBERS OF CHRIST AND ALL MEN

So close is the union of Christ with the members of his Church
that what we do to them, we do to him. This was brought home
to Saul on the road to Damascus as he was on his way to persecute the early Christians—Christ said, "Saul, Saul, why do you
persecute me?" (Acts 22, 7). Christ himself tells us pointedly how
he will judge us one day: **Read Matthew 25, 34-40.**

Since we are joined with one another in Christ's body, what we
do to another we also do to ourselves. When we hurt another, we
hurt ourselves, making it harder for both of us to achieve happiness. "For no man ever hates his own flesh, but nourishes and
cherishes it, as Christ does the Church . . ." (Ephesians 5, 29).

Love, therefore, is the test of being a Christian. It is the Spirit
which must infuse anyone who claims to be a Christian—and it is
the Spirit who is Love within us. We must love others just as we
would Christ, and as we love ourselves.

Christians should witness to love by loving their fellow members of the Church in a special way. Because Christians should be conscious of their union in Christ, people today should be able to say of us as of the first Christians, "See how they love one another!" We should work and pray especially for full Christian unity, that all Christians will one day show the united, universal love for which Christ prayed.

But we treat all men as we would Christ himself, with love. Christ died for all men, not just Christians. Others may be called partial or "hidden" members of Christ's Church. We know they often show a great deal of love in their lives. They can be brought to fully appreciate Christ's love by your love.

The true Christian, then, treats everyone with kindness, regardless of race, class, nationality, politics or religion. In his daily actions, at work, at home or school, he tries to avoid anger, and particularly deliberate hatred or seeking of revenge, just as he would avoid injuring Christ himself. In his speech, he is careful of any calumny or detraction. He associates with all, particularly those who need a friend: "Who is weak, and I am not weak?" says St. Paul.

The true Christian is mindful of today's particular test of love. Any refusal to work with, live with, or associate with someone because of his race is a rejection of Christ himself.

In Chicago, a neighborhood group of Christians from several denominations joined with their priests and ministers in going from door to door to block a group of unscrupulous real estate speculators who were panicking people into selling their homes, which would then be sold to Negroes at an exorbitantly high profit. The canvassing was a difficult task, but now, by the common effort of these Christians, the neighborhood is peacefully integrating.

The true Christian is honest in his dealing with others. In dealing with them, he recalls, he is dealing with Christ himself. Cheating, lying, or any form of dishonesty is unworthy of a member of Christ. "Therefore, putting away falsehood, let everyone speak the truth with his neighbor, for we are members one of another" (Ephesians 4, 25).

Finally, the true Christian respects his body and the bodies of others, by temperance and sexual self-control. Our bodies are united to Christ. When we abuse them, we abuse Christ himself: Read 1 Corinthians 6, 15-18.

SOME SUGGESTIONS FOR ...

DISCUSSION

Can you understand the necessity of a worldwide unity among Christ's followers?
Can you see how the Church, in its true, inner reality, is Christ among us?
What for you right now would be a concrete test of Christian love?

FURTHER VIEWING

A *Time for Burning* (Contemporary Films, Inc., 267 W. 25th St., New York, N.Y. 10001)—A 58-minute, dramatic portrayal of a midwestern Lutheran minister's struggle to achieve a racially integrated congregation.
Bloodstrike (Paulist Productions, 17575 Pacific Coast Hwy., Pacific Palisades, Calif. 90272). A dramatic exposition of a Dorothy Day/Mother Theresa type of sanctity among the poorest of the poor. 28 minutes.
Images of the Church (Paulist Productions). Three dramatic episodes which explore the contemporary understanding of the Church. 13 minutes.

PERSONAL REFLECTION

Christ lives in my fellow human beings, even the most lowly and despicable. He thinks enough of them to die for them, and to live now in a most intimate union with them. Trying to see Christ in all men, especially those who seem most unlike him, is reaching out for a great reality.

I might perform an act of kindness, if possible, toward someone different from myself: someone retarded; one of another race who needs help in obtaining decent housing or a good job; one of another religious belief that I have difficulty understanding, or of another political persuasion with whom I have clashed.

10
Those Who Serve as Our Guides

What is the origin of the pope and bishops of the Church? How can a human be infallible? What place does authority have in religion?

CHRIST CHOOSES THE APOSTLES AND PETER

God's way has been to come to us through other human beings. While each man must find him in his own heart, yet God gives us his love and help most often through others. He uses other men to draw us to himself. We realize his presence to the extent that we are loved by others and give love to others.

In the Old Testament God always taught his people and led them through men specially chosen by him—the patriarchs, kings, priests, and prophets. This is the pattern of God's plan. Christ also chose men to spread his teachings and his grace.

Christ chose the twelve apostles as leaders, among God's new People, to give his teachings and grace to mankind. They are the leaders of the faithful remnant who began spreading God's kingdom among men. An apostle is a witness of the resurrection sent by Christ to testify to this. More than twelve were apostles, but the Twelve were the nucleus mentioned in all the gospels; as Israel's twelve sons had founded the twelve tribes, so the twelve apostles would lead the new Israel, Christ's Church.

Most of the twelve apostles were simple Galilean fishermen. One, Matthew, was a tax-collector. Another, Judas, betrayed Christ; after he hanged himself, Matthias was chosen in his place. The greatest apostle, Paul, not one of the Twelve, was a persecutor of Christ's Church whom Christ converted on the road to Damascus. Christ's choice of Simon Peter, the leader of the apos-

tles, his brother Andrew, and Matthew, is related by Luke: **Read
Luke 5, 1-11 and 27-28.**

While on this earth Jesus Christ travelled only through the
small country of Palestine, and spoke to comparatively few
people. He was concerned with bringing God's kingdom among
men, rather than setting up an organization. The Twelve and the
others he chose would work out the best way of carrying his
teachings to others, guided by the Spirit. Luke tells how he set
the Twelve apart after a night of prayer: **Read Luke 6, 12-16.**

**The apostles were to carry on Christ's own work as prophet,
priest, and king.** They were to teach all mankind, as prophets of
the new law of love:

> He who receives you, receives me; and he who receives me,
> receives him who sent me. He who receives a prophet because he
> is a prophet, shall receive a prophet's reward; and he who re-
> ceives a just man because he is a just man, shall receive a just
> man's reward (Matthew 10, 40-41). And Jesus drew near and
> spoke to them saying, "All power in heaven and on earth has
> been given to me. Go, therefore, and make disciples of all na-
> tions, baptizing them in the name of the Father, and of the Son,
> and of the Holy Spirit, teaching them to observe all that I have
> commanded you; and behold, I am with you all days, even unto
> the consummation of the world" (Matthew 28, 18-20).

They were to teach with Christ's own authority, to share in his
kingly power: "He who hears you, hears me; and he who rejects
you, rejects me; and he who rejects me, rejects him who sent me"
(Luke 10, 6). ". . . whatever you bind on earth shall be bound in
heaven, and whatever you loose on earth shall be loosed in
heaven" (Matthew 18, 18).

**They would continue Christ's priestly work of offering worship
to the Father,** and giving his grace to man. They were to be his
instruments, as when he told them to forgive sins: "As the Father
has sent me, even so I send you . . . Receive the Holy Spirit. If
you forgive the sins of any, they are forgiven . . ." (John 20, 21-
23). He would use them to make himself present in a special way
and to offer a sacrifice commemorating his death: "This is my
body . . . this cup is the new covenant in my blood. Do this, as
often as you drink it, in remembrance of me." Of this St. Paul

comments, "For as often as you eat this bread and drink the cup, you proclaim the Lord's death until he comes" (1 Corinthians 11, 23-26).

When the Spirit came upon the Christian community at Pentecost, they went forth under the leadership of the apostles, to spread Christ's teachings. Before Pentecost they were confused and frightened; afterward, though still imperfect men who could quarrel among themselves, they taught clearly and fearlessly. The community ". . . devoted themselves to the apostles' teaching . . ." (Acts 2, 42). After Samaria had been evangelized, "the apostles who were at Jerusalem sent there Peter and John . . ." (Acts 8, 14). Also Paul, though chosen personally by Christ to be an apostle, yet wanted to be united and recognized by the apostolic group of Jerusalem (Galatians 1).

The apostles taught with a clear authority. When a dispute arose, the apostles met in Jerusalem and issued a decree which began ". . . the Holy Spirit and we have decided . . ." (Acts 15, 28); they knew they could speak with the authority of the Spirit. John wrote of himself and the other apostles: "We are of God. He who knows God listens to us. He who is not of God does not listen to us. By this we know the Spirit of truth and the spirit of error" (1 John 4, 6; 2 John 1, 10).

The apostle Paul forcefully reminded his converts of his authority when he wrote about a faction that opposed him: Read Galatians 1, 6-9.

Finally, whenever people join together to accomplish anything there is usually one person in charge. A nation has a president; a city, its mayor; a business firm its president or chairman of the board; in a family, the father has the final authority. In the Old Testament God was represented among his people by some leader, a patriarch, king, or high priest. So too Christ chose one man as the leader of his followers. This would assure unity, that all might work together to spread his teachings.

Christ chose Simon Peter as the leader of the twelve apostles. A reading of the gospels shows clearly that Peter was the leader of the group—he is mentioned six times as often as any other, is listed first and is the one who speaks for the others. Three of the gospels tell us how Christ singled out Peter and gave him a special authority over the others. These testimonies come from

different parts of the Church and this despite the fact that all
knew he had denied Christ. John and Luke describe Christ's first
meeting with him at which he changed his name from Simon, son
of John to Peter which means "rock" in the language spoken by
Christ (John 1, 42; Luke 6, 14).

Matthew described Christ's choice of Peter as leader in this
incident: **Read Matthew 16, 13-19.**

> A rock is strong, permanent, the base which holds a structure
> together; to the Jews of Christ's time *the* rock was Mount Sion
> which according to legend shut off the underworld and therefore
> provided protection against the devil's powers. The keys given
> Peter symbolize authority, power (Cf. Isaiah 22, 22; Revelation
> 1, 18). To bind and loose means a law-making power.

Luke describes Christ at the last supper telling Peter to
strengthen the other apostles, and this despite the fact that Peter
will deny him: ". . . when you have turned again, strengthen your
brethren" (Luke 21, 32). John portrays Christ after his resurrection making Peter the shepherd or leader over his flock, his followers: **Read John 21, 15-17.**

> Christ had often referred to himself as a good shepherd and his
> followers as his flock (Cf. John 10, 11ff; Luke 15, 1-7; Luke 12,
> 32; Matthew 10, 16; Acts 20, 28). Later, others came to be
> called shepherds or pastors (1 Peter 5, 1-3). To "feed" expresses
> teaching, ruling; the triple repetition means a solemn, binding
> affirmation, like a modern oath.

**Peter went eventually to Rome where his position as leader of
the early Christian Church was passed on to his successors, the
bishops of Rome.** Peter's leadership is evident in the early
Church, yet not as one endowed with supreme jurisdiction; all
the apostles had been commissioned by Christ and evidently felt
little need to refer to Peter. They spread the faith independently
of each other. Peter went to Rome, because it was the center of
the civilized world, and was martyred there. As time went on and
the Church grew throughout the world, the unifying authority
of Peter's successors grew with it and they become recognized as
the leaders of the Christian Church, eventually called popes.

Peter's leadership is shown by his presiding over the election of Matthias; he also works the first miracle, is the first to preach the gospel, the first to receive a pagan convert, and he constantly speaks for the others. On starting his ministry, Paul visited Jerusalem to speak to Peter (Galatians 1, 18); when Paul "opposed him to his face" because of his vacillating conduct, this description of the incident (Galatians 2, 11) shows Peter's special position—though he certainly did not exercise the authority the popes would a few centuries later.

THE COLLEGE OF BISHOPS

From the early years of the Church there has been a hierarchy, that is, different degrees of authority: bishops, priests, deacons. Bishops have the full power of the apostles, priests some of the powers, and deacons lesser powers. As in the Church of the Old Testament, and as in any organization, so there are various offices in Christ's Church.

The organization of the early Church, however, was formed only gradually. Many offices are mentioned in Paul's epistles and in the Acts, but the terms do not always have the precise significance that they have today; elders, presbyters, bishops, priests, shepherds, superintendents, presidents, deacons. Some if not most local communities were governed by a college of "presbyter-bishops" of whom one was the president or overseer, and all had been appointed by the apostles or their delegates.

Actually, in the very early Church, there seems to have been two types of organization, one hierarchical and the other not. Luke pictures Paul as appointing presbyter-bishops in the communities where he worked (Acts 14, 23; 20, 17), and Paul in Philippians 1, 1 mentions bishops in the church he had founded there. On the other hand, the church at Corinth had no evident hierarchical leader, but people with different charisms. What soon prevailed, however, was the hierarchical form. (At the end of the first century, for instance, a letter of Clement of Rome to Corinth shows bishops leading the church there.)

In John's writings the bishop (or "angel") leads and personifies the whole community. This concept may have come from the Essenes at Qumran who had one overseer or "shepherd" over their whole group. At any rate what emerges is a "monarchical" episcopate: the bishop presides as the head of the local Church and the priests form a college around him, assisting him. Thus

Ignatius, bishop of Antioch in 69 A.D., writes: "You must all follow the lead of the bishops as Jesus Christ followed that of the Father; follow the presbyterium (college of priests) as you would the apostles . . . Let no one do anything touching the Church apart from the bishop . . . Where the bishop appears there let the people be, just as where Jesus Christ is there is the Catholic Church" *(Letter to the Smyrnaeans* 8; cf. also the *Constitution on the Church, no. 20).*

A bishop is the leader of the local Church or diocese, its spiritual father and center of unity. Each diocese is the Church in miniature: each is a family under the bishop's fatherly guidance; as in any family, the talents of the members of the diocese are to be used for the good of all; each must contribute what he can.

A common early method of selecting bishops was election by the local congregation. Soon local choices had to be approved by the more important "metropolitan" bishops or archbishops, in the West by the bishop of Rome—this to safeguard the episcopacy from unfit men. Since the early Middle Ages bishops have been selected by the pope usually upon recommendation of the other bishops of the area. Civil rulers have often had—and a few still have—a voice in selecting bishops, sometimes with unfortunate results. Today there is discussion of again giving the local people of God, perhaps through select clergy and laity, a voice in choosing their bishop.

The "College of Bishops" is the successor of the group of apostles. Although the bishops are appointed by the pope, they are not his agents, nor do they get their authority from him. It is as a member of the group of bishops, the successor of the group of apostles commissioned by Christ, that the bishop has authority.

Each bishop also has a responsibility toward the whole Church. The apostles and their delegates worked jointly for the conversion of the whole world, and the early bishops showed great charity even to distant Churches. This responsibility of the bishops, obscured for a time, has been stressed again by Vatican Council II:

Each of them . . . is to be solicitous for the whole Church . . . to instruct the faithful in love for the whole mystical body of Christ,

especially for its poor and sorrowing members and for those who
are suffering persecution . . . and to supply to the missions both
workers and also spiritual and material aid, and . . . to gladly extend their fraternal aid to other churches, especially to neighboring
and more needy dioceses . . . (*Constitution on the Church*, no. 23).

The bishop, by the laying on of hands, shares some of his
powers and duties with priests and in some cases with deacons.
Just as Moses was helped by many elders when he led the
Israelites through the desert, as a priesthood always existed in
Israel, as Christ chose other disciples besides the twelve leaders,
so too the bishop is helped particularly by his priests and sometimes by deacons. They assist in worshipping God and bringing
his grace-presence and teaching to men.

THE PAPACY

The bishop of Rome, the pope, is Peter's successor among the
bishops and the visible leader of Christ's Church on earth. Later
we shall see how the pope is chosen.

The title "pope" means "father of fathers" and was once used
for the heads of all important dioceses; it came to be used solely
of the Roman bishop in the 11th century. The popes have rejected other titles such as "universal bishop," which might seem
to derogate from the position of their brother bishops. "Pontiff,"
which has been sometimes used, comes from Imperial Rome and
means "bridge-builder" or priest connecting God and man.

The pre-eminent authority of the Roman Church was recognized from the early centuries by most of the Christian world.
Ancient Christian documents tell us that the Roman Church was
the only one that claimed a primacy over the others, as the center
of unity and settler of disputes. It was the only one recognized as
universal leader, at least to some extent, by the Christian world in
general. It consistently upheld what came to be recognized as
orthodox Christian teaching.

As the Christian Church developed, the great dioceses became leaders of their areas and centers of unity. In the East these were particularly Alexandria, Antioch, and Constantinople. Their bishops were called metropolitans, archbishops, or patriarchs. The other bishops became to some extent limited; for example, the metropolitan had to consent to their election. Rome, the only apostolic patriarchate in the West, thus developed as the unifying center and leader of Italy and the West.

Its actions showed that Rome more and more considered itself pre-eminent throughout the whole Christian Church. Near the end of the 1st century, for instance, Clement, Peter's third successor, settled a dispute at Corinth in Greece. Irenaeus of Lyons near the end of the 2nd century expressed the growing conviction that it was necessary to be united to the Roman Church to have the true teaching of the apostles: ". . . the superior pre-eminence of that Church is such that every Church—I mean the faithful of any country whatsoever—necessarily agrees with her, that is, every Church in any country in which the apostolic tradition has been preserved without interruption" (*Adv. Haer.*, III, 3.2). Rome came to be considered more and more the center of Christian unity and its teaching the test of orthodoxy; many accused of heresy, for instance, felt obliged to explain their teachings to the bishop of Rome.

However, during the first four centuries recourse to Rome by the Eastern Churches particularly was rare. It became more frequent from the 5th century on when the strong leadership of the papacy as we know it began to take form; thus the bishops assembled for the Council of Chalcedon in 451 stated their acceptance of the view of the current pope, Leo: "Peter has spoken through Leo."

It was natural that Rome should develop as the leader of the Christian world. The Roman empire's traditions of stability, law and order, practical justice and discipline, its penchant for institutionalism and its conservative regard for tradition—all these worked to make the Church of Rome the stabilizing influence and center of unity of a developing Christendom. Particularly after the barbarian invasions, it became evident that the Roman Church was the only one that could effectively reform and reorganize the often scandal-ridden, weakened local Churches. Catholics see in this developing authority of the Roman Church an evolution planned by God to give a center of unity and certainty to his Church as it grew.

Jesus Christ himself working through his Spirit is the real leader of the Church; the pope is his vicar or visible representative. Christ is the true rock, the one shepherd, and all human authority only represents him and is his instrument. The hier-

archy of human leaders is necessary, but it is only temporary until
Christ comes again in glory.

The college of bishops under the leadership of the pope has the
authority of governing Christ's Church. The pope has supreme
power, but when he uses it he acts on behalf of the whole college
of bishops; the episcopal college has full power, but the "keys" to
the use of the power are in the hands of the head of the college,
Peter's successor, so that it can never be used against his will.

This authority can be used in several ways. The bishops can
exercise their supreme power in union with their head, the pope,
as in an ecumenical council. Or the bishops can teach or act in
union with the pope while remaining dispersed throughout the
world. Or again, the pope himself can teach or legislate for the
whole Church, speaking for all bishops, but not dependent upon
the consent of the Church or of the bishops, though he does consult the Church and particularly the bishops before he speaks.

Vatican Council II thus sums up the governing authority of the
Church:

Just as in the gospel . . . St. Peter and the other apostles consti-
tute one apostolic college, so in a similar way the Roman Pontiff,
the successor of St. Peter, and the bishops, the successors of the
apostles, are joined together (carrying on) the very ancient practice whereby bishops . . . in all parts of the world were in communion with one another and with the Bishop of Rome in a bond
of unity, charity and peace. In virtue of his office . . . as vicar of
Christ and pastor of the whole Church, the Roman Pontiff has
full, supreme and universal power over the Church. And he is
always free to exercise this power. The order of bishops, which
succeeds to the College of Apostles . . . is also the subject of
supreme and full power over the universal Church, together with
its head, the Roman Pontiff, and never without this head. This
power can only be exercised with the consent of the Roman
Pontiff . . . This college, insofar as it is composed of many expresses the variety and universality of the people of God, but
insofar as it is assembled under one head it expresses the unity
of the flock of Christ (*Constitution on the Church, no. 22*).

An ecumenical council, a gathering of the bishops of the world
in union with the pope, best shows this "collegiality" or co-
responsibility of the bishops and pope for teaching and guiding
the Church. Such a council is to be called by the pope, presided
over by him or his delegates, and its decrees approved by him.

Councils have undergone an historical development. Some early councils were convoked by the emperors and presided over by them or their representatives, though the papal delegates had positions of honor, and the popes' previous attitudes guided the orthodox course of most councils; conciliar decrees were often promulgated by the councils on their own authority, receiving papal approbation later. For a council to be truly ecumenical, then, it must have been representative of the bishops of the whole Church, and its decrees at least eventually accepted by the pope.

Today many wish to have future councils or their equivalent open to lay participation, pointing out that a council should truly represent the whole Church. The Church itself is the "council" called together by God, comprising the whole people of God. As many levels as possible should be present at these gatherings, pope, hierarchy, priests, religious, and people of all sorts: married, unmarried, scientists, laborers, etc. Early and medieval councils had lay participation and when the present church law is changed, they may once again.

Vatican Council II was held from 1962 to 1965, with approximately 2,500 bishops in attendance. It was the major event in the Church's history in this century. It was the twenty-first ecumenical council of the Church (by the reckoning of most authorities). Only the bishops voted, but much influence for its decrees came from the Church's leading theologians, non-Catholic observer-delegates, and lay people and religious who were also invited to give their views.

A "synod" of bishops meets regularly with the pope to help him guide the Church. Most of these bishops are elected by national bishops' groups around the world, and their smaller number enables them to function as a "senate" within the Church, perhaps to eventually supplant ecumenical councils. Commissions of bishops from all over the world are also carrying out the decrees of Vatican Council II; some are meeting regularly with clerical and lay experts in various fields.

THE GIFTS OF ALL TO SERVE ALL

Christ showed his followers how to use their authority by being the servants of others. He gave himself totally in serving others, even to dying for them. He told his apostles: "You know that the rulers of the Gentiles lord it over them, and their great men exercise authority over them. It shall not be so among you; but whoever would be great among you must be your servant, and whoever would be first among you must be your slave; even as the Son of Man came not to be served but to serve . . ." (Matthew 20, 25-28).

Just before he died, he dramatically showed Peter and the other apostles that their authority should be humble service (this ceremony is re-enacted in the Holy Thursday liturgy each year by the pope and by many bishops): **Read John 13, 2-16.**

Christ's followers realized they were to serve not only God but others. They served God by serving others. Paul constantly calls himself a "slave" who does not want to "lord it over" others. "Be servants of one another," he says (Galatians 5, 13). Peter exhorts the elders to "tend the flock. . . . not as domineering over those in your charge but being examples of the flock" (1 Peter 5, 2). The usual New Testament word for authority, used again and again, is "diakonia," i.e., service, ministry.

Some, the hierarchy, are to be leaders in service. They lead in order to unify, structure, and organize the service of all, so that it can be truly communal and effective; they are chosen to be mediators, priests, instruments in a special way. Their service is to be given in a more intense manner—sometimes as a model to their flock by dying for them, as their master did and many have done through history.

The pope is called "the servant of the servants of God." He is the "shepherd" who leads, but he leads only in order to take care of the Church, to serve it, and perhaps to die for it. The Caesars killed thirty of the first popes, almost one after another. Many others have suffered much, as they bore the burdens of Christendom's leading figure.

Unfortunately popes and bishops have not always remembered their duty of service. Particularly in medieval times, they were more often worldly lords than spiritual leaders serving their people. Much of this was historically inevitable as European civilization developed, but great evils came to the Church because Christ's representatives ruled in an autocratic manner.

Recent popes and bishops have been much more conscious of this duty of service. Vatican Council II says of the bishops' mission: That duty, which the Lord committed to the shepherds of his people, is a true service, which in sacred literature is significantly called "diakonia" or ministry *(Constitution on the Church, no. 24)*.

The Church is a living community of people with different gifts or "charisms" for the service of all: Read 1 Corinthians 12, 4-11.

Vatican Council II has stressed these gifts of the Spirit once again: "The Spirit... equips and directs the Church with various hierarchical and charismatic gifts... Among these gifts the grace of the apostles is pre-eminent . . . (but) he distributes special graces among the faithful of every rank . . . These charisms, whether they be the more outstanding or the more simple and widely diffused, are to be received with thanksgiving and consolation, for they are perfectly suited to and useful for the needs of the Church" *(Constitution on the Church, nos. 4, 7, 12)*.

Each member of the Church, clergy and laity, has something to contribute. We saw how each member of Christ's body has a vital function, how the Spirit dwells in each member. Some of the extraordinary gifts St. Paul mentions above existed primarily in apostolic times, to help the Church get underway. But many exist today in modern form, together with other gifts particularly suited to our present needs.

Each must try to use his gifts. Some are called to be leaders, administrators or organizers, while others have gifts for taking care of the "little ones," the poor, sick, neurotic. Some excel in teaching, others in works of charity, art, or Christian witness. One is gifted in speaking out boldly, another tempers our works by prudent observations, and still another does day-to-day tasks extraordinarily well.

The greatest gifts are those of loving, not those of authority. Christ makes clear that we will one day be judged on our works of charity, not on our status (Matthew 25, 31ff). St. Paul says, "Love never ends; as for prophecy, it will pass away; as for tongues, they will cease; as for knowledge, it will pass away" (1 Corinthians 13, 8). The most notable member of the Church is a woman, Christ's mother Mary, who never exercised any hierarchical function. Ultimately, only holiness matters.

The leaders of the Church must try to be aware of, judge, and use the gifts of all. Much of what is best in the Church has been initiated by the Spirit among the laity and priests, reaching the attention of the bishops only later. The bishop's role is to engage in a continual dialogue with his people, trying to be open to the Spirit who often speaks through their gifts. "Judgment as to their genuineness and proper use belongs to those who are appointed leaders in the Church, to whose special competence it belongs, not indeed to extinguish the Spirit, but to test all things and hold fast to that which is good" (Constitution on the Church, no. 12; 1 Thessalonians, 5, 12: 19, 21).

The Church, then, exists to serve God and the world. Its organization, which will one day pass away, exists only that it might better serve by witnessing to truth and love. It must imitate its founder in service particularly to the "little ones," the poor, sick, ignorant, and in trying to further the good in all men.

THE GIFT OF INFALLIBILITY

We would expect that Christ would give his followers some guidance when they set out to spread his teachings. Even the most brilliant men can disagree or be mistaken, and Christ's followers were to communicate God's own special revelation of truth. To be sure men would get his message, and to avoid confusion, Christ gave his Church infallibility.

Infallibility means Christ's guidance of the Church through the Holy Spirit so that it cannot make a mistake in teaching his message. We saw how Matthew shows Christ telling the apostles as a group, and Peter as an individual: "Whatever you bind on earth shall be bound in heaven, and whatever you loose on earth shall be loosed in heaven" (16, 19: 18, 18). Sending them out to teach, he says, "He who hears you, hears me. . . ." (Luke 10, 16). Before leaving his followers Christ told them that he would be with them "always, to the close of the age" (Matthew 28, 19). He promised them also that the Father would give "another Counselor, to be with you forever, the Spirit of truth . . ." (John 14, 16-17). The apostles knew that they had the authority to speak for God himself, as we saw; Paul thus speaks of "the

Church of the living God, the pillar and bulwark of the truth" (1 Timothy 3, 15).

Infallibility is expressed by the belief of the people of the Church who are in union with the pope and bishops. When the people as a whole believe a doctrine, it must be true. "The entire body of the faithful, anointed as they are by the Holy One . . . cannot err in matters of belief" (Constitution on the Church, no. 12).

The people sometimes express the faith better than their leaders. Cardinal Newman has shown, for instance, that during the 4th century it was the belief of the people that was largely responsible for keeping the true Christian doctrine about the nature of Christ's divinity, while the bishops were either silent or divided (Cf. Newman, On Consulting the Faithful in Matters of Doctrine (New York: Sheed & Ward, 1961).

Christ's infallible guidance also passed on from Peter and the apostles to the popes and bishops. It was inevitable that disagreements and confusion would creep in among Christians, particularly as we get further from the time of Christ. Therefore the successors of the apostles and Peter would have an even greater need of an infallible guidance.

Infallibility is expressed by the bishops as a group, as a college. As the successors of the apostles they use this charism when teaching or protecting Christ's revelation concerning belief or morality. Sometimes they teach "solemnly," in an extraordinary way, gathered in an ecumenical council together with the pope. Usually they exercise "ordinary infallibility," that is, they separately teach the same doctrine throughout the world.

Infallibility is expressed by the pope when teaching "ex cathedra," that is, under these conditions: when he teaches as the visible head of the Church, to all Catholics, on a matter of religion or morality, intending to use his full authority and give an unchangeable decision. Infallibility refers only to the pope's power or charism of correctly teaching Christ's revelation to mankind. In personal belief or morality, in science, politics, etc., the pope can be wrong. He can sin, and make mistakes—and many have—in governing the Church.

By this power the pope does not give new revelation, but rather serves and protects the revelation Christ has given us. It is not something of which the pope is proud; it is no guarantee of the soundness of his personal faith, good judgment or prudence. It is rather a testimony to his, and our, human weakness that needs this guidance.

In using this power the pope is the "mouthpiece" of the Church. He speaks on behalf of all the bishops and the believing people. He does not act arbitrarily, pulling teachings out of the air. He rather expresses more clearly a teaching already within the life of the Church; assisted by the Holy Spirit, he can clarify or bring out further implications in what the Church has been believing.

Infallible teachings about God's revelation (dogmas) are the Church's basic, unchanging beliefs. Catholics see a proof of God's guidance in the Church's use of infallibility over the centuries, for the popes and councils have never contradicted the solemn infallible teaching of other popes and councils. Considering the evident weaknesses of some popes and bishops of history, their corrupt lives, the pressures upon them and the fact that some personally held erroneous beliefs, such consistency in infallible teaching is seen to be truly extraordinary.

There is a development of doctrine in the Church, however, a deepening understanding and clearer expression of the doctrines revealed to the apostles. Though the Church's basic teachings are unalterable and can never be negated, their formulation can change, grow, develop to express the truth more fully. As one entering a darkened room gradually makes out the shapes of the furniture, etc., or as a film being developed gradually becomes clearer, so the Church's teachings develop. The Church might be compared to a flowerbox in which many seeds—God's revelation to man—have been planted; some are now blossoming, others are partly grown, and others have only just begun to appear—so the Church's teachings are in various stages of development.

A doctrine is proclaimed solemnly only when there seems need to do so, usually when it is attacked, and only after long study and careful consideration. The doctrine of papal infallibility was itself not solemnly proclaimed until the year 1870—it took that long for it to be clearly formulated and its solemn proclamation considered necessary—although it can be seen in the Church from the early centuries as a part of the developing concept of papal authority.

By its infallibility the Church does not claim to possess the whole truth of God and his relationship to man, but only what we humans are able to see of his revelation at this particular point in history. Any teaching—or even all of them—while true, cannot claim to express the whole truth; they must be understood in their historical context, for example, in relation to the errors they condemn. Actually the Church's infallible teachings, while giving us a measure of certainty in our service of God, say very little. "Now we see in a mirror dimly, but then face to face. Now I know in part; then I shall understand fully, even as I have been fully understood" (1 Corinthians 13, 12).

Catholics also follow the guidance of the pope and their bishops in religious matters when they are not teaching infallibly. These are the more common laws of the Church. Some have greater authority than others. They can and do change, according to the circumstances and needs of the times. They are given in decrees, encyclical letters, etc. Most of what an ecumenical council deals with concerns non-infallible or disciplinary matters. All that Vatican Council II dealt with were these.

It is obvious that we must have these, too, just as a city must have health regulations, parking laws, etc., which good citizens obey. To have unity instead of confusion we have this authority to which all give their free allegiance.

Among the Church's teachings some are more important and meaningful than others. The Church's basic teachings about the nature of God, Christ, our salvation by Christ, the bible, baptism and the eucharist are a far greater part of an educated Catholic's life than, for instance, truths about Mary and the saints, the nature of purgatory, or papal infallibility. ". . . in Catholic doctrine there exists an order or 'hierarchy' of truths, since they vary in their relation to the foundation of the Christian faith" (Decree on Ecumenism, no. 11).

IN THE LITURGY

Pentecost Sunday, fifty days after Easter, is the feast on which we commemorate the coming of the Holy Spirit on the apostles. It is often called the birthday of the Church.

At Mass in the beginning of one of the eucharistic prayers we offer our gifts "in the first place . . . for your holy Catholic Church throughout the whole world . . . together with your servant our pope, with our bishop, and with all who faithfully teach the Catholic apostolic faith." Since these men are God's special instruments, they need special help.

Then we recall the fellowship we have with "your holy apostles and martyrs, Peter and Paul, Andrew . . . Linus, Cletus, Clement (the first successors of Peter) . . ."—reminding us that this is the same Mass in the same Church as that of the apostles and Peter.

A "novena" is nine days of public or private prayer in preparation for some feast. This practice comes from the nine days the apostles prepared after Christ's ascension for the coming of the Holy Spirit at Pentecost.

DAILY LIVING: OUR ATTITUDE TOWARD AUTHORITY

To the Catholic believer an infallible authority is natural and what one would expect from God. If God has come among us to teach us a way to himself, we would expect him to provide us with a certain amount of surety in knowing his teachings. In human affairs, we always try to come as close as we can to an infallible truth—if one has a disease, he wants a doctor who knows as much as possible about curing it—and it is obviously much more important to have at least a minimum of truth about God and eternal happiness.

An infallible authority, far from limiting our freedom, can give us greater freedom. Christ says of his teaching, "You will know the truth, and the truth will make you free" (John 8, 32). Knowing the truth about anything frees us from ignorance, doubt, insecurity—if we know our watch is correct, we are freed from uncertainty about the time. The more truths science discovers about man and the universe, the greater freedom we can have from disease and calamities. A Catholic, following the infallible authority of his Church, can have a basic freedom from ignorance and error in the most important of all things.

On the other hand the more truth we possess, the greater is our

152

Christ Among Us

responsibility. Now that nations control the power of the atom, we can also destroy ourselves; we must use this knowledge for the good of all. So, too, God expects those who have his infallible guidance to love more, to use their insights and bring others to his truth and love.

Obedience to authority is natural, too, in less important, non-infallible matters. All day long we obey authorities, sometimes reluctantly, but seeing the necessity for it—conforming to parking laws, paying taxes, obeying those we love or those over us at work, school, etc. We realize that we are free to disobey but then we must face the consequences. We realize, too, that we must live with the weaknesses and inequalities of any human authority.

There may be extraordinary situations in which a Catholic, after sincere attempts and discussion with theological teachers, cannot make his own some authoritative, non-infallible teaching (e.g. the present papal teaching on birth control); he cannot reconcile it with his grasp of the total gospel preached by the Church. He should then tell his convictions to his spiritual leaders and responsibly work toward a revision of the Church's position. This can be a difficult process in which one has no certitude about how to proceed.

In all of this one's conscience must be his ultimate guide. When papal infallibility was defined in 1870, Cardinal Newman was asked what he would do if the pope declared infallibly something that violated his conscience. He unhesitatingly replied that he would obey his conscience first and the pope second. Authority, then, is a guide for one's conscience, but can never substitute for it.

One's attitude toward religious authority is conditioned by his lifelong relationships to other authorities. One who has experienced little loving authority in his personal life will rarely be able to relate to a Church that speaks with authority. Another might have a personal need for constant authoritarian "props" and so will be overly dependent on a structured religious system. Between these extremes people vary in their need for or independence of religious authority.

A Catholic gives his free obedience to the Church's authority.

He tries to be open, ready to learn, to make the teaching his own. He knows that his bishops are gifted by the Spirit to pass on Christ's saving truth. He tries to obey as intelligently as he can.

But this obedience is not just a blind keeping of rules, obeying minimal laws which make a person's decisions for him. Rather it is an openness to guidance in making decisions oneself, a readiness to apply to oneself the general principles of authority, an openness to the Spirit as he acts in our life.

SOME SUGGESTIONS FOR . . .

DISCUSSION

Does it seem logical that the Church should have a center of authority and unity?

What to you are the advantages—and/or liabilities—of an infallible guide?

Can you see the reasonableness of a development of doctrine in the Church?

FURTHER READING

* *Faith and Doctrine,* Baum (Newman Press, 1969)—An excellent apologetic for the Catholic-Christian faith in contemporary terms.
** *Introduction to Christianity,* Ratzinger (Herder, 1971)—A clear, solid presentation of the ground of our faith: God, Christ, and the Church, given in a modern setting by a well-known German theologian.
* *The Roman Catholic Church,* McKenzie (Holt, Rinehart & Winston, 1969)—A perceptive, in-depth look at the Church's structure, worship, belief, and works.
** *Infallible? An Inquiry,* Kung (Doubleday, 1971)—A liberal theologian's call for a reassessment of the concept of infallibility and the substitution for it of the concept of indefectibility. With the above should be read: *The Infallibility Debate,* Baum, Lindbeck, McBrien, McSorley (Paulist Press, 1971)— Four theologians, three Catholics, and a Lutheran, give incisive critiques of Kung's book.

154 *Christ Among Us*

* *Church, the Continuing Quest,* McBrien (Paulist Press, 1969) —A fine, brief presentation of various views of the Church, particularly of Vatican II and the developments since then, including a persuasive vision of the Church's mission in the world.
* *Do We Need the Church,* McBrien (Harper & Row, 1969)— An excellent presentation of the various ways of viewing the Church, particularly as seen in today's theology, and a commentary on questions like salvation, mixed marriages, intercommunion, the meaning of Church membership, etc.
** *The Church,* Kung (Sheed & Ward, 1967)—This has been called "the best single-volume study of the Church," yet "too narrowly circumscribed by . . . biblicism and Lutheran separatism." If the cautions are kept in mind, it is well worth reading.
** *Priest and Bishop, Biblical Reflections,* Brown (Paulist Press, 1970)—A brief and excellent study by an outstanding biblical scholar on the biblical background of the priesthood and the hierarchy of the Church.
** *Authority in the Church,* McKenzie (Sheed & Ward, 1966)— An incisive study by one of our best scripture scholars showing that the Church's use of authority cannot be modelled after political forms, and that when this has been obscured both Christian authority and Christian freedom have suffered.
** *The Documents of Vatican II,* Abbott, ed. (Angelus Book, 1966)—The documents of Vatican Council II, with an explanatory introduction to each and comments by non-Catholic authorities.

PERSONAL REFLECTION

To attain salvation we all need the help of others. I should try to realize that some guiding authority is natural and necessary, and in giving it my free allegiance I follow, not just the men involved, but ultimately God. I will humbly seek whatever guidance I feel necessary to reach God and his truth.

The Apostles' Creed is the ancient Christian profession of faith, having come to us from the time of the apostles. It is a good prayer to say frequently as a profession of Christian faith.

I believe in God, the Father almighty, Creator of heaven and earth, and in Jesus Christ, his only Son, our Lord, who was conceived by the Holy Spirit, born of the Virgin Mary, suffered under Pontius Pilate, was crucified, died, and was buried. He descended into hell; the third day he arose again from the dead. He ascended into heaven, and sits at the right hand of God, the Father almighty; from thence he shall come to judge the living and the dead. I believe in the Holy Spirit, the holy, catholic Church, the communion of saints, the forgiveness of sins, the resurrection of the dead, and life everlasting. Amen.

11

The Great Book in Which We Meet God

Why is the bible a special book? How can one better understand the bible? How can one be helped by reading the bible?

THE BIBLE, GOD'S WORD AND MAN'S TOO

We have seen how God revealed himself and his plan to mankind through the men and events of the Old Testament, and then finally revealed himself fully in Jesus Christ. God's revelation to man culminated in the teachings of Jesus Christ as set down in the New Testament. We saw that over the centuries the Church has been developing new insights into his teachings, and he is himself continually among us, revealing himself to his followers in a number of ways. But the basic source of what we know about God and Jesus Christ, the Church's great contact by which all other claims to contact with God are tested, is the revelation given us in the bible.

The teachings of Christianity and of the Catholic Church have their basis in the bible. This was dramatically demonstrated at Vatican Council II when, each day, the book of gospels was solemnly placed before the assembled bishops at the start of their deliberations. Near the close of its last session the Council thus summed up the Church's dependence on the bible:

... All the preaching of the Church must be nourished and regulated by Sacred Scripture. For in the Sacred Books, the Father who is in heaven meets his children with great love and speaks with them; and the force and the power in the Word of God is so great that it stands as the support and the energy of the

156

Church, the strength of faith for her sons, the food of the soul, and the pure and everlasting source of spiritual life. *(Constitution on Divine Revelation, no. 21).*

The bible is called the "Word" of God because through it God communicates himself, expresses himself, to us. As we communicate ourselves to others through our words, so by the bible God communicates himself to us.

The Second Person of the Trinity is the almighty Word, the perfect expression of the Father. The bible is God's created Word. He expresses himself through it by guiding the human authors. The Word-made-flesh, Jesus Christ, and the Word-that-is-the-bible, are mysteriously and intimately connected: Today's theology speaks of the "sacramentality" of the bible, because through it man is offered a special opportunity to encounter God in Jesus Christ. This is brought about by the bible's direct contact with the human intellect, imagination, and emotions. In some ways it can excel the encounter with God that comes through the sacraments because it is more tangible and offers more substance to man.

The bible is inspired by God, that is, he guided the human authors so that they wrote what he wanted. Even though the human authors sometimes may not have been aware of his guidance, nevertheless they set down in their writings what he wanted them to. Thus we read it as the world's most sacred and special book.

The bible is also the work of men who expressed their own thoughts as they wrote in their own way. The human authors were not merely passive instruments of God, but wrote freely, using the language and style of their time and culture to communicate their message in the way that seemed most appropriate to them. The writers were like us, sinful, subject to error. Sometimes they did not grasp the fullness of God's revelation.

The prophet, Jeremiah, shows an awareness of his human limitations by opening his book thus: "The words of Jeremiah . . . to whom the word of the Lord came." (Jeremiah 1, 1-2) Luke in his prologue (1, 1-4) wrote: "Inasmuch as many have undertaken to compile a narrative of the things . . . it seemed good to me also . . . to write an orderly account. . . ." Thus the scripture is the words of men seeking to express the word of God which had come to them.

The bible gives the inspired record of God's revelation from the time when the revelation was originally given. God guided his Church to put together the bible because he wanted us to have his teachings in the actual form in which they were first given—when the great, "breakthrough" events of our salvation were still fresh in men's minds—so that down through the centuries we might draw inspiration from them.

A person might set down in a diary an account of some great event in his life soon after it took place, and then years later upon rereading it, be deeply stirred. Reading the words of the bible makes God's great actions seem very close to us—and helps us realize that he is just as truly acting in our lives today.

The bible is a special type of literature and its books must be understood as God and the human authors intended. It contains many different kinds of writing, or literary forms, each of which presents the truth but in its own way—e.g., poetry, parables, hyperbole, metaphors, satire, etc. "Since God speaks in Sacred Scripture through men in human fashion, the interpreter of Sacred Scripture, in order to see clearly what God wanted to communicate to us, should carefully investigate what meaning the sacred writers really intended, and what God wanted to manifest by means of their words" (**Constitution on Divine Revelation, no. 12**).

We saw previously the purpose of the bible and its style of writing. Cf. "The Source of Our Story" in chapter 2. To understand particularly the literary style of the New Testament, cf. "The Coming of Jesus Christ," chapter 6.

The reliability of the historical setting of the books of the bible, once challenged by critics, has been confirmed again and again by modern archeological findings. Just as Christian scholars have come to see the importance of understanding the literary forms of the biblical books, so the discoveries of modern archeology have confirmed the bible's antiquity and the authenticity of the historical setting in which its events took place.

In 1947, the "greatest manuscript discovery of modern times" occurred in the finding of the first of a collection of ancient scrolls in a cave near the Dead Sea. Since then, ten additional caves within a radius of a few miles of Qumran have yielded more material. To date there have been found the remains of some 600 manuscripts, consisting of about a dozen complete scrolls and thousands of fragments dating from the third century B.C. to the early Christian decades. About a fourth of the material comprises copies of the Hebrew Scriptures including a well-preserved scroll of Isaiah and manuscripts representing every Old Testament book except Esther. Of the deuterocanonical books, fragments of Tobit, Sirach, and the Letter of Jeremiah were found. These ancient writings were used by the Essenes, a separatist Jewish sect living in a monastic community at Qumran. The other writings of this priceless discovery consisted of commentaries on various books of the Old Testament, the theology of the sect, and the organization of the community and their disciplines.

These momentous discoveries gave us a Hebrew text of much of the Old Testament over a thousand years older than anything that previously existed. They showed that the final redaction of the Hebrew text was considerably older than what some textual critics had held heretofore. New Testament scholarship has been strikingly illuminated by the material containing the theology and disciplines of the Essenes. It has been held by some that Jesus was strongly influenced by the sectarians of Qumran. Responsible scholarship today does admit to some similarity in his teachings, but the resemblances are outweighed by the differences; the objectives, ideals, and motivation of Christianity greatly differed from that of the Essenes, though quite possibly John the Baptist had some early connection with them, and probably many of them were numbered among the first Christians.

In early 1972 the announcement was made of the discovery of several tiny fragments of St. Mark's gospel, dating from about 50 A.D., among the Dead Sea Scrolls; the oldest New Testament fragment previously found was dated about 135 A.D. by bible scholars.

There have been further discoveries of manuscripts and papyri in Israel and Egypt that are shedding further light on biblical times. Scientific archeology, a relatively new discipline, has added new dimensions to bible study. With the excavation of numerous biblical sites throughout the Near East, new data on many aspects of ancient life and biblical history are available to modern scholars.

None of the original manuscripts of the Old or New Testament books remain today, but our copies are more ancient and numerous than any other books of that period. Our earliest copy of Horace, for instance, is dated 900 years after his death; of Plato, almost 1,300 years. But we have a complete copy of the gospels dated 250 years after its writing, an almost-complete copy dated 100 years earlier, plus fragments from the 2nd century. Compared to the few dozen ancient copies we possess of the best-preserved classics, we have a few thousand of the scriptures. Also, in other early Christian writers we find thousands of biblical quotations and citations, from the New Testament particularly, all testifying to its authenticity.

Because the biblical authors did not write a scientific detailed history in our modern sense, some critics have said that we cannot arrive at a true picture of the historical Christ. They say that what we have in the New Testament particularly are only testimonies of the writers' faith, fragmentary and mythological accounts. However, a conclusive majority of Christian scholars, while agreeing that the faith of the Christian community shaped the writing of the New Testament, and that it does use some mythology, nevertheless hold firmly that at the basis of the gospel accounts is a real person, Jesus Christ, who said and did certain definite things.

One writer puts it: "Faith in Christ is not a spontaneous creation, a satellite which never had a launching pad." The evangelists wrote within the early Christian community, amid either eye-witnesses or those who had intimately known eye-witnesses. There is no explaining the faith and influence of these Christians unless the Christ portrayed in the gospels is real. Otherwise no one would believe in such a totally unique character, preaching such a doctrine: perfect and yet very human, claiming to be the unique revelation of God among men, assuming absolute authority over the sacred Law of Judaism, demanding that men change their lives for him even to loving one's enemies and dying for him, finally going to his death and appearing alive again as proof of his teaching.

Unless this portrayal is real, there is no logical reason why Christians should ever have believed in him or convinced so many others of his teachings. There is no other explanation of his great impact and following.

THE BIBLE'S ORIGIN AND DEVELOPMENT

The scriptures used by the apostles and the primitive Christian Church was a Greek translation of the Old Testament called the Septuagint. This translation had been originally made of the then-existing writings of the Old Testament in the 3rd century B.C. at Alexandria in Egypt for the Jews of the diaspora (those living in foreign lands away from Palestine and the temple). Certain other sacred writings were added to this original translation in the next century and a half (some Psalms, Daniel, Esther, Tobias, Judith, Wisdom, Sirach, Baruch, and 1 and 2 Maccabees). When the Christian Church expanded beyond Palestine and began to evangelize the Hellenistic world, this Greek bible was used with great enthusiasm. It became the bible of the Church during its first generation.

The New Testament canon, the Christian writings considered the inspired Word of God, was slow in developing. At first the early Christians were not concerned with providing written records for posterity because they believed that Christ's second coming would occur in their immediate lifetime. With this in mind, missionary efforts were primarily directed toward preaching the oral gospel. Not until the death of most of the first generation Christians—the apostles and others who were actual witnesses of Christ's public ministry, passion, and resurrection—did a concern arise to preserve the gospel for future generations.

With the last half of the first century Christian literature began to develop. Some of these writings would eventually make up the New Testament. St. Paul's first letter to the Thessalonians is the earliest of all New Testament writings to reach us in its original form. It was written from Corinth about 50 A.D. Paul followed this with additional letters to various and scattered groups that he had converted to Christianity. His letters were written for the practical purpose of encouraging, instructing, and admonishing these far-flung churches.

The earliest gospel that we have in its original form is Mark. Written sometime after 64 A.D., it is historically the most important of the gospels, for it is the earliest surviving record of Jesus' life and virtually the only record; it is the basis of most of Matthew and Luke and it underlies John.

Irenaeus, an historian of the late 2nd century, says that "after the deaths of Peter and Paul, Mark, the disciple and interpreter of Peter, also handed down in writing the things which Peter had proclaimed." (Harper Bible Dictionary).

From this point on there was a great increase in Christian writings. The other extant gospels were written within a decade or two. Many other writings were highly regarded by local churches, *e.g.*, The Epistle of Clement, the Didache, Gospel of St. Thomas, Shepherd of Hermas, etc. But it was almost unanimously held that the writings which had some apostolic origin were to be placed in a special category. Between 150 and 200 A.D. our pres-

ent New Testament books came to be basically accepted by the
Christian world, though some books were not widely used.

*There is a development in Christian theology among the books
of the New Testament.* From its earliest book, Paul's first epistle
to the Thessalonians, to the second epistle of Peter, the last to be
written, there is an evident development in the Church's understanding of Christ and his teachings. Under the influence of the
Holy Spirit, Christ's first followers were coming to understand
and set down in words what God had done in Christ.

**The canon or list of books of the Old and New Testaments was
established by the end of the 4th century** for all practical purposes. Certain early Church "fathers," scholarly and holy churchmen who were often bishops, particularly influenced the selection
of the books that would comprise the New Testament. More and
more these 27 books were used by the Church, and the other
writings fell into comparative disuse.

> Clement of Alexandria (150-215 A.D.), Eusebius (d.c. 340
> A.D.), and Jerome (d.c. 420 A.D.) were some of these Church
> fathers. Athanasius in 367 A.D. issued a list of 27 books which is
> the same as our present New Testament; this was accepted as
> canonical by the synods of Hippo (393) and Carthage (397,
> 419). About this time Pope Damasus I commissioned Jerome to
> translate the Septuagint and the canonical Christian writings
> from Greek to Latin, the spoken language of the Roman empire.
> This translation is known as the Vulgate and was used as the
> Church's official version until recently.

**The Catholic Church, within whose influence the bible was
formed, has always reverenced it, and today especially the
Church urges her people to read it daily.** The bible has always
been the basis of the Church's teachings and of her liturgy. Its
use was not as widespread in past centuries as today, mostly
because people generally could not read and understand it. Yet
before the Reformation there were translations of the bible into
almost every modern language, and many in Latin which was
understood by most educated people.

The Church, however, particularly in post-Reformation times,
banned certain translations of the bible because they were considered to have distorted some passages or were being used to
teach erroneous doctrines. Because of this defensive mentality,

the post-Reformation Church placed too little emphasis on the bible, and sometimes discouraged private bible reading altogether.

Today there is a great biblical revival in the Church, and the bible has become the great force for Christian unity. Christian scholars of all faiths are working together on the ancient biblical manuscripts, sharing their discoveries with one another. They are in almost unanimous agreement on the bible's translation, and the more biblical studies progress the closer they draw together on its meaning.

Regarding vernacular translations of the bible in modern languages:

Before the Reformation there were a number of versions of the bible available to the people in French, Spanish, Italian, and German; these were translations from the Latin Vulgate.

Beginning with Tyndale's translation in 1526, there appeared in rapid succession eight English versions of the bible, culminating in the King James version in 1611. One of these was the Douay-Rheims bible translated from the Latin by Roman Catholic scholars—the New Testament in 1582 and the Old Testament in 1609. This version became the official bible for English speaking Roman Catholics, and the source for the later Knox and Confraternity translations.

The English bible owes more to William Tyndale than to any other man, not only because he was the first to translate the bible from the original Hebrew and Greek, but because the basic structure of his translation has endured through all subsequent changes. The King James version used much of his translation. One third of the New Testament is worded exactly as Tyndale's and the balance follows his general underlying structure.

The King James version came to be called the authorized version of the English people. For two and one half centuries it remained unchallenged. In 1870 a revised version was made in which something like 36,000 corrections were entered; other revisions have been published since.

In America the most widely used edition today is the Revised Standard Version; the New Testament was published in 1946, the Old Testament in 1952, and the Apocrypha in 1957. This is the authorized version of the National Council of Churches. The **Oxford Annotated Edition** with Apocrypha has excellent footnotes, maps, and supplementary information. Both of these bibles are available in Roman Catholic editions.

The New American Bible completed in 1970 is the first translation of the entire bible from the original language into English under Roman Catholic auspices. It replaces the Confraternity edition, and it has been authorized for the readings used in the Mass. Because of this, it will probably become the most widely used bible by American Roman Catholics. It is in modern English and some editions have excellent footnotes.

The Jerusalem Bible, translated by English Roman Catholic scholars in 1966, is another modern English text with a wealth of explanatory notes and other supplementary information. It is unexcelled in its marginal cross references to other parts of the bible which contribute to an understanding of the text.

In 1970 the **New English Bible,** authorized by the Church of Scotland and other British churches, was completed. It is exceptionally effective in its use of modern English. Yet, it retains a continuity with the older versions that have been hallowed with centuries of use. Another very fine translation in modern English is the **J. B. Phillips New Testament.**

Good News for Modern Man, the New Testament in Today's English, published by the American Bible Society in 1966, has surpassed all records as a best selling paperback. It has outsold the best seller of every year since its publication, and its total sales exceed any book ever sold. A companion volume of the Old Testament is being prepared because of the overwhelming success of the New Testament.

In recent years bible scholarship has been bringing together men of all faiths in cooperative ventures. An example of this is the scholarly **Anchor Bible** being published with an extensive commentary, one book at a time. It is being translated by the most renowned scripture experts of Judaism, Protestantism, Catholicism, and Orthodoxy.

In the Old Testament, Catholic bibles have seven more books than most non-Catholic versions. There is no substantial difference in the New Testament. Though some early Christian writers had reservations about the seven Old Testament books, scholars today agree that they were generally accepted and used throughout the Christian Church from the beginning. The books, called the Apocrypha or deutero-canonical books, are Tobias, Judith, Wisdom, Sirach (Ecclesiasticus), 1 and 2 Maccabees, and parts of Daniel and Esther.

The difference of opinion about the books is an ancient one:

The Jews at the time of Christ had no fixed list of books. The theory that the Greek Septuagint, translated and used by the Jews of the diaspora, had a fixed canon which was eventually adopted by the early Christian Church is questioned today. The great codices of the Septuagint—Vaticanus, Sinaiticus, and Alexandrinus —which should bear witness to this supposedly fixed collection, are in disagreement. The same situation existed among the Palestinian Jews, and is attested to by the fact that the Essenes of the Dead Sea included some of the deuterocanonical books in their collection of scripture. It is generally believed that the Rabbinical schools of Palestine, because of the growing controversy with early Christianity and the development of Christian writings being used as scripture, did establish a canon in the late second century—although there are echoes in rabbinic literature well into the third century of individuals questioning the status of some of the writings.

The Jewish historian, Josephus, alludes to a rabbinical tradition that Ezra closed the canon of the bible; this tradition which is in fact unfounded is probably an attack on the Septuagint. Another rabbinical tradition attributes the delineation of the canon to a synod at Jamnia in Palestine about 100 A.D., but there is little reliable information on the activities of this synod.

At the time of the Reformation, Martin Luther made a translation of the bible using the Palestinian canon as the basis for his Old Testament—thus eliminating Judith, Tobias, Wisdom, Sirach, Baruch, 1 and 2 Maccabees, and parts of Daniel and Esther. These books were placed in an appendix to the Old Testament. He also rejected Jude, Hebrews, James, and Revelation from the New Testament. The other Reformation churches, however, did not dispute the New Testament canon, and Lutherans returned to the traditional New Testament listings in the 17th century. By the end of the 19th century most bibles published by non-Catholic sources did not include the disputed seven books of the Old Testament.

The Catholic bishops at the counter-reformation Council of Trent declared in 1546 that the 73 books which had been used to that time by the Christian Church were canonical and the inspired Word of God.

"The quarrels over the authority of the Apocrypha are now

largely matters of the past. A generation that has witnessed the discovery of the Dead Sea scrolls will probably agree with the statement by Prof. Frank C. Porter, in Hastings' **Dictionary of the Bible** (1901), that 'modern historical interest . . . is putting the Apocrypha in their true place as significant documents of a most important era in religious history' " (Preface of Thos. Nelson & Sons R.S.V. Apocrypha).

> Most of the best recent versions of non-Catholic bibles are available in editions with the Apocryphal books. To quote E. Jacob: "These books do not appear to be a roadblock but rather a bridge between the two testaments. Certain doctrines such as the resurrection of the dead, angelology, the concept of retribution, have assumed in the apocryphal (deuterocanonical) literature the aspect under which they materialize in the New Testament. To not include them is to run the risk of removing a precious link in the web that constitutes the unity of revelation." This prominent European Protestant bible scholar goes on to say that it is highly desirable that these books be inserted at the end of the Old Testament, as they were during reformation times.
>
> Catholics and Protestants are now working together to produce common bibles, especially in the minor languages of the mission fields, and these bibles will contain the apocryphal (deuterocanonical) books.

THE CHURCH'S TRADITION INTERPRETS THE BIBLE

Christ did not leave his followers a religion in the sense of a "package" of clear, well-defined truths. His teaching was to be completed by the Holy Spirit and undergo development in the course of centuries. While he gave us the fullness of God's revelation, yet much was implicit, not able to be grasped by the ones to whom it was given—and today much is not able to be grasped by us. To help each age understand Christ's teachings, his Church must adapt their expression to the mentality of that time. The teachings remain basically the same, but we progressively see into them more fully, more relevantly. The Holy Spirit guides each generation to add its own understanding to them.

Nor did the apostles sit down and write a handbook of the Christian faith. Their religion was still "finding itself," growing in an understanding of its true mission—sometimes through painful controversy, as in the battle over the "Judaizers" who would have kept Christianity an aspect of the Jewish faith. These were the problems of the humans who tried to carry on after Christ. They were inspired by the Spirit, but still remained very human.

The primitive Church developed through the oral teachings of the apostles and others who were the witnesses to the great events of Christ's life. The Christian writings which later made up the New Testament were comparatively slow in developing, so that in the first decades of Christianity the faith was based solely upon oral apostolic traditions. In fact the people based their faith almost entirely on the preaching Church until near the end of the 2nd century. The basic elements of the faith were being revealed during the full period of the apostolic age. Only slowly did the Church arrive at a definite creed in the sense of a clearly defined set of truths.

An example of the development of revelation can be seen in the formula for baptism. In the earliest oral proclamation as recorded in the sermons of the book of Acts, the apostles stated that one must be "baptized in the name of Jesus Christ" (Acts 2, 38; 8, 16). As a deeper understanding of the faith was revealed to them, they baptized "in the name of the Father, and of the Son, and of the Holy Spirit" (Matthew 28, 19).

Christian traditions were expressed in both oral and written form. St. Paul wrote to the Church in Thessalonica, "So then, brethren, stand firm and hold to the traditions which you were taught by us, either by word of mouth or by letter" (2 Thessalonians 2, 15). Christianity did not simply become a religion of a book. The Church often asserted apostolic sanction for traditions and usages that could not be traced to apostolic writings.

The bible came from the living Church—the Old Testament from the living community of God's people, Israel, and the New Testament from the apostolic community that Christ founded, his Church, the new Israel. The books accepted as part of the New Testament, particularly, had to be orthodox, to match the belief of the Church. For every accepted book, the Church rejected a similar one. God's truths are revealed to us in the bible, but to understand them in their fullness, they must be seen along with the traditions of the Church from which they first came.

Tradition is the way Christ's Church understands and lives his teachings. It is not merely the quaint customs of the Church, things like our practice of shaking hands upon meeting a friend. It is the way Christ's teachings were and are lived by his Church.

Tradition comes from many things: The Church's creeds, the records of the Church's worship and liturgical practices, the writings of scholars and Church leaders, the decrees of popes and councils, the prayers of the Church's people, etc.

The Church pays particular attention to the tradition that comes from the ancient Church, from those who were closest to Christ. This is called "apostolic tradition." It is found in the early records of the Church's worship, the writings of the early Church "Fathers," ancient Christian inscriptions, paintings, etc.—anything that tells us what Christians believed and did from the time of the apostles.

Tradition is also continuing and developing today. It is the way the Church here and now understands and lives Christ's teaching. It is going on now, in the writings of scholars, the decrees of Church authorities, the practices of the liturgy, the Christian practices and devotions of the people, etc. Since Christ and his Spirit guide the Church, they are continually forming this tradition.

Tradition, then, is the way in which the teachings of the bible are understood and put into living application in the Church. The teachings of the Church, contained in the bible, are interpreted for us by the Church's tradition. To understand Christ's teachings we look both to the bible for the "Word" and to tradition for the "Spirit" in the interpretation of sacred scripture. It is something like looking at a house from the outside and from the inside—in either case you are looking at the whole house, but both points of view are necessary to grasp it fully.

While the bible contains God's original revelation, yet the bible cannot be understood alone. The Church's living tradition is necessary to understand it. Sometimes all that it gives us is a hint of a particular teaching, and while some of its teachings are explicit, others are only implicit. To try to interpret the bible without the aid of Christian tradition would be like trying to interpret the American Constitution while ignoring the other writings of the Founding Fathers, the constitutional interpretations of the courts, commentaries of legal scholars, etc.

None of the biblical authors had any idea of writing a book which would of itself give us all of God's revelation. John wrote the last and longest gospel and says at the end of it: "There are, however, many other things that Jesus did; but if every one of these should be written, not even the world itself, I think, could hold the books that would have to be written" (John 21, 25). St. Paul says, ". . . hold the teachings that you have learned, whether by word or by letter of ours." (2 Thessalonians 2, 15). We saw that Christianity was in existence almost two hundred years before the biblical writings were known throughout the Christian world, and even after this the books were accepted and passed on under the aegis of the Church's authority.

So we cannot arbitrarily use biblical texts to "prove" a teaching apart from the Church's tradition. Through the centuries men have tried to "prove" almost everything by quoting biblical texts without regard for the living tradition of the Church. We recognize that each individual cannot be given his own copy of the American Constitution to interpret and live as he sees fit; so we cannot understand and live the teachings of the bible without the traditions of the Church.

"There exists a close connection and communication between sacred tradition and sacred scripture. For both of them, flowing from the same divine wellspring, in a certain way merge into a unity and tend toward the same end. Sacred tradition and sacred scripture form one sacred deposit of the Word of God committed to the Church." (*Constitution on Divine Revelation,* no. 9).

God's revelation, then, is something that is happening to God's people today, as well as what the Church has possessed from the beginning. In the events of their daily lives, Christians should be making personal contact with Christ revealing himself to them. They should experience this especially when they gather together for the liturgy, as we shall see, or when they pray, or when they encounter God in some deed of kindness, justice, fortitude, etc. For the committed believer, everything that happens is divine.

AN OUTLINE OF THE BIBLE

The Old Testament tells the story of God's revelation of himself and of his plan leading up to the coming of Christ. It contains forty-six books, written by various authors over a period of many centuries. (The older, alternate titles of the books are shown in parentheses. The books are arranged in the order of their appearance):

The Pentateuch, the first five books—Genesis, Exodus, Leviticus, Numbers and Deuteronomy—also called the Law (Torah)—
   This begins with a primitive history of mankind presented in a mythological setting. It continues with God's choice of his people, given in an historical setting. Its high point is the making of the old covenant. It also contains religious legislation covering the way of life of God's chosen people.

The Historical Narratives
   Joshua (Josue), Judges, Ruth, 1 Samuel (1 Kings), 2 Samuel (2 Kings), 1 Kings (3 Kings), 2 Kings (4 Kings), 1 Chronicles (1 Paralipomenon), 2 Chronicles (2 Paralipomenon), Ezra (1 Esdras), Nehemiah (2 Esdras), Tobit (Tobias), Judith, and Esther—
   These books give a general history of Israel. They tell us of the conquest of the promised land, Canaan, the development of the kingdom of Israel as an ancient world power under the reign of Kings David and Solomon, and the divided kingdoms of Israel and Judah, the destruction of these kingdoms, followed by the captivity in Babylon, and finally the return and attempt to rebuild Jerusalem and the temple to their former glory.

Wisdom Literature and Poetry
   Job, Psalms, Proverbs, Ecclesiastes (Qoheleth), Song of Solomon (**Canticle of** Canticles), Wisdom, Sirach (Ecclesiasticus)—
   Historically these books have been classified as the seven "sapiental books," or collections of wisdom sayings, though they contain poetry, prayer, liturgy, and love songs as well.

The Written Prophets
   Isaiah (Isaias), Jeremiah (Jeremias), Lamentations, Baruch, Ezekiel (Ezechiel), Daniel, Hosea (Osee), Joel, Amos, Obadiah (Abdias), Jonah (Jonas), Micah (Micheas), Nahum, Habakkuk (Habacuc), Zephaniah (Sophonias), Haggai (Aggeus), Zechariah (Zacharias)—
   These men of God are unique not only among the men of ancient times but in the entire literary history of the world.

Their office was not filled by human choice but by God. Occasionally and rarely predictors of the future, their main concern was the current situation among God's people. They were a comparative handful of extraordinary preachers who dramatically exhorted, inspired, and tried to reform God's people at times of great crisis.

An historical bridge to the New Testament: 1 and 2 Maccabees (Machabees)—Saga of the period in Israel's life from 166 to 37 B.C.

The New Testament gives the early Christian Church's view of Christ's life and teachings. It contains 27 books, written between 50 A.D. and the early years of the 2nd century A.D.

The four gospels, as we saw, give a rough outline of Christ's life and teachings. The first three, called the synoptic gospels, closely resemble one another; in their composition there was some copying, either from one another or from identical sources, though each author has his own distinctive arrangement and purpose.

Matthew was written particularly to show that Christ is the promised Messiah, the new Moses. It therefore stresses how Christ fulfilled the messianic prophecies, and it arranges things according to five booklets as does the Pentateuch. It was probably written in Syria or Palestine in the 80's A.D. Both Matthew and Luke show that they got much material from Mark, and some material from another source which is now lost (designated as "Q," from the German word quelle = source). Matthew is the first gospel in the sense that it was the one most widly read in Christian assemblies and so did more than any other gospel to form the Christian image of Jesus.

Mark, the oldest and shortest gospel, is very descriptive, and is mainly concerned to show that God has come and saved us in Jesus; everything leads up to the climax: Christ's suffering, death, and resurrection. It was probably written in Rome and shows an awareness of its Gentile Christian readers.

Luke, described as a physician and disciple of Paul, shows Christ as the friend of the poor, the sinner, the sufferer. His is the most complete of the gospels, and has something about almost everybody. This gospel was probably written at about the same time as Matthew, perhaps at Rome, but unlike Matthew it has in mind Gentile Christian readers.

John, written from the viewpoint of one who loved Christ very much, is the loftiest of the gospels. It is quite different from the other three. Its purpose is to show that Jesus is the eternal Son of God, and shows a developing Christian theology about Christ— hence it probably comes from the last decade of the first century. It stresses Christ's "signs" and particularly the sacraments of baptism and the eucharist.

The Acts of the Apostles also written by Luke, takes up where the third gospel stops. It tells of some outstanding incidents in the beginning of the Christian Church. The second part is concerned chiefly with Paul. This book is fascinating and easy to read from beginning to end.

The fourteen epistles attributed to St. Paul are letters written to early Christian communities or to individuals. They are letters of instruction, guidance, and admonition, written to strengthen the faith of the early converts and to put down errors. They were either dictated by Paul himself, or were written by his followers from the teachings he gave them. In their pages is a summary of Christian theology as presented by the great apostle of the Gentiles.

The seven "catholic" epistles are letters addressed to the Church in general, one of James, two of Peter, three of John, and one of Jude. Attributed to these apostles and reflecting their thought, these letters were written mostly by their followers.

Revelation or the Apocalypse, concerns the "hidden things," and gives a series of figurative visions in symbolic and mysterious language. It concerns the time between the Ascension of Christ and his return at the end of the world, and was especially meant to console the early Christians struggling against imperial Roman paganism.

IN THE LITURGY

The bible forms the basis of our worship. Most of the prayers of the Mass, the sacraments, the daily prayer of priests and religious, etc., are composed of prayers from scripture.

The best way to receive God's Word is when the scriptures are read to us at Mass. The first part of the Mass is called the Liturgy of the Word, because it gives us God's Word, especially in the scripture readings and the sermon which should be based on these. It is then that God addresses his Word to his people. At Mt. Sinai, the chosen people assembled to hear God's Word read to them; they then agreed to his Word and a covenant was established by sacrifice. God's people assembled today at Mass likewise listen first to his Word, and then show their acceptance by taking part in the renewal of Christ's perfect new covenant sacrifice.

Sacred Scripture, then, is at the heart of the Mass. Just as we receive Christ in the sacrament, so also we receive Christ in the "Word." There are now normally three scripture readings in the Sunday Mass. The first is from the Old Testament, and is chosen for its relationship to the Gospel, thus stressing the unity of the Old and the New Testaments. The second reading consists of semi-continuous passages from the letters of Paul and James. The Gospel, the final reading, follows the theme of the liturgical season. The lectionary of the Mass provides a more varied reading of the bible by arranging the texts in a three-year cycle.

> "We are fully confident that priests and faithful alike will prepare their hearts together more earnestly for the Lord's Supper, meditating more thoughtfully on sacred scripture, nourishing themselves daily with the words of the Lord. The fulfillment of the wishes of the Second Vatican Council will be inevitably the consequence of this experience of God's word: sacred scripture will become a perpetual source of spiritual life, and an important instrument for transmitting Christian teachings, and the center of theological teachings." (Introduction to the Lectionary, Chapter I, Part IX.)

DAILY LIVING: THE BIBLE IN OUR LIFE

When we meditatively read the bible and try to apply its words to our lives, God communicates with us. He helps us to know what to do and have the courage to do it. The bible's words are addressed to us as much as to the men among whom it was written. The deeds related in the bible are meant to show us that God is continually present among his people, that he acts to help us here and now as he once helped them.

The bible's power in one man's life is illustrated by this real-

life story: Raised as a midwest minister's son, a young man was accustomed to daily bible reading in the home, but upon attaining adulthood and financial success he abandoned any practice of the Christian faith. Then a crisis caused the breakup of his marriage and he gradually turned again to reading his deceased father's bible. Eventually he was converted to Catholicism, and now, several years later, he leads an outstanding group of lay apostles and is in constant demand for his penetrating talks on the bible.

SOME SUGGESTIONS FOR . . .

FURTHER READING—

BIBLE STUDY AIDS

Many persons become discouraged in their bible reading because they are using an older version in which the style and language are obsolete and difficult to follow. Thus it is important to have one of the newer versions of the bible. A number of these are listed earlier in this chapter. In addition, there are other study aids available:

A **bible dictionary** is a collection of articles offering facts and data about persons, places, ideas, words, and themes from the bible. It provides pertinent information from other sources dealing with history, geography, archeology, and language studies that can further illuminate one's bible study. Recommended texts in this category are McKenzie's **Dictionary of the Bible,** and Harper's **Bible Dictionary.**

A **bible atlas** contains maps of important historical periods in bible history, with a commentary on the events occurring in those eras. Among the many good atlases available are Grollenberg's **Atlas of the Bible,** and **The Oxford Bible Atlas.**

A **concordance** lists alphabetically all the words that are found in the bible. This helps one find particular bible verses, and also helps locate material topically. Some good concordances are **Cruden's, Young's,** and **Strong's.**

A **commentary** provides an explanation of the bible passages book by book and verse by verse. It illuminates difficult and obscure passages, and gives an interpretation of the meaning. One of the best available today in one volume is the **Jerome**

Biblical Commentary. The Interpreter's One-Volume Commentary of the Bible is also excellent.

DISCUSSION

Can you understand how Christ's teachings spread and the natural and gradual development of the bible?
Does it seem natural to you that God's revelation should be continuing today in our lives?
What part or book(s) of the bible are the most meaningful to you?

PERSONAL REFLECTION

We should all read a bit of the bible each day, asking the Holy Spirit to open our mind as we do so. Below are suggested readings, with a prayerful response to each. As I read one of the suggested sections, I should ask myself "What is God saying to me here?"

When temptations are great read Matthew 4, 1-11; James 1. Pray Psalm 139 (140).
If you have fallen into serious sin read Luke 7, 36-50; 1 John 1 or 2. Pray Psalm 50 (51). Then express your sorrow as perfectly as you can to God whom you love.
When you need strength to overcome your weakness read Romans 8; Ephesians 6, 10-24. Pray Psalm 31 (32).
If you need reassurance read 1 John 3. Pray Psalm 26 (27) or 90 (91).
When you are lonely read John 14. Pray Psalm 22 (23).
If you are facing a crisis read Colossians 1 or 1 Peter 1. Pray Psalm 15 (16) or 120 (121).
When ill or in pain read 2 Corinthians Chaps. 1, 4, or 12, 1-10 or James 5. Pray Psalm 40 (41).
If you fear death read John 11 or 20 or 2 Corinthians 5, or Revelation (Apocalypse) 14, 12-13. Pray Psalm 85 (86).
When you are bereaved read Wisdom 3, 1-9 or 1 Corinthians 15 or 1 Thessalonians 4, 13-18, or Revelation 21 or 22. Pray Psalm 102 (103) or 115 (116).
When following the crowd seems easier than following God read 2 Corinthians 6. Pray Psalm 36 (37).

12
The Great Signs in Which We Meet God

Can we reach God by our worship? How can we be sure of his presence in our lives? Of what value are religious ceremonies?

THE SACRED LITURGY, CHRIST'S SIGNS OF LOVE

We have just studied the bible which tells us of God's great works among his people in times past. Now we will take up the sacred liturgy, in which God is present and acting among us today. We can meditate on the bible, but far better, we can actually relive its great events ourselves by taking part in the ceremonies of the liturgy.

To understand the sacred liturgy, we must have some appreciation of the meaning of love. Love is not only the basic concept of Christianity, but indeed of all human existence. We cannot be happy, even in this life, unless we are loved and can give love. Love means giving ourselves to the one we love, in order to be united with our beloved, to bring our beloved happiness.

Christianity is simply a love affair between God and us. God first gave himself to us, and we respond by giving ourselves to him. Through this intimate, mutual giving, we attain union with God and happiness forever.

God draws us to himself by giving us his teaching and his grace. He teaches us how to come to him and he gives us his own presence, grace, to raise us to himself.

We give ourselves to God by worshipping him. We saw that this is man's basic, most natural attitude before God—to honor him, to try to make contact, to ask his help.

It is by being united with Christ that we worship God and

receive his grace and teaching. We saw that Christ is our Savior and Mediator, risen and living among us in his Church, acting through his Spirit. God gives himself to us to the extent that we are united with Christ, and we can give ourselves to God only in and through Christ. Many do not know Christ, but are united to him as "anonymous Christians."

The believer, united to Christ, can meet God as an individual, worshipping him by himself and receiving his grace and truth. He might do this in the prayer of his own heart, in the silence of his room or in the stillness of a forest. Or he can meet God in his fellow man—by an act of kindness or courage or honesty—worshipping God by this and being more filled with his presence.

The Christian, however, can unite himself with the worship of the whole Church—meeting God in the sacred liturgy. No longer does he approach God merely as an individual. Now he is united in a special way to Christ and to all the members of the Church. His poor pleadings become those of Christ and everyone in the Church.

The sacred liturgy is the signs or ceremonies by which Christ and his Church worship God and are filled with his grace-presence. In the sacred liturgy, we express our love together by signs or ceremonies. Signs, symbols, ceremonies play a great part in anyone's life. Often they express our feelings and particularly our love better than words can.

By a "sign" we mean something visible, some action, which conveys our inner feelings, our love. A kiss is a visible sign of love which is something spiritual, invisible. A handshake is a sign of friendship. Because we are human, it is natural and necessary for us to express our love and be assured of God's love by means of visible signs. A child spontaneously shows his regard for his father by many little actions, a husband expresses his affection for his wife. So our love affair with God expresses itself in the signs and ceremonies of the liturgy.

Christ is present in a special way in the sacred liturgy, acting on our behalf, joining us to himself. His worship becomes ours. We receive grace as part of him. We no longer appear alone and inadequate before God the Father, for now Christ is pleading for us. We are behind him, in a sense, in his shadow. He is our High Priest, ". . . able at all times to save those who come to God

through him, since he lives always to make intercession for them"
(Hebrews 7, 25). To take part in the liturgy, Christians receive a
"character," a special power joining them to Christ so they can
share in his work as priest and mediator.

**When we take part in liturgy, our worship has a great, new
power to help others as well as ourselves.** The worship of the
whole Church is now with us and becomes ours. We pray in the
name of the whole Church, with its power behind us, like an
ambassador speaking for his country. ". . . every liturgical celebration, because it is an action of Christ the priest and of his
body, the Church, is a sacred action surpassing all others; no
other action of the Church can equal its efficacy . . ." **(Constitution on the Sacred Liturgy, no. 8).**

**The liturgy is the worship of the whole Church and comes from
the Church.** It is the Church's official, "public" worship. To have
liturgy, with all its power, requires more than assembling a group
of Christians to pray together; although Christ would surely be in
their midst, yet his presence in the liturgy is more. The Church
determines what is liturgy, for the liturgy belongs to all of us, to
the whole Church. It has a sacredness, a power transcending any
individual or group. This is why it must be guided by the spirit
and rules of the Church.

The liturgy is the greatest thing we have in the Church. "The
liturgy is the summit toward which the activity of the Church is
directed; at the same time it is the fount from which all her
power flows . . . (It) is the outstanding means whereby the
faithful may express in their lives and manifest to others the
mystery of Christ and the real nature of the true Church. . . ."
(Constitution on the Sacred Liturgy, Introduction and no. 10).

The Vatican Council further sums up how the liturgy shows
what Christ is and what his Church is: ". . . she is both human
and divine, visible and yet invisibly equipped, eager to act and
yet intent on contemplation, present in this world and yet not at
home in it. . . . In her the human is directed and subordinated to
the divine, the visible to the invisible, action to contemplation,
and this present world to that city yet to come which we seek"
(*Constitution on the Liturgy, no. 2*).

*When we take part in the liturgy we are plunged into the past
and are also living in the future.* Mysteriously the liturgy brings
together past, present, and future. Time, relative even to us, can-

not restrict God. By the ceremonies of the liturgy time is "stretched out" for us. Christ conveys to us here and now the actions by which he saved us 2,000 years ago—and by these same signs we are actually beginning now our life in eternity, the future "heavenly liturgy," the worship and love that will absorb us forever. Of all the moments of our life, then, we are the most in contact with God, the most "in eternity," when we are taking part in the liturgy.

Through the liturgy Christ prolongs through the centuries his death and resurrection, his great acts of love for us, so we can share in them. Through the ceremonies and feasts of the liturgy we live "in Christ," actually taking part in these great events of his life. We continually die with him to sin and rise with him to the new life of grace, offering perfect worship with him and growing more and more in love.

The liturgy is, then, the great way in which Christ speaks to us now and tells us of his love, not only by the words of scripture but by actions or signs of his love. As a couple in love dwell on each other's words and gestures, even those that appear to others the most ordinary, so to the Christian in love with God the words and ceremonies of the liturgy convey God's own personal and tender love. As God in the Old Testament reassured and strengthened his people assembled together, at Mt. Sinai, for example, and as Christ spoke so lovingly and intimately to his followers at the last supper, so today he speaks to us, tells us of his love by his Word given us in the liturgy. And more than this, God through his Son is communicating his love to us in each ceremony of the liturgy—each is meant to be a sign of himself and his love reaching out for us—and each has a meaning for the Christian truly in love with him.

The rites and ceremonies of the liturgy must express our inner love also. Without a sincere attempt to love, the ceremonies are valueless. Christ stresses that we must adore God "in spirit and truth." He continually condemned the Pharisees, the "whited sepulchres," "hypocrites," whose lives were a mere external observance of rituals which lacked inner meaning.

. . . in order that the liturgy may be able to produce its full effects, it is necessary that the faithful come to it with proper dispositions, that their minds should be attuned to their voices, and that they should cooperate with divine grace, lest they receive it in vain. (*Constitution on the Liturgy, no. 11*).

The ceremonies of the liturgy are the great ways we join ourselves to Christ, to exchange love with God and be united to him. We give God the best worship possible, and he assures us of his grace-presence and teaching by which we attain union with him here and forever.

The Mass and the seven sacraments are the great ceremonies of the liturgy. We prepare for them by the "little things" of the liturgy, the sacramentals.

THE SACRAMENTALS—REACHING OUT FOR CHRIST

Little children were brought to him then that he might lay his hands on them and pray; but the disciples rebuked them. But Jesus said to them, "Let the little children be, and do not hinder them from coming to me, for of such is the kingdom of heaven." And when he had laid his hands on them, he departed from that place (Matthew 19, 13-15).

Just as Christ himself did during his life on earth, so today his Church calls down his blessing on us at different times in our lives. The story of creation concludes, "God saw that all he had made was very good." The Church asks God to bless not only ourselves but many of the ordinary things of life, so that they might lead us to him.

A sacramental is the Church's prayer asking Christ's blessing on someone or something, or it is an object that is thereby "blessed." The Church's prayer asking Christ's blessing is usually given by a priest; however, parents can bless their children, people ask God's blessing on their food, or bless themselves with the sign of the cross. Some blessings are given to dedicate a thing to a sacred use.

Some of the more common sacramentals are: the sign of the cross, blessed candles, blessed pictures, statues, medals, scapulars, holy water, the rosary, the stations of the cross, benediction of the blessed sacrament, the Divine Office.

Statues, pictures, etc., are not prayed to as having power of themselves; rather they remind us of God's presence. God commanded the Jews long ago: "Make two cherubim of beaten gold ... which you shall then place on top of the ark" (Exodus 25, 18-20). Christian art from the early centuries has used images of Christ and the saints to stimulate devotion.

Some sacramentals are given on certain days during the year: Candles are blessed and distributed on Candlemas Day, February 2nd; throats are blessed on St. Blaise Day, February 3rd; on Ash Wednesday, blessed ashes are placed on our foreheads; palms are distributed on Palm Sunday; fields are blessed on August 5th. Other blessings are given at any time, e.g., the blessing of a mother before or after childbirth.

A sacramental is a reminder, but it is also something more: it is a special way of putting ourself in Christ's presence, asking his help and blessing. The woman who reached out for Christ acted as we might in using a sacramental: Read Luke 8, 40-48.

When we use a sacramental with faith and devotion, we reach out for Christ—and the entire Church joins us in petitioning him. We can be sure that he will help us in some way. When a mother receives the Church's blessing on herself and her newborn child, she comes into Christ's presence, asking his blessing on herself and her baby. Having our automobile blessed, with a determination to drive carefully, is asking Christ to drive with us and protect us.

We should use the sacramentals reverently, but also avoiding superstition. What we derive from them depends on God's will, the Church's prayer, and our own faith and devotion. We must be careful not to look on them as magical, producing effects automatically. If we use them with a living faith, they are wonderful ways to make us aware of God's presence in our everyday lives, in everyone and everything around us.

The sacramentals are particularly meant to prepare us for the sacraments, which are the all-important signs by which we come into a most intimate grace-giving contact with Christ. The sacramentals are the less important signs by which we reach out for Christ. They prepare us for our meeting with Christ in the sacraments by stirring our faith and devotion, and they prolong the effect of the sacraments in our lives.

The difference between these was instinctively understood by a woman, not a Christian, who recently visited a Catholic priest. Her husband, unfaithful for years, had gone off with another woman, leaving her to care for their four children. Introduced to the rosary by a Catholic friend, it had been a great comfort to her for several turbulent years. But recently she had been attending Mass and now yearned to take part in holy communion, realizing that this would be the best possible help for her and her family. One had led to the other.

CHRIST'S SEVEN SACRAMENTS—OUR GREAT, INTIMATE CONTACTS WITH HIM

After relating Christ's healing of the woman with a hemorrhage, Luke continues with the incident of the dying twelve-year-old daughter of Jairus: **Read Luke 8, 49-56.**

While visibly present on earth, Christ often used physical actions, his own ceremonies, as instruments of his divine power. In this incident he gives life by calling out to the girl, taking her hand, raising her up.

Christ also communicates the divine life of grace through ceremonies or signs. Just as his human body was the instrument of his divinity 2,000 years ago, so today he uses the human members of his body, the Church, to give us the life of grace through these ceremonies. These are the all-important signs of the liturgy, the seven sacraments.

A sacrament is a sacred sign of worship by which we come into intimate personal contact with Christ and receive his grace—a ceremony in which we meet Christ most intimately and receive his grace—and by which we join with Christ particularly in his great action of dying and rising.

> By these meetings with Christ we are joined most intimately with the whole Trinity. It is the Spirit within us that unites us with Christ in the sacraments, and they join us ultimately with the Father. Our love relationship with each Person is deepened by each sacrament.

Christ gave us the sacraments two thousand years ago. He instituted them, that is, he provided that his grace would be given especially by some suitable signs. These he left mostly to his Church to determine.

Christ gives us the sacraments here and now. Through them we

come into intimate, personal contact with him giving us grace—each is a "sacramental meeting" or "encounter" with him, like the meeting on the road to Emmaus: Read Luke 24, 15-32.

When we take part in a sacrament, Christ's presence is also concealed, but he is there, affecting us intimately by his love. We on earth cannot yet bear to look upon Christ glorified in heaven—but in each sacrament he is with us, using this ceremony to reach out to us, taking hold of us as one in love embraces his beloved, as a mother embraces her child. We know that sometimes a single contact with one we love, even a glance or smile, can greatly affect and even change our life—so Christ in his sacrament can totally renew us.

Christ uses human beings within his Church, usually bishops and priests, to give us his sacraments. But the man who gives the sacrament is only Christ's instrument; Christ himself communicates his grace to us through the words and actions. The goodness or badness of the human instrument makes no difference as far as our receiving grace is concerned. We are always assured of contact with Christ, of deepening God's grace-presence within us.

> *Christ is the "sacrament" of God, and his Church is the "sacrament" of Christ.* We saw that a liturgical sign is something visible that conveys a spiritual reality. In Christ we meet visibly, palpably, the invisible God. And through Christ's visible Church we make contact today with Christ among us. The Church's sacraments are Christ's actions among us.

The seven sacraments are "signs" in this way: when the visible ceremony takes place, Christ brings about an invisible spiritual change within us. Every sign or ceremony conveys an idea, but it does not actually produce an internal change—a handshake conveys the idea of friendship, but it does not make two men friends. The sign of a sacrament, however, not only tells us about the spiritual change taking place within us—Christ uses it actually to produce that change. A sacrament gives the grace it signifies. In baptism, for instance, as the priest pours the water and says the words, Christ is bringing about an invisible change in us—we are receiving grace and being freed from sin.

Christ gives us these visible signs so that when we go through
them, we can be sure we have been in contact with him
and have received his grace. The ceremony assures us that he is
there. Just as it is not enough for a child merely to know of its
mother's love, but needs her actual embrace, just as a husband
and wife need to show their love by signs of affection, so we need
these sacramental signs of Christ's presence and love.

> Vatican Council II sums up what the sacraments do for us:
> "The purpose of the sacraments is to sanctify men, to build up
> the body of Christ, and . . . to give worship to God. Because they
> are signs they also instruct. They not only presuppose faith, but
> . . . they also nourish, strengthen, and express it" (*Constitution on
> the Sacred Liturgy, no. 59*).

A sacrament, if entered into with faith and love, always affects
us interiorly, always gives us grace. It is Christ's powerful gesture
of love, causing us to respond, as a firm handshake compels a
firm grip in return. Christ always gives us grace unless we deliberately block him. One might block Christ's grace by receiving
certain sacraments in serious sin, e.g., confirmation, holy orders,
marriage; if the sin is later forgiven, Christ then can give us
the grace.

The sacraments intensify our faith and our love for God and
our fellow man, as well as making our sufferings bearable and
meaningful. They unite us to the humiliated and glorified Christ.
They do not eliminate suffering from our lives, but they help us
bear it. They deepen our Christian joy, assuring us of our ultimate resurrection with Christ.

Each sacrament, then, makes us more like Christ, assimilates us
to himself so that his thoughts and words and actions become
ours—or rather, ours become his. The more we share in his
sacramental life, the more we are transformed, drawn to him.
Through the sacraments we gradually acquire his love, his sensitivity for others, his zeal and passion for justice, his compassion
for the sick and "little ones," his single-mindedness in doing his
Father's will.

The sign or ceremony of each sacrament teaches us about its
special effect upon us. While all the sacraments increase God's
presence within us Christ does something special for us in each.

The ceremonies are often difficult to understand today, but originally were taken from the people's ordinary life and given a religious meaning.

> *The basic rites, while particularly meaningful to the people of the bible, are fundamental human symbols found in almost every culture;* e.g., washing with water, placing hands on another's head, eating a symbolic meal together, anointing with oil. Obviously many symbols that came from a simpler pastoral society, or from among people accustomed to court ceremonial, are not as meaningful to an urban, democratic, mechanistic culture like ours.
>
> Many now think that much of this symbolism, which is based on the old cultural forms of the Mediterranean area, should be replaced by signs more obvious to today's people. It will take much patient and prayerful effort to develop signs that keep our link with the past and yet are meaningful in the present. The Church must supervise this development, and the Council has given a basic norm for this: "The rites should be distinguished by a noble simplicity; they should be short, clear, and unencumbered by useless repetitions; they should be within the people's powers of comprehension, and normally should not require explanation" *(Constitution on the Sacred Liturgy, no. 34).*

Through his Church, Christ tells us how his sacraments should be given. Christ's Church is the guardian and giver of his sacraments. He has let his Church choose the sign which best expresses the grace he has attached to a particular sacrament (except the eucharist and probably baptism whose signs seem to have come from Christ himself); thus the essential sign of some sacraments has changed in the Church's usage over the centuries.

The power to give a sacrament is communicated to men especially chosen by Christ's Church in the sacrament of holy orders. A man must be empowered by this sacrament—a special laying on of hands—in order to communicate Christ's grace sacramentally to others (except for baptism and matrimony).

> *In each sacrament Christ unites us in a particular way with the other members of the Church, so we can help and be helped by them. He uses the sacraments to build up his Church.* Baptism joins us to Christ's body, his Church. Confirmation makes us adult Christians, specially empowering us to help spread Christ's body. The eucharist unites us most intimately not only with Christ, but with the other members of his Church. Penance gives us the for-

giveness of the Mystical Body which we have offended by our sins. The anointing of the sick either restores us to the Church on earth or it prepares us to enter the Church in heaven. Holy orders and marriage provide for the continuation of Christ's Church on earth.

A sacrament is a sign of our worshipping love. Our part is vital in this meeting with Christ. When we take part in a sacrament, we express our faith, love, and worship. The greater our faith and love, the more sincere our worship, the more of his grace-presence Christ can fill us with.

Therefore, we should prepare well to meet Christ in each sacrament. We must come to it with the proper intention, with sorrow for our sins, with faith and love. A sacrament is not a mechanical "thing," something magic, that gives us grace automatically without any contribution on our part. It is a meeting in which we must respond to Christ reaching out for us. As we would prepare ourselves for any special meeting with one we love, so the better we prepare the more we will receive from our meetings with Christ in the sacraments.

To help us prepare and to bring out its full meaning, each sacrament has some lesser signs, or sacramentals, along with its essential sign. The ceremony by which each sacrament is given, including the prayers and sacramentals connected with it, is called the "rite" of the sacrament.

Christ's help for us in the sacraments is intensified or weakened by our everyday actions, and vice versa. The more we consciously try to get strength from the sacraments, the more they help us to use countless other daily opportunities to grow in grace—much as a soldier in combat might derive strength from the memory of his last meeting with his loved ones. A sacrament is a powerful beginning—comparable to the first stage of a missile—whose purpose is to impel us to a more Christian life moment by moment.

The sacraments are the great ways in which Christ encounters us and gives us his grace, but he also uses many other ways. Like a stone thrown into a pond, making ripples that spread out in continuous circles, so grace flows from Christ's Church to mankind: the inner, distinct circles are the sacraments, beyond these are the less clearly defined sacramentals, and still further from the center are the other good actions of men.

One might experience God more intensely and receive grace more fully outside the sacraments, but normally they are the great moments at which Christ meets us and helps us on our way to heaven. A boy and girl in love, separated for several months, finally come together again—their meeting is a special moment of sharing in love, to which our encounter with God in the sacraments is comparable.

Christ gives us the sacraments, then, to help us at the important moments of life. Men have always surrounded the great moments of life with sacred symbols and ceremonies. Christ uses these occasions to give us his saving grace: birth, growth to maturity, our daily need for nourishment, moral failure, marriage, serious illness and death, a need of human help to reach God— these are the pivotal points of our lives on earth and at these Christ stands with his sacraments.

These are the seven sacraments, and briefly, what Christ does through each:

Baptism joins us to Christ and his Church, gives us grace, and takes away all sin.

Confirmation makes us adult apostles for Christ.

The Holy Eucharist is Christ himself coming to us under the appearance of bread and wine.

Penance Christ uses to forgive us our sins after baptism.

The Anointing of the Sick Christ uses to strengthen us in serious illness.

Holy Orders is the way Christ ordains priests for his Church.

Marriage is the way Christ unites a Christian man and woman in a lifelong union.

Among the sacraments, baptism and the eucharist are the most important. Baptism begins in us the Christian life, and the eucharist is our main source of strength along the way.

WORD AND SACRAMENT

To sum up: The great means by which God gives himself to us are the bible and the liturgy—"Word and Sacrament." Each is a special meeting with Christ and the Trinity. God uses them above all else to give us his grace and teaching. Together they form the Christian's way to God.

There has always been an intimate connection between the Word of God and the worship of God. The books of the bible, both Old and New Testaments, came from the community's liturgy in the sense that the scriptural narratives, hymns, and prayers were either meant to be used at worship or they came from the actual worship services of God's people. Even the New Testament epistles or letters were intended to be read when the Christian community assembled for the liturgy. (Cf. 1 Thessalonians 5, 27.)

The bible gives us God's teaching, and at the same time prepares us to receive his grace in the sacraments. Christ speaks to us through the scriptures, arousing faith in us, leading us to respond by the sacraments. The better prepared we are by the scriptures, the better is our worship and the more of God's grace-presence the sacraments bring us.

It is in the liturgy, on the other hand, that we best hear, understand, and respond to God's Word given in the bible. The ceremonies of the liturgy not only teach us in a living way the sacred events of the bible, they also enable us actually to take part in them here and now. Our reading of the bible is meant to lead to the sacraments in which our most powerful and most lasting bond with Christ and our fellow Christians is established.

DAILY LIVING: SIGNS OF GOD'S PRESENCE

If we believe in God, in Christ, we should have some sign of this in our home. Many people find that they need some reminder of God's presence, particularly since our lives today are becoming more and more secularized.

One might in one's home have a cross or crucifix, a bible placed where we will read it, or perhaps a picture or statue that appeals to us and will inspire us.

We should also take advantage of what the Church has to visibly remind us of God's presence. Anyone, including one who is not Catholic, can receive the sacramentals of the Church. If used with sincere faith they can help anyone to be aware of God's presence.

> . . . for the well-disposed members of the faithful, the liturgy of the sacraments and sacramentals sanctifies almost every event in their lives. . . . There is hardly any proper use of material things

which cannot thus be directed toward the sanctification of men
and the praise of God. *(Constitution on the Sacred Liturgy, no. 61).*

SOME SUGGESTIONS FOR . . . DISCUSSION

Can you understand the naturalness of using signs to express our feelings, in the liturgy as well as in our daily life?
Do the sacramentals of the Church seem meaningful?
What sign of God's presence seems particularly meaningful to you?

FURTHER READING

** *Liturgy and Doctrine*, Davis (Sheed & Ward, 1960)—A clearly-
written, brief, but profound work on the meaning of liturgy
in the Christian life, this book says a great deal in relatively
few pages.

** *Christ, The Sacrament of the Encounter with God*, Schillebeeckx (Sheed & Ward, 1963)—A theological classic for
those who want a thorough understanding of the notion of
sacrament; shows how Christ is the sacrament of God, the
Church the sacrament of Christ, and the reality and depth of
the Church's seven sacraments.

* *Signs of Life*, Louvel and Putz (Fides, 1970)—An excellent,
concrete, and fairly brief presentation of the sacraments, with
pertinent discussion questions at the end of each chapter.

* *Christian Sacraments and Christian Personality*, Cooke (Holt,
Rinehart, and Winston, 1965)—A study by a very relevant
American theologian of how the sacraments fulfill us as they
unite us with Christ and others.

PERSONAL REFLECTION

Each time I look at an inspiring cross or crucifix, or work of
religious art, I should be reminded of God's presence in my daily
life.

If I am alert to them, there are many other signs of God's
presence around me: the beauty of a landscape, a sunset, the
laughter of a child, the peaceful countenances of an old couple,
the eager joy of young lovers, the infinite patience of a face worn
with suffering, the quiet dignity of many of the poor.

13

Christ Unites Us to Himself and One Another by Baptism

Why is baptism so important? What is the meaning of the ceremony of baptism? What is meant by saying that a person is converted? What of most of the human race who are not baptized as Christians?

WHAT CHRIST DOES FOR US IN BAPTISM

We saw how God uses the signs of the sacred liturgy, particularly the sacraments, to come into our lives today. By entering into these signs we meet Christ most intimately and go with him to the Father. These are the great meetings by which we are filled with his grace-presence.

The first of these great signs is baptism. Here Christ unites us with himself in a new, deeper way, to live more truly and fully with him. Somehow, mysteriously but really, we now go with Christ through the great actions of his life, particularly his death and resurrection. We begin journeying with him to the Father. We will suffer and die with him, and one day we shall rise with him to our real, full life after death.

Baptism is the sacrament in which Christ joins us to himself as a member of his Church. Baptism is often called a "christening," expressing how we are made one with Christ, a completely new person. St. Paul tells how baptism unites us to Christ, so that we are "in" him as in a garment:

> For all you who have been baptized into Christ, have put on Christ. There is neither Jew nor Greek; there is neither slave nor freeman; there is neither male nor female. For you are all one in Christ Jesus (Galatians 3, 27-28).

Scripture tells us how Baptism is to be given. Matthew attributes to Christ himself this ancient formula:

Jesus . . . said, 'all power in heaven and on earth has been given to me. Go, therefore, and make disciples of all nations, baptizing them in the name of the Father, and of the Son, and of the Holy Spirit. . . .' (Matthew 28, 17-19).

The sign or ceremony of baptism is to pour water on the person's forehead while saying the words, "I baptize you in the name of the Father, and of the Son, and of the Holy Spirit." To "baptize" means to wash with, to immerse in water. The water is ordinarily poured on the person's forehead, but baptism can also be given by immersing a person in water while saying the words— the ordinary way it was done in the early centuries—or by sprinkling water on the forehead while saying the words.

By baptism, Christ initiates us into his Church, joins us to his body, the Christian community. He thereby gives us the ability to take part fully in the other sacraments. "For in one Spirit," says St. Paul, "we were all baptized into one body, whether Jews or Gentiles, whether slaves or free" (1 Corinthians 12, 13).

In baptism the new Christian is pledged to the Christian community and the community in turn pledges itself to him. It is the entrance into the Christian family with a pledging of love and service on both sides. The new Christian now will seek God particularly within this Church community, and the community promises its love, prayers, and help to him. Just as belonging to a natural family is far better than being an orphan, so being a part of the Christian family can give love and support one would not have on one's own. The growing custom of baptizing at the Sunday eucharist brings out beautifully this mutual pledge of love and service.

Baptism gives the new life of grace to one who does not have it: Read John 3, 1-6.

The new birth of which Christ speaks is baptism; the new life it gives us is sanctifying grace, God's living and loving presence within us.

By baptism Christ forgives us all our sins. If we are truly converted, we make a fresh start, we begin living a new life with and in Christ. ". . . if anyone is in Christ, he is a new creation"

(2 Corinthians 5, 17). All our sins are totally made up for; it is as
if we had never sinned. When Peter on Pentecost preached the
gospel to its first hearers, they were ". . . cut to the heart" and
asked, "Brethren, what shall we do?" He replied:

> Repent, and be baptized everyone of you in the name of Jesus
> Christ for the forgiveness of your sins; and you shall receive the
> gift of the Holy Spirit" (Acts 2, 37-38).

**Christ frees us from sin and gives us grace in baptism by
joining us to himself in his own death and resurrection.** We saw
that his death and resurrection was the great action by which he
freed us from the power of sin to keep us from heaven, and by
which he obtained for our whole race the new life of God's
grace-presence. By baptism we first unite ourselves to Christ's
death and resurrection. St. Paul explains: **Read Romans 6, 3-11.**

**Sin's power "dies" within us and is "buried" as we go under the
water, and we rise to a new life of grace as we come up out of
the water.** We are thus united with Christ's death which overcame sin, and to his resurrection which brought us the new life
of grace. The ordinary ancient way of baptizing fully expressed
this: the person was immersed or "buried" in water and then
drawn out of it.

**The ceremony of baptism fulfills in a perfect way the deliver-
ance to life and freedom that was begun in the Old Testament.**
God's people were saved by the waters of the Red Sea from
Pharaoh's army, and given a new life of freedom. Christ leads us
through the waters of baptism to free us from sin and death and
give us the new and eternal life of grace. Baptism is our Christian
passover, our own personal exodus.

> The use of water to overcome death and slavery and give new
> life is often foreshadowed. Water has always been a symbol both
> of death and of life; the ancient Hebrews feared the waters of the
> sea, and yet as a desert people they knew that water also meant life.

By baptism one is drawn into the new covenant. Under the old
covenant God was present among his people in the Ark of the
Covenant which they brought with them through the desert and
later enshrined in the temple at Jerusalem. Now, under the new

covenant, God lives within each of his people, most intimately, and they in him. He is himself the new promised land; instead of a geographical territory, he gives us himself—and for all eternity.

Baptism, then, is the sign of our true, interior life, God's grace-presence within us. Now we are publicly (and consciously, if old enough) pledged to live with an awareness of this presence within us: the Persons of God are within us, transforming us, giving a new meaning and power to everything we do. Mysteriously, wonderfully, we are joined in a particular and intimate way to each of the Three Persons. Within us, surrounding us, filling us, guiding and loving us, the Trinity draws us into their own life. This is the "indwelling" of the Blessed Trinity—it is heaven already begun within us.

> "Grace" is simply our relationship to the divine Persons, the "state," the life situation in which the Persons come to us, live with us and love us. By this we have a special relationship to each of the Persons. Now that we have penetrated further into God's plan, and have seen something of the actions of the divine Persons in human history, we might reread the part of Chapter 7 dealing with our personal relationship to each Person. This should now have a deeper meaning.

Like any personal love relationship that fulfills, elevates and transforms one, so grace makes us more and more like God. A deep friendship, the love of a man and woman—these raise and fulfill one's personality wonderfully. We become fuller persons ourselves, even as we take on more and more of the characteristics of our friend or loved one. So here we are raised to the very level of God, transformed more and more into him. ". . . it is no longer I who live, but Christ who lives in me" (Galatians 2, 20).

This is the "kingdom of God" which Christ preached: God's grace-presence within us. To have God's grace-presence within us is to belong to the kingdom, to submit to his loving guidance from within. When we believe in him and try to do his will, we belong to this kingdom. We might recall what Christ said about this kingdom: the poor, the humble, the oppressed are the happy ones, and the one law in the kingdom is that of love. The kingdom is not yet completed—we must suffer and work for its fulfillment, that God's grace-presence will fill all men—and so we pray

". . . thy kingdom come, thy will be done on earth as it is in heaven."

To help us live the Christian life, Christ gives us special powers: the virtues. The virtues are powers or attitudes within us: faith, hope, charity; they are explained in detail in the next chapter. Christ also promises us all the day-by-day helps, the "actual graces" necessary to live as his followers. One's Christianity may never develop, through no fault of his own; Christ guides him through life nevertheless, giving him more than sufficient help to attain heaven.

At baptism the Christian receives the power to share in Christ's own work as priest, prophet, and king. This is the "priesthood of the laity," the power to offer Mass fully with Christ and take part in the other sacraments, to act as a mediator in prayer and other ways. It is a prophetic and kingly power in that we must now openly witness to the faith, hope, and love within us—to the kingdom of God, God's grace-presence within us.

WHO CAN BE BAPTIZED?

For those who know about and believe in Christ's teaching, baptism with water is the necessary first step Christ has given us to eternal happiness. The words of Christ to Nicodemus express this clearly: ". . . unless a man be born again of water and the Spirit, he cannot enter the kingdom of God" (John 3, 5). This has been the Church's belief from the beginning, as is evident again and again in the Acts of the Apostles, the epistles, and other early Christian writings.

Therefore we baptize infants, so they can begin growing in the life of grace within the Christian community. Infant baptism has been practiced in the Christian Church from the beginning, as early Christian documents testify (Cf., for instance, Warren Carr, **Baptism: Conscience and Clue for the Church** (New York: Holt, Rinehart, and Winston, 1963).

> *An infant being baptized* should not be looked upon as if he were somehow interiorly evil, needing to be washed "clean" by the waters of the sacrament. Rather he is good and beautiful in God's eyes, and certainly free of moral fault. But he shares the inherent human weakness that we call original sin, and will suffer

from its effects all his life. He experiences what it is to be un-loved, beginning in the womb, and will be unloving in return. Baptism sets up a new relationship, gives him a new orientation, pointing him in the direction of God through Christ and the Church—now the vision of God and a new perfect world is before him. Baptism is thus a new birth, to eternal life, and a new crea-tion, for by it one shares in the vision of a new universe. Now it is up to his parents and the Christian community to tell him of this Christian vision, and to help him activate his powers to do his part to make that vision a reality.

While most today favor the traditional practice of infant bap-tism, some feel that there should be a conscious commitment, whenever possible, on the part of the one being bapitized. Some want children at the age of reason (about seven years) to learn about and go through the ancient rites of initiation into the Christian community—baptism, confirmation, and the eucharist—and the Church has given permission for this in a few places.

Regarding what happens to unbaptized infants, we have no clear teaching of Christ or doctrine of the Church. Some scholars have thought that they go to "limbo," which they regard as a state of perfect, unending, "natural" happiness, but much less than the happiness of heaven. They point out, however, that we need not think of heaven and this possible state of limbo as being totally separated places, as are the U.S. and Europe; one in limbo could be with his parents and loved ones, but not as aware of God nor as penetratingly happy—as a child approaching com-munion with his mother would grasp something of its reality, but not as much as she. Most today, however, think that the faith and love of the parents, for instance, would supply for the infant and it would at-tain heaven. They point out that God accepts each of us (unless we have fully rejected him by serious sin) and our response is secondary, and therefore not necessary in the case of these innocent little ones. It should be pointed out, incidentally, that an infant attaining heaven would be a full-grown adult, capable of growing endlessly in knowl-edge and love.

A priest usually gives baptism. However, in case of danger of death anyone can baptize, even one who is not a Christian. He must, of course, baptize correctly and have the intention of giving Christian baptism.

National news bulletins several years ago told how Shirley O'Neill, a Catholic college student, baptized her companion, Albert Kogler, who had been attacked by a shark off a San Francisco beach. She swam to rescue him, towed him ashore, and then poured water over his head from her cupped hands while she said the words of baptism. Two hours later Albert Kogler died. Later it was learned that he had been taking instructions to enter the Catholic Church. Shirley eventually received a medal from the President for her heroism. The incident graphically demonstrated to the nation the faith of a devout Christian.

At baptism we have sponsors or godparents—a Catholic man and woman chosen to help their godchild live his Catholic faith fully. An adult convert usually has one sponsor of the same sex. A sponsor must be a practicing Catholic, at least fourteen years of age.

A sponsor must be someone other than one's parents or marriage partner. Also, a non-Catholic Christian cannot be a sponsor at a Catholic baptism, since the sponsor is the representative of the community of the Catholic faithful, the guarantor of the Catholic faith of the candidate.

It is a privilege to be a baptismal sponsor and involves a sacred duty. A sponsor should be an active, zealous Catholic, who realizes that he must keep in touch with his godchild, and help him grow in the faith, especially by his own good example.

An infant is usually baptized in the parish of its parents; an adult convert where he takes instructions. A convert is baptized when the one instructing him judges him ready. An infant should be baptized within two or three weeks after birth, or as soon thereafter as possible.

A *priest may have to refuse to baptize someone* if he judges that the person will probably not live a good Catholic life. Baptism is not just a ceremony—it is the beginning of a new way of life. A priest might therefore have to refuse to baptize the children of fallen-away Catholics, or of those "married outside the Church," unless there is a sufficient guarantee that the children will be brought up as good Catholics.

Since we have become a new person at baptism we normally take a new name, that of a saint. This saint becomes our patron, a lifelong model to imitate as he or she imitated Christ. St. Paul says, ". . . be imitators of me, as I am of Christ" (1 Corinthians 4,

16). An adult may retain his own name, whether or not it is that of a saint.

We should learn something about our patron saint in order to better imitate him. Our patron, in turn, is vitally interested in us and helps us attain heaven, as will be explained.

If one who was baptized a Christian wanted to become a Catholic, he would not be baptized again, unless there was doubt about the validity of the previous baptism, *i.e.,* whether it had been done correctly. If there is a real doubt, the priest would baptize conditionally with these words, "If you are not baptized, I baptize you in the name of the Father, etc." One previously baptized as a Christian should obtain a certificate of this baptism, so the information can be entered on the records of the Catholic church at which he becomes a Catholic.

The already-baptized Christian who wishes to become a Catholic would *make a Profession of Faith,* a statement of his belief in the teachings of the Catholic Church, before a priest and a witness (usually an adult of the same sex who can act as his "sponsor," helping him to adjust to his new faith). Vatican Council II provided that a new rite be composed for the reception of such a person into full communion with the Church; at present, the sacramentals which are part of the present adult baptismal rite may be used for such an occasion, or it might be done in the setting of a bible service.

BEFORE BAPTISM, CONVERSION AND A PROFESSION OF FAITH

The Acts of the Apostles tells how the deacon Philip one day met an official of the Queen of Ethiopia and told him the good news about Christ, as they were driving along the road from Jerusalem. They came to a stream, and the official said, "See, here is water; what is there to prevent my being baptized?" Philip said, "If you believe with all your heart, you may." And the official answered: "I believe that Jesus Christ is the Son of God." Then they stopped the chariot and went down into the water where Philip baptized him (Cf. Acts, 8, 26-39).

In this incident Philip asked that the official believe "with all his heart" before being baptized. So anyone wishing to be baptized must not only accept intellectually the teachings of the Church, believing them to be true—and a course of instructions is naturally necessary for this—he must also believe with all his heart, that is, be converted, determined to live up to those teachings. Peter's Pentecost sermon expresses it. "Repent (convert, have a change of mind and heart) and be baptized. . . ." (Acts 2, 38). St. Paul reminds his converts ". . . how we entered among you, and how you turned to God from idols, to serve the living and true God. . . ." (1 Thessalonians 1, 9).

A conversion, therefore, is a total "turning" toward Christ and a new way of life. We accept the Church's teachings as true, and, repenting of our sins, are determined to live a good Christian life. It is a total interior change of mind and heart. With all our heart we turn away from our sins, toward Christ and his Church. We make a total commitment of ourselves to Christ. We may have sincerely tried to serve God before, but now we are determined to do so to the full extent of our new and fuller knowledge of the truth.

Conversion means a firm determination, but not a certainty that one will never sin again. Perhaps the convert is realistically fearful, even quite certain that he will fall again into his old sins, but he commits himself nevertheless, trusting in God to help him and pick him up should he fall.

The power to be converted is given by God, and is often called the "gift of faith." It presupposes our own sincere efforts, as we shall see. But it is God who first attracts us, motivates us, "calls" us by a loving invitation that is perhaps gradual but nonetheless persistent to turn completely to himself.

To express his conversion an adult convert to Catholicism makes a Profession or Act of Faith. If he is to be baptized this is done immediately before baptism. He solemnly reads this profession before a priest, affirming his acceptance of the Church's basic teachings and his commitment to live by them.

The priest who is conducting the person's instructions judges whether he is ready to make his Profession of Faith and be baptized into the Church. If one cannot accept the Church's basic teachings as true, and commit himself to try to live a good Catholic life, he should not be baptized a Catholic.

IN THE LITURGY

The full rite of baptism, including the sacramentals that are a part of it, brings out its meaning for the new Christian. Ideally the baptism of an adult, or his reception into the Church, is prepared for by a catechumenate—a series of preparatory sessions, during which the rite of baptism may be given in stages to better bring home its meaning.

At the Easter Vigil service each year, the climax of the Church's liturgy, the whole congregation joins in a renewal of baptismal vows by renouncing Satan and professing their belief in the teaching of the Church.

The baptism of converts may take place during this service, which was the ordinary time for their reception into the early Christian Church. After baptism, they assist at Mass for the first time as Catholics, sharing fully now in offering Christ and receiving the full graces of the Mass as they receive him in their first holy communion.

During the week after Easter (its "octave") particularly, the prayers of the Church's liturgy reflect the intimate connection between the resurrection of Christ and our own "resurrection" by baptism.

The use of holy water, particularly when making the sign of the cross upon entering or leaving church, is a reminder of the water of our baptism; as it cleansed us originally from sin, so now we are reminded to live free of sin. Holy water is ordinary water blessed by a priest with the official prayer of the Church that whoever uses it reverently will remain cleansed of sin. The "Asperges" ("Sprinkling") of the congregation before some Masses also indicates this.

THE MAJORITY WHO ARE NOT BAPTIZED

There are other ways of being united to God besides baptism. Most of the human race has never heard of or cannot believe in Christ or baptism. And as the world population increases, Christians become proportionately less. The Christian life begun by baptism is becoming more and more the privilege and the responsibility of a few. Most of humanity is united with God in other ways.

An adult who believes in God and basically desires to do his will, and who has sorrow for his sins out of love of God, has

God's grace-presence by this sincere desire. His sins would
be forgiven. This is called "baptism of desire." So, too, a potential
convert would receive grace if he desired to receive baptism
and had sorrow for his sins out of love of God; if such a person
died before baptism he would attain heaven. Also an unbaptized
person who gives his life for his belief in God or some Christian
teaching—though he may not recognize it as Christian—is said to
be "baptized" in his own blood and thereby receives grace and
salvation.

**Many men come to God in this way through other, non-Chris-
tian religions.** They would not normally have available the fullness of helps which Christ gives to his Church. Since he is "the
way, the truth, and the life," the privilege and responsibility of
being fully and consciously united with him belongs to Christians. But God is present among these others, as Vatican Council
II points out:

> The Catholic Church rejects nothing that is true and holy in these
> religions. She regards with sincere reverence those ways of con-
> duct and of life, those precepts and teachings which, though
> differing in many aspects from the ones she holds and sets forth,
> nonetheless often reflect a ray of that Truth which enlightens all
> men." *(Constitution on the Church in the Modern World, no. 2).*

**So, too, one who cannot believe in a personal God, through no
fault of his own, but is committed to following his conscience,
receives God's grace-presence.** The basic orientation of his life
would be to some worthy ideal outside himself, perhaps the
good of society or the welfare of those he loves. In seeking this
he is unknowingly seeking God—and God comes to him.

> Some who sincerely seek truth oppose Christ and his Church,
> sometimes to the point of actively persecuting it. Often they have
> a false image of Christ or his Church. Perhaps they have en-
> countered believers whose behavior is blatantly unchristian, and
> who, as Vatican Council II says, "conceal rather than reveal the
> authentic face of God and religion." Perhaps they see the glaring
> deficiencies in the Church's institutional framework, while not
> realizing how the framework can foster what is best in man. God
> lives within many of these unbelievers, though they may oppose
> him or those who try to work for him.

But these other ways of being united to God's grace-presence do not normally produce the full, deep union that can begin by Christian baptism. The baptized Christian knows more of the basic truths about God, man, the universe, and the purpose of life. He has the power to share in Christ's priesthood in a special way, to act consciously as a mediator between God and men. He can share fully in Christ's death and resurrection by taking part in the sacraments and the Mass. He can witness to Christ consciously and grow to know him more fully. The Christian community is there to be his constant help.

One who knows about and believes in Christ's sacrament of baptism must receive it, with all its privileges and responsibilities. Otherwise he would be untrue to his conscience, and he should realize that he will have to answer for this, not only to himself but to God. It would be tragic to refuse Christ when he invites one in a special way, as he did his first disciples: "Come, follow me!" (Mark 1, 17; Matthew 9, 9).

Yet Christian baptism is only the beginning. Its power can be frustrated by an unchristian upbringing or environment, or by a deliberate rejection of its consequences. Unfortunately some baptized Christians live as if they are inoculated by their Christianization against true Christianity—they have long since convinced themselves that they are living as Christians, but by their smugly sinful lives they are hardened against its message. On the other hand, some who are not baptized may by their sincere and open lives grow much more fully in God's presence and spread far more love in the world.

DAILY LIVING: RENEWING OUR BAPTISMAL CONVERSION

Baptism does not permanently give faith and enable one to live a truly Christian life unless one continually cooperates with what God has begun within him. One must recommit himself, reaffirm his baptismal commitment, make it his own. He must continually be open, investigating, trying to learn more and to form an adult faith. Sometimes this comes about only through doubt, perhaps after a period of "falling away" from one's baptismal belief.

A Christian's life is one of continual reconversion. He fails in his baptismal commitment, and he falls, perhaps into serious sin, and perhaps again and again. But he is sorry, he renews his commitment, humbly asks God's help and begins again. If he is wise, he knows that God's love is endless as it draws him on and on.

SOME SUGGESTIONS FOR...

DISCUSSION

Can you understand the significance of the sacrament of baptism?
Can you see the need of a true conversion before an adult's baptism or Profession of Faith?
What advantages and responsibilities does one who is baptized normally have in contrast to one who is not?

PERSONAL REFLECTION

The grace received in baptism, or by the sincere desire to do what God wants, is the only important thing in life. It is God's intimate presence within me, the beginning of heaven itself. It is lost by the deliberate state of serious sin. I should resolve to do all in my power to avoid sin, particularly serious sin which would rob me of God's love and cut me off from others.

14
The Inner Life of a Christian

How can one obtain faith, and why do some people have more faith than others? What sums up the whole of Christ's teaching? How can one get help from prayer?

We have seen how baptism is the climax of one's conversion and the beginning of a totally new life. God lives his own life within us—we share in his life. To live and grow in this life he gives us new powers.

The virtues are attitudes, powers, relationships that we have as a result of God's presence within us. The virtues help us to look at things differently, to act differently, to relate differently to others—to conform ourselves to Christ's way of thinking and acting. They are sometimes called habits, because they make it easier for us to act as Christians should.

The three fundamental virtues of a Christian are faith, hope, and charity or love. They make it easier for us to give ourselves to God, to trust him, and to love him and our neighbor. Those who are not Christians may also have these powers as a result of God's grace-presence within them, but the Christian should be more aware of them, better able to grow in them and thereby witness to Christ's life within himself.

These virtues are meant to grow stronger by our developing them, as any attitude or relationship should between those in love. The virtues are not static "things" but living ways in which we express the grace-life within us. Every time, for instance, that we express our faith by our words and actions, the attitude of faith grows within us and makes easier our next act of faith.

FAITH—ACCEPTANCE AND COMMITMENT

Faith is our saying "yes" to God as he reveals himself to us. It is our response to Christ—he invites us and faith is our acceptance of his invitation. It is something lasting—an attitude, a relationship to God by which we open ourselves to him.

Faith is the power, the ability to say "I believe" to God in whatever he teaches and to commit ourselves to live by his teachings. When people generally speak of "faith" they mean accepting something on the word of someone else. Daily we make countless acts of this sort of faith: that the food we eat is nourishing and not poisoned, that the car we drive is safe, etc. We do not test these things for ourselves, but take another's word. By the virtue of faith we take God's word for something we cannot prove for ourselves.

There are several aspects or steps to a person's faith: first, faith is a personal contact with Christ, an intimate "meeting" or "encounter" with him. This usually happens gradually, and one's awareness of it is vague, unrecognized. Perhaps one will never recognize it explicitly. But the experience is real, profound, and bit by bit we are changed by it. Through Christ we gradually come into contact with the Triune God.

Then, by faith we believe that what God tells us is true not because we see the evidence for ourselves, but simply because we realize that he is telling us. We become certain that what he has revealed is true, even though we cannot fully understand it. Yet, knowing with a certain degree of clarity that God has spoken is one thing; faith is something further . . .

Faith is ultimately a commitment, a free choice by which we give ourselves to Christ and begin living a whole new way of life. It is a free and personal decision to abandon ourselves to the living God. We are converted, we turn fully toward him, a changed person.

Faith is perhaps best looked at as a dynamic relationship, a living and continual encounter between God and oneself, by which we continually grow in knowledge of him and his will for us, and commit ourselves to live by this.

We have great need of faith because it is the basis of our life with God. Without it we cannot accept God's teachings, nor can we commit ourselves to live by them. Our minds are obviously limited, especially when faced with the mysteries of the infinite God, and our wills are weak.

Faith is like a telescope enabling us to see his design in the smallest things—though by faith we do not see clearly, but rather "in a mirror dimly, but then (in heaven) face to face" (1 Corinthians 13, 12). It can be compared, also, to a powerful magnet that draws us to God.

There are degrees of this faith-relationship. One person might be able to believe only in God, another might be able to accept the divinity of Jesus Christ, and yet another perceive the role of the Church—with all sorts of degrees in between.

One might have some faith before being baptized, responding to what he can accept of the truth. Upon becoming a Christian —and particularly upon becoming a Catholic—his faith is broadened, deepened. He is able to accept more of Christ's teachings and commit himself more fully to live them. He is now a conscious, contributing member of God's people and has the Christian community's help to grow in faith.

The faith necessary to be a Catholic—the "gift of faith"—is the power to believe God in whatever he teaches us through his Church, and to commit ourselves to live by those teachings. It is our response to what we now see is the fullness of God's revelation. We see that this is more than we have believed before, and we are determined to live by this new knowledge. We realize that we had many good things before, but now we see that we are getting more. We feel, somehow, that God wants us to embrace this. We feel that our spiritual "home" is now in the Catholic Church. Difficulties remain, of course, things in Catholicism which do not appeal to us. But we see that these are peripheral, relatively unimportant. We know too that we will often fail to live our belief, that we will sin, but we are determined to do our best. We are inwardly converted, we want to turn more fully toward Christ as a part of the Catholic Church.

If we have faith, we will show it by a life of love, by good works. "In Christ Jesus," Paul says, the only thing that avails is "faith working through love" (Galatians 5, 6). The faith that would not result in works of love would be counterfeit, spurious, a hypocritical delusion on the part of the "believer": **Read James 2, 14-18.**

"This faith needs to prove its fruitfulness by penetrating the believer's entire life . . . and by activating him toward justice and love, especially regarding the needy." *(Constitution on the Church in the Modern World, no. 21.)*

Faith is not an assurance that we are already "saved" regardless of our actions. If our faith is genuine, good works will follow— but one can always fall away from faith. "I chastise my body," says Paul, "and bring it into subjection, lest perhaps after preaching to others I myself should be rejected" (1 Corinthians 9, 27; cf. 1 Corinthians 10, 12; 13, 2; Philippians 2, 12; James 2, 14-26). On the other hand, we cannot "work" ourselves to heaven; God's gift of grace is necessary, initially and continually, that we might freely cooperate with him, that we might have the encounter of faith.

Some "unbelievers" show that they have more faith than some who profess Christianity. Their works of mercy and their exemplary lives prove this. Often they put to shame their Christian neighbors. They live according to their conscience, responding to God's call, but without an explicit awareness of it. However, moral goodness is not always a sign of a sincere faith; it might come at least in part from a self-justifying pride.

> Sometimes an unbeliever's rejection of Christianity is ". . . in reality a protest against the evident lack of faith in his Christian surroundings, and an expression of his deeply rooted yearning for the genuine dedication of a lively faith . . . It is also possible that his self-evident moral endeavors are subconscious pretenses which arise from his disturbed conscience whereby he justifies his defection from the faith." Bernard Häring, *Christian Renewal in a Changing World,* p. 107).

On the other hand many believers reveal their weak faith by constantly failing in charity. They may attend Church services and keep most of the Church's "rules" but in a time of testing they act primarily out of self-interest or they "follow the crowd." They might, for instance, oppose Negroes in their neighborhood, object to fair housing or aid to the underprivileged, or they adopt as their major goal in life the achieving of a certain material status.

HOW ONE COMES TO FAITH

The way faith comes to an adult is a mysterious, individual, and awesome process. One must be careful here of preconceptions, of assuming that God would or would not act in a particular way. Both the one who is seeking a possible faith and the one who seeks to lead him to faith must hold themselves open to the infinitely free action of the Spirit.

Faith, we know, is a free gift of God which we cannot earn by ourselves. It is God who enables us to have the attitude of faith toward him. Others may help to bring one to faith, but only because God wills to use them for this. "For by grace you have been saved through faith; and this is not your own doing, it is the gift of God—not because of works, lest any man should boast" (Ephesians 2, 8-9).

But we can and must do our part to obtain faith by humbly praying to know the truth and be able to live by it. St. Paul assures us that God ". . . desires all men to be saved and to come to the knowledge of the truth" (1 Timothy 2, 4). St. Mark's gospel tells the story of the father who brought his boy possessed with convulsions to Jesus and asked: "'. . . if you can do anything, have pity on us and help us.' And Jesus said to him, 'If you can! All things are possible to him who believes.' At once the father of the boy cried out, and said with tears, 'I believe; help my unbelief!'" (Mark 9, 21-23). Jesus then cured the boy, showing us that a sincere plea for faith will not go unanswered.

"Ask and you shall receive," said Christ—and humility is vitally necessary: "Truly, I say to you, whoever does not receive the kingdom of God like a child shall not enter it" (Luke 18, 17). ". . . I thank thee, Father, Lord of heaven and earth, that thou hast hidden these things from the wise and understanding and revealed them to babes" (Matthew 11, 25).

We must also study, sincerely and open-mindedly seeking the truth. In Christ's words, "Seek and you shall find . . ." We must use our minds, and be always open to truth wherever it may be found. Some have preconceived notions, prejudices that blind them. Christ refused to work miracles in his own town of Nazareth, for the people there had the unshakable idea that he was nothing more than a carpenter. Herod was convinced that Christ was merely a great magician; no matter what miracle Christ worked, Herod would only be confirmed in his opinion; so Christ scornfully "made no answer" to his questioning (Luke 23, 6-9).

To obtain faith we must live up to what we already believe.
People often cannot see the truth of the Church's teachings because they are clinging to habits of sin. The blatantly immoral
Herod and the hypocritical Jewish leaders of Christ's times are
examples of this. We must live up to what we see of God's will
in order to grasp more: "If anyone desires to do his will, he will
know of the teaching whether it is from God . . ." (John 7, 17).

A person can reject the faith that God is offering him, perhaps
because he is proud and unwilling to seek it sincerely, perhaps
because he is unwilling to live as he knows he should. God
always respects our free will, and never forces himself upon us.

**An adult comes to faith in the Church usually gradually and
often painfully.** It means facing oneself honestly, critically, perhaps breaking old habits, overcoming the fear that one cannot
live his new life. Like Christ, one struggles to do the Father's
will. And like him, one must die—not physically, but interiorly
and often as painfully—in order to live the new life of faith.

Our coming to faith might be like that of the Samaritan woman
who met Christ, was upset and embarrassed by him, gradually
accepted him, and ended by bringing others to him: **Read John
4, 1-30.**

Faith is a risk, a "leap." The evidence is never so clear that one
is forced to believe. A natural explanation can always be given
for any divine intervention. To believe is to take a risk—it is the
risk, really, of giving oneself to another in total love. The truly
convinced believer is willing to risk all that he is sure of, even
life itself, for a new life of love with Christ.

Elements of doubt always remain to plague him, and so there is
conflict, a struggle over this choice: On the one hand there is the
attraction of Christ and the unseen life he promises. On the other,
the visible reality and concrete allurements of life here and now.

Some expect a "sign," a special experience or good feeling to
assure them of God's presence. But usually God does not work
this way. Often he prepares one for faith by allowing one to feel a
great need, a discontent, an irritation, a helplessness. Slowly, by
humble prayer, by study, and by trying to live a good life, faith
usually comes—when we are ready for it and can appreciate it.

*Often the example of those who have given all for their belief
helps* to persuade the sincere seeker—those who give their lives to
serve others, truly dedicated and unselfish missionaries, those who
are living a day-by-day martyrdom with a self-centered and perhaps neurotic marriage partner, those who do not marry in order

to better serve others, or those who commit themselves to working among the poor and uneducated.

Many have been helped in their search for faith by reading the experiences of others who sought and found faith. There are available a number of interesting biographies and reflections of converts and other seekers of the truth, many in paperback editions.

Often believing friends or loved ones can be a great help in arriving at faith. By their love, prayer and exemplary lives they win God's grace for the seeker, and show how to believe. They can make God's love real for the one who is seeking, sometimes supplying for an earlier lack of love that makes God seem remote, unreal. If there is any way to overcome deeply-rooted erroneous notions or previous unpleasant experiences, it is through close contact with a genuine believer, cleric or layperson.

DOUBTING AND GROWING IN FAITH

The extent of one's faith depends on the circumstances of one's life, besides God's gift and one's own free response. Faith comes to anyone who is baptized, yet its growth depends on one's background, love relationships, education, etc. It may always remain stunted, through no fault of one's own. God only expects us to respond to the extent that we are able.

Faith is not something that is possessed once and for all, but rather must be constantly renewed. It is a personal relationship that must continually grow, or else it weakens, perhaps dies. It is each instant a free gift of God for which we must continually ask.

We grow in faith by praying for a stronger faith, by publicly expressing our beliefs when opportunities arise, and particularly by trying to live according to our beliefs. Faith is not a flight from a sinful world, nor a sentiment to be kept within our hearts. If it remains only interior, it will die within us. The true Christian realizes that he must freely and openly express his beliefs to others, hoping to bring them as well to a further faith, to love a bit more.

The Christian's commitment of faith is strengthened or weakened by whether or not he lives the Christian life of love. The immoral, uncharitable Christian will soon find that he cannot accept many things in the belief he professes.

The believer must continue to learn more about his beliefs, particularly in our age of rapid change, new knowledge, and

210 Christ Among Us

consequent confusion. Learning more not only deepens our own faith, but enables us to communicate it to others. The humble and realistic Christian knows that he cannot be constantly concerned with material things and this-worldly knowledge, however good, and yet expect the unseen world of faith to mean much to him.

Uncertainty and doubt will always co-exist with our faith. Faith is not knowledge that frees us from the proddings of doubt. Faith rather gives a certain deep direction, a meaning, illumination, purposefulness to our life. God will never overwhelm us with proofs that will force us to believe. An unbeliever can always give a logical, rational explanation for any of God's actions in history. This is because God loves us—he seeks to persuade rather than compel our assent.

The believer bred in the Christian faith must often painfully discard the uncomplicated faith of childhood and adolescence, and form a new, adult, simpler, deeper, more mature and realistic belief. This means for many a "crisis of faith"—usually in the late teens or early twenties, though it can come earlier or later—often involving a rejection of many of the Church's "rules" and structures.

The believer for the first time faces a challenge to what he has always accepted. He sees now that he must be personally involved in and committed to living what he professes. He examines his beliefs critically, testing their power and relevance in his life. He sees the weaknesses of the Church, the mediocrity of many Christians, and the dedication of many unbelievers. He may find the Church's moral code difficult to live with and he wonders if it is not largely unrealistic. He must now distinguish the core of Christian belief from what is peripheral, the teachings of Christ from the weak human instruments who propose them, the Christian faith as he may have been taught it from what it really is.

The mature person will realize his own weakness and his critical need of guidance during this period of massive doubt. He will realize that he must now study his faith on an adult level, that he cannot solve the problems of a sophisticated adulthood with an adolescent's knowledge of religion. He will also face his own moral weaknesses, and realize that he is open to the promptings of pride and sensuality and the enticements of material success. He will humbly pray, ". . . help my unbelief!" (Mark 9, 23). Finally, hopefully, he will emerge from this period of crisis recommitted to a new, mature and realistic Christian faith.

Vatican Council II took note of modern conditions which are causing growing numbers of people to abandon religious practices, but pointed out that this also results in "a more critical ability to distinguish religion from a magical view of the world and from the superstitions which still circulate, purifies (religion), and exacts day by day a more personal and explicit adherence to faith. As a result many persons are achieving a more vivid sense of God" (Constitution on the Church in the Modern World, no. 7).

IN THE LITURGY

The Church provides many opportunities for publicly renewing our commitment of faith. The choice of faith made at baptism is reaffirmed by us whenever we take part in any of the sacraments, but particularly in confirmation and at Mass. A renewal of baptismal promises is part of the Easter Vigil service, the high point of the Church's yearly liturgy. Taking part in a parish mission, a retreat, or cursillo are other ways of renewing one's faith.

HOPE—A CONFIDENT YEARNING

Linked to faith is the virtue of hope, an attitude of deep yearning for God joined to confidence or trust in him. God gives us this power: it is basically a deep desire for God and for the consummation of his plan, that all men might be united in perfect love with him and with one another. Then, hope is the confidence that God will give us all the help necessary to attain our eternal destiny—and indeed that he will take care of all our needs, and will never abandon us for an instant.

By our attitude of hope we put our lives into his hands, confident that he will forgive our sins, and will turn even misfortune and suffering to mankind's eternal advantage. Paul describes the effects of hope in his own life when he says, "Now may the God of hope fill you with joy and peace in believing . . ." (Romans 15, 13).

Despair and presumption are the two attitudes by which people reject God's gift of hope. Despair is a loss of hope in God's mercy, the depressing conviction that one is rejected by God or that God is not interested in us. It is the most tragic of attitudes, because it forgets that God has revealed himself to be above all else a God of merciful love, willing to undergo a humiliating death to convince us that he cares for each of us.

A presumptuous person, on the other hand, counts on obtaining heaven while doing little or nothing to overcome his sins. He considers God the "man upstairs" who "understands" his unrepentent wrongdoing. Such a person acts like a spoiled child and must sooner or later mature and face the living God.

People especially need hope in today's world because of the tensions and insecurity, the crimes, wars, and suffering of the innocent which we see all around us. To avoid discouragement or bitterness, to realize that good will come from the evil about us we need the joyful trust that is hope. "Cast all your anxiety upon him, because he cares for you" (1 Peter 5, 7).

The way to grow in hope is to pray for it and confidently and expectantly to live according to our beliefs. We should pray for this attitude of confidence in God especially during times of temptation, when depressed, in mental or physical suffering. St. Paul suffered as few of us will, but he wrote from his imprisonment:

". . . no one took my part; all deserted me. May it not be charged against them! But the Lord stood by me and gave me strength to proclaim the Word fully, that all the Gentiles might hear it. So I was rescued from the lion's mouth. The Lord will rescue me from every evil and save me for his heavenly kingdom. To him be the glory forever and ever. Amen" (2 Timothy 4, 16-18).

LOVE—THE ONE THING NECESSARY

The central point in Christ's teaching, the topic to which he returned again and again, is love. No religion or philosophy before or since has taught love as Christ did. It distinguishes his teaching from all others. Only Christianity presents a transcendent, all powerful God who is yet so loving that he becomes one of us, is disgraced and dies for us, and sums up his whole teaching in love: **Read Matthew 22, 34-40.**

> Again he said: "A new commandment I give to you, that you love one another; even as I have loved you, that you also love one another. By this all men will know that you are my disciples, if you have love for one another!" (John 13, 34-35).

The greatest virtue, then, is charity or love: the power given us by God to love him above all things, and to love our neighbors as ourselves. "So faith, hope, love abide, these three; but the greatest of these is love" (1 Corinthians 13, 13). Love is not merely an emotion or feeling; it is not only physical or sexual; it is primarily spiritual, something that comes from God himself. "God is love," says St. John. The more of him we have in our life, the more we truly love—and the more we have of true love in our life, the more of him we possess.

Love is concern for another's happiness. Consider human love: when we are truly in love, we are primarily concerned with making another happy. It is the very opposite of selfish concern for oneself. We want to please our beloved in every way possible.

When we love, we want to be united with the one we love. We gladly give ourselves, seeking to be united with our beloved. The more we give ourselves, the more we fulfill ourselves—this is the paradox of love. We give ourselves in order to make the one we love happy. Their happiness, in turn, brings us the greatest happiness.

By the virtue of love we give ourselves to God and our neighbor, to make them happy. We are primarily concerned with what God wants, and the happiness of our neighbor. We give ourselves to God, either directly or through our neighbor, in order to be united with him. And in this, paradoxically, we fulfill ourselves and attain limitless, eternal happiness.

God has shown us how to love by loving us first and totally. He has given us everything we have, our life, our talents, our destiny. Above all he has given us himself—the root meaning of "charity" is the total gift of oneself. When man was unfaithful to him, he became one of us and died to prove his love for us. "In this is love, not that we loved God but that he loved us and sent his Son to be the expiation for our sins" (1 John 4, 10).

Though he has no need of us whatever, he yet gives us a share in his own life. He is constantly concerned with our happiness, and wants us to be united with himself. His love knows no limits, for he is willing to forgive us again and again.

We love God above all things by making him the center of our life, by trying to please him in everything we do. As a man would love the one woman who really matters to him, and she him, so we should try to love God. We will think of him each morning, offering ourselves to him. We are united with him especially by worshipping him, showing our love before others, celebrating it at special times. We respect his name, as a boy would tolerate no one speaking disrespectfully of the girl he loves.

We want to know more about him, his desires, his friends, his innermost life, as a boy and girl falling in love take joy in discovering more and more about each other; the bible particularly tells us about him. We know that love is tested, not in the initial glow of romance but in the long hours of suffering, and so we are willing to bear the cross with him. As the center of our life, God will always come first: our family, friends, work, recreation should never cause us to do anything that would lead us away from him. We should be able to face him honestly each night, ask his pardon for any selfishness, and quietly, peacefully renew our profession of love.

If we truly love God, we will also love our neighbor, our fellow human beings. It is impossible to love God and not love our neighbor. "Beloved, if God so loved us, we also ought to love one another. . . . If anyone says, 'I love God,' and hates his brother, he is a liar. . . ." (1 John 4, 11, 19). Everyone else has been created by God for heaven, just as we; they have the same dignity, are redeemed by Christ, and have God living within them.

Our neighbor is everyone, whatever his race, color, background, belief, or talents. Christ made this clear in the famous parable of the Good Samaritan: Read Luke 10, 29-37.

We should note that this story, Christ's great example of love of neighbor, concerns love between men of different racial and religious backgrounds. Christ's fellow Jews looked on the Samaritans as an inferior breed and as heretics. Christ told the Samaritan woman that "salvation is from the Jews," but he significantly chooses a Samaritan as his great example of brotherly love.

Any form of prejudice or discrimination is a rejection of Christian love: if we do not associate with our neighbor because of his race, his lack of social position, his past moral failings, Christ makes clear that at the end we will be judged by the way we treat our "least" brethren: **Read Matthew 25, 35-40.**

Everyone must consider his every neighbor without exception as another self. . . . In our times a special obligation binds us to make ourselves the neighbor of every person without exception, and of actively helping him when he comes across our path, whether he be an old person abandoned by all, a foreign laborer unjustly looked down upon, a refugee, a child born of an unlawful union and wrongly suffering for a sin he did not commit, or a hungry person who disturbs our conscience by recalling the voice of the Lord, "As long as you did it for one of these the least of my brethren, you did it for me" (Matthew 25, 40). (*Constitution on the Church in the Modern World, no. 27*).

We fail to love our neighbor by not respecting him: by anger, by jealousy or envy of his good fortune, and particularly by hatred or desiring revenge. If we love our neighbor we will also respect his right to the truth and to his good name: lying, calumny, and detraction—we should remember that we have no right to repeat something uncharitable, even if true—are thoroughly unchristian.

Our Christian love of our neighbor should manifest itself in certain ways, often called the four "moral virtues." These are four aspects our love of others should include: prudence, by which we form our right judgment as to what to do or not do; justice, by which we give everyone what is due him; fortitude, courageously facing opposition to our Christian ideals; and temperance, controlling our passions so as to use them more fully to truly love.

True love means that we respect the one we love, especially in the use of the power of sex. If we truly love another, we do not ever want to treat that person as a "thing," as the outlet for our passions. True love cannot be forced, as for example a boy demanding that a girl give in to him. Nor can it be bought, as a girl might confusedly try to do in giving herself to a boy. Even a couple deeply in love, who experience how naturally sexual intimacies can express their love, must realize that a true and mature love requires discipline and sacrifice. They will fully express their love sexually only when the marriage commitment has been made.

The love of our enemies is the test of a truly committed follower of Christ. This is as difficult for us today as when Christ first proposed it. Sometimes we may have to defend ourselves or others against our enemies, but always and only to the extent that we must, never using immoral means, and always ready to forgive without exacting vengeance. Christ said simply that if almighty God puts up with their sins, so should we: **Read Matthew, 5, 43-48.**

Christ as he hung dying at the hands of his enemies gave us a strong hint as to why we should forgive those who have hurt us: "Father, forgive them; for they know not what they do" (Luke 23, 34). People rarely, if ever, hurt us with full deliberation—and even then they may think their action is for our good. Usually people bring to their actions all sorts of personality traits, pressures, and drives from their background and daily environment. Only if we are fully aware of these can we judge them—and God alone knows all that is within us, driving us on. So Christ says, "Judge not, that you be not judged" (Matthew 7, 1).

> *A modern poet/monk/mystic gives this insight about love:* "All life is love. . . . Men love, whether they know it or not, and never cease loving . . . Love is. All else is not, because in the same measure in which things partake of being, they partake of love. All that is not love, is not. . . . The conflicts which beset our world are not caused by the absence of love, but by a love which refuses to acknowledge itself as such, a love which has become ill because it fails to recognize its true nature and has lost sight of its object. . . . Cruelty is misdirected love, and hate is frustrated love. . . ." (Thomas Merton's introduction to Ernesto Cardinal's *To Live is to Love.*)

CHRISTIAN PRAYER

By prayer we communicate with God, open ourselves to him, find out his will for us and obtain the strength to live as we should. In the first chapter we saw the vital necessity of praying.

We can never know God or ourselves unless we pray. In its daily necessity prayer can be compared to eating: sometimes it is enjoyable, sometimes not; it is more enjoyable for some than for others, but a daily necessity for everyone; as physical nourishment is more pleasurable if prepared well, so will our prayer be if we prepare by reading and reflection.

The prayer of a Christian has a new meaning and new power. The Christian knows that his prayer is joined to Christ's prayer by the power of the lay priesthood he received in baptism. He knows that Christ's prayer is already answered, that it can never fail to bring about good. The more we are consciously united in prayer to Christ, the more God can communicate himself to us and spread love in the world.

A Christian's prayer is especially powerful when he is united with Christ's whole body in the prayers of the liturgy. Whenever one unites with other believers in prayer, Christ promises his special help: "Where two or three are gathered in my name, there am I in the midst of them" (Matthew 18, 20). But the private individual prayer of a Christian also has special power:

> "The spiritual life . . . is not limited solely to participation in the liturgy. The Christian is called to pray with his brethren, but he must also enter into his chamber to pray to the Father in secret (Matthew 6, 6); further, according to the teaching of the apostle, he should pray without ceasing" (1 Thessalonians 5, 17). (*Constitution on the Sacred Liturgy*, no. 12).

Prayer is the great way in which God allows us to work with him in saving ourselves and others, in spreading love in the world. We do not pray to ask God for something he does not know we need; nor is prayer a cringing before a whimsical deity, coaxing him into giving what we want; nor is it something we give to God, "bargaining" with him, that he might proportionately help us in return. Rather it is our small but real contribution to the love which runs the universe. God wills that we shall obtain certain things for ourselves and others if we do our part, contribute our love, by expressing our reliance on him in prayer. He treats us like adults, with dignity and even reverence, giving us a part in the working out of our salvation.

The most important moments of our life are the moments of

prayer—and someday we may come to see this. We can learn more in one second of pure prayer than in all the books ever written. We can accomplish more by one fervent moment of prayer than we might otherwise in a lifetime of effort. "The man of prayer is a worker of miracles" (Léon Bloy).

In the heart of Manhattan there is a convent of contemplative nuns whose lives are devoted to praying and doing penance for that vast city. Unnoticed, this little group of women have a sublime and joyous faith that God is using them to bring his love to others. In almost every metropolitan center of the free world a group like this lives a life of prayer and strict asceticism, to open the hearts of the rest of us to God's love.

When we pray we try to make contact with God, become aware of him, open ourselves to his love and his desires for us. We can never become aware of his will for us unless we pause to pray. This is our basic human need—to give ourselves to the will of the Father, who after all knows what is best for us. So underlying our every prayer must be Christ's prayer. "My Father . . . not as I will, but as thou wilt" (Matthew 26, 39).

How does prayer for others "work"? Here we are before a great mystery, so we cannot analyze prayer in a mechanistic way. But we can say this: When we pray for others, our love reaches out to them through God—when we speak to him about them, his all-powerful love is joined to our poor, stumbling love, and now our joint love enfolds them. Our prayer for others also changes ourselves, so that we are more open and loving toward those others and toward God.

We should not pray to God, however, to do what we should do ourselves. Sometimes, instead of asking him to help someone or remedy some situation, we should be doing something about it ourselves. Our prayer should normally thank him for making us such wonderful and capable human beings, who can do such great things in partnership with him, and a plea that we might use our talents in the best way possible. At times, however, our weakness overwhelms us and we can only beg for his all-powerful help.

It is often hard to pray, and we must discipline ourselves to do

it. Our sins keep us from prayer and disturb us when we do pray. In praying we must learn humble, loving adoration before our infinite God; pride resists this, inciting us to rely on our own efforts. Our minds are usually undisciplined, at least in trying to contact the Infinite, and so distractions are natural. We must mobilize our divided faculties, and compel them to pay attention to what God is doing in us. Prayer usually does not develop spontaneously, but is learned by persevering practice.

Christ tells us how to pray: first, confidently and perseveringly. We must remind ourselves that God always answers, in some way, every sincere prayer. Christ's parable is plain: **Read Luke 18, 1-7.**

We must be humble and reverent as we pray. We are sinners putting ourselves in the presence of the infinite God. Moses took off his shoes to approach the burning bush, and the Church uses Jacob's cry to describe a house of prayer: "Terrible is this place!" We sign ourselves and take holy water to remind ourselves that we are coming into God's presence to pray. We often kneel when we pray, an ancient, spontaneous attitude of reverence. We realize our sinfulness, but we are like the child who knows it is loved and trusts in its Father's forgiveness: **Read Luke 18, 10-14.**

Christ also reminds us that our prayer should be simple and sincere—the best prayers are usually those in our own words. "And in praying do not heap up empty phrases as the Gentiles do, for they think that they will be heard for their many words" (Matthew 6, 7). We may say just a few, simple, stumbling words—reaching out, to make contact, to realize his presence.

Perhaps we will form no words, but just have a quiet awareness of his presence. Prayer can be seeing God at work in the things that happen each day, a peaceful realization that he is intimately with us, concerned about us. "Be still, and know that I am God!" (Psalm 46, 10).

The Church's pattern for prayer is an ancient one: to God the Father, through Jesus Christ, in union with the Holy Spirit within us. We are children weak but loved, coming before our all-powerful Father. We try to unite ourselves with Christ, our Brother—he is there leading us to the Father—and we realize that it is the Spirit within us who is actually praying, who gives form, power and meaning to our prayers—so we try to hold ourselves open to the Spirit.

The Church often prays by prepared formulas which are meant to help us. These are most often prayers that have helped billions of people throughout Christian history, and so might be helpful to us as well. Sometimes it is hard to become used to praying in set words, especially when the prayer is gone through rapidly. Anything done over and over tends to become hurried, but we should remember that the attention of the will is what is important, the attempt to make contact with God—just as a couple in love may talk for hours and later are unable to tell what they discussed.

We should pray often, several times a day if possible. Prayer should be habit but not routine. We read how Christ many times "withdrew . . . and prayed" (Luke 5, 16; Matthew 14, 23; Mark 6, 46, etc.) and sometimes he spent the night in prayer. Our prayers need not be lengthy, as long as we try to have some sense of "making contact" with God. Nor should we feel obligated to say a particular formula of prayer which is no longer meaningful.

Some good times to pray are in the morning upon arising and in the evening before retiring; when in special need of help, as in time of temptation, or before making an important decision; also, before and after meals. The family might gather for a moment in the morning before going off to work or school, or particularly before supper. Some couples pray for a few moments before going out on a date.

We will get much more out of our prayer if we prepare for it by reading spiritual books, particularly the bible. It is only natural that prayer will be difficult if we put no spiritual thoughts into our minds. "Meditative reading" is an excellent way of doing this: reading a bit, thinking over what we have read, then speaking to God in our own words whatever comes to mind.

Many times we will get nothing out of our attempts to pray. Everyone who seriously tries to reach God experiences this. Our prayer has no fervor: it seems to be cold, mechanical repetition. Often God himself seems to have disappeared, and we may even wonder whether he exists at all. We should expect this: God "hides" from us, perhaps so that we realize how much we need him and so that we will reach out for him all the more. He wants us to mature spiritually, to grow in "naked faith," and so he takes away our feelings of fervor. We are sharing in Christ's desolation, in this worst of his sufferings—and as with him, this is the very time when we are accomplishing the most to spread love in the world.

We should pray for everyone and anyone—for all mankind, especially those close to us, those for whom we have a responsibility, those who need it the most, sinners, those for whom God is not real, and for our enemies. Our prayer can also embrace all creatures, including those who may be on other planets, that they too will attain their destiny with God. Our prayer truly has no limits.

Often the greatest help we can give someone is to pray for him. A crippled person may need help in standing and we reach out and help him up, or someone may be in pain or sorrow and we comfort him with words of sympathy—or we extend to him the love-power of our prayer and we help him as much and perhaps more.

We should remember that worship is our highest form of prayer—adoring, praising, thanking God for his goodness, instead of constantly asking for help. The great "practitioners of prayer," the saints and mystics, prayed mostly by pouring out their gratitude, admiration, and awe before the Lord.

DAILY LIVING: LOVE IN OUR LIFE

Our life with God, with his grace-presence within us, gives us fantastic new powers. By the virtues we can live the very life of Christ—the life of heaven already is a part of us. The whole purpose of our life is to grow in grace and the virtues, especially in love.

To be a successful Christian there is only one thing we have to do: love. Faith is meant to end in love, and the whole purpose of prayer is to make us love more. Conversely, if a Christian does not truly love, his Christianity is in vain. We might profess our beliefs and keep all the Church's rules, but unless we honestly love it is all a sham.

We cannot prove our love of God except by loving our fellow man. Jesus Christ loved God precisely by loving his fellow man. In his act of dying he loved God perfectly, by loving us to the extent of giving his life for us.

We cannot love everyone at once. But perhaps we could try to commit ourselves to one other person who is unlike us in some way, someone to whom we normally would not be attracted, but who needs our help, and whom circumstances have brought into our life. At the very least we can try to be aware of someone in our life who is in need of love, whom we can consistently treat with kindness: someone insecure, or hypersensitive, or narrow and unimaginative, or perhaps one who is moody or melancholy—someone whom we can say is "the least of my brethren" (Matthew 26, 40).

The way some try to show love is illustrated by a letter from a Christian couple to a woman who made a highly-publicized trip to Europe a few years ago to have an abortion of her deformed "thalidomide baby." The letter read in part:

"We have read that you have been advised to kill this unborn child because it might not be normal . . . We have eight children and feel that we are about due to care for one who is handicapped. If your baby is born with handicaps, we will be happy to take him and raise him as our own. He will have ten of us to love him. I told the older children of the situation, and asked them if they would be willing to give up something they might want, in order that this child be allowed to live and be loved and be given the care he'll need . . . I asked them if they would love our little one less if he didn't have arms or legs, and the incredulous looks told me they couldn't understand how that would make any difference . . . If you should decide to let us adopt your baby, please get in touch with us through . . ." (*America* magazine, Dec. 15, 1962).

Their letter went unanswered. The woman had her abortion. But the world was richer for the Christian love manifested by this family.

SOME SUGGESTIONS FOR . . .

DISCUSSION:

Can you understand why coming to faith, and growing in faith, are often painful?
What aspect of loving one's neighbor do you find the most difficult?

What particularly do you find the most helpful in your attempts to pray?

FURTHER READING

* *Prayers,* Quoist (Sheed & Ward, 1963)—A very popular, profitable, well-arranged, book of suggested prayers.
* *Life for a Wanderer,* Greeley (Doubleday, 1969)—Reflections on the virtues as vital forces making life more meaningful and pleasant.
* *Meeting God in Man,* Boros (Herder & Herder, 1969)—The virtues leading us to God and man: respect, reverence, joy, love, serenity.
* *Dynamic Contemplation,* Hinnebusch (Sheed & Ward, 1970) —Why and how man must recover his ability to speak with God if he is to remain a person.
* *God is More Present Than You Think,* Ochs (Paulist Press, 1970)—A brief and incisive little book giving some insights into prayer.
** *Prayer, the Problem of Dialogue with God,* Mooney ed. (Paulist Press, 1969)—An excellent collection of incisive essays on various aspects of prayer and its possibilities.
* *Prayer of Christians,* the American Interim Breviary (Catholic Book Publishing Co., 1971)—A shorter, modern version of the Divine Office—psalms, prayers, readings, hymns of praise, etc.—an excellent book for someone who wants to undertake systematic daily prayer in union with the liturgy and the great traditions of Christianity.
* *We Are Future,* Boros (Herder & Herder, 1970)—Meditations by a popular author on hope as the indispensable condition for engaging in Christian life.
* *Contemplation in a World of Action,* Merton (New Directions)—A practical treatment of contemplation in today's world.
* *Meditations,* Dorothy Day (Newman, 1970)—Hard-hitting and prayerful reflections written by the prophetic woman who for several decades has inspired us all.
* *Contemplative Prayer,* Merton (Herder, 1969)—A practical study of prayer and contemplation by one of the great spiritual writers of our time.

FURTHER VIEWING

Bird on the Mast (Paulist Productions, 17575 Pacific Coast Hwy., Pacific Palisades, Calif. 90272)—27 minutes, in color—Dramatic exploration of modern man's search for God and approaches to contemporary prayer.

Ride the Turquoise Pony (Paulist Productions)—27 minutes, in color—A teenage girl confronts a crisis of faith when she returns from Vista with her horizons broadened.

Old King Cole (Paulist Productions)—27 minutes, in color—Five "losers" who have been running away from life discover hope and freedom when a blind little girl almost abandons both.

PERSONAL REFLECTION

I should treat at least one other person with true Christian love. I might reread the story of the Good Samaritan (Luke 10, 29-37) and then pray that I might honestly put it into practice in the next few days.

15
Our Christian Presence in the World

What of Christians who are concerned only with getting themselves to heaven? What practical things can one do to show concern for others? What can the average Christian do to bear witness to his faith?

OUR CHRISTIAN PRESENCE

A self-centered Christian is no Christian at all. We cannot attain heaven alone. Following Christ, our God who came to share what he had with us, we must work and pray to share our faith with others. Millions today are without any strong religious convictions. Often their bewilderment and confusion are painfully evident. We should be alert to opportunities to help them.

Every Christian is meant to be an apostle, one who witnesses to his convictions by his words and actions. The original twelve apostles had a unique role as witnesses of the resurrection and founders of the Church. But each baptized Christian shares in the privilege of being Christ's chosen representative, speaking about him in his name and bringing others to him. This was stated clearly by Vatican Council II:

> The laity derive the right and duty with respect to the apostolate from their union with Christ their head. . . . Through baptism and strengthened by the power of the Holy Spirit through confirmation, they are assigned to the apostolate by the Lord himself. They are consecrated into a royal priesthood and a holy people (cf. 1 Peter 2, 4-10) in order that they may offer spiritual sacrifices through everything they do, and may witness to Christ throughout the world. . . . On all Christians therefore is laid the splendid burden of working to make the divine message of salvation known and accepted by all men throughout the world (*Decree on the Apostolate of the Laity*, no. 3).

Some ways in which a Christian might profess and share his beliefs are:

Praying that everyone may come to know Christ and his Church.

Offering up his sufferings for those outside the Church and those within it who do not appreciate it fully.

Stating his belief in Christ and the Church's teachings when opportunities arise, quietly, without rancor, but courageously. "Therefore, everyone who acknowledges me before men, I also will acknowledge him before my Father in heaven. But whoever disowns me before men, I in turn will disown him before my Father in heaven" (Matthew 10, 32-33).

Giving good example. "You are the light of the world. . . . Even so let your light shine before men, in order that they may see your good works and give glory to your Father in heaven" (Matthew 5, 14-16).

Taking part in works of charity, especially to the neglected and underprivileged. "As long as you did it for one of these, the least of my brethren, you did it for me" (Matthew 25, 40).

Aiding particularly the apostolic works of the Church by prayers, offerings, and, if possible, by taking part oneself in some apostolic work.

What some are doing today: A 14-year-old girl in East Germany, whose parents were killed in the war, gathered neighboring refugee children in a barn each Sunday, pinned a picture of Christ to the wall, and taught them about God and how to pray. A man from Kentucky, his wife, and ten children, gave up a comfortable life on a farm to go to Alaska for two years as lay missionaries. He said, "We've been blessed so much, we figure we owe something back." A dozen lay apostles in Minneapolis, working two and three evenings a week after their daily jobs, have been instrumental in bringing over 1,000 people to Christ's Church besides helping numerous other people regain their religious commitment.

A witness for Christ will first try to be truly competent in his job or profession, using his talents, doing as good a job as possible. Then his witness will be all the more effective.

Some are called to be lay apostles in a special sense: They have a particularly apostolic spirit, are qualified, and undergo training. The Spirit works within them in a special way. Tactful and competent, they have the "apostolic urge," and give freely of their time and energies to bring Christ to others. The Church simply could not function without such people—and they are urgently needed today as never before.

Groups, formal and informal, work in the Church today in every type of activity: teaching writing, nursing, instructing, doing parish census work, planning liturgies, social activist concerns, helping the poor, etc. New groups continually start, and their work is tested by time. Some groups are full-time callings, others ask much less. One who feels qualified can usually find a group suitable to his talents.

Some groups of specialized "lay apostles" are: the Confraternity of Christian Doctrine and the Legion of Mary. Many older organizations of lay people are adapting themselves to the lay apostolate, e.g., the Sodality, the Third Orders.

Some groups train lay people for the missions in foreign lands or here at home. These lay missionaries may be either married or single, and they usually volunteer for a few years. Examples of these are Grail, the Extension Lay Volunteers, the Papal Volunteers for Latin America, the Association for International Development, the Lay Mission-Helpers Association, the International Catholic Auxiliaries, the Young Christian Workers, the Women Volunteers for Africa, etc.

A current phenomenon of great significance is the increasing number of informal groups that are spontaneously forming themselves in many places. Sometimes these have clerical participation, sometimes not. They are highly informal, "open," "accepting," and composed often of young people with common concerns to make their religion relevant in today's world.

IN GOD'S WORLD AND OURS

The Christian must be concerned to develop the world in which he lives, not only religiously but materially. It would be childishly immature, and a rejection of Christian love, to be unconcerned with bettering our world, our country, our neighborhood. God created the world and "saw that all he had made was very good" (Genesis 1, 31). He came to live upon it and died to redeem it. We cannot be less concerned than he.

One cannot be a good Christian if he is concerned only with bringing himself and others to God, and not with making our world a better place. Particularly today, says Vatican Council II, profound and rapid changes make it more necessary that no one, ignoring the trend of events or drugged by laziness, content himself with a merely individualistic morality. Each person must ". . . according to his own abilities and the needs of others . . . promote and assist the public and private institutions dedicated to bettering the conditions of human life" (**Constitution on the Church in the Modern World,** no. 30).

Vatican Council II says further: "They are mistaken who, knowing that we have here no abiding city but seek one which is to come, think that they may therefore shirk their earthly responsibilities. For they are forgetting that by the faith itself they are more obliged than ever to measure up to these duties, each according to his proper vocation. . . . The Christian who neglects his temporal duties, neglects his duties toward his neighbor and even God, and jeopardizes his eternal salvation." (*Constitution on the Church in the Modern World,* no. 43).

There are many problems that especially concern us, that challenge our Christian response: Underdeveloped nations, world hunger and overpopulation, world peace and disarmament, totalitarianism and the oppression of minorities, racial injustice, etc.

Pope John XXIII, who was himself so concerned with the good of all the world challenged each of us: "There is an immense task incumbent on all men of goodwill . . . the task of restoring the relations of the human family in truth, in justice, in love and in freedom: the relations between individual human beings, between citizens and their respective political communities, between intermediate associations and political communities on the one hand, and the world community on the other. This is a most exalted task, for it is the task of bringing about true peace in the order established by God" (Encyclical, *Pacem in terris*).

Pope Paul VI echoes his predecessor's words: "We are responsible for our times, for the life of our brother, and we are responsible before our Christian conscience. We are responsible before Christ, before the face of God."

Pope Paul dramatically illustrated his concern for the good of the whole world when he flew to the United Nations in late 1965, to show his faith in it at a time when many considered its prestige ebbing. "Let unanimous trust in this institution grow," he said, "let its authority increase. . . . This organization represents the obligatory path of modern civilization and of world peace. . . . The people of the earth turn to the United Nations as the last hope of concord and peace."

Vatican Council II makes clear what we should strive for: ". . . there must be made available to all men everything necessary for leading a life truly human, such as food, clothing and shelter; the right to choose a state of life freely and to found a family, the right to education, to employment, to a good reputation, to respect, to appropriate information, to activity in accord with the upright norm of one's own conscience, to protection of privacy, and to rightful freedom, even in matters religious" (**Constitution on the Church in the Modern World,** no. 26).

There is the "black rage" of the people of our ghettoes—urban and rural—who live in anguish and frustration, often with little hope of bettering their condition. Their housing and diet are inadequate, their education inferior, exploitation and immorality their constant companions, and the temptation to violence ever present—and this in the wealthiest nation on earth. The Chicanos and Indians in our midst have also been suffering exploitation for a long time at the hands of the white majority—as are many of the poor whites who have not "made it" in our achievement-oriented, materialistic society. There is a cynical and totally unchristian tendency today to look down on anyone who cannot "pull himself up by his own bootstraps." The committed Christian will give of his time and effort wherever he can to help these people who are suffering in our midst.

Pope Paul VI's encyclical, "On the Development of Peoples," concerns the critical situation of the growing imbalance between the "have" and "have not" peoples of the world. It spells out practical norms for worldwide Christian social action, and should be studied in detail by one wanting to be a Christian in today's world.

> *The central message of the encyclical is a call for social and economic justice on a global scale:* "It is not just a matter of eliminating hunger, or even of reducing poverty. The struggle against destitution, though urgent and necessary, is not enough. It is a

question, rather, of building a world where every man, no matter what his race, religion or nationality, can live a fully human life, freed from servitude imposed on him by other men or by natural forces over which he has not sufficient control; a world where freedom is not an empty word and where the poor man Lazarus can sit down at the same table with the rich man."

Then the pope challenges our well fed complacency with some practical tests of our Christianity and humanity: "Let each man examine his conscience, a conscience that conveys a new message for our times. Is he prepared to support out of his own pocket works and undertakings organized in favor of the most destitute? Is he ready to pay higher taxes so that the public authorities can intensify their efforts in favor of development? Is he ready to pay a higher price for imported goods so that the producer may be more justly rewarded? . . . When so many people are hungry, when so many families suffer from destitution, when so many remain steeped in ignorance, when so many schools, hospitals and homes worthy of the name remain to be built, all public or private squandering of wealth, all expenditure prompted by motives of national personal ostentation, every exhausting armaments race, becomes an intolerable scandal. We are conscious of our duty to denounce it. Would that those in authority listen to our words before it is too late."

The Christian should take an active interest in political affairs, those of his country, state, city or town. Patriotism is a virtue. Christ himself reminded us that just as we render God his due, we should also "render to Caesar the things that are Caesar's" (Matthew 22, 21).

Voting is the privilege and duty of every Christian. We should take time to inform ourselves about the candidates and their positions about the issues involved, and then vote as we judge best—remembering that even one ballot is important.

Some ways in which Christians can be active in civic and social affairs are: Working for better neighborhood housing and better educational facilities, taking an active part in one's labor union, combatting racial discrimination in employment and housing, combatting quick-profit building, etc.

Instead of being overcome by the hugeness of the problems and doing nothing, we can always do something constructive, however little. The handful of apostles must have been staggered by Christ's command to "teach the whole world." They did not give up because they could reach only a few people during their lifetime, but inspired by the Spirit with a long-range, optimistic view, they began spreading the belief that has guided billions and changed history.

Among many real-life examples of what just one person has done is that of a painfully shy mail carrier, self-conscious even when speaking in his own home; spurred on by a desire to improve working conditions, he took a leadership course, overcame his shyness, and eventually represented his fellow workers before a Congressional Committee to improve labor legislation.

CHRIST SENDS US THE HOLY SPIRIT IN CONFIRMATION

At baptism we were united to Christ and born into the life of grace. We came forth as children of God from the "womb" of baptismal water. Yet, as we know from everyday life, a child is concerned primarily with taking care of himself. Gradually he must mature, become an adult. He must become concerned with others, share what he has. So we must mature spiritually. Christ has given us the way whereby we become spiritual adults, aware of our responsibilities, sharing our spiritual riches with others. This is his sacrament of confirmation.

Confirmation is the sacrament in which Christ sends the Holy Spirit to make us adult apostles for our faith. We become "adults," not in physical age or psychological maturity, but spiritually mature, able to share our spiritual life with others. Confirmation is the public expression or celebration of this emerging spiritual maturity.

Confirmation is the completion of baptism, the giving of the full power of a Christian. "Confirmation" means a strengthening —this sacrament strengthens and increases what we receive at baptism, particularly the power of bearing witness to Christ. To emphasize this, the ceremony of confirmation includes a renewal of our baptismal promises. We now become full-fledged members of the Church, lay apostles in the fullest sense.

The sign or ceremony of confirmation is the imposition of the bishop's hands and anointing of the forehead with chrism. The bishop and priests present impose their hands on those being confirmed—the ancient biblical gesture by which the gift of the

Spirit is invoked. Then the bishop anoints the forehead of each with chrism (a perfumed oil blessed by the bishop), and says, "N., be sealed with the Holy Spirit, the gift of the Father."

Oil symbolizes strength, and this oil particularly symbolizes the strength we are given to share in Christ's work as prophet, priest, and king. We are given the strength to teach in his name with greater power, to share more fully his priesthood, and to lead others to his kingdom. The name of this oil, chrism, and the word Christ have the same root. Oil was used in ancient times by soldiers in preparation for battle, and by athletes, and today it is used by people to make their bodies limber and strong.

At confirmation Christ sends the Holy Spirit in a fuller outpouring of his indwelling presence. At baptism we had received by grace the presence of the Trinity within us. Now we receive a great increase of God's grace-presence, and particularly an increase of the presence of the Holy Spirit.

The Holy Spirit is especially associated with bearing witness, with publicly professing God's truth. The Spirit often moved the Old Testament prophets to bear witness. Luke points out how the Spirit inspired those associated with Christ's coming: Mary, Elizabeth, Zachary, Simeon (chapters 1 and 2).

Christ himself is given the Spirit by his Father. When he goes forth to preach the gospel, the Spirit inspires him:

> Now . . . when Jesus also had been baptized and was praying, heaven was opened, and the Holy Spirit descended upon him in bodily form, as a dove. . . . And Jesus, full of the Holy Spirit, returned from the Jordan, and was led by the Spirit for forty days in the wilderness. . . . (Luke 3, 21-22 and 4, 1).

> And Jesus returned in the power of the Spirit into Galilee; and a report concerning him went out through all the surrounding country. And he taught in their synagogues, being glorified by all. And he came to Nazareth . . . and he went to the synagogue . . . on the sabbath day. And he stood up to read . . . the book of the prophet Isaiah. . . . The Spirit of the Lord is upon me, because he had anointed me to preach good news to the poor. . . . (Luke 4, 14-18).

When Christ sends his apostles to carry on his mission, he predicts that they will be persecuted, but the Spirit will sustain them and speak through them: **Read Matthew 10, 16-22.**

Christ promised to his Church the Holy Spirit that he had received from the Father. He told the apostles that "the Spirit of truth" would be with them forever (John 14, 16). After his resurrection the Spirit came in his fullness to Christ. Then, about to leave his apostles, he gave them the great promise:

> But you shall receive power when the Holy Spirit has come upon you, and you shall be my witness in Jerusalem and in all Judea and Samaria, and to the ends of the earth (Acts 1, 8).

We saw how Christ fulfilled his promise and sent the Holy Spirit on Pentecost, transforming the fearful and confused apostles into courageous and eloquent witnesses. Amid a violent wind and tongues of fire, they "were all filled with the Holy Spirit" (Acts 2, 4). This was their confirmation.

On another occasion after this "they were all filled with the Holy Spirit and spoke the Word of God with boldness" (Acts 4, 31). Threatened by the authorities, they answered, ". . . we cannot but speak of what we have seen and heard. . . . We must obey God rather than men!" (Acts 4, 20; 5, 29). Scourged by the authorities, "they departed from the presence of the council, rejoicing that they were counted worthy to suffer dishonor for the name (of Jesus). And every day in the temple and at home they did not cease teaching and preaching Jesus as the Christ" (Acts 4, 41-42).

The incident of Stephen, the Church's first martyr, is typical. Courageously professing his faith in Christ, he underwent death by stoning, "being full of the Holy Spirit" (Acts 7, 55). Especially during the first three centuries, a time of almost continuous persecution and courageous witnessing, we read of the activity of the Holy Spirit.

The apostles gave others the Holy Spirit in confirmation by the ordinary ancient way of imposing hands on them. From time immemorial the laying on of hands had been connected with the gift of the Spirit among God's people; it was only natural, then, for the apostles to use this for what was to become confirmation. We see this, for instance, after some converts had been baptized in Samaria: **Read Acts 8, 14-17.**

At our confirmation the Holy Spirit comes to us, giving us too the power to profess and spread our faith. Confirmation is our personal Pentecost. As at baptism the mystery of Christ's passing from death to life becomes visible in our life, so by the ceremony of confirmation the event of Pentecost happens to us.

As the apostles gave the Holy Spirit by imposing hands on those who were baptized, so today the bishop and priests present lay their hands on those to be confirmed. Then each is anointed with oil on the forehead. This ceremony gradually developed over the centuries as the essential part of the sacrament, best expressing the interior coming of the Spirit with power and strength.

The Holy Spirit works within us by means of his seven gifts, seven "instincts" which make us open to his guidance. Given us for the first time in baptism, they are enlarged or sharpened at confirmation. They help us accept and follow the inspirations of the Spirit. They can be compared to sails on a boat that receive the wind that moves the boat—or a TV set that is turned on to receive a program. (They are predicted in regard to Christ, who had them fully, in Isaiah 11, 2-3).

These are the gifts of the Holy Spirit—we might note the one we particularly need:

Wisdom is the gift by which the Holy Spirit enables us to judge all things as God sees them.

Understanding helps us understand better what God has revealed.

Knowledge enables us to see the things of the world as they really are.

Counsel helps us to know what to do in particular difficult situations.

Fortitude gives us the courage to do what is right, joyfully, in a difficult situation.

Piety helps our worship of God and our regard for people and things connected with God.

Fear of the Lord strengthens in us the wholesome fear of offending God and being separated from him whom we love.

The more we try to be aware of the Spirit within us and ask for an increase of the gifts we need, the more he will guide us in our everyday life.

The Holy Spirit also illumines our minds, so that we may better understand and explain the things of God. He deepens our faith, so that we can more clearly proclaim it to others: Read 1 Corinthians 2, 9-13.

We should have confidence when we speak of our religion, remembering "It is not you that speak, but the Spirit of your Father that speaketh in you" (Matthew 10, 20). There is little danger that people today will become "fanatics" in speaking of their faith—but there is a real danger of underconfidence, diffidence, hesitancy. Often a quiet word, a bit of good example, can be a great help to another who is struggling within himself. The power of God himself can ride on our seemingly stumbling words. We are his instruments.

Each person has special gifts that the Holy Spirit can use for the good of all, for the whole Church. Everyone has talents and opportunities to help the Church and the world. The Spirit inspires our efforts, unifies them, and makes them truly effective. "Now there are varieties of gifts, but the same Spirit . . . varieties of service . . . for the common good" (1 Corinthians 12, 4-7). (We touched on these in chapter 9). "Each believer has the right and duty to use them in the Church and in the world for the good of mankind and for the upbuilding of the Church" (**Decree on the Apostolate of the Laity, no. 3**).

> To one is given through the Spirit the utterance of wisdom, and to another the utterance of knowledge according to the same Spirit, to another faith by the same Spirit, to another gifts of healing by the one Spirit, to another the working of gifts of healing by the one Spirit, to another the working of miracles, to another prophecy, to another the ability to distinguish between spirits, to another various kinds of tongues, to another the interpretation of tongues. All these are inspired by one and the same Spirit, who apportions to each one individually as he wills (1 Corinthians 12, 8-11).

In response to Vatican Council II, which stressed the vital need of laypeople taking part in Church affairs, diocesan and parish councils of clergy and laity have been set up in many places. In this way the clergy and laity consult regularly with one another and with the bishop, and the gifts and talents of all can be used for the good of the parish, the diocese, and in the nation and world as well. (Cf. also Chapter 21). The Vatican Council said of this:

> In dioceses, as far as possible, there should be councils which assist the apostolic work of the Church either in the field of making the gospel known and men holy, or in the charitable, social, or other spheres. To this end, clergy and religious should appropriately cooperate with laity. . . . Councils of this type should be established as far as possible also on the parochial, interparochial, and interdiocesan level as well as in the national or international sphere. Some special secretariat, moreover, should be established at the Holy See for the service and encouragement of the lay apostolate. . . . (*Decree on the Apostolate of the Laity, no. 26*).
> In many places where such councils have been set up, they are functioning well. In other places, unfortunately, these councils are not yet functioning, usually because of an authoritarian fear on the part of the bishop or parish clergy, or because of apathy on the part of the laypeople.

By confirmation the Holy Spirit inspires and aids us to help develop the society in which we live. It is the social sacrament. It makes us more aware of our opportunities and responsibilities as members of society. We develop the powers of our confirmation by trying to make the world a better place—by prayer, study, and by joining with others to bring this about. Some professions are particularly vital: teachers, writers, those in social work, medicine, communications, labor, etc. Some contribute by taking part in the Peace Corps or similar domestic programs.

Vatican Council II comments succinctly about often-overlooked virtues that confirmed Christians should have in today's world: "They should also hold in high esteem professional skill, family and civic spirit, and the virtues relating to social behavior, namely, honesty, justice, sincerity, kindness, and courage. . . ." (Decree on the Apostolate of the Laity, no. 4).

By confirmation we share more fully in Christ's priestly powers, deriving more from the Mass and sacraments. We can now particularly pray for those who do not have his truth, and bring them his grace. We are changed interiorly, and this change within us is called the "character" of confirmation. By our baptismal character we received the power to take part in the Mass and other sacraments; by this character of confirmation we can take part in them as adult apostles.

By confirmation we share particularly in the prophetic work of Christ, teaching and bearing witness as he did. As baptism gave us the Spirit to be the source of our new Christian life, so confirmation confers the Spirit giving prophetic power to witness to Christ. Whether we realize it or not, however poor our words seem, we have something of Christ's own power and forcefulness in witnessing.

In today's Church many laymen and women, particularly writers, are outstandingly using their prophetic gifts. While the prophetic function of teaching the truth belongs to the authorities of the Church, it belongs as well to the whole Church and particularly to those gifted with this charism. A modern theologian writes:

Prophecy within the Church is a remedy against corruption on all levels. There are times when the officers of the Church fail to speak as they ought; those who utter the authentic voice of the Church in such moments are prophets. There are times when the hierarchy itself needs to be redeemed from corruption; those who rebuke it are prophets. Prophecy in such times of need can be either speech or action. Prophecy is not found in any class or level in the Church; and it is not limited to men. . . . However . . . there are true prophets and false prophets. . . . The true prophet is recognized not only by the criterion of concord with the traditional faith of the Church, but also by whether his message supports unity in faith and in love, or whether it makes for disunity. The prophetic mission is undertaken with risk, for, even if the prophet has a genuine call, he may delude himself in the course of his mission. The officers of the Church have no uncertainty about their call because they are authentic officers by appointment. But they are no better protected than the prophet against self-deception in the execution of their mission (John L. McKenzie, *Authority in the Church* New York: Sheed & Ward, 1966, pp. 153-55).

We receive confirmation only once, because it permanently changes us (like baptism), marking us for eternity with new powers and social responsibilities. It can take a lifetime of Christian living to appreciate the staggering interior change that confirmation begins to bring about.

The bishop ordinarily gives confirmation. However, a pastor may confirm his parishioners in danger of death, as can hospital chaplains their patients, and any priest if empowered.

Since confirmation completes baptism, it was given in the ancient Church immediately after baptism, as part of the same ceremony. In that age of persecution, adults particularly needed the sacrament immediately to bear witness to their faith. Gradually, in the West, the two sacraments became separated, and confirmation would usually be given when a child began to mature, about the age of puberty. Some, however, have kept the practice of infant confirmation: in the Eastern Rites and in some parts of the Latin church it is given immediately after baptism. Many today favor giving it shortly after a child's first communion; others prefer that it be given when one is a teenager; some wish it to be a sacrament of "recommitment" that one might receive when he wished to in his early adult years.

One should be confirmed at his earliest opportunity. While he need not be confirmed to attain heaven—and it is not necessary before marriage—without it he would be deprived of much grace and truth.

If one who has already received "confirmation" in a Protestant Church should desire to become a Catholic, he would receive the Catholic sacrament of confirmation sometime after his reception into the Catholic Church. The two "confirmations" are not the same thing.

We take the name of a saint at confirmation—in addition to the one taken at baptism—as an additional patron and model to bring us closer to Christ. We should choose someone whose life inspires us in an apostolic way.

There is a sponsor at confirmation. As in baptism, the sponsor should be a practicing Catholic, of the same sex as the one being confirmed, at least 14 years old—but a different person than our baptismal sponsor. Sometimes when a group is confirmed, there is one sponsor for all the men and one for all the women, chosen by the pastor.

The more faith and love we bring to our confirmation, the more we will receive from it. Like all the sacraments it is an act of worship, an intimate, personal meeting with God—and especially with the Holy Spirit. The better we prepare ourselves by prayer and study, the more power we will receive from it.

Adults who are being baptized into the Catholic Church are now confirmed along with their baptism—thus reviving today the ancient, full rite of initiation into the Church: baptism, confirmation, and the eucharist.

Confirmation is now normally given at Mass, to stress the fact that it empowers one for a fuller participation in the eucharist.

A good confession should also be made before one is confirmed, as a penitential recommitment of oneself to Christ and the Christian community. It goes without saying that receiving the Holy Spirit in a condition of unforgiven serious sin blocks the full effect of his grace; one doing so, however, would still be confirmed, and he could later receive the full, special grace of confirmation after a good confession.

DAILY LIVING: BEING OPEN TO THE SPIRIT

Each Christian must encounter the Holy Spirit in his own life. Each has the Spirit within him, with the power to make his life and actions truly superhuman. But if he is not aware of this indwelling power, or is afraid to submit to it, the Spirit's work in him will be handicapped. Each of our lives is a constant struggle between our weakened self and the Holy Spirit within.

The Spirit is the one who, in the practical situations of life, inspires our choices, our willing, our actions—if we but let him. He moves us to see how we should react to the events of our life. In Christ's life there was a particular moment for everything, and so there is in ours. It is the Spirit who prompts us in what we must do, with Christ, when the time comes. He is the one who stirs within us the grace of conversion, of understanding, and gives us courage to act as we know we should.

Sometimes we are confused, troubled, and then we should particularly ask the Spirit for help. Sometimes we find it difficult even to pray for guidance, but ". . . the Spirit himself intercedes for us with sighs too deep for words. And he who searches the hearts of men knows what is the mind of the Spirit, because the Spirit intercedes for the saints according to the will of God" (Romans 8, 26-27).

The Spirit "opens" the scriptures to us, helping us draw guidance and strength from them. The bible was written under the guidance of the Holy Spirit, and he is there constantly to help those who read it. It is his book. That we might interpret it correctly, he also guides us by his presence in the Church—through the Church's teachers he helps us understand what is beyond our comprehension. On one of the first pages of any Catholic bible there is a suggested prayer to the Holy Spirit.

Today especially it seems that the Holy Spirit's work is becoming more evident. Pope John, the old man who brought new life to the Catholic Church, said that our day is a "new Pentecost." He called our time (as have many others recently) the age of the Holy Spirit. If we try to be open to the Spirit, he will guide us in using the new knowledge and fresh insights that are constantly coming upon us.

> *For instance, some Christians of a C.F.M. group,* inspired by the current renewal within the Church, asked themselves what they could do to take part. They concluded that the most critical need of their neighborhood was passage of a fair-housing law before their city council. Despite opposition, they calmly, factually, persistently gathered signatures and other support for the measure, which was passed and is gradually and successfully being implemented.

Each of us should set aside a period of prayer with the Holy Spirit. The saintly Belgian Cardinal Mercier, admired by all Europe at the time of World War I, practiced daily a "secret of sanctity": five minutes alone in a quiet place asking the Spirit for help and guidance. Countless others who have practiced something like this have found a new awareness of God and a sense of guidance in their lives.

A current evidence for many, of the Spirit's presence among us today, is the "Pentecostal" movement within the Church. This is a "charismatic renewal" reminiscent of the early Church when the Spirit was particularly active through various charisms or gifts. Catholic Pentecostals gather, often with other Christians, to pray with each other and to experience the Spirit in their midst, particularly through different charisms such as speaking in tongues or healing. These people have all experienced a "baptism" of the Spirit, a sensible coming of the Spirit and his gifts which has transformed their lives. While this seems to be a particular gift, and therefore not for everyone, many thousands have been moved in this way to become more loving Christians.

SOME SUGGESTIONS FOR . . .

DISCUSSION

How do you feel you can most effectively bear witness to your beliefs in your particular life situation?

What do you think is the one most critical need in our world today—and what could we do to help?

Can you think of a recent event in your life in which the prompting of the Holy Spirit was evident?

FURTHER READING

* *Catholic Pentecostals,* Ranaghan (Paulist Press, 1969)—A presentation by those whose lives have been changed by the Catholic Pentecostal movement.

* *Humanism and Christianity,* D'Arcy (World Publishers, 1971)—A presentation of the conditions for an authentic Christian humanism vis-a-vis the secular variety.

  Poverty: Sign of Our Times, Schwartz (Alba House, 1970) —Why the Church must face the challenge of poverty, and become the Church of the Poor.

* *Revolution Through Peace,* Camara (Harper & Row, 1971) —An outstanding, renowned modern bishop's presentation of the Church's mission in the temporal as well as the spiritual world.

* *The Social Aspects of the Christian Faith Contained in Mater et Magistra and Pacem in Terris,* Haipt (Paulist Press Deus Book, 1965)—A brief study of Pope John's great encyclicals giving the Christian view of modern social problems; an excellent guide to reading the encyclicals themselves.

* *On the Development of Peoples* ("Populorum Progressio"), Pope Paul VI (Paulist Press, 1967)—The hard-hitting encyclical of Pope Paul spelling out particularly what we of the "have" nations must do to help the "have not" peoples of the world. This is "must" reading for anyone who would call himself a Christian today.

(For more reading along this line, Cf. chapters 22 & 24.)

PERSONAL REFLECTION

A test of our openness to the prompting of the Spirit is whether we are witnessing for Christ by joining in needed social action. I might ask myself whether I have tried recently to join with others to bring about some social good, e.g., helping someone I know who is poor, handicapped, or retarded, or joining with others to obtain fair housing or employment for those deprived, or helping someone of another race find the housing or the job he deserves to live decently or to become a part of the community.

16
The Meal of Christ's Sacrifice — The Mass

What is the meaning of the Mass? Why is the Mass arranged the way it is? How can one derive real value from the Mass?

WE TAKE PART IN CHRIST'S GREATEST ACT

We have seen God's love for us and his desire to be with us. He came among us in Jesus Christ. He lives among us today in his Church. He reaches out to us through the sacraments: baptism, by which he unites us to himself, and confirmation by which he sends us his Spirit.

Wonderful though it is that God should come among us, more wonderful yet is the destiny he has prepared for us. He wants to raise us to himself, to the very level of divinity, to know and love him most intimately in unending happiness.

Mankind had rejected the grace that made this possible, but Christ came and redeemed us, making it possible once more. This, our salvation by Christ, was the greatest act of his life and the central event of all history. By it mankind could attain union with God, face to face, forever.

Yet in order to profit by this great act of Christ's love, we must unite ourselves to it. We must make it our own. We must somehow take part in Christ's death and resurrection in order to attain heaven. This is because he loves us and wants us to be with him, freely and most intimately.

It is natural to share in the things that happen to those we love, and particularly in the great events of their life. We want to be with those we love, particularly, in their great moments of joy or suffering. A husband wants to be by the bedside of his critically ill wife, parents want to take part in their child's graduation, friends take part in one another's weddings, etc.

Christ in his love has made it possible for us to share in what happened to him. We can relive his life, mysteriously but really. We try to imitate him, but even more we can actually go through —with him—what he did. His actions become our own. So says St. Paul: "I have been crucified with Christ. It is no longer I who live, but Christ who lives in me. . . ." (Galatians 2, 20).

Above all, Christ wants us to take part with him in his death and resurrection. He wants us to share his own "passage" his going back to the Father and eternal happiness. We saw how Christ unites us for the first time to his death and resurrection by baptism. After baptism, each sacrament unites us in a special way to Christ as he saves us. But the greatest partaking possible is by the sacrament of the holy eucharist.

The holy eucharist is Jesus Christ living among us under the appearance of bread and wine. When the priest at Mass says over the bread and wine Christ's words, "This is my body . . . This is the chalice of my blood. . . ." the bread and wine are changed into the body and blood of Christ. By the power of Christ working through the priest the bread and wine, though still appearing to be bread and wine, become Christ.

> We are aware that this sounds strange indeed to some and is open to misunderstanding. When we say that the bread and wine "become Christ" we are not saying that bread and wine are Christ, nor are we practicing some sort of cannibalism when we take this in communion. What we mean is that the bread and wine are a sign of Christ present, here, in a special way—not in a mere physical way, as if condensed into a wafer; somehow his presence has "taken over" the bread and wine, so that, for us who believe, it is no longer merely bread that is present, but Christ himself. And Christ is here present, not just to be eaten as if in a cannibalistic sense, but rather present and doing something for us, putting us in touch with and causing us to share in his death and resurrection.

When Jesus Christ living among us in the holy eucharist prolongs his death and resurrection so we can take part, this is the Mass. Christ's going to the Father is made present under the appearance of bread and wine so that Christians till the end of time can take part continually, gradually going with him to the Father. The Mass is to be the great way we are drawn to God, and our great source of strength for the journey to him.

> "Recalling thus the mysteries of redemption, the Church opens to the faithful the riches of her Lord's powers and merits, so that these are in some way made present for all time, and the faithful are enabled to lay hold upon them and become filled with saving grace" (*Constitution on the Sacred Liturgy*, no. 102).

There are various ways in which we can take part in a great event, for example, the 1965 American civil rights march from Selma, Alabama, to Montgomery. We might hear of it, or we might see movies of it on TV; we might watch it from afar, or from nearby; or we might have actually been a part of the march. The more one enters into it, the more one is involved in it, the more he gets out of it, the more it means to him and to the others with whom he comes into contact.

At Mass, we are not only present at Christ's actual death and resurrection, we can actually take part in them to the extent that we want to. Christ's death and resurrection are here, we are present at them, but they are hidden—they are present here through the signs of bread and wine—and the more these signs mean to us, the more we want to enter into the great struggle of Christ's death and resurrection, the more we actually are a part of them, the more our life and pain become meaningful, the more love we spread in the world, the closer we come to eternity and God.

THIS IS OUR COVENANT MEAL

The night before he died Christ gave us the great way of continually sharing in his death and resurrection—by means of a meal, the last supper: Read 1 Corinthians 11, 23-29.—To understand this incident we must remember that this meal was the passover meal, eaten to commemorate the salvation of God's people from slavery and death, and the old covenant of Mt. Sinai. Whenever the Jews ate this meal they looked forward to a new passover to come, a new salvation, a new exodus to a new freedom. Our redemption was Christ's great new passover, from death to life, from this world to the Father—and he began it by eating this paschal meal, his last supper. He gave this paschal meal a new power and new meaning. He made it the way his followers could actually share in his passover, in his death and resurrection.

By the words, "This is my body. . . . This cup is the new covenant in my blood," Christ changed the bread and wine into his living body and blood—this is the sacrament of the holy eucharist. The bread and wine, though still appearing to be bread and wine, were now Christ himself. Christ was now present in a new way, under the appearance of bread and wine. And it was the whole living Christ present under the appearance of bread, not only his body, and the whole living Christ present under the appearance of wine.

But above all, Christ was presenting before his apostles his death and resurrection. The bread was his body which would be given in death for them the next day. The cup was his blood which he would shed the next day to establish the new covenant. By these words he made present at the last supper, mysteriously but really, his bloody death and his resurrection. It was a preview of what would happen the next day, Good Friday, and on Easter Sunday morning.

This meal by which Christ began his passover also began the events by which he made his new, perfect covenant. "This cup is the new covenant in my blood," he said. As he and his apostles ate the meal which commemorated the old covenant, he was looking forward to the new covenant which he would shortly begin. Then as Moses had once sealed the old covenant by sacrifice and the sprinkling of animals' blood, Christ shed his blood in sacrifice on Good Friday to begin the new covenant. As the greatest event of the Old Testament had been celebrated by a meal, so Christ made this meal the occasion of celebrating the greatest event of his life and of all history.

Then Christ gave his apostles the power to do what he had done, to make present his death and resurrection after changing the bread and wine into himself—"Do this in remembrance of me," he said. By this he gave his apostles the power to prolong his sacrifice, to extend it, to somehow continue it down through history. Each time this took place, his passover, his covenant would be renewed again. Every other action of history is bound by limitations of time and space, except this.

Every priest by his ordination receives the power of making Christ present and re-presenting his death and resurrection. This power has been passed on in the Church from the apostles by the sacrament of ordination, holy orders. By giving this power to his priests, Christ provides that his Church down through the centuries can continually take part in the great events of our salvation. Christ chose his apostles to be the first priests of the new testament, just as God had chosen Aaron and his sons as the first priests of the old testament. As the powers of a special priesthood were passed on in Israel, so the full powers of Christ's priesthood are passed on today to those he chooses through his Church.

Every Christian also shares in Christ's priesthood and in this offering of himself which is his death and resurrection prolonged. We saw how, by baptism and confirmation, each Christian receives this power of the lay priesthood. The ordained priests of the Church, the successors of the apostles, act as Christ's instruments making him present in the eucharist. Then the whole Christian congregation uses its priestly powers to offer him, and itself with him, to the Father.

. . . AND OUR PERFECT SACRIFICE . . .

One way of understanding the Mass is to recall that the great events of life are celebrated by giving gifts or presents—as on birthdays, weddings, anniversaries. Giving gifts is as old as humanity and as widespread. Our gift can express many things: love, praise, thanks, repentance, and it can implicitly ask for something. A gift stands for the giver—accepting a gift often means acceptance of the one who gives it, as when a girl accepts a ring from a boy. A gift, then, particularly expresses our desire to be united in love with the one to whom it is given.

From ancient times, we saw, men have offered gifts in sacrifice to God (or their concept of God). They have done this to show their feelings toward him and their desire to be united with him. We saw in the Old Testament sacrifices how God helped his people express their feelings toward him, guiding them to offer their gifts to him.

Sacrifice means offering a gift through a priest, changing it in some way, and sometimes eating of it. People would take some gift that represented themselves, and offer it to God by means of their representative, a priest. He would change or transform the gift to signify that they were giving it to God, that it no longer belonged to them—often he would kill a living gift or victim—and then he might burn it to further show God's acceptance and possession of it. Sometimes there would be a meal or banquet, a communion, to further signify their union with God by eating of what was now divine.

Something was lacking even in the Old Testament sacrifices. Men never had a suitable gift for almighty God, nor did they have a worthy priest; then, too, they were unable to be as fully united with God as they wished.

> "If I were hungry, I should not tell you, for mine are the world and its fullness. Do I eat the flesh of strong bulls, or is the blood of goats my drink?" (Psalm 49, 12-13).

When mankind was ready, Jesus Christ offered the perfect sacrifice by his death and resurrection. He was the perfect gift and the perfect priest making this offering. The best gift, after all, is that of a living person, as when a couple give themselves to one another in marriage—and Christ is the divine Son giving himself to the Father. By his death he gave himself to his Father; his resurrection and ascension showed that the Father accepted his gift.

Christ gave us the power to offer this same perfect gift, himself, to continually share in his death and resurrection by the holy eucharist. We would expect that Christ would not leave his followers without a way of communicating with God by sacrifice. But he went beyond our greatest expectations. He gave us the holy eucharist, his living presence among us, so we could join ourselves to him and continually share in his own great sacrifice.

The Mass, then, is the renewal of Christ's sacrifice, of his passover, and new covenant, by him and us, his Church. At each Mass Christ becomes present; he prolongs and renews his sacrifice so we can be a part of it, so we can pass with him through this world to eternity, and with him continually renew our own covenant.

Christ is present among us at Mass with the same intention or desire to give himself for us, but now he shows this by the separate signs of bread and wine. Instead of showing it by a bloody death, he now expresses his giving of himself by this ceremony with bread and wine. In our own actions for example, it is our inner intention, our sincere willingness to do something, that really matters. There is a great difference between a person giving up his life voluntarily and one who is forced to die. Christ becomes present among us at Mass with the same inner intention, the same desire to be sacrificed for us that he had on Calvary 2,000 years ago. However, now, instead of carrying out his intention by a bloody death, he expresses it by the separate signs of bread and wine.

> A person can show his love by giving his life, or equally by being ready and willing to do so. Christ is present at Mass with the same willingness, the same desire to give his life for us that he had when he actually died. It is somewhat as if our war dead could come back alive on Veterans' Day, inspired by the same interior willingness to give their lives, and go through a pageant reenacting the way they died, that we might now unite our feelings with theirs. "Do this for a remembrance of me," said Christ —the Mass is a living remembrance, a living memorial which brings the past into the present.

At Mass Christ does not suffer or die again. Rather he represents, prolongs, continues, renews his great moment of sacrifice down through the centuries so that we can be a part of it. There are millions of Masses, but only one sacrifice of Christ. If we at Mass were to close our eyes it would be the same as if Christ's followers on Calvary closed theirs; the same great action is taking place before us and we are able to be an intimate part of it.

Through the Mass Christ does many things for us. Above all, he enables us to offer perfect worship and be perfectly united with God. The men of the Old Testament strove to bring this about but never could. Now at Mass we are joined with Christ as he appears before his Father and ours. The Father no longer sees the poor actions of mere men—you and me with our sins and weaknesses—but only the gift that God himself cannot resist.

If our eyes could see what is really happening at any Mass, we would see Christ at the altar and among us, leading us and drawing us all into himself. Then, with him, we ascend to the Father's presence. We would also see the Holy Spirit within each of us, uniting us, inspiring our offering. We would see the Father giving us in return his Son, Jesus Christ, the best gift God can give mortal man, and we would see ourselves being drawn into an indescribable union with divinity.

THE MASS IS GOD'S WORD, OUR GIFT, AND HIS GIFT

When giving a gift, there is conversation, some sort of preparation to bring out its meaning and significance. We do not merely thrust our gift at its recipient. Particularly if it is a noteworthy gift, there is conversation and ceremony with it. When a national hero is presented with the Medal of Honor there are speeches, music, etc. So too we prepare to offer our gift in sacrifice to God by conversation with him, by listening to his Word, and by ceremony.

God had called his people together at Mt. Sinai to hear his Word and respond to it by sacrifice. (Cf. Exodus 24, 7-8). This assembly of the Israelites established the old covenant, making them his people. This "assembly of Yahweh" is the same as the New Testament word for "Church." The basic meaning of a Church, then, is this: God's people assembled by him to hear his Word and respond to it by sacrifice.

After Christ's ascension his followers assembled to receive his teaching from the apostles and offer the eucharistic sacrifice. This is the Church of the New Testament. The eucharistic meal, called the "breaking of the bread," and the teaching that went with it would gradually develop into the pattern of worship that would be the Mass.

And they devoted themselves to the apostles' teaching and fellowship, to the breaking of bread and the prayers (Acts 2, 42). On the first day of the week, when they were gathered together to break bread, Paul talked with them, intending to depart on the morrow; and he prolonged his speech until midnight . . . And when Paul had gone up and had broken bread and eaten, he conversed with them a long while, until daybreak, and so departed (Acts 20, 7. 11).

Many scripture scholars see in the 6th chapter of John's gospel an excerpt from an early Christian liturgical service; John himself may have conducted primitive services in this way. Verses 35-50 give the doctrine or teaching, and verses 51-58 the eucharistic part of the service. This, then is the pattern: The Word of God followed by the eucharist.

The Mass, then, is the assembly of God's new people, his Church, called together by him to hear his Word and to take part in his perfect sacrifice. When we come together for Mass we are not only going to church—we are a Church. The Mass welds us into one people as we renew our common covenant, offer our gift and share our meal which is Christ. It is by the Mass that the Church is continually renewed in what it is.

The Mass as the meal which renews Christ's sacrifice can be compared to the main meal of a family. First, the family comes home; they wash up, and talk to one another, learning the events of the day. The table is set and the food is prepared. Then the family prays together over their food, offering thanks to God for all he has given them. Finally, they eat together, taking part in the food and in one another's companionship.

So too at Mass we first come together and prepare ourselves, cleansing ourselves of sin, speaking with God, and learning from him the great events of our salvation. Then we prepare our food, the bread and wine. We then join in the great eucharistic prayer of thanksgiving to God over our food which is now Christ his Son. Finally, we take part together in our meal of holy communion, nourishing ourselves on Christ and joined with one another in the companionship of our Christian family love.

The arrangement of the Mass also expresses the fact that it is an exchange of love:

God gives to us—his Word, the scriptural teaching.

We give to God—our sacrifice-offering of thanksgiving, Christ, and ourselves with him.

God gives to us—his Word, the eucharistic Christ.

The Mass begins with some introductory prayers, usually recalling our sins and asking God's pardon that we may be worthy to worship him, and briefly praising him for what he is and has given us.

The first main part of the Mass is the Liturgy of the Word, the scripture readings. We have assembled together as God's people and have prepared ourselves by prayer. Now God addresses his Word to us. Later we will respond to his Word by our sacrifice. This, we saw, was the way God's people worshipped in the Old Testament, and the way Christ's first followers continued to worship. Christ himself had followed this pattern when he prepared his apostles by his last discourse (John, chapters 13-17), and then went forth to his death and resurrection. The first Christians originally adopted this part from the Jewish synagogue service of prayers, readings, and commentary.

Faith is aroused and we are enlightened and made eager for Christ by the scripture readings and the preaching that follows. Before our gifts of bread and wine are changed into Christ, our hearts must be changed, opened, by this instruction. Usually there are three readings: the first is from the Old Testament; the second is from one of the New Testament epistles; and the third reading is from one of the gospels. In the sermon or homily Christ addresses his message to us through the priest who represents him.

The importance of this first part of the Mass is stressed by Vatican Council II when it says that here "God speaks to his people and Christ is still proclaiming his gospel" (**Constitution on the Sacred Liturgy,** no. 33). And again, "From the table of both the Word of God and the body of Christ . . . the Church unceasingly receives and offers to the faithful the bread of life" (**Constitution on Divine Revelation,** no. 21).

We then respond to God's Word on Sundays and great feasts by professing our faith, saying together the Creed. Then, in the Prayer of the Faithful, we respond to the exhortations of the scriptures and the sermon by praying for all those who need help and for the things we and the world particularly need.

The second main part of the Mass is the Liturgy of the Eucharist (or the Liturgy of Sacrifice). Here we prepare our gifts, they are transformed into Christ, and through him and with him we offer ourselves in thanksgiving to the Father. The Father, in return, gives us the same perfect gift, Jesus Christ, who unites us to himself and to one another.

We begin our sacrifice with the offertory during which we prepare our gifts, the bread and wine, and make them ours by uniting ourselves to them. As a mother prepares a meal for her family, as Christ sent his apostles to prepare for the last supper so we do here. We also unite ourselves and all we wish to pray for with these gifts, so that later when they have become Christ we will be united to him in his offering to the Father.

With the preface we begin the great eucharistic prayer, or canon, during which our gifts are transformed into Christ and we offer him in thanksgiving to the Father. This is the most solemn part of the Mass. We call this the eucharist, that is, an offering of thanksgiving, because it is to thank the Father for his love toward us that we are offering him Christ, our best possible gift, and ourselves with him. The term comes from the long prayer of thanksgiving said by the Jews at the end of a meal, which recounted God's mighty deeds for his people. So it was that Christ at the last supper, ". . . took bread and when he had given thanks he broke it and gave it to them saying, 'This is my body . . .'" (Luke 22, 19).

During the eucharistic prayer we remember everyone and everything, joining all creation in our offering. We pray sometimes for the Church, its leaders and people, and we ask its members who have passed into eternity to join our worship. Then we ask the Father to accept our offering.

At the center of this prayer is the consecration. Our gifts are transformed into Christ and we are particularly reminded of his death for us. The separate consecrations of bread and wine bring home to us how his blood was separated from his body as he hung dying for us on the cross. First is the consecration of the bread: the priest says over it:

"The day before he suffered he took bread into his holy and venerable hands and with eyes lifted up to heaven to you, God, his almighty Father, giving thanks to you he blessed, broke, and gave it to his disciples saying 'Take and eat this, all of you, for this is my body.'"

Then follows the consecration of the wine, as the priest says over the chalice:

"Likewise after the supper, he also took this glorious cup into his holy and venerable hands; he gave thanks to you again and blessed the cup and handed it to his disciples saying 'Take and drink this, all of you, for this is the chalice of my blood of the new and everlasting covenant, the mystery of faith. It shall be shed for you and for many to atone for sins. Whenever you do these things, you will do them in memory of me.' "

By the words, "This is my body. . . . This is the chalice of my blood," Christ has become present under the appearance of bread and wine. The whole living Christ is present both under the appearance of bread and under that of wine. But by the separate words and separate signs of bread and wine, we are vividly reminded of how he really spilled his blood for us when he died for us. He is present among us with the same willingness to die for us as on Calvary, but now he shows it by these separate signs of bread and wine.

Then come the memorial prayer, the invocation of the Holy Spirit, and several intercessions. We call to mind the death, resurrection and ascension of Christ, and offer him to the Father. We call on the Holy Spirit to unite us. Then we may ask to be united with the saints in heaven, we may pray for the dead, and for the welfare of the Church on earth.

Our eucharistic prayer culminates in the offering of ourselves and of all creation with Christ to the Father. Christ has taken our poor gifts and transformed them into himself. Now, joined with him, everything we are and have is offered in a great thanksgiving gift. This prayer concludes:

"Through him, with him, in him, in the unity of the Holy Spirit, all glory and honor is yours, almighty Father, for ever and ever." The congregation responds with their great "Amen!"—"So be it!"

Our gift has been offered in sacrifice, and now we prepare for our sacrificial meal, holy communion, God's gift to us. God now shows us strikingly that he has accepted our gift, that we are truly united with him. He comes to us himself in the form of food—something of which men in times past would not even dream. This is the greatest gift he could give us. He unites each of us to himself in the most intimate way possible, through Christ his Son. Christ comes to us in this sign of food to bring home to us that he is our spiritual strength and nourishment.

We say together the prayer that Christ himself taught us, the

Lord's Prayer or "Our Father." Then we pray for freedom from sin and anxiety "as we wait in joyful hope for the coming of our Savior, Jesus Christ."

With the prayer for peace we give the handshake or embrace of peace to one another. This is an outward sign of the peace and unity which we are attempting to have as a Christian community. Then the priest breaks a particle off the large "host" and drops it in the chalice to symbolize our unity through this eucharist (in the ancient Church a particle from the host used at the bishop's Mass was sometimes taken to the other churches and dropped in the chalice as a sign of the unity of the Church)—and also this reminds us that the Mass is the ancient "breaking of bread."

Now Christ unites himself with each of us through holy communion. First the priest takes part in communion under the form of bread and then under the form of wine—as at the last supper, the priest always takes both the host and the chalice. Then the people take part in communion, usually under the appearance of the smaller round hosts of bread—and on certain occasions they may also take part under both forms.

Holy communion is our great and joyous meal of love, unity, and thanksgiving. People have always expressed their happiness, friendship, thanksgiving, and particularly their unity by having a meal together. We saw that the joining of two parties in a covenant was often celebrated by a meal together: today a couple has a wedding meal, often, to celebrate their lifelong covenant of love. We saw that Israel celebrated its union with God through the old covenant by the passover meal which also looked forward to a new, more perfect union. Now we have a far more intimate and perfect union with God in this sacrificial meal of the new covenant. But this is not all Christ does:

> The cup of blessing which we bless, is it not a participation in the blood of Christ? The bread which we break, is it not a participation in the body of Christ? Because there is one loaf, we who are many are one body, for we all partake of the same loaf. Consider the practice of Israel; are not those who eat the sacrifices partners in the altar? (1 Corinthians 10, 16-18).

Christ through holy communion also unites us with one another, making us "one body," one Church. Just as many grains

make one bread, so we, by eating the eucharist, become one.
Eating together draws people together, especially when celebrating a great event, as Christmas or Thanksgiving dinner, a wedding breakfast, or a banquet. A family meal is normally the center
of its life together.

Christ chose this custom of eating together to draw his followers together, to unite us not only with himself but with one another. Holy communion, then, is the great banquet of God's family, his Church, by which the members are drawn together in
love. We are so truly united with one another that St. Augustine
could say, "You are the body of Christ, and when you receive the
body of Christ you receive yourselves." Singing together when
taking part in communion particularly emphasizes our unity.

**The communion meal is the part of the Mass that particularly
reminds us of Christ's resurrection.** A meal symbolizes life—we
must eat to live. This eucharistic meal not only symbolizes but
gives us Christ resurrected, living again, communicating to us his
own life of grace.

> Christ usually appeared after his resurrection during meals and
> ate with his followers. The authentic witnesses of the resurrec-
> tion, says Peter, are those "who were chosen by God as witnesses,
> who ate and drank with him after he rose from the dead" (Acts
> 10, 41). When Christ appeared to two of his followers on the
> road to Emmaus, they did not realize who it was until "he took
> the bread and blessed, and broke it, and gave it to them. And
> their eyes were opened and they recognized him . . ." (Luke 24,
> 30-31). After his ascension Christ's followers felt that he was living
> in their midst especially when they gathered for the eucharistic
> meal, and they looked for his second coming one day at this event.

**After the communion, the Mass concludes with a few prayers
of thanksgiving and the final blessing.** Strengthened and united
with Christ and one another, we are now sent back into our daily
lives to live the life of Christ.

**This, then, is the Mass—the wonderful way in which Christ
continually joins us to the great actions by which he saved us, the
greatest events of human history.** Now we can take part in them
most intimately, continually drawing strength from them for our
journey to the Father. We who take part in Mass today are as
truly a part of Christ's greatest deeds as if we were his followers

standing on Calvary, and in some respects we can join in even more intimately. This privilege is ours as Christians—for many, it is their privilege every day.

DAILY LIVING: THE MASS AND OUR DAILY LIFE

All the actions of a Catholic's daily life should lead up to the Mass and flow from it. When we take part in the Mass, we unite ourselves with Christ and through him we reach out and are drawn to God. This act of worship is certainly the most significant and important action of the day and of the week.

At Mass we personally renew our covenant with God for that week. The more we prepare for it, and try to remember and prolong it in our daily life, the more truly Christian—Christ-filled—our life will be.

Our offering at Mass must be interior and sincere. Christ sacrifices himself at Mass by his interior desire to give himself for us. The more we unite ourselves interiorly, by our own sincere desire, to Christ's offering—the more we offer something that is really of ourselves—the more effect the Mass will have on our daily lives.

SOME SUGGESTIONS FOR . . .

DISCUSSION

Can you understand the idea of the Mass, as a sacrifice and as a meal?

Can you understand why the Mass is arranged the way it is?

How, in your opinion, could one get more out of the Mass?

PERSONAL REFLECTION

Each Mass is a renewal of my covenant with God. He pledges himself to give me eternal and unimaginable happiness, if I will only be faithful this little while here on earth. I should take every occasion I can to renew my covenant with him, to open myself in sincere acceptance of his love. The Mass is the great way in which I can do this.

17

The Eucharist in
Christ's Church Today

Why is the Mass changing today? What further developments might we expect in the Mass? How are Christians drawing closer in their worship? Why do we call the Mass the greatest thing in Catholicism?

HOW THE MASS DEVELOPED

The Mass at first was a simple service that took place after a meal, as at the last supper. The meal was the "agape" and the eucharistic service was called the "breaking of the bread" or the "Lord's supper." In Jerusalem the first Christians continued to attend the temple together, but then "breaking bread in their homes, they partook of food with glad and generous hearts" (Acts 2, 46). We read of Paul's visit to Troas: "On the first day of the week, when we were gathered together to break bread, Paul talked with them. . . ." (Acts 20, 7ff).

Soon, however, abuses crept in, and gradually the eucharistic service was separated from the agape-meal: Read 1 Corinthians 11, 17-22. When the eucharistic meal became a separate service and gradually took on a regular form, it was begun by the reading of the Word of God and prayers. The Christians at first had continued taking part in the Jewish service of prayer and instruction in the temple or synagogue; now this became a part of their own service in their homes. We saw how the gospels came from the narratives, prayers, and hymns used at worship, and the epistles were written to be read at the assembly's worship.

An early Christian writer has left us the first full description of a Christian Mass celebration, about the year 150 at Rome:

". . . And on that day which is called after the sun, all who are in the towns and in the country gather together for a communal celebration. And then the memoirs of the apostles or the writings of the prophets are read, as long as time permits. After the reader has finished his task, the one presiding gives an address, urgently admonishing his hearers to practice these beautiful teachings in their lives. Then all stand up together and recite prayers. After the end of the prayers . . . the bread and wine mixed with water are brought, and the president offers up prayers and thanksgivings, as much as in him lies. The people chime in with an Amen. Then takes place the distribution, to all attending, of the things over which the thanksgiving has been spoken, and the deacons bring a portion to the absent. (He had previously remarked, '. . . this food itself is known amongst us as the eucharist. No one may partake of it unless he is convinced of the truth of our teachings and is cleansed in the bath of baptism. . .'). Besides, those who are well-to-do give whatever they will. What is gathered is deposited with the one presiding, who therewith helps orphans and widows. . . ." (Justin Martyr, *First Apology,* c. 67).

As time passed, other prayers were added, but the pattern of worship was: God's Word, the eucharistic offering of thanks, and the eucharistic meal. In the first several centuries of Christianity, the Mass was at its best: the key actions were central, done in comparative simplicity; everyone stood closely about and had an active part in the ceremonies, which were in the people's language.

Then gradually the Mass became more complicated and distant from the people. By the early Middle Ages, many court ceremonies had become incorporated into Christian worship in an attempt to make it more solemn: genuflections, bowing, kissing, incensing, etc. Then too the Arian heresy which denied the divinity of Christ became widespread; to stress Christ's divine presence, altars gradually were moved away from the people, the priest turned his back on the people and alone said the eucharistic prayers, communion railings went up to separate the sanctuary from the people, at which they knelt to receive the consecrated bread from the priest who alone could touch it, and prayers expressing our unworthiness became common in the Mass. Also, to weld together the various conquered tribes, the Franks had imposed on them the Latin language and liturgy which was less and less understood by the people.

By the high Middle Ages the Mass had become largely separated from the people and the business almost exclusively of the clergy, who often did little more than say "their" Mass which was felt to have an almost automatic value. The great cathedrals of Europe reflect the devotion of the people but also their growing distance from the mysteries of worship. Communion became less and less frequent and was taken more and more under only one form. The sacrifice aspect of the Mass was overstressed. Private devotional practices multiplied, especially those to the saints, and began to partake of superstition; relics were sold and stolen. The clergy in many places became smug and corrupt in their status. The the inevitable happened—the Reformation took place. Luther's first demands included the reform of the clergy and Mass in the vernacular.

The Church reacted at the reform Council of Trent by curbing the abuses that had crept into its worship as well as other aspects of its life. However, in the Church's view the reformers had gone too far in setting aside the separate, hierarchical priesthood and the sacrificial aspect of the Mass. Its Counter-Reformation, though, swung the pendulum too far—it "froze" the ceremonies of the Mass, the use of Latin, the stylized role of the priest and the silent and non-scriptural participation (or non-participation) of the people.

With the beginning of the 20th century, however, a healthy counteraction began: Under Pope Pius X the Church began gradually moving toward restoring the Mass to its early, ideal form. But the progress was sporadic and only among a comparative few. Few had any idea of the great reform that would shortly take place.

The Constitution on the Sacred Liturgy of Vatican Council II was the culmination of the work of those who were trying to make our worship more meaningful. It has been called by many, non-Catholics as well as Catholics, the most revolutionary and far-reaching document of its kind in the Church's history. Some of its main points follow:

Full and active participation by all the people is the aim to be considered before all else. . . . The Christian people, so far as possible, should be able to understand (the texts and rites) with ease and take part in them fully, actively, and as befits a community. . . . The people as well as the priest have different functions, and ". . . the people should be encouraged to take part by means of acclamations, responses, psalmody, antiphons and songs, as well as by actions, gestures, etc."

There is to be more reading from holy scripture and it is to be more varied and suitable. . . . The ministry of preaching is to be fulfilled with exactitude and fidelity. . . .

The rites should be distinguished by a noble simplicity; they should be short, clear, and unencumbered by useless repetitions; they should be within the people's powers of comprehension, and normally should not require much explanation. . . .

The use of the mother tongue . . . frequently may be of great advantage . . . The Church has no wish to impose a rigid uniformity . . . (and) elements from the traditions and cultures of individual peoples might appropriately be admitted into divine worship.

The reforms of the Council have had a good beginning in the Church, but there is much to be done in the years ahead. Much experimenting will have to be done to arrive at ceremonies that will retain the meaningful things of 2,000 years of worship, and yet be meaningful to contemporary man. The American bishops have asked for the broadest possible powers to experiment with different types of Masses. The liturgical authorities at Rome have the final decision about when and what major changes should take place, so as to keep a certain uniformity throughout the changing Church.

The ceremonies and language of the Mass may differ from place to place, according to the Church's different "rites" or liturgies. There are several dozen different rites, most as ancient or more so than the Latin, especially among the churches deriving from the Middle East. But the essential actions of the Mass are the same throughout the worldwide Church. A Latin Rite Catholic would derive a good deal of profit from taking part in an Eastern Rite Mass.

The Mass throughout most of the Church is in the Latin Rite, but the Latin language has been replaced by the vernacular so the people can better take part. Latin was retained over the centuries as a reminder of the antiquity and universal sameness of the Mass; today, however, it is seen that universal unity does not depend on uniformity of language and ceremonies.

The vestments worn by the priest at Mass remind us of the antiquity of the Mass, and also that Christ is present working through the priest. In a sense the vestments "hide" the priest, bringing home to us that he stands at the altar as Christ's instrument. They came originally from the ordinary clothes worn in the early centuries when the Mass began. Today many want to simplify these, particularly when Mass is said in homes, so it will be more meaningful to modern worshippers.

The setting, solemnity, music, etc., of the Mass can vary greatly. In a solemn high Mass, usually celebrated only on special occasions, the priest celebrant is assisted by a deacon and sub-deacon, incense is used (a symbol of our prayers rising, pleasing to God) and there are other marks of special solemnity. Or, to have a special solemnity when only one ordained minister is present certain parts of the Mass may be sung or chanted by him, with the choir and congregation responding (sometimes called a sung Mass).

Today, however, the singing or chanting done by the priest and people can vary a good deal from place to place; it is hard to apply the old labels to our developing liturgy.

> *Mass is sometimes "concelebrated,"* that is, a group of priests may take part with the presiding celebrant, sharing in the prayers and readings and all exercising their power to consecrate. This brings out strikingly the unity of the priesthood, particularly in its great role of celebrating the eucharist.

Today there are often different types of Masses for different groups, with the prayers and readings adapted to the particular group—e.g., school children, teenagers, college students, office workers, those in the inner city, suburbanites, professional people, etc.—besides being adapted to the occasion on which the Mass is celebrated.

One modern development, very meaningful to many, is the folk Mass in which popular folk music is sung in a religious context; for the young, particularly, this type of Mass can be deeply stirring. Also, in some places, during the Liturgy of the Word, slides, films, dancing, and brief dramatic presentations are being used to instruct the people and bring home to them the lessons of God's Word.

A close sense of participation is usually best attained when Mass is celebrated among smaller groups. For this reason, and to make the Mass more available to people, many favor Mass being celebrated regularly in homes, in small halls, etc. So that all could attend one of these smaller celebrations, people might gather on a day other than Sunday and come together periodically on Sunday as the larger parish family.

THE MASS AND CHRISTIAN UNITY

Since the worship of God is the greatest thing we can do on this earth, the way we worship is vitally important. When giving someone a present, we try to find out what will please that person, how we can best express our love by our gift. God in his love helps our worship by showing us how best to do it. As he once guided the Israelites in their worship (cf. Exodus, Leviticus), so now he guides our worship through his Church. Through Christ he gave us the best way we could possibly worship him, the eucharistic service, which developed in the Church as the Mass. This is why many Christians, and especially Catholics, have always been particular about worshipping with other church groups.

However, worship among separated Christians can express the unity we have and also powerfully ask God to unite us further. The Vatican Council here opened new doors: "In certain special circumstances, such as in prayer services for unity and during ecumenical gatherings, it is allowable, indeed desirable that Catholics should join in prayer with their separated brethren" (**Decree on Ecumenism, no. 8**). Nothing is as effective as praying together, to make us experience the unity we have and to make us yearn for further unity.

"There are two main principles upon which the practice of such common worship depends: first, that of the unity of the Church which ought to be expressed; and second, that of the sharing in means of grace. The expression of unity very generally forbids common worship. Grace to be obtained sometimes commends it. The concrete course to be adopted . . . is left to the prudent decision of the local episcopal authority . . . the Bishops' Conference . . . or the Holy See. . . ." (*Decree on Ecumenism, no. 8*).

Intercommunions between Catholics and other Christians is not yet normally allowed, since this has always been considered the fullest expression of Christian unity—and we are as yet disunited on some basic teachings. However, there could be circumstances in which the grace to be gained by such a practice would outweigh any wrong impression of a premature unity, and intercommunion might be allowed; the eucharist could be a means of unity as well as a sign of it. The Catholic Ecumenical Directory of 1970 allows priests to give the eucharist to non-Catholic Christians who request it, in certain "emergency" situations, and also on other special occasions that might be determined by the bishop. Intercommunion among Catholics and Orthodox was allowed by Vatican Council II (if no church of one's own tradition was available) because both have the same Mass and priesthood by apostolic succession; in the U.S., however, this is not yet acceptable to both groups. Being unable to communicate together should make Christians yearn for the day when they can do so in full unity—and make them work all the harder for ecumenical understanding.

In the Catholic view the full sacramental sign of unity and grace comes about only through the instrumentality of a priest, at Mass. Yet when the eucharist is celebrated in another Church there is present in some way the reality of the eucharistic mystery; despite the frequent lack of valid priestly orders which express the unity of the Church, there is yet some real presence of Christ in these "other eucharists." A devout non-Catholic receiving the eucharist in his church might have more of the reality of the eucharist than a lukewarm Catholic. (Cf. *Decree on Ecumenism*, no. 22).

In 1971, the theological dialogues between Roman Catholic and Anglican theologians, and also between Catholic and Lutheran theologians, produced statements saying, in effect, that their churches were in substantial agreement in their teaching on the eucharist, and recommending that steps be taken toward intercommunion between their churches.

Certainly a Christian who truly desires to be united with Christ and his fellow Christians through communion, and who has sorrow for his sins and love in his heart, is really united in love with Christ and the rest of the Church when he takes part in communion in his own particular church. Perhaps, then, one great thing that all Christians can do to bring about unity among themselves is to take part in communion in their own churches whenever they can.

Many today, particularly young people, feel that if they can work together as Christians, they should also, at least on occasion, worship and take part in communion together—and they are simply ignoring the prohibitions against intercommunion. The theological issues that so divided their elders seem to them to be of no immediate importance, while the need to express Christian unity in worship and intercommunion seems to them to be a movement of the Spirit through all the Churches.

Christians today are drawing closer and closer in their forms of worship. Vatican Council II stressed things dear to non-Catholic Christians: Christ's presence among the people at worship, their full participation, the Word of God read and preached upon, an openness to spontaneity and change in worship, etc. Protestant Christians, on the other hand, are stressing more and more things Catholics consider vital, particularly the inclusion of the eucharistic prayer and communion as a regular part of the liturgy, and belief in the presence in some way of Christ's unique sacrifice in the eucharistic act.

Speaking of an interdenominational meeting concerning this, one churchman has said, "Surprisingly, it became apparent that the old battle between the Reformers and the Roman Catholic Church over the eucharist as sacrifice is no more." (Lance Webb, **The Christian Century**, Sept. 1, 1965.)

CHRIST AMONG US AT MASS

When Christ becomes present among us in the eucharist, it is not as if he were coming among his followers for the first time. Christ is already present in the hearts of his people by faith, grace, and love, when they come together to take part in the Mass.

At Mass Christ is among us in several ways. He is in the signs of the eucharist prolonging his sacrifice, and uniting us with himself in his passage to the Father; this great action, we saw, is what the Mass basically is. But Christ is also present in the priest who represents him and who leads the people in worship. He is present speaking to us and opening our hearts through the scripture readings and sermon. And he is present in the communion meal by which he comes to us as food.

Christ is present also in the Christian community as it worships. He is in the midst of his brothers and sisters, the Christian people, worshipping the Father in and through them. He is in each and all, inspiring their love of one another and of the whole human family. "Where two or three are gathered together in my name, there am I in the midst of them" (Matthew 18, 20; cf. Constitution on the Sacred Liturgy, no. 7).

The presence of Christ in these various ways should make us realize why the Mass is so important. Christ loves us so much that he uses all these ways to communicate himself to us, to become united with us, to strengthen us, and to give us his love. "Christ is present from the first word to the last, from one wall of the church to the other" (Fr. Bernard Cooke).

Christ is with us at Mass in all these ways above all to unite us, the Christian community, as one body. He unites us to his sacrifice, presides through the priest, speaks to us in the scriptures, comes to us as food—all in order that we might be truly united in love, that we might become one body with him and with one another. It is at Mass above all that we are united. It is at Mass that we best show our unity. And it is at Mass that we become the presence of Christ in the world.

At Mass we are continually becoming a Church. We saw that the Church is not a static "thing," but the growing, developing way we are united to Christ and one another. It is basically a love relationship, and like any such relationship it must express itself, continually grow and develop. The Mass is the great way the Church grows. Here the Church is continually renewed, cemented, strengthened. Here it worships, grows in love, and receives God's love and teaching.

Were Mass no longer celebrated, the Church would cease to exist. A good gauge of the spiritual health of the Church is the participation of the people in the Mass. Historically, those who have attacked the Church have almost always begun by prohibiting the Mass. "It's the Mass that matters" is an old adage that sums up its place in the Church.

THE CHRISTIAN PEOPLE AT MASS

In the liturgy we pray and sing together because, though many, we are one—and we want to become one. The liturgy should bring about a great awareness of one another—that we need one another and are helped by one another, in worship as in life. We are joined together as we offer our common gift and receive God's gift to us. We join our incompleteness to that of others, and together, as a worshipping family, we most perfectly express our stumbling attempts at union with divinity.

The Mass, then, is not only the best sign of our unity—it also is the great cause of our unity, particularly when we partake together of our great family meal, the "Lord's Supper" (1 Corinthians 10, 17). During the week we are scattered in our homes, factories, schools, and offices. At Mass we come together for the great banquet that makes us one. The more closely we take part in it the more we will appreciate and love our fellow Christians. Christ is here among us in the closest possible way, joining us with himself and one another.

The Mass is our great weekly Christian social event, the family worship of God's people gathered together with Christ. The priest who leads the people never prays in his own name or for himself alone, and the congregation's prayers also are for one another: "The Lord be with you . . . Let us pray . . . Let us give thanks to God. . . ." The frequent "Amen" of the whole congregation perfectly expresses their unity in love and offering.

Particularly at Mass God's new chosen people use the power of their "royal priesthood." By their baptism, and again by confirmation, they share in the priesthood of the laity, able to offer perfect worship to God for themselves and others and to bring his graces to the world. They do not claim to be holier than others, but they know Christ is in their midst, using them in a special way, poor instruments though they may be, to spread his love to others. What was said of the Israelites in the Old Testament is now said in the fullest sense of the Christians of the New Testament: **Read 1 Peter 2, 4-10.**

The Mass is meant to bring out the true unity in catholicity of the Church. All races, classes, and social strata should be one in this worship. When we gather together for Mass we should heed St. James' reminder to the first Christians: **Read James 2, 1-4.**

Since the Mass is a family worshipping and eating together, each member has a part to play. Christ is among us, invisibly present as our real head and leader. The bishop is his visible representative who guides our worship so that it is truly a part of the liturgy of the whole Church. The ordained priest is Christ's representative and instrument, and also the leader of the people at this particular Mass; through his Word Christ becomes present in the eucharist, and then he leads us all in offering Christ and ourselves to the Father.

The people's part is to respond to God's Word, to unite themselves to the offering of Christ and to join in the banquet of holy communion. They express their part by praying and singing together, by contributing in some way to the offering, by responding to the great prayers of offering, and above all by taking part together in the eucharist.

> "The Church . . . earnestly desires that Christ's faithful, when present at this mystery of faith, should not be there as strangers or silent spectators; on the contrary, through a good understanding of the rites and prayers they should take part in the sacred action, conscious of what they are doing, with devotion and full collaboration. They should be instructed by God's Word and be nourished at the table of the Lord's body; they should give thanks to God; by offering the immaculate victim, not only through the hands of the priest, but also with him, they should learn also to offer themselves; through Christ the Mediator, they should be drawn day by day into ever more perfect union with God and with each other. . . ." (*Constitution on the Sacred Liturgy,* no. 48).

Some of the people have special roles, proclaiming the scripture readings, or other readings, assisting the priest, commentating, leading the singing, bringing up the offerings, etc.

> *It takes time to appreciate the liturgy fully, to feel at ease in community worship and to participate actively.* The Mass prayers will be led by priests at varying speeds; the Mass becomes so much a part of a priest that it reflects his temperament and background. Some congregations respond with more uniformity and seeming devotion than others. Distractions occur constantly. To adjust to the great reality behind all this takes time and patience.
>
> We should remember, too, that while the Mass is a social event, at times we will want to—and should—pray in our own way during it, to express our most personal feelings toward God, our deep longings, our particular needs, our secret fears and joys. There are normally periods of silence in the Mass to allow this.

Catholics are expected to assemble for Mass each Sunday, and also on the holydays scattered throughout the year. Only a Catholic with a poor understanding of the meaning of the Mass would take this responsibility lightly. Of course, important work, sickness in the family, etc. excuse us from taking part, though perhaps one could join in the Mass prayers at home, or take part on another day. In most places the Sunday or holyday Mass may now be anticipated on the previous evening to make it more meaningful for those taking part.

The holydays in the United States are six: Christmas (Dec. 25), the Octave of Christmas (New Year's Day, Jan. 1st), Ascension Thursday (40th day after Easter), the Assumption of Mary (Aug. 15th), All Saints (Nov. 1st), and the Immaculate Conception of Mary (Dec. 8th).

We can offer our Mass for anyone, living or dead or for any good intention. Naturally we derive from the Mass what we bring to it. The more faith and love in our worship, the more it will unite us with God and help others. The prayers of the liturgy are not just external ceremonies but actions into which we must enter with our minds and hearts. Two people might attend Mass, one getting a great deal from it, and the other almost nothing.

Even if it is impossible for us to attend Mass daily we should unite ourselves by our sincere intention with Christ's offering in all the Masses of that day throughout the world. During the day, working, suffering, struggling to be good, we can offer ourselves with Christ for the salvation of others, uniting ourselves to his continuing sacrifice.

The priest usually offers each Mass for some particular person or intention, and people sometimes ask a priest to offer Mass for their intention. It has been customary for the person requesting this to make an offering of money (a "stipend") to the priest—not to pay for the Mass, but to help support the priest and the church. This custom comes from the early Church when the people brought to the Mass the things necessary for the sacrifice, for the support of the priests, the poor, etc. St. Paul wrote, ". . . the Lord directed that those who preach the gospel should have their living from the gospel" (1 Corinthians 9, 13-14).

Every Mass, however, is an offering to the whole Church, and the whole Church and each member benefits from each Mass. To better emphasize this, and for other practical reasons, many today want to abolish the practice of Mass stipends, and to provide for the support of priests by a larger regular salary.

The eucharist and the Mass, then, are the center of the Catholic faith. The other sacraments converge on this. Baptism and confirmation lead up to it; penance and the anointing of the sick prepare one for it; holy orders is given at Mass, and a Catholic couple offers the nuptial Mass when united in marriage. After

death one's body is brought to the church for a requiem Mass.
Nothing else has meaning or power except in relation to the
eucharist and the Mass. This was brought out at Vatican Council
II when each day's session began with a Mass in which all the
assembled bishops took part.

Each day Mass is celebrated in every Catholic parish. It can be
a source of daily grace to that whole neighborhood. The Mass is
the center of the priest's day, from which he draws strength for
his other activities. Many Catholics take part in Mass on weekdays, and some come daily to draw help from it for their daily
lives.

RELIVING CHRIST'S LIFE THROUGH THE LITURGICAL YEAR

Since Christ's life and sacrifice is such a tremendous, infinite
reality, we cannot grasp it all at once. It takes time to grasp and
be changed by it. The Church in the liturgy presents Christ's life
and sacrifice in parts, so that we can live them out event by
event.

The liturgical year is the way we relive each year the great
events of Christ's life. It is the way the Church each year teaches
us in a living way about these events. It is the Church's yearly
cycle of feasts, beginning with the first Sunday of Advent (the
4th Sunday before Christmas) and ending with the last Sunday
after Pentecost.

Each Mass has an ordinary or unchanging part, and a proper or
changing part which varies according to the liturgical year. Some
of the proper or changing prayers may be said or chanted together by the people: the entrance antiphon, the gradual (or
tract or alleluia), the offertory antiphon, and the communion
antiphon. The lay lector reads the epistle for that day, and the
priest or deacon the gospel. The priest reads the collect, the
prayer over the gifts, and the prayer after communion.

Through the events of the liturgical year we actually relive,
with Christ, the events of his life, death and resurrection. People
attend a movie or a play or watch a TV presentation that reenacts the events in the life of a great person. Through the liturgical year we reenact the events of Christ's life—but unlike a
movie, Christ is actually present in each Mass, and we not only

watch, we actually take part in the great events of his life. He is present in a special way at each feast, communicating something special to us each time.

> The liturgical year . . . is not a cold and lifeless representation of the events of the past, or a simple and bare record of a former age. It is rather Christ himself who is ever living in his Church. Here he continues that journey of immense mercy which he lovingly began in his mortal life, going about doing good with the desire of bringing men to know his mysteries and . . . live by them. (Pope Pius XII, *Mediator Dei*).

Through the liturgical year the Church systematically brings forth before us God's Word, the bible. The most significant passages are selected and arranged to best bring home to us the great events of our salvation. An expanded selection of scripture readings, replacing the present one-year-cycle, is being developed to bring more of the bible into our worship.

The liturgical year is built around the two great feasts of Christmas and Easter. Each of these has a period of preparation, the central feast itself with two minor feasts, and a continuation or prolongation of the spirit of the feast:

I. THE CHRISTMAS SEASON—Theme: The Coming of Christ —the Incarnation

Preparation in Advent—Four Sundays before Christmas—(violet vestments). Through prayer and self-discipline we repent of our sins and prepare for the coming of Christ.

Celebration—Christmas, December 25th, and its two lesser feasts, the Octave on January 1st, and the Epiphany on January 6th— (white vestments). We rejoice that God has come among us and that we have been born with him into the new life of grace.

Continuation—the Sundays after Epiphany—(green vestments). As the Gentiles were called to Christianity, so we are thankful for our faith and seek deeper faith. This season ends with the last Sunday after the Epiphany.

II. THE EASTER SEASON—Theme: Christ's Death and New Life—Our Salvation

Preparation from Ash Wednesday and on through Lent—(violet vestments). Through this time of prayer, fasting, and voluntary self-discipline, we make up for our sins which caused Christ's sufferings.

During Holy Week, the last week of Lent, we reenact in the liturgy the sufferings and death of Christ, taking part in them, whereby we can bear our sufferings and repent because of our sins which made Christ suffer so greatly.

Celebration of the Triumphal Resurrection of Christ at Easter— the greatest feast of the Church, and the basis of our faith—the two lesser feasts following upon this are the Ascension (40 days after Easter) and Pentecost Sunday (50 days after)—(white vestments, except for the red of Pentecost). Through the Sundays after Easter we rejoice at Christ's new life and the triumph of our faith; we try to rise with him from a life dead in sin to one of new fervor and holiness.

*Continuation—the Sundays after Pentecost—*24 to 28 weeks, through summer and fall, ending with the last Sunday after Pentecost—(green vestments). We ask to grow in the love and practice of our faith, guided by the Holy Spirit, imitating Christ and looking forward to his second coming.

There is also the Proper of the Saints, the liturgical cycle of lesser importance; on most dates throughout the year the Church celebrates the feast of some saint, one of God's heroes. Often, the date is the day of the saint's death, his "birthday" into eternal life. The Proper of the Mass changes on that day, according to the particular saint; a "Common" is a Proper for a particular type of saint and may be used for a number of similar saints. By bringing before our minds these different saints, the Church wants to teach us that we can imitate Christ's suffering and glorification as they did.

There are ranks of feasts in the Church's liturgy, the most important taking precedence. Sometimes a lesser feast is commemorated by adding some of its prayers to the Proper used that day. Any missal gives the rank of feasts, and includes a calendar telling what Proper is to be used on a particular day. The Proper of the Saints is also in the process of simplification today.

The Divine Office is the daily prayer of the Church by which she prepares for and prolongs the spirit of the Mass. As Christ prayed before and during his death, so does the Church. The office is composed mainly of the psalms, and other parts of scripture, and outstanding writings from the Church's tradition. It is arranged according to the Church year, and is divided into various "hours" to prepare for and prolong the worship of the Mass. It is recited particularly by priests, and is chanted in choir by monks and other religious.

CHRIST AMONG US IN THE EUCHARIST

Christ's presence among us in the eucharist has always been a key teaching of the Christian faith. It has been the constant teaching of the Church from the beginning; the clear belief found in early Christian documents is overwhelming. (Cf., for instance, Palmer, **The Sources of Christian Theology,** Newman, 1955, Vol. 1). Through bread and wine Christ becomes present in the eucharistic celebration; somehow Christ himself is now truly present under this form of food as St. Paul says succinctly: **Read 1 Corinthians 11, 27-30.**

Theologians today stress a dynamic or existentialist view of Christ's presence in the eucharist, that he is present with a purpose. He is not just a passive presence in the host, but rather he is present doing something to the Christian communicant, meeting him person-to-person, bringing him life and love. And only one who meets Christ in the eucharist with faith and love derives something from this.

There can be degrees of one person's presence to another: one might vaguely notice a person across the street, or he might pass close to him, he might have a deep conversation with him, etc.— the more each gives of himself, the greater is his communication of himself to another in understanding and love. In the eucharist Christ comes to us in the fullest possible expression and communication of his love. The more we try to be aware of him and what he is doing for us, the more we try to give ourselves to him as we meet him in communion, the more intimate will be our union with him, the greater will be the love and grace we will receive, and the more we will be transformed into him by this experience.

Another way of looking at this is to see the eucharistic meal as a sign through which we meet Christ and by which he expresses or "signifies" his love for us. A man might best express himself and his feelings by playing a violin for us; we would more fully "meet" him by listening to him play than by merely having him present. As the violin is an extension of the violinist, so the consecrated bread and wine are an extension of Christ through which we meet him most fully and are changed by him. Sharing

in food expresses refreshment, strength, and a sharing in love—
so Christ expresses these things to us, in an infinitely greater way,
through the eucharistic food. Through this food Christ expresses
himself and his love for us in the most intimate way possible. The
more we try to express our love as we take part in communion,
the greater our love will grow through it.

**We need not confess before taking part in holy communion
unless we are sure we are in the state of alienation from God
and the community by serious sin.** To take part in communion
knowingly before confessing one's alienated state of serious sin
would be a grievous act of hypocrisy; one would be publicly proclaiming his unity with the rest of the Church by taking part in
the eucharist, but all the while he would be interiorly cut off from
them. The purpose of confession is to reconcile such a one to the
Church.

It might happen, however, that one conscious of being in a state
of serious alienation would find it necessary to take part in communion—it might, for instance, be quite embarrassing not to—
and he could not go to confession; in this case he should express
his sorrow as best he can out of love, and then take part in communion. Christ's desire would surely be for him to take part.

> *Confession should be available to a child before first communion,*
> according to a Vatican decree of June, 1973. Certainly there is no
> obligation for a child to confess unless he is in serious sin, any more
> than there is for an adult; and many skilled in child psychology ques-
> tion the ability of a young child to sin seriously. Young children
> might be introduced to this sacrament, and express their sorrow for
> their sins, through communal penitential rites, as is being done in
> many places.

**We fast before taking part in holy communion, to help us
prepare for it.** We normally do not eat or drink for one hour
before communion (water or medicine, however, may be taken at
any time). Just as one would not spoil his appetite by eating before
a special meal, so we sharpen our spiritual appetite for Christ by
this bit of self-discipline.

**Catholics of the Latin rite usually take communion only under
the appearance of bread.** This became customary in the late Middle Ages when the meal aspect of the Mass was being largely
overlooked. It is usually more convenient to take part in communion under one form, especially where large city congregations

are involved; the whole living Christ is present either under the appearance of bread or that of wine, so it is only necessary to take part in one form.

However, taking part under both forms brings out more fully our sharing in the eucharistic meal as Christ instituted it, and Vatican Council II has once again revived this for special occasions in the Latin rite; the Eastern rites of Catholicism have always communicated under both forms.

On certain occasions, then, Latin rite Catholics take part in communion under both forms. This brings out more fully our sharing in the eucharistic meal as Christ instituted it. The Eastern rites of Catholicism, incidentally, have always done this. Also, a sick person, for instance, might now receive the eucharist under the appearance of wine alone, if unable to do so under the form of bread.

In some areas of the Church the custom is growing today of taking communion in one's hand. Although not yet officially approved for all parts of the Church, this practice is a return to the way in which communion was received throughout most of the Church's history. For many this practice is a visible, reverent expression of their need to feed themselves on the body of Christ.

A Catholic's "Easter duty" means that he must take part in communion once a year, during the Easter season, *i.e.*, from the first Sunday of Lent until Trinity Sunday. Otherwise, while still a Catholic he would not be considered a practicing one, because he has refused to take part in the greatest thing the Church has for him—the help toward which all the other helps of his religion are directed. Christ said: "Truly, truly, I say to you, unless you eat the flesh of the Son of man and drink his blood, you have no life in you . . ." (John 6, 53).

A good Catholic should take part in communion at least weekly— normally at Sunday Mass, our great Christian family meal. Unfortunately some, from faulty training or timidity, hold back from the eucharist when they could easily take part. They realize they are unworthy, but they should remember what Christ said: "Those who are well have no need of a physician, but those who are sick" (Luke 5, 31). Not to take part in communion is to expect God to accept our gift while refusing his gift.

What Christ does for us in holy communion is shown by this sacrament's sign: he comes to us in the form of a meal, of food. As we must eat to maintain life, to grow and remain strong, so this food is the great means of growing in the life of grace. A preview of this food was the manna by which God kept the Israelites alive in the desert; Christ refers to this and then tells us that he himself will be the food which sustains the infinitely greater and eternal life of grace. Read Exodus 16, 4-21.

Read John 6, 47-59. Christ in the eucharist, then, is our "living bread," our greatest way of growing in God's grace-presence, his life within us. As a good meal can have an immediate effect of contentment and satisfaction, so we may sometimes experience a certain spiritual peace and strength after taking part in communion. As food builds energy and strength for the future, so Christ here strengthens us for further temptations. As we are sometimes hungrier, perhaps from hard work, than at other times, so we sometimes need more spiritual strength and should receive Christ more often.

Food must be taken frequently; so our spiritual growth requires frequent reception of the eucharist. Paradoxically this food satisfies, but also increases our hunger: the more we receive Christ, the more we inevitably hunger for God.

Our eucharistic meal is above all our greatest way of being united to one another in the Church. The more we eat together with our family and friends, the more we get to know and understand one another, the stronger our love should grow. So too with this meal. Its greatest effect is the unity of Christ's body, his Church.

By frequently taking part in the eucharist we are gradually transformed into Christ. We share the very life and personality of the risen Christ. We gradually shed our weaknesses and assume something of his own strength. His outlook, his reactions bit by bit become ours. Because we have here a real contact with Christ's risen body, this sacrament is the most effective way of keeping our bodily passions under control; many Christians can testify that it is for them the best way of remedying abuses of sex, drinking, anger, etc.

The more of ourselves we put into celebrating the Mass and partaking of the eucharist, the more we will derive from it. Christ is present in the priest and in the people, as we read and listen, preach and sing, and as we offer the great eucharistic prayer of thanks. The better we try to do these things, the more consciously we join ourselves to him, the more we will receive from our union with him in holy communion. The eucharist can be the most intimate, personal, and meaningful union with Christ possible—if we prepare for it and generously give ourselves to him. He gives us himself totally. The rest is up to us.

The eucharist is the greatest way to grow in the Christian life. Each time we take part in the eucharist we repledge ourselves to our baptismal commitment to Christ. The eucharist is the greatest way we grow in faith, hope, and love, the greatest source of light and strength for our prayer, and the surest way to grow in appreciation of the world around us.

Through the eucharist we are already beginning the life of heaven. We are on our way to the final resurrection and our eternal glorification with the Father. Heaven is often referred to in scripture as a banquet, a wedding feast. Now, through this food that is Christ, we are already beginning to take part in it.

Christ's presence in the eucharist in the tabernacle of every Catholic church is a way in which God today dwells among his people with special closeness. This is why our churches are open daily, why people often drop in for a "visit" to share their joys and sorrows with Christ, or just to talk things over. We saw how God was present among the Israelites, invisibly hovering over the Ark of the Covenant in his tabernacle. Today we have God become man in our midst. "And my tabernacle shall be with them and I will be their God, and they shall be my people" (Ezechiel 37, 27).

Because of this presence of Christ, upon entering their churches Catholics sometimes genuflect (go down on the right knee) as an act of adoration before entering the pew. In some places, a bow of the head is made to the tabernacle. Also, the candle kept burning day and night near the altar, usually in a red glass container, signifies this eucharistic presence of Christ in our midst.

We honor Christ in the holy eucharist in many ways: on Holy Thursday each year we celebrate with special liturgical services the great feast of Christ's institution of the holy eucharist at the last supper. On the Sunday after Trinity Sunday we celebrate the feast of Corpus Christi (the body of Christ).

The "Forty Hours Devotion" is a special service of honor and reparation to Christ in the eucharist, held in many Catholic parishes each year; by special Masses, processions, prayers, and preaching we pay him homage. This devotion commemorates the forty hours during which Christ's body was in the tomb before Easter Sunday. During this time, the host is exposed in the monstrance on the altar.

The service of Benediction ("Blessing") consists of putting a large host in a gold monstrance; it is then put on the altar for all to adore, hymns of praise are sung, and the host is incensed; then the priest blesses the people by making the sign of the cross over them with the monstrance containing the host.

The vigil lights or votive candles which one sometimes sees in churches are there to "keep watch" with Christ in place of the people who must be elsewhere. They represent our desire to be with him.

DAILY LIVING: ONE BREAD MAKES US ONE BODY
(1 Corinthians 10, 17)

On the occasion of the first eucharist Christ said, "By this shall all men know that you are my disciples, if you have love for one another." The great thing we should get from the eucharist is a greater love—not only of God but of our neighbor. We prepare best for Mass by attempting to practice some kindness or forgiveness in our daily life—and we best prolong the Mass in our daily life by this same concrete love.

Sincerely and actively taking part in the Mass should make us dynamic, socially-minded Christians. If we are sharing in the Mass as we should, we will become aware of how we are joined with God's family throughout the world. Those who cry for social justice, who are deprived of racial equality, the underprivileged of our city, the poor of other nations, the billions who will never hear of Christ and his love—these needs become ours.

People sometimes remark on Christians who worship on Sunday, but live unchristian lives the rest of the week. All too often this is so. Sometimes it is the result of a wrong emphasis in one's religious upbringing, a stressing of external obligations to the neglect of their inner spirit. However, we should remember Christ's warning not to judge, "that you be not judged." Sometimes seemingly immoral people are struggling against tremendous odds of background, deprivation, strong passions—and at least they manage to worship God and reach out for his help. They might be much worse without Mass.

Also, some cheat themselves of much of Christ's help by not taking part in communion when they attend Mass. They realize their unworthiness, but forget Christ's loving mercy and his desire to come and be their strength. Then, too, those who do communicate regularly may show no striking improvement in their lives, but might be undergoing a gradual, almost imperceptible growth in holiness.

The way many people come to desire union with Christ's Church is by taking part in the Mass. The disciples at Emmaus recognized Christ only in the "breaking of the bread"; they then realized why their hearts were burning within them. So too, many today come to recognize Christ in his Church, and want to be an active part of it, by regularly taking part in the Mass.

SOME SUGGESTIONS FOR . . .
DISCUSSION

Can you understand how the Mass developed and why changes are taking place today?

Can you understand how the Mass and the eucharist are the center of our Catholic faith, and our great way of having Christ among us?

How might one deepen his appreciation of the Mass, and bring from it more love into his daily life?

FURTHER READING

** *Eucharistic Theology,* Powers (Herder, 1967)—A detailed biblical and historical treatment of the theology of the Eucharist.

* *Christ Present and Yet to Come,* Champlin (Orbis Books, 1971)—Some practical suggestions for priest and people as to how parish liturgy can be more meaningful.

* *Children and God: Communion, Confession and Confirmation,* Buckley (Dimension Books)—An excellent book on the preparation of children for first communion, confession and confirmation.

* *New St. Joseph Weekday Missal* (for 1974, etc.) (Catholic Book Publishing Co.)—A complete daily missal, issued new each year, of all the Mass prayers and readings for each day; handy and inexpensive.

FURTHER VIEWING

The Eucharist (Franciscan Productions, Santee Street, Los Angeles, Calif.)—10 minutes, in color—An excellent documentary treatment of the Mass and its relationship to the modern world.

PERSONAL REFLECTION

A "communion of desire" (less appropriately called a "spiritual communion") can be made by one who cannot take part sacramentally in the eucharistic meal. One does this simply by telling Christ that he believes in his presence in the eucharist, is sorry for his sins, and desires to be united with him. This can deepen one's intimate union with Christ and one's neighbor.

If I cannot be united with Christ sacramentally, I might resolve to do so by desire at Mass this Sunday.

I might also drop into some Catholic church during the week to make a "visit" with Christ in his eucharistic presence—perhaps just sitting there quietly, thinking, and talking things over with him.

18
Sin and What It Can Do to Us

SIN IN OUR LIFE

What is sin? How does it affect us? Why do we sin? How can we overcome our sins? Everyone at one time or another asks himself these things. To understand sin we must try to appreciate God's love which it rejects.

Read Luke 19, 41-44. The gospel picture of Christ weeping over Jerusalem is striking. He loved this city and its people, but he foresaw that because of their rejection of his warnings the city would be utterly destroyed. It was in 70 A.D. with the slaughter of a million people. Here is strikingly shown the effect of sin, of rejecting God's love.

We are the most fortunate beings in creation, for we are loved by the infinite God. He has given us life, an eternal destiny with him, and has himself come to save us. By baptism, we become his specially adopted children. In return, we should constantly desire to please him, to respond to his love. Yet often we do not. We sin against him.

Sin is a rejection of God's love, a refusal of an opportunity to accept his love and pass it on to others. All day long he gives us opportunities to respond to his love by our love—sin is a knowing neglect of these. It is as if God says, "Here is an opportunity to spread love in the world, to grow yourself in love and happiness" —and we refuse, we reject his loving guidance. Ultimately sin is a personal rebuff to our loving Father, to Christ our Brother and Savior, to the Spirit who is love within us. Incredibly, the infinite God is concerned with our rejection of his love. Christ tells us, also, ". . . as you did it to one of these, the least of my brethren, you did it to me" (Matthew 25, 40).

Despite continued attempts to explain away the notion of sin,

people today feel guilty about their moral failings. A poll of
modern American adults revealed that they worry about personal
failings, e.g., not going to church regularly, overeating, incon-
siderateness, wasting time, not being active in the community,
not contributing to charity, etc. The pollsters concluded that
"worries about such personal failings beset some of the population almost all of the time, and all of the population some of
the time" (Newsweek, June 21, 1965).

But people are often fearful of facing their sins, of honestly
acknowledging their sinfulness. Christ longs to help them if only
they would humbly turn to him. His entire life and teaching
divides people into two classes: those who admit they are sinners
—and these he goes out of his way to forgive, again and again—
and those who refuse to acknowledge their sins—and these he
castigates, "Woe to you, Scribes and Pharisees, hypocrites. . . ."

Sin is immaturity, destroys our personality, leads to ultimate
frustration. By sinning, we yield to selfish, primitive urges. We
refuse to recognize our personal relationship with God, our dependence on him, and we form an unreal concept of ourselves,
making ourselves and our desires the supreme guide for our actions. Ironically, when we reject the demands of God's love, we
spurn the one thing that can perfect our own personality and
fulfill our aspirations.

Sin, then, is a failure to fulfill ourselves, to grow, to develop, to
realize our potential. We fail to fulfill our capacity for good, for
love, for lasting self-achievement in this particular situation. We
miss a chance to achieve what we could. Read Genesis 3, 1-5.

Pride is at the root of all sin—and pride, if unchecked, is the
one thing that might cut us off from God forever. As Lucifer had
said, "I will ascend above the height of the clouds, I will be like
the Most High," so in the story of the first human sin the devil
promised Adam and Eve, "You shall be like God. . . ." Pride
rejects the love that would bring us out of our egotistical little
world, into union with God and his other children.

We should remember, incidentally, that a thought or desire
can be sinful, as well as neglecting to do something we should.
Christ says of lustful thoughts: ". . . whoever looks with lust at a
woman has already committed adultery with her in his heart"
(Matthew 5, 28). Sinful, too, would be a desire to harm someone,

have revenge on him, bearing a grudge, etc. Many people sin by neglecting to do what they should—parents, for example, who neglect to guide their children, those who have no concern for the poor, who deliberately refuse to worship the God they know they should.

One who continually and deliberately indulges in the same sin finds it harder and harder to stop, and gradually becomes the slave of sin. Bit by bit he can blind himself to God's truth and deafen himself to the promptings of grace. His sin becomes a habit, a vice. Scripture says of such: "For what the true proverb says has happened to them—a dog returns to his vomit, and a sow even after washing wallows in the filth" (2 Peter 2, 22).

JUDGING THE SERIOUSNESS OF SIN

Read Matthew 26, 20-24. Some sins are obviously worse than others. We recognize the terrible malice of Judas' betrayal of Christ. So, too, hatred of another is worse than an impatient word and embezzling millions is more serious than stealing a few dollars. Some sins more deeply reject God.

As in human love, there are slight offenses—a boy might be carelessly late in picking up his fiancée. Or the offense can be a more serious rejection of her love—he might begin dating another girl. Ultimately, the love relationship might be destroyed altogether.

Facing the fact of man's weakness and sinfulness, and the human tendency to become discouraged at keeping the moral law, there developed over the centuries in Catholic theology the legally-based notions of mortal and venial sin. Inadequate as is this categorizing of sin, these notions still can provide us with a basis for making realistic judgments about our moral faults.

A mortal sin is a fundamental rejection of God's love. By it we drive his grace-presence from us. "Mortal" means "death-dealing" —this sin kills God's life and love within us. "Then desire when it has conceived gives birth to sin; and sin when it is full-grown brings forth death. . . . All wrongdoing is sin, but there is sin which is not mortal" (James 1, 15; 1 John 5, 16).

To sin mortally, our offense must be seriously wrong, we must fully realize it is seriously wrong, and we must fully want to choose our way over God's. In sinning mortally one makes a basic choice of his own way over God's, and is willing to repudiate his friendship with God over this choice. He thus wants this thing or person more than God. Such a choice must engage one's whole person to the depths of his being.

Not all serious wrongs are mortal sins. Many people do seriously wrong things without fully realizing they are such, e.g., the millions who have little or no knowledge of Christ's moral teachings, the many nominal Catholics who do not sufficiently know their religion, or some converts before studying Catholicism. Some do seriously wrong things, but do not fully want to do them; people often act under pressing mental strain, or from deeply-rooted bad habits. Most would rarely, if ever, make a fundamental and lasting choice of their way over God's.

Mortal sin, then, is a fundamental choice of ourself over God that engages us to the depths of our being. Rather than thinking of mortal sin as a particular action, we should see it as a fundamental option, an attitude, a state of living, contrary to God, that we knowingly and deliberately choose.

> Some might conclude that it is impossible to choose to live in mortal sin, to fully and deliberately reject God's will for us—so that even serious sins need not be taken too seriously. But mortal sin is an attitude of rejecting God that is built up by continual sinning. Each sinful act turns us further from God, hardens us in our basic attitude which is becoming one of rejection. So each must be taken seriously. One might become so hardened, bit by bit, that he does recognize the point of ultimate rejection.

Mortal sin is the one real evil of our universe. A person in mortal sin cuts himself off from God's love, rejects Christ, is a detriment to his fellow man and a source of disruption in the universe. While in this state, he is rejecting love, and rendering useless for himself Christ's sufferings and death. He paralyzes the power of his own acts of love, his prayers, good works, acts of worship, sacraments, etc. God's love—actual graces—still surround him, but he is a lonely, self-centered, spiritually starving individual.

The vast majority of sins are less serious rejections of God's

love, called venial ("easily forgiven") sins. The offense is not serious, or the person does not fully know or fully want to do a serious wrong. A venial sin weakens our love for God and our neighbor. It is like a spiritual sickness or wound which hurts but does not kill or lessen God's grace-presence within us. A venial sin can be lesser or greater, as a sickness can, according as we realize its evil more clearly or consent more willingly.

Even our less serious sins should not be taken lightly. Deliberate, continual venial sin, like a virus, can leave us prey to the deadly infection of mortal sin. People who try only to avoid mortal sin and are unconcerned about venial sins have a relationship with God like that of a married couple who, though living together, argue ceaselessly. Their love is weak and stunted.

Each person must follow his own conscience in judging whether an action is sinful, and how serious it might be. One's personality, moral awareness, and other circumstances surrounding our sinful acts have a bearing on their seriousness. One's conscience usually considers these things. Our conscience, however, is influenced by many things—environment, passion, lack of knowledge etc.—so that we obviously need guidance in forming a true conscience about sin.

Christ through his Church helps us form a true conscience, to best express our love and arrive at heaven. Like anyone in love, we want to know how best to express our love, and how to avoid anything that might disrupt our love. We can look at the Church's moral teachings like a roadmap and set of directions given us for an auto trip; they may seem negative, restrictive, warning us to avoid certain things—but only to bring us and our fellow travelers more easily and safely to our destination.

Christ's Church points out some actions that are considered seriously wrong. Long study by the teachers of the Church, reflecting on Christ's teaching given in the scriptures, shows that these things normally are serious rejections of God's love:

Deliberately refusing to worship the God one believes in; blasphemy; hating or seriously injuring the reputation of another; refusing to help someone in serious need; adultery, or sexual intercourse outside of a marriage commitment; scandal, stealing, lying, drunkenness, racial or religious discrimination or segrega-

tion when these do serious harm; lustful or hateful thoughts that
are deliberately prolonged and fully wanted; seriously neglecting
one's duties to family, job, country, the underprivileged, etc.

If a person should do one of these things while fully realizing its
serious wrong, and fully wanting to choose his own way over
God's, to reject God in doing it, he would commit a mortal sin,
cutting himself off from God's grace-presence.

**One judging himself to be in mortal sin must confess his sin
and be reconciled to Christ and the Church before he can take
part in the eucharist.** It would be a living lie—a sacrilege—to proclaim our union with Christ and our brethren by taking part in
communion, if all the while we were cut off from them by an un-
confessed mortal sin. The purpose of confession is to reconcile us
to the Church.

**God will forgive any sin again and again—even the most
serious—as long as we are truly sorry.** ". . . if your sins be as
scarlet, they shall be made white as snow; and if they be red as
crimson, they shall be white as wool" (Isaiah 1, 18). We shall see
that Christ has given us the sacrament of penance within his
Church, by which he forgives our sins.

> *Concerning the guilt of one's sinful actions,* sometimes uncon-
> scious or semi-conscious emotional drives carry people toward
> sin, inhibiting free will and reducing responsibility. Many com-
> pulsively reach out for what they can get here and now. Though
> their action is objectively sinful, they may have little or no guilt
> in God's eyes. St. Paul experienced this: "I do not understand my
> own actions. For I do not do what I want, but I do the very thing
> I hate... So then it is no longer I that do it, but sin which dwells
> within me... I can will what is right but I cannot do it. For I do
> not do the good I want, but the evil I do not want is what I do"
> (Romans 8, 15-19).
>
> *Some people have an overdeveloped sense of sin. They are
> scrupulous—judging things to be sins that are not, exaggerating
> their guilt,* constantly fearful of offending God, hounded by guilt
> feelings. They have an emotional problem, in need of counseling
> and often professional treatment. From childhood they have
> never been loved properly, so they find it hard to believe in God's
> love and mercy. Usually they can grasp the fact of God's love
> only through others who accept and love them.
>
> *Many people today, however, have an underdeveloped sense
> of sin: they do not consider things to be sinful that actually are.*

Some may not be subjectively guilty before God, but they injure their fellow man and hinder the spread of God's love in the world. Some are guilty of insincerely preferring to remain in ignorance, rather than trying to find God's will. The saints who loved God most perfectly had a most profound awareness of their sinfulness.

THE CONCEPT OF HELL

"If thy hand is an occasion of sin to thee, cut it off! . . . And if the eye is an occasion of sin to thee, pluck it out! It is better for thee to enter the kingdom of God with one eye, than, having two eyes, to be cast into hellfire"—these harsh words of the usually gentle Christ emphasize the Church's teaching on hell: **Read Mark 9, 42-47.**

Hell, in Christian tradition, is the eternal state or situation of those who die totally turned away from God, in which they continue to reject him forever, in unimaginable pain, deprived of all happiness. The concept of an eternal, personal punishment after death took many centuries to develop. Israel had no clear notion of this. It came when men were ready and might better appreciate what totally rejecting his love could mean. Christ spoke of it in the primitive imagery of his time, for instance, as a place "where the worm dies not" and "the fire is not quenched" (Cf. Matthew 13, 36ff; Matthew 25, 41ff; 2 Thessalonians 1, 7-9; Revelation 14, 11). Reflecting on Christ's words, and spurred by an early novel opinion (of Origen) that hell was not eternal, the early Christian Church came to teach its eternity.

Reflecting on the concept of hell, its greatest suffering is the realization that one has forever cut himself off from God for whom he longs with his whole being. Christ most often speaks of hell, not in terms of bodily torment but as rejection, eternal isolation: "Then he will say to those on his left hand, 'Depart from me, accursed ones, into the everlasting fire which was prepared for the devil and his angels' " (Matthew 25, 41). The damned soul reaches out for God with his whole being and at the same time must reject God, for he has chosen himself over God.

One might now glimpse hell, in a sense, if he deliberately cuts himself off from God by continually living in a state of serious sin, clinging to some sinful situation while realizing fully that he is choosing it over God. Then, if God had been at all real in his life, he is not able to talk with him any longer. Prayer becomes an impossible situation. He wants God, loves him, but can't reach him—and the torment of this state can be the beginning of hell.

One in hell is seen as eternally alone. It is complete alienation. There is no love, no sympathy, no sense of companionship, only emptiness and hatred—of oneself, of the other damned, of all creation, of God. One ceaselessly turns within himself, finding only emptiness and an endless, frustrating restlessness. He fully realizes that he is utterly rejected by the good God. A faint image of this might be the anguish of a child told repeatedly by his parents that they wish he had not been born.

Some wonder how a merciful God could send anyone to hell eternally. It would seem that, if anyone is in hell, he has put himself there, and God only respects his free choice. One who has made himself totally the center of his world, who refuses to love anything beyond and greater than himself, could not be happy in heaven, for heaven is giving totally in love and being loved. God would not force such a one to love, since love cannot be forced. At death he would have for all eternity what he wanted—himself and only himself—and this would be hell.

We should not fear hell in a morbid way, nor make this fear the motive for living a Christian life. "God who wishes all men to be saved" assures us over and over that he loves us and will give us a superabundance of graces to attain heaven. He gives us many chances, warnings, proddings, to accept his love. His whole revelation of himself as a loving God makes it clear that no one will go to hell except one who, with full awareness, fundamentally and permanently rejects God with his total being.

It is perhaps significant that while the Church proclaims a large number of saints to have attained heaven, she has never declared anyone damned. Guilt-ridden people, particularly, with an image from childhood of a stern and punishing God, should put aside thoughts of hell and try to learn of God's love.

Even the very possibility of hell should make us realize how much we crave to be united with God. There must be good reason for God's bringing the concept of hell to our attention. Perhaps even its possibility, of what it could mean to be rejected by God, will make us realize how terrible is any separation from him by sin. For those who truly love, the thought of losing their beloved, however remote, will spur them on to greater appreciation and love.

Theology has no complete answer as to how, or even whether anyone may be damned forever. Many scholars, and ordinary people as well, feel that no one is damned; they cannot conceive of a person choosing with full knowledge and deliberation to be cut off from God forever. Nor can they conceive of a loving God damning anyone forever. Some people believe they make their hell here on earth, through their alienation from God, others and even themselves. Two things God has revealed: his loving will is that we all be with him forever, and there is a state of hell for any who reject him. How to reconcile these is a mystery we may never be able to resolve. This we can be sure of: if any are damned, it is fully their own fault, and God's love surrounds each of us with countless helps toward heaven.

MAKING UP FOR SIN

Read Luke 7, 36-50. The penitent prostitute fell at Christ's feet, bathed them with her tears, and anointed them with the most expensive ointments. She tried to show her gratitude for Christ's forgiveness of her sins by making up for them in this touching way. So our love should impel us to do something to make up for the sins God forgives us.

When God forgives us, he forgives thoroughly and asks nothing in return. He is not like a judge imposing a sentence for a crime. He "blots out" our sins, "forgets" them, "hurls them into the sea." When the scriptures picture him threatening punishment for sin, it is a way of saying that his people are bringing punishment on

themselves—"Salvation is mine, O Israel, destruction is thy own."
Read Psalm 103, 8-14.

**Though God does not demand that we make up for our sins,
there is a necessity within ourselves to do so,** to rebuild the love
between us. When one has offended someone he truly loves—and
especially when he realizes his beloved is so much more loving
than himself—he cannot be happy until he has made up for his
offenses.

**We make up for our sins by uniting ourselves to Christ who has
made up for them.** We particularly join ourselves to Christ's great
act of healing love, his death and resurrection. By this we simply
express our sincere willingness to let ourselves again be loved by
him.

**United with Christ, we can make up for our sins in many
ways:** by acts of worship, particularly the Mass, by the sacraments, deep sorrow in confession, prayer, offering up our sufferings, doing "penance" for our sins by any good action performed in the state of grace.

> *An "indulgence"* has reference to a practice that began in the
> early Church: the bishop would lessen a sinner's public penance
> if a martyr would offer his sufferings to help make up for the
> penitent's sins. Gradually the Church declared that certain prayers
> or good works could gain an "indulgence," usually stated as the
> equivalent of a certain period of penance in the early Church.
> With the very long penances of the medieval Church, indulgences
> became a practical necessity to make them livable; with the token
> penances of recent times, this is no longer the case. Indulgences
> were never considered "automatic" ways of making up for sin—
> one had to be in the state of grace and sorry for his sins to gain
> them, and their effectiveness ultimately depended on God and
> one's own faith and love—but they were greatly abused and even
> sold by some medieval preachers, occasioning Luther's original
> and rightful protest.
>
> Today indulgences are seen as of minor importance in Catholi-
> cism. At Vatican Council II new, more meaningful interpretations
> of indulgences were proposed, but the question was not declared
> upon. Recently, the whole practice was simplified by new regula-
> tions—but the relevance of indulgences to modern Christians is
> highly questionable. In practice, indulgences can be viewed
> simply as the Church's recommendation of a particular prayer or
> good work.

If at our death we have not yet made up for our sins, we must make up for them in the next life, by passing through the state called purgatory. Our love may still be too weak for us to be taken up into God's all-consuming love. In the view of some, this is our shattering meeting with God in the experience of death. We shall see this in more detail in the last chapter.

IN THE LITURGY

The Mass prayers several times remind us of our sinfulness: the opening confession of our sins, the Lord's Prayer, the "Lamb of God, have mercy on us," etc.

Besides the use of the sacrament of penance, the Church sets aside certain seasons to particularly make up for our sins: Advent, Lent, the Ember Days, and the devotion of the "First Fridays."

DAILY LIVING: OVERCOMING SIN

Read Matthew 4, 1-11. At the beginning of Christ's public life, the devil was there to tempt him—to an empty display of power by turning stones to bread, to challenge his Father's providence by hurling himself from the temple, to throw in his lot with the devil and thereby receive power over the whole world. He was tempted as each of us is, continually, but far more excruciatingly.

So strong was this initial temptation of Christ that "angels came and ministered to him." During the agony before his death, Luke tells us, he underwent a bloody sweat. On the cross he cried out from a terrible sense of abandonment: "My God, My God, why have you forsaken me?"

Temptations—attractions or enticements to sin—are inevitable. God permits us to have these, not that we might sin, but that by overcoming them we might be strengthened spiritually. Soldiers are toughened by obstacle courses; cars are tested on rough roads, not to weaken them, but to make them stronger. Temptations also humble us, making us realize how much we need God's help. When St. Paul complained of a constant temptation, Christ told him, "My grace is sufficient for you, for my power is made perfect in weakness" (2 Corinthians 12, 9). **Read 1 Peter 5, 8-10.**

We are attracted to sin by the pleasures of the material world, the weakness of our own flesh, and the influence of the devil. We must recognize our weakness: inclined by original sin, we are further weakened by our past personal sins. We may also be trying to compensate for a lack of love in our life; God may not be very real, and sinful human loves are.

The devil, the mysterious power of evil among us, exploits these weaknesses. Many sinful acts do bring a certain happiness. But eventually sin leaves only a deep uneasiness within us. We may try to ignore the "still, small voice" of conscience, or attempt to drown it out, but it persists.

When we are tempted, a good rule is to pray quickly for help, and then calmly turn our attention to doing something else, thinking or talking of something else, etc. God is always there, giving us the strength to overcome temptation. "God is faithful and he will not let you be tempted beyond your strength, but with the temptation will also provide the way to escape that you may be able to endure it" (1 Corinthians 10, 13).

Even when one falls into sinful acts again and again, God's grace is always there to save us from sinning with full deliberation, inspiring us to start over again and again—perhaps until our deathbed.

To overcome sin, we must obviously avoid situations that might normally lead us to sin. It is seriously wrong to put ourselves in situations where we would probably commit serious sin. Such might be: a married man going out with another woman, an alcoholic going to a bar, a morally weak young couple parking together, or one's gossiping with another who consistently encourages serious uncharitableness.

The mature Christian, however, concentrates on doing good, rather than merely avoiding sin. If one flies from New York to Chicago, looking forward to seeing someone he loves, what motivates his travel is the positive desire to be in Chicago, not merely an urge to leave New York. So we should desire to show our love for God and our neighbor in our actions, instead of merely trying to avoid hurting them.

The life of a Christian should be a personal, free, loving response to God's love—doing good out of love, not because we feel forced to. In Exodus, before God lists the commandments that his people are to observe, he reminds them of how he has shown his love for them: "I, the Lord, am your God, who brought you out of the land of Egypt, that place of slavery. . . ." Realizing how much God has loved us, even to dying for us, we spontaneously want to please him, like anyone in love.

We should never become discouraged about overcoming even the worst habit of sin. It was not Judas' betrayal of Christ that ruined him, but his despair: **Read Matthew 27, 3-5.**

Here we see the one lasting tragedy of sin—the conviction that it is no use trying any longer. God does not ask that we succeed, but only that we sincerely try. It may take years, even a lifetime of struggle, but God's grace will always sustain our efforts.

> At a meeting of Alcoholics Anonymous in New York, a man told how he had battled alcoholism for thirty years, losing job after job, taking a "cure" three times, in and out of A.A., alienating his family and friends. But now, with perseverance in using the sacraments and returning to A.A., he has been "dry" for several years, with a job he is capable of, happy amid his children and grandchildren. He may possibly fall again, but he has already achieved more than he once even hoped for.

Often the hardest battle is the initial decision to renounce one's sin, to start over. Countless people over the past 1,500 years have echoed St. Augustine's classic description of the clinging power of sin:

> The very toys of toys, the vanities of vanities, my old mistresses, still held me; they plucked my fleshy garment, and whispered softly, "Do you cast me off? And from this moment shall we no more be with thee forever?" . . . I hesitated to break away and shake myself free from them, and to lean over to where I was called. A violent habit said to me, "Thinkest thou, that thou canst live without them?" (*Confessions,* Bk. 8)

Our sins can be turned to profit. Through sorrow and repentance, the experience of sinning can teach us much: humility, our weakness and need of God's helping grace, understanding and tolerance of others, gratitude for God's love which receives us back again and again.

SOME SUGGESTIONS FOR . . .

DISCUSSION

Why do you think people are reluctant to face their sins and try to do something about them?
Can you understand how some sins are worse than others?
Have you found an effective way of dealing with temptations?

FURTHER READING

** *Sin, Liberty, and Law,* Monden (Sheed & Ward, 1969)—An excellent book dealing in a new way with problems of sin, our fundamental option, conscience, freedom, determinism, situation ethics, etc. The author shows a deep understanding of human nature.

** *The World to Come,* Gleason (Sheed & Ward)—A somewhat dated, yet interesting and insightful presentation of sin, hell, purgatory, etc.

FURTHER VIEWING

Graduation Day (Paulist Productions, 17575 Pacific Coast Hwy., Pacific Palisades, Calif. 90272)—The pressures of maturing as faced by an 18 year old today, i.e., drugs, "sexual freedom" and parental misunderstanding are explored in this 28-minute drama.

Night and Fog (Contemporary Films, Inc., 267 W. 25th St., New York, N.Y. 10001)—A powerful, half-hour documentary on the concentration and extermination camps of World War II, showing the results of sin at its worst.

PERSONAL REFLECTION

Since Adam and Eve, sin has weakened our whole race and brought the fearfulness of death, endless pain and inhumanity to our world. Serious sin can cut me off from God and turn me against my fellow human beings. I should meditate frequently on how God has shown his love for me in my life, and consider what

I can do to show my love for him—and others—in return. Such thoughts are the best way to defeat temptations to sin.

To appreciate what our sins can do, I might also reread in Chapter 8 "What This Cost and Why." Christ took on our sins and suffered and died to show us sin's ultimate absurdity.

Before retiring I might examine my conscience, concluding with an expression of sincere sorrow and a firm resolution to turn away from at least any serious sin.

19

The Christian's Continuing Conversion

What can we do when we have sinned, and we also know that we will surely sin again? How can we be helped by confessing to a priest? What does a Catholic do in confession?

OUR NEED OF CONTINUAL CONVERSION

Read Luke 15, 1-24. Christ recognized that the life of the average Christian would be a humiliating process of falling and rising and falling again,—of sinning and continual reconversion. By this parable of the sinful son's return, Christ brings home to us God's immense love and joy at our return from sin. We plunge into sin, like going down into the grave, but Christ is always there to raise us up again. All God asks is that we sincerely continue to try, to be converted again, and never despair.

"Then Peter came up to him and said, 'Lord, how often shall my brother sin against me, and I forgive him? Up to seven times?'" (Matthew 18, 21). In Peter's question "seven times" means an indefinite number. Christ's answer is even more emphatic: "seventy times seven"—that is, we should never cease to forgive. Why? Because God never ceases to forgive us.

GOD WANTS TO FORGIVE OUR SINS

The assurance of forgiveness and reconciliation is a vital part of love. Couples in love often experience the wonder of mutual forgiveness after an argument; in fact, some of the deepest moments of love come after making up. On the other hand, a refusal to forgive can be a terrible thing. A recent news story told of a woman on her deathbed refusing to forgive her unfaithful husband, though he knelt tearfully beside her begging forgiveness. Ancient peoples often thought that the gods would not forgive men's offenses, and throughout history men have considered themselves damned by an implacable deity or rejected by a blind, unfeeling fate.

Many sincere people today, realizing their moral failings, feel that they ought to do something about them. They know that they have been selfish, insincere, immoderate, and have hurt others, even those they love. They vaguely wish for a chance to acknowledge their guilt, to be assured of understanding and forgiveness, and the strength to make a "fresh start." They may not realize it, but they are looking for God's forgiveness, for his understanding acceptance, and an assurance of his help to do better.

God has revealed himself to be, above all, understanding, merciful, and forgiving. Centuries ago his inspired psalmist proclaimed, "Not according to our sins does he deal with us, nor does he requite us according to our crimes." The prophet Hosea, from the example of his own life, portrays God as a husband who loves his wife and forgives her even when she degrades herself by prostitution. The book of Jonah describes in a delightfully human way how this prophet was scandalized because God did not destroy the sinful Ninevites, but allowed them to repent.

Micah says God "delights in mercy . . . he will put away our iniquities, and he will cast all our sins into the bottom of the sea" (7, 18-19). And the Lord bade Ezechiel to answer the sinful Israelites:

> You people say, 'Our crimes and our sins weigh us down; we are rotting because of them. How can we survive?' Answer them: 'As I live, says that Lord God, I swear to take no pleasure in the death of the wicked man, but rather in his conversion, that he may live' (Ezechiel 33, 10-11).

Read Luke 7, 36-50. Christ above all revealed God's merciful, forgiving love, by associating with sinners, and particularly by forgiving their sins. He welcomed this sinful woman who came weeping to him in Simon's house, and silenced his host's objections: "'. . . her sins, many as they are, shall be forgiven her, because she has loved much.' And he said to her, 'Thy sins are forgiven.'" He often proclaimed that he was sent particularly to sinners, the "lost sheep." He scandalized the influential leaders of his people by his continual association with sinners.

Read Luke 5, 18-26. As an assurance that he could forgive sins, he cured the paralytic, ". . . that you may know that the Son of Man has power on earth to forgive sins . . . I say to thee, arise, take up thy pallet and go to thy house." This same assurance of forgiveness and reconciliation can be ours today when we submit ourselves to his merciful forgiveness.

CHRIST FORGIVES AND RECONCILES THROUGH HIS CHURCH

Christ continues to forgive our sins today through the sacrament of penance. John describes how Christ passed on to his apostles, the first bishops of his Church, the power of forgiving sins in his name: Read John 20, 19-23.

The apostles passed their power of forgiving on to others, the bishops and priests of Christ's Church. When a man is ordained a priest he receives this power of acting as Christ's instrument, giving his assurance of forgiveness to men.

Penance—or the rite of reconciliation—often called "confession"—is the sacrament in which Christ forgives our sins and reconciles us to our fellow Christians. Its sign or ceremony is the sinner's showing his sorrow by acknowledging his sins and the priest's words of forgiveness and reconciliation in Christ's name. While Christ is no longer visibly among us to assure us, "Thy sins are forgiven thee!", he is with us in this sacrament, speaking through the priest, giving us his loving assurance of forgiveness.

The sinner confesses to the priest, the representative of the Church, because he has offended the whole Church by his sins, and comes to be reconciled to his fellow Christians. Sin, we saw, is essentially selfish and alienating. Even one's secret sins deprive his fellow Christians of love and helps toward heaven, and serious sin may cut one off from them. So the ceremony which restores our full love-union with them is public and social: our confession may be private, but we appear in church, before our fellow Christians, to acknowledge that our sins have affected them as well as us and that we wish to be reconciled to them.

An acknowledgment of one's guilt before others has usually been the first step in receiving God's forgiveness. Those who came for forgiveness to John the Baptist, Christ's precursor, "were baptized by him in the river Jordan, confessing their sins" (Matthew 3, 6). Over and over again sinners came to Christ himself, acknowledged their sinfulness, and received his forgiveness. When Paul preached Christ at Ephesus, "many also of those who were now believers came, confessing and divulging their practices" (Acts 19, 18). And St. James exhorts, "Confess, therefore, your sins to one another, and pray for one another, that you may be saved" (James 5, 16).

We can acknowledge our guilt, ask forgiveness, and be reconciled either privately or publicly. We might come and acknowledge our sins to the priest in secret, in the confessional, or some private room, or publicly, in a penitential service. When we go to confession privately, we confess our sins in confidence and receive forgiveness and reconciliation, but we come to the priest as the representative of the Christian community to acknowledge that our sins have upset our relationship of love to the other members of the community. If we take part in a public penitential service, we show before all that we are sinners and that our sins have affected them.

From the earliest days of Christianity the Church has had a ceremony of reconciliation by which sins were forgiven. Confession was generally public, infrequent, and only for the most serious sins, with long penances before forgiveness. A Christian guilty of serious sin, when publicly known, was excluded from communion with the Church. Then, after a long period of public penance, he was reconciled to the community. These ceremonies were usually done by the bishop, as spiritual father, before the assembled community. Today, incidentally, a priest must normally have "faculties" from the bishop to exercise his power of forgiving. Along with this was the secret confession of secret sins, a private forgiveness, and a private penance.

Pope Clement at the end of the 1st century urges those who had instigated a schism in the Corinthian Church to "submit to the presbyters and be corrected unto repentance." The 2nd century Church leaders, Ignatius of Antioch, Irenaeus of Lyons, and Polycarp of Smyrna, speak of sinners confessing before the Church and receiving forgiveness and reconciliation from the bishop. The 3rd century scholar, Origen, speaks of private confessions and penance which was then beginning to replace the public form, and urges sinners to seek out an understanding confessor as they would a competent physician.

In the 4th century the Spanish Church leader, Pacian, answered the objection that the Church could not forgive certain sins: ". . . this, you say, only God can do. This is true; but what he does through his priest is the exercise of his own power. For what else is the meaning of that which he says to the apostles: 'Whatever you shall loose on earth shall be loosed in heaven,' and 'whatever you shall bind on earth shall be bound in heaven?' Why this, if it was not permitted to men to bind and loose?" (Cf. *Sources of Christian Theology*, Palmer Vol. II).

Read Luke 22, 54-62. In each act of penance, the one we really come to meet is Christ. Though he is invisible, we encounter his look of love, and like Peter after his denial, we are penetrated by sorrow for our sins. Then through the assuring words of the priest we know that Christ is forgiving us. There is the silent and wonderful realization that he joyfully welcomes us back as he did Peter: "When they had finished breakfast, Jesus said to Simon Peter, 'Simon, son of John, do you love me more than these?' He said to him, 'Yes, Lord, you know that I love you.' He said to him, 'Feed my lambs'" (John 21, 15).

In penance Jesus Christ forgives us, restores God's grace-presence if we have lost it by mortal sin, and strengthens us to avoid future sins. Each confession also helps us to make up for our sins, to renew the bond of love between ourselves and Christ and our fellow man. Of course, all this depends on how sorry we are and how determined to avoid sin in the future. Each confession should bring home to us our selfish ingratitude in sinning, and our need of God's constant help, besides reminding us again of Christ's love in dying for our sins.

Confession of our sins makes us face our sins and helps us do something definite about them. Rather than forgetting them, we are made conscious of them, of our weakness and need of God's help. The trained and experienced priest can help us face our sins without equivocation, make us see that we must do something about them, and perhaps give suggestions for overcoming them.

Penance gives us, above all, the assurance that our sins are actually forgiven. If we have tried to make a sincere confession, the priest's words of forgiveness give us the same assurance as if we heard them from the lips of Christ himself: "Thy sins are forgiven thee."

The urge to confess one's wrongdoings to a trusted and helpful friend is natural. There can be psychological benefits in confessing—but these should not be exaggerated. Confession can relieve the natural sense of guilt that follows sin, and might temporarily decrease some neurotic guilt feelings. But the functions of confessor and psychiatrist should not be confused: the psychiatrist deals with unconscious, neurotic guilt, while the confessor is concerned with conscious guilt.

Confession particularly gives one a special sense of personal contact with God. One can express his personal sorrow in his own way for the sins that are his particular burden, and his personal need of God's help. Many a priest—and many a Catholic—can testify that this can be an extraordinary, penetrating experience. Perhaps this is why many Christian churches today are again making confession available for their people.

To safeguard this sacrament no priest is ever allowed to reveal, directly or indirectly, anything he has heard in confession. It is a remarkable fact of history how few instances there have been of the violation of this confessional "seal," despite priests' human weakness, persecution, etc.

> In the history of the Church certain priests have had an extraordinary influence as confessors. During the mid-1800's hundreds of thousands of people flocked to Ars, a village in southern France, to confess to the parish priest, John Vianney. An extraordinary ascetic whose daily diet was often only a few potatoes, he would sometimes hear confessions for seventeen or eighteen hours per day, amazing all by his wisdom and insights. Awarded the Legion of Honor before his death, and afterward declared a saint of the Church, he is credited with renewing the morals of much of France of his day.

SORROW, THE ONE THING NECESSARY

Read Luke, 8, 9-14. Our Lord's parable is a glimpse into the life of the Pharisee and publican. Undoubtedly there were many times when their real life counterparts played out this scene—the Pharisee proudly enumerating his good works, while the publican could only acknowledge sorrowfully that he was a sinner—yet it was the publican who merited God's loving approbation.

When we ask God's forgiveness, the first and most important thing we must have is sorrow or contrition—as in any breach of human love. Without true sorrow there can be no forgiveness, and any ceremony of reconciliation would be a mockery.

True sorrow need not be felt. It is basically the will to be sorry. A feeling of sadness, tears, etc., are emotional reactions that may accompany some people's sorrow, but sorrow is essentially one's willing or wanting to be sorry.

The test of true sorrow is our determination not to sin again. We must be determined to avoid at least all serious sins and the situations that lead to them, to seek more help from prayer, the sacraments, etc.

We should try to be sorry primarily because of our love for God. We call this "perfect" sorrow. We may have other motives as well, but we are sorry most of all because we have offended one who is so good, who deserves all our love—simply because we want to love him and know that he loves us.

When we are sorry primarily because of love, our sins are forgiven immediately, and God's grace-presence is restored if we have lost it. This is the way most people's sins are forgiven. So if we realize that we are in a state of serious sin, we should try to express our sorrow out of love as soon as possible.

For a Catholic this perfect sorrow includes a determination to take part in the sacrament of penance as soon as normally possible. He realizes that his sin has offended the whole Church, that he is alienated, and he must therefore come to be reconciled.

One who is sure he is in a state of serious alienation should confess before taking part in holy communion. It would be a living lie to take part in this greatest sign of our unity while yet cut off from one's fellow Christians by a state of serious sin.

But otherwise we need not confess before taking part in holy communion. We need do so only if we are sure of being in the state of serious alienating sin. If a normally conscientious Catholic doubts whether he is in serious sin, he can simply express his sorrow out of love of God, and then take part in the eucharist without confessing. He may mention his doubtful state in his next confession, but need not do so.

We might be sorry primarily because of what our sins have done to us—a wholesome fear of losing heaven and going to hell, a sorrow because of the punishment we are inflicting on ourselves by our sin. This relatively selfish sorrow is sometimes the most a poor sinner can arouse.

Though we should try to be sorry from a motive of love when confessing, this less perfect sorrow is sufficient to obtain forgiveness. The sacramental grace Christ gives us makes up for our deficient sorrow and raises it to a perfect sorrow. This is a great advantage of penance—a sinner who could arouse only imperfect sorrow could still be assured of forgiveness because of his special meeting with the merciful Christ in this sacrament.

THE RITE OF RECONCILIATION

The first step in making this "fresh start" is to examine our conscience, asking the Holy Spirit particularly to help us be sensitive to our state of sinfulness. Then we run through in our mind our Christian duties, considering particularly any sinful attitudes we may have acquired. We might consider some of the things mentioned in Chapter 25, *Living Daily the Christian Life*. One who has any sort of sensitive Christian conscience is usually quite aware of his main sinful attitudes, and need not review every possible sin.

One should note particularly any seriously sinful attitudes, and how often we give in to these in our daily lives—any actions or neglect that deeply alienate us from God and from others. The purpose of this sacrament is especially to assure us of forgiveness for these and to effect our reconciliation to the Christian community. Most people who come to this sacrament are aware of a less serious, or venial state of sin—one that disrupts their relationships of love rather than deeply alienating them. This sacrament gives us a chance to acknowledge even our less serious sinful attitudes— but we should bear in mind that they are also forgiven, and we are reconciled for these in many other ways: by taking part in any of the sacraments, particularly the eucharist; by an act of sorrow, a work of charity, etc.

In confessing, we should "talk a bit" about the sinful attitudes we confess, and counsel with the priest about why we have done them, what we are going to do to correct them, etc. Confession face-to-face is obviously suited for this. To be particularly avoided is the "grocery list" type of confession in which the penitent recited every possible fault he could think of, with no attempt at assessing his basic sinful attitudes and what he could do about them.

The traditional way of confessing has been for the penitent to come to the priest in the confessional "box" and to confess anonymously through a "screen." The new penitential rite, however, envisions the use of a comfortable room in which the priest and penitent sit face to face—though provision may also be made for those who wish to confess anonymously.

The new rite of reconciliation is a great step forward in making this sacrament more meaningful to people today. The rite for private reconciliation of one penitent is as follows: After an opening prayer there is read an appropriate passage from Scripture. Then the penitent confesses his sins to the priest, who will counsel with him about what he can do to improve, and asks him to do some "penance" as a sign of a renewed way of life. The priest then invites the penitent to pray with him (The Lord's Prayer, for instance). Then the priest places his hand(s) over the penitent, and says, "In the name of our Lord Jesus Christ, who by his passion and resurrection reconciled the world to his Father, and by the power of the Holy Spirit, I absolve you from your sins, and I reconcile you with the Church." The penitent responds with his "Amen!" There may be a final prayer, and the penitent is told to "go in peace."

The "penance" the priest asks the penitent to do is usually some prayers or good work—a symbolic sign or token of our desire to make up for our sins, of our new attitude. The prayer or action asked of us is meant to be the first of many in our renewed way of life. Now we are a new person. We have left Christ's presence, renewed as if by his words, "Go, now, and sin no more!"

Today the social nature of this sacrament is being stressed once again, at public celebrations of penance. These bring out the fact that we are a community of sinners, that we affect one another by our sins, and are coming to be reconciled to one another. People do not reveal their sins publicly, but they come together as sinners to examine their conscience and ask forgiveness and reconciliation.

The usual form of a public or communal penitential rite is: An opening prayer; a reading of Scripture, followed by a homily; the examination of conscience, followed by prayers of all asking forgiveness; a prayer calling down the grace of the Holy Spirit on all, said by the priest(s) with hands extended over the penitents; then there is individual confession of sin by those who wish or who feel they are in serious sin, and the words of absolution and reconciliation said over them by the priest; finally, some closing words or prayer by the priest and people.

The words of absolution and reconciliation may also be said by the priest over the whole congregation—a "general" absolution. The Church, however, asks anyone who is conscious of being deeply alienated from God or the community, i.e., one in the state of serious sin, to confess this sin individually to the priest, in order to receive help and guidance for the future along with the assurance of forgiveness and reconciliation.

In the liturgy at the beginning of the Mass today there is usually held a brief penitential service, during which all silently examine their conscience and then together express sorrow for their sins, as a preparation for their worship of God.

Confessions are heard at these times in the average Catholic parish: during the afternoon and evening each Saturday, and where possible on weekdays—perhaps before or after daily Mass. One should check his local parish schedule.

How often one should confess depends on his individual need. There are special circumstances and special times. One might have committed some upsetting sin or a series of sins, and wants to express his sorrow and be reconciled; one might feel a particular need for Christ's special help to do something about some sinful attitude, or one might feel that he needs to again recommit himself to a fervent Christian life. Or there might be a special occasion for which one wishes to prepare by confessing: a birthday, anniversary, special feast or some other important event in one's life.

Most today are making use of private confession much less frequently than formerly—they may attend communal penitential services regularly—but are making their private confessions much more meaningfully when they do come. They confess perhaps once or twice yearly, but it is often a deeply renewing experience, during which they examine themselves extensively and show a profound intention of changing their life.

A person who feels sure of being in a state of serious sin should, of course, be reconciled as soon as possible, so he can return to the eucharist with a clear conscience. If such a one did not go to the eucharist for a year, he would no longer be considered a practicing Catholic.

It is natural to be somewhat nervous and ashamed when confessing, particularly when one is not used to it. This, however, is a sign that our sinful pride is being lessened. In a very rare case a person might, through shame, deliberately conceal a serious wrong in confession; the whole confession is then useless, as are any future confessions until he confesses the concealment.

If, however, one forgets to mention some serious wrongdoing it is still forgiven: he need not return to the sacrament, nor refrain from communion; he should try to remember it when next he takes part in the sacrament.

To get the most out of each confessional-encounter with Christ, we should prepare well, but not indulge in anxious soul searching. We should try to arouse in ourselves a deep, true sorrow for our sins, realizing the sufferings they have caused God who loves us infinitely, and how they have hurt our fellow men who so need our help. On the other hand, we should not try to ferret out each and every sin— serious attitudes of sin will usually come to mind immediately. Nor should we waste time in useless regrets, but rather make a confident, thought-out resolution to avoid whatever might lead to future sin.

Some find it helpful to confess regularly to the same priest, one who seems to understand and help them. Envisioned by the new rite is a "relaxed" type of face-to-face confession in which priest and penitent can discuss in some depth the penitent's spiritual problems. If one prefers to confess anonymously, unseen by the priest, it is still good to tell him one's age, state of life, and other relevant facts that will help him help the penitent.

DAILY LIVING: DOING PENANCE FOR OUR SINS

The test of our sincere desire to recommit ourselves is our willingness to "do penance for our sins—by the sacraments, prayer, works of love, and self-discipline. If we are truly sorry for offending a loved one, we go out of our way to be kind to him in the future. We try, in this way, to repair the damage to our relationship. St. Paul unequivocally states his need of bodily penance: "I chastise my body and bring it into subjection, lest perhaps after preaching to others I myself should be rejected" (1 Corinthians 9, 27).

Since the penance given us is usually only a token atonement for our sins, it is necessary for us to do more, especially if we have sinned seriously. Love will impel us to do further penance for the harm we have done—if not in this life, then in a purgatory-state after death.

A particular way of doing penance is to fast and abstain. Fasting means eating less at meal time and not eating between meals; abstinence is refraining from eating meat. In the United States, Ash Wednesday and Good Friday are days of fast and abstinence for those from 21 to 60 years of age; the Fridays of Lent are also days of abstinence for those 14 and over. Many people realize their need of voluntarily fasting on occasion, particularly during Lent.

The best way of doing penance, of course, is to perform some act of charity or kindness to another. We cannot make up to Christ, for he has totally forgiven and forgotten our sin, but we can make up to him in other people who need our love and kindness—often almost desperately. A kind word, a bit of sincere interest, a favor done someone, even just patiently listening to someone—these can often go a long, long way.

To summarize, the one great lesson for us all is that we should never become discouraged about our sins. We may fall into sin again and again, and there seems no way of stopping. We are harassed by past falls, and perhaps our present situation demands of us heroism of which we are incapable. We are tempted to despair, to turn from God, saying like Peter, "Depart from me, for I am a sinful man, O Lord!" But God's purpose in all this is to make us nakedly face our sinfulness, our nothingness.

The only possible solution, then, is to flee to him in a supreme act of trust, to tell him that we are so sure of his love that we dare to come to him even as unfaithful as we are, that we know he loves even our worst weakness. We accept our sinful selves and throw ourselves on his love, determined to keep trying, though we may never cease falling—we know that at every moment, including our last, we can always return home to him. He is our Father who will always be waiting.

SOME SUGGESTIONS FOR . . .

DISCUSSION

What is the most important thing to do when one recognizes that he is a sinner?
Can you see the value and/or necessity of confession?
Can you understand how "doing penance" can help to restore our love?

FURTHER READING

* *It Is the Lord, Sin and Confession Revisited,* Bausch (Fides, 1970)—A good presentation of the history of penance, modern man's concept of sin, and sin and its relation to God's community of love, together with suggestions for celebration of penance.

PERSONAL REFLECTION

The only thing in life that really matters is to strive continually to have God's grace-presence with us, to grow in his love. Unrepented mortal sin is the one thing that can ruin us.

A brief daily examination of my conscience, and a sincere expression of sorrow and recommitment to Christ by a specific resolution, can be the most realistic thing I do all day.

If I am truly penetrated by sorrow I will want to do something —preferably some act of love or kindness—to make up for the harm of my sins.

20
When Illness Comes to a Christian

Why is there so much sickness in the world and what purpose can it serve? What help does God give us in sickness? How can one have a better attitude toward sickness?

THE POWER OF SICKNESS OVER US

Read John 9, 1-3. Sickness, particularly when serious and debilitating, is often regarded as evidence that God is not really loving and forgiving after all. Many people cannot understand why a good God would allow sickness in his universe, particularly the sufferings of the innocent, and because of this they sometimes reject the existence of a personal and loving God.

Public opinion in Israel in Christ's time—and of many people since—held that sickness always comes upon us because of our sins. It is God's way of punishing us. Job's friends remonstrated with him because of his afflictions, and Christ's disciples spontaneously asked whether the blind man's condition was due to his sin or that of his parents. Christ rejected this overly simple solution. We might bring suffering on ourselves by some sins, as intemperance or stubborn pride—but the good can also suffer, as exemplified above all by Christ himself.

Sickness shows the influence of the power of evil in the world. In the gospels the cures of diabolic possession and of disease were considered the same—defeats for Satan.

When our body is weak we can be tempted to despair or unbelief. Satan's influence always appears, not in vitality and joy and peace, but in misery, boredom, and pain. Sickness, therefore, should be looked on like any temptation—it can be an occasion for growing in love, but it is basically bad and to be avoided as far as possible. Every cure of sickness is a setback for the power of evil. A Christian should never be dumbly resigned to sickness, but should do all he reasonably can to be cured.

CHRIST'S POWER OVER SICKNESS

Read Luke 7, 20-23. Christ's life was unceasingly devoted to curing the sick. Such cures were to be a sign to the Jews of the messianic age, and Christ pointed to his cures as proof of his divine mission: "Go and report to John what you have heard and seen: the blind see, the lame walk, the lepers are cleansed, the deaf hear, the dead rise. . . ." By his touch or by a simple command, he performed all sorts of healings.

Christ sent out his apostles with power to heal the sick: ". . . He gave them power and authority over all demons, with the power to heal diseases. And he sent them to proclaim the kingdom of God and to heal. . . ." (Luke 9, 1-2). These cures were done in two ways: the apostles laid on hands, and they "anointed many sick persons with oil, and healed them" (Mark 6, 13). Among the Christians of the first few centuries, particularly, special powers of healing appeared quite often.

Above all, Christ conquered the power of sickness over us, so that we can now use it to bring ourselves and others to heaven. Most of the sick he did not cure, and he did not abolish sickness, death, or drudgery. But far more important, these can now be "offered up" in union with his sacrifice to accomplish great good. We can overcome Satan in the very misery of sickness.

THE ANOINTING OF THE SICK

From the beginning Christ's followers used the power he had given them over sickness, anointing the sick with oil to heal the body and forgive sins: Read James 5, 13-16.

The presbyters (priests, bishops) were to pray over the sick person "after anointing him with oil in the name of the Lord," and this would "raise up" the sufferer and forgive his sins. The description shows this to be the ordinary sacramental rite for the sick, distinct from the extraordinary and miraculous gift of healing that some had in the early Church.

In the sacrament of the anointing of the sick, Christ uses the anointing and prayers of the priest to give comfort and strength to the soul and sometimes to the body of one seriously ill. We meet Christ here to receive his healing comfort, strength, and pardon. Anyone who is seriously ill, mentally or physically, may take part in it—or one who is weak from old age.

The rite of anointing the sick today is this: the priest prays over the sick person, lays hands on him, and then anoints with oil his forehead and hands, saying, "Through this holy anointing and his great love and kindness, may the Lord fill you with the power of his Holy Spirit. In his goodness may he ease your suffering and extend his saving grace to you, freed from all power of sin."

The full ceremony of anointing is designed to comfort and inspire: the priest blesses with holy water the one to be anointed; together they pray that God will have mercy and forgive our sins; comforting passages from Scripture may be read, after which the priest may give a short exhortation and then prays over the sick person. Then follow the laying on of hands, the anointing with oil, and a final prayer.

Ideally the ceremony is celebrated before the whole community, preferably at the Sunday eucharist, so that the prayers of all might aid the sick in their midst. The oil used, incidentally, is a special oil of the sick blessed by the bishop on Holy Thursday (but it may be blessed by the priest during the anointing ceremony).

In this sacrament Christ's power may help to heal the sick—if it is for their good and they have sufficient faith—and it always strengthens and comforts them to bear their illness. The oil signifies what it produces—a soothing, comforting healing—in the way that we might use sunburn oil or certain linaments. The sick person will be healed to the extent that God sees it is for their spiritual good; and also, as one gospel of anointing says, "It shall be done in answer to your faith." But more importantly it gives one peace, strength to offer up this illness, to put aside fear and bitterness and entrust himself to God.

By this anointing Christ forgives the sick person's sins if he cannot confess but is interiorly sorry—as when unconscious or unable to respond. Even if his sorrow is mostly out of fear, Christ's power in this sacrament raises it to the sorrow out of love that unites him with God. If he is able, however, he makes his confession, since this is the particular sacrament of forgiveness and recommitment.

This sacrament is the prayer of the Church-family, represented by the priest, that the sick person will soon return to his place among them as they worship and work together. It assures him of the healing love of Christ and his fellow Christians. It should help him have the will to live, to be back with his friends who miss him, joined with them again in the eucharist. The priest prays, "In your mercy give him health . . . that he may once more be able to take up his work . . . and give him back to your holy Church, with all that is needed for his welfare."

But if the sickness is our last, this sacrament will help us toward the great family of heaven. It should never be delayed—otherwise we may be deprived of the strength, resignation, and purifying love Christ wishes to give through it. It helps us die as a totally committed Christian. It gives us the prayers of our friends, joined with Christ, making easier our passage into eternity.

This is primarily Christ's sacrament of sickness, not of death, and should be given as soon as possible in a serious illness. Like all the sacraments, the more we can put into it of faith and love the more benefit we will receive from it. Though it has a special power to help the dying, it is primarily Christ's rite of healing, meant to help us overcome and profit from our illness.

Holy Viaticum is meant to be the sacrament of the dying. To wait until a person is dying before calling the priest to anoint him deprives him of help for his recovery, of peace, and the profitable bearing of his suffering. One should take part in this sacrament whenever he suffers from something serious, from which he could die, even if he is not in immediate danger.

Anyone can take part in this sacrament who is seriously ill from mental or physical sickness, old age, or accident. One must have been capable of personal sin, so it is not given to young children, or the totally mentally deficient. It is given only once during an illness, but if a new danger arises, it can be given again.

Through this sacrament, then, Christ gives us the power not only to overcome the power of evil in our sickness, but to grow spiritually, to make up for our past sins, and to overcome sin's power now and in the future.

DAILY LIVING: OUR ATTITUDE TOWARD SICKNESS

Read 2 Corinthians 12, 7-10. Our sickness when "offered up" makes us more like Christ. When St. Paul complained of his sickness, the "messenger of Satan," Christ reminded him, "My strength is made perfect in your weakness." We should try to overcome sickness, but when it must come, our attitude should be more than mere resignation. Our sickness should be looked upon as an opportunity for Christ to gradually take over our life.

"We bear at all times in our body the sufferings of the death of Jesus, that the life of Jesus also may be manifested in our body." Suffering like him and with him, we die to selfish egotism, become aware of our utter need for the Father's help, and are also made more understanding toward other's weaknesses.

Sickness can be a power given to us to spread love in the world, to help others toward heaven, to make up for their sins, and open them to God's love. Realizing this, Paul could say: "I rejoice now in the sufferings I bear for your sake; and what is lacking of the sufferings of Christ, I fill up in my flesh for his body which is the Church" (Colossians 1, 24).

A *stirring example of the use of suffering* is the electronics company on Long Island, New York, founded by a man born without legs, and employing only disabled persons. Here each makes his contribution, motivated by love, knowing that he is accepted. "Love," says the founder, "gives our incredible, wonderful crew a right to share—to know what is going on in the work of which they are part, to understand its problems, to learn new ways in which to do better. . . ."

A great opportunity for genuine Christian living is to help others in their illness, caring for them, visiting them, consoling them and their families. The sick are especially in need of our loving attention, and few people are more appreciative. Christ assures us, "As long as you did it for one of these, the least of my brethren, you did it for me" (Matthew 25, 40.)

A particular need of our time is to recognize the human and Christian dignity of "exceptional" people. Most of us view the physically and emotionally handicapped as difficult to deal with, and we tend to avoid them in our daily lives. Perhaps we are uncomfortable in their presence because of our own inability to perceive the simple dignity and spiritual depth which often lies beneath their "different" appearance.

An especially pressing need today is sincere interest in the mentally ill. So often we avoid emotionally disturbed people, when what they need is a bit of friendship, someone to be concerned about them. Love is the best therapy, and one we can all give.

SOME SUGGESTIONS FOR . . .

DISCUSSION

> What should be the Christian attitude toward sickness? Can you understand how the anointing of the sick can help one who is seriously ill?

PERSONAL REFLECTION

Christ accomplished the greatest deed of history, our salvation, through suffering. Offering up my sufferings and frustrations with his may be the greatest thing I will accomplish in my life. Christ, I know, lives particularly in those who are sick. I might visit someone who is ill, mentally or physically, or one who is neglected.

21

Christ Joins a Christian Man
and Woman in Marriage

What is unique about Christian marriage? How can one have a
happy marriage? What about divorce? Planning a family? Can
mixed marriages work?

NOTE: While the insights of many lay people, Catholic and
non-Catholic, are used throughout this book, this chapter particularly is the product of several married people whose joyous,
courageous, fruitful lives have long been admired by the author.

WHY MARRIAGE?

God originated marriage as the basic way of giving and growing in love and together attaining salvation. He created us in such
a way that we would find happiness in each other. We are not
meant to live in isolation, but to find and fulfill ourselves through
the love of others. The figurative story of Genesis conveys how
close was the union of the first man and wife: **Read Genesis 2, 18
and 21-25.**

Marriage is God's way of bringing new human persons into
existence. Genesis pictures God saying to the first man and
woman, "Be fruitful and multiply, and fill the earth and subdue
it. . . ." (1, 28). Through the union of marriage, God's human
creatures come to be, to grow in knowledge and love and eventually attain perfect union with him forever. Marriage is thus a
continuing, living sign of God's love for human beings.

A loving family, then, is God's purpose in originating marriage,
and should be the reason why a couple marry. Neither by itself
is sufficient: love while excluding children is not marital love—
and neither is the mere desire for children sufficient. The love and

the family obviously take time to achieve—and sometimes cannot
be fully achieved. The love of a couple must grow, day by day.
And sometimes a couple cannot have children of their own. What
is important is that the couple want to be united to achieve these,
and are determined to do nothing to exclude them—or else they
simply should not marry.

**Throughout the history of his dealings with men, God shows
his constant regard for the marriage union.** The nuptial theme is
woven throughout scripture: Israel is the spouse of God, he
pledges her his unending love by the covenant-bond, and even
when Israel is unfaithful he takes her back again and again.
Scripture often speaks of the nobility and joys of marriage:
"Happy the husband of a good wife, twice lengthened are his
days; a worthy wife brings joy to her husband, peaceful and full
is his life" (Sirach, 26, 1-2).

Marriage is a covenant, ideally monogamous and permanent.
Two people pledge themselves to each other for life. Polygamy,
polyandry, divorce and remarriage appear as exceptions to God's
desires for marriage: "A man cleaves to his wife and they become
as one flesh" (Genesis 2, 24). When questioned about divorce
Christ said, "For the hardness of your heart Moses allowed you
to divorce your wives, but from the beginning it was not so"
(Matthew 19, 8).

Throughout most of history, marriages were arranged by the
family or society in which the couple lived, the bride especially
having little to say about it. In recent times, since prospective
partners are better educated and presumably more capable, the
commitment to each other is made by the couple themselves.
Thus their great responsibility to prepare themselves well; the
choice is ultimately theirs alone.

WHAT IS CHRISTIAN MARRIAGE?

It is significant that Christ's first miracle was performed—
before he was ready to begin his ministry, it seems—to help a
young couple on their wedding day. **Read John 2, 1-11.**

**Christ made marriage a sacrament, giving it a new meaning, a
new power and new beauty.** He made marriage one of the great
ways of encountering him and receiving his grace. When two

people take one another in marriage, they are uniting themselves not only to one another, but to Christ. Further, by this they become a living example of Christ's love-union with his Church. Their relationship is a miniature of Christ's bond with his Church. The husband should love his wife as Christ does us, and the wife should love her husband as we are to love Christ: **Read Ephesians 5, 21-33.**

Marriage is the sacrament by which Christ joins a Christian man and woman in a grace-giving, lifelong union. Thus any two baptized people capable of marriage, when they are freely and legally married thereby receive the sacrament of marriage. Christ joins them together and guarantees them all the help they need to make their union a success. Of course they must be capable of receiving his grace—thus the vital necessity of a couple being sorry for their sins, in order to have God's forgiveness and grace-presence when they are married and throughout their whole life together.

The couple give the sacrament of marriage to each other in what is probably the most important exercise of their priesthood. As the ordained priest is Christ's instrument in bringing about the eucharist or in giving Christ's forgiveness in confession, so the husband gives this sacrament to his wife, and she to him. The priest acts as the official witness of the Church to their union, and brings to the marriage the Church's blessing.

The power of Christ's action in this sacrament only begins when the couple are joined by their mutual "I do." His grace continues to strengthen them each day and hour of their married life as they continue to give this sacrament to each other. Each sacrifice, each act of love, each bit of work for their common good is used by Christ to communicate more of his love. As they give themselves more and more to each other, he gives himself more fully to them.

Christian marriage is not only a goal in itself, but the way in which a couple will attain their ultimate goal of eternal life. This is their vocation, their call from God, the state by which they will attain heaven; they enter marriage just as a priest or nun would enter his or her state of life, as a most important part of God's plan for their salvation. As a couple work at their marriage they grow in love of God as well as one another.

A Christian marriage is a sign to the world of Christ's presence among us. Marriage partners accept the responsibility not only for their own salvation, but for that of their mate and for each member of their family. The family, in turn, is responsible for showing the world that total and enduring love is possible in this life. In this way the Christian couple take on at marriage a' lifelong commitment to be a missionary of Christ's love in the world.

> The Christian family, which springs from marriage as a reflection of the loving convenant uniting Christ with the Church, and as a participation in that covenant, will manifest to all men Christ's living presence in the world and the genuine nature of the Church. (*Church in the Modern World*, no. 48).

Permanence is of the very nature of Christian marriage. We saw that each Christian marriage is a miniature of Christ's union with his Church. Just as there is no divorce between Christ and his Church, so there should be none between the Christian husband and wife: "Is Christ divided?" says St. Paul. This is a lifelong commitment, requiring one's best efforts for years—which emphasizes the need of care in choosing one's partner.

In order to properly raise a family of children a marriage must have the assurance of being lifelong—and in order that a couple's mutual love not be frustrated, they must determine to have a permanent union. Marriage needs to be a permanent commitment, in order that the couple can give themselves fully to one another without the possibility that one or the other will leave when the going gets difficult. One reason why today so many marriages break up—one out of three in the United States—is because the couple enter the marriage with an implicit reservation about possible divorce; these obviously will not give themselves as fully and perseveringly as those for whom divorce and remarriage is out of the question. People are free to enter into this agreement or not, but once decided, the choice should be for life. "Until death do us part" should mean just that.

The Catholic Church has taught for centuries that there could be no divorce and remarriage for Christians. Read Matthew 19, 3-11. Here Christ is evidently changing the Mosaic law which allowed divorce, restoring it to what it was "from the beginning."

The phrase, "except for unchastity" (v. 9), is taken by most Catholic scholars today to mean the legal uncleanness of marrying within the degrees of kinship forbidden by Jewish law (Cf. 1 Corinthians 5, 1)—such a marriage would not be a real and valid marriage and therefore one could separate and remarry. There is no exception mentioned in the earlier version of Mark (10, 2-12), in Luke (16, 18), or in St. Paul (1 Corinthians 7, 10-11 and 39).

It should be noted that Jesus is laying down the ideal of Christian married life when he excludes divorce—but he is obviously not specifying the exact marital laws which would be appropriate for his followers in attempting to carry out that ideal in practice.

But some couples must face the agony of divorce—they realize they are destroying themselves and perhaps their children and have no alternative but to separate and begin a new life. Particularly today, in our unstable society, this is often the decision—painful but courageous—that many people will have to make.

Separation and divorce without remarriage is sometimes allowed by the Church for a serious reason. The local bishop is the judge of this. Catholics may be allowed to go through the formality of a civil divorce (or separation) to settle custody of children, property, support, alimony, etc.—but not to remarry. And since separation is against the very nature of marriage, this can be done only for a very serious reason. St. Paul says:

> To the married I give charge, not I but the Lord, that the wife should not separate from her husband (but if she does, let her remain single or else be reconciled to her husband)—and that the husband should not divorce his wife (1 Corinthians 7, 10-11).

Divorce and remarriage is also not allowed in the Eastern Churches united with Rome, but it was (and is) tolerated by some Eastern Churches during the several centuries that these churches (now mostly Orthodox) were in union with Rome; vindicating reasons were "moral death," *e.g.*, long separation, incurable disease, or adultery; and remarried persons had to undergo a period of penance before they would be readmitted to the sacraments. There are also instances of this in the Western Church.

Some bishops at Vatican Council II and some prominent canon lawyers today, as well as many couples, are urging that the Church reconsider its position on remarriage in cases of desertion, lack of mental as well as physical consummation, etc.

To many in the Church it seems inhuman to require that divorced people, except for the few exceptions, remain unmarried for the rest of their lives. While the Church needs to uphold the permanence of marriage as the ideal for the ultimate good of human society, it would seem that it has to realistically recognize that some cannot live up to this ideal, particularly in today's unstable society.

One solution proposed by some theologians today is that if one has remarried "outside" the Church, has been living for some time in this second marriage, and it seems that the union is a good thing morally and spiritually, and one wishes to fully practice his Catholic faith (and particularly if there are children), a priest in confession might allow that person to once again take part in the sacraments—providing, of course, that no public scandal would be caused. Those who propose this solution point to a practice of the Church through the centuries allowing truly repentant people in these situations to return to the sacraments.

As far as Catholic teaching is concerned, the marriages of non-Catholics are real marriages and are valid until death (on condition, obviously, that they were free to marry—not married before, etc.—and did so freely and legally, intending to enter a permanent union). Obviously the Church cannot judge the conscience before God of a divorced and remarried person, Catholic or non-Catholic.

The Church may dissolve a valid marriage when one (or both) of the parties is not baptized as a Christian. This practice dates from the early Church. (Paul mentions it in 1 Corinthians 7, 12-15—hence the name "Pauline Privilege" given to some of these cases), and is predicated upon one of the parties sincerely wanting to become a Catholic and marry a Catholic. This second marriage is allowed because of the advantage to the partners and their children of Christians being married to other Christians rather than to persons who do not share their faith. Much investigation is usually required for this, and hence a priest should be consulted early in the relationship if one thinks this may apply to his or her situation.

An annulment is a declaration of the Church that no marriage bond existed in the first place. An annulment might be given if the partners to a marriage never intended to enter a permanent union, intended never to have any children, if one partner substantially deceived the other in relation to the marriage ("lack of moral rectitude"), married only to legitimize a baby—or if a Catholic were to marry without permission before a justice or a non-Catholic minister—or for a number of other causes that might affect the validity of the marriage.

It is wise to consult a priest before attempting to judge whether someone's marriage is valid and permanent or not in the eyes of the Catholic Church. Often an understanding priest can be a great help to one trying to work out his or her marriage situation. Though greatly simplified today, the Church's marriage laws are often as complicated as those of the state—marriage is society's basic institution and all sorts of possible situations can arise. The Church has its own system of marriage courts, staffed by trained priests and laymen whose duty it is to investigate and judge these situations; the Church's investigation is always confidential, and in most countries (including America) has no legal effect, so one should not hesitate to seek advice.

BEFORE MARRIAGE

A couple should be mature—ready and able to assume the responsibilities of married life, the daily struggles as well as the joys, the financial and social obligations that will come.

A couple should pray each day for a happy marriage and frequently take part in communion, asking for God's insights and blessings upon their union. "God is love," says St. John, and the more of God they have in their union, the more love there will be.

A wise couple will seek out some sort of pre-marital instruction or counselling, to prepare them for this greatest venture of their lives. They should particularly examine their religious convictions, especially if they are entering an interfaith marriage—this is often the most open time of their lives—and in most places competent adult religious instruction or discussion are available today. Many places have a series of lectures or discussions to prepare couples regarding the different aspects of marriage: spiritual, psychological, sexual, financial, etc.

A couple should be mature enough to seek advice—of a competent and trained minister, marriage counselor, or anyone trained in this field—if there is some continual, upsetting difficulty which

they are not resolving, if there are deep conflicts with either's
family, inability to attain a measure of sexual discipline, doubts
about financial capabilities, or anything else that is causing either
of them worry.

In their developing relationship with one another, a mature
couple grow to respect the individuality of the other. They try
to learn about one another—likes and dislikes, hopes and fears,
strengths and weaknesses—and then, each tries by loving respect
to encourage and foster what is best in the other. Each listens
with respect and takes seriously the views of the other, particularly in such matters as religion, the raising of a family, and life's
goals. One should never enter marriage with the object of changing the deep-seated convictions of one's partner; this is a fatal
lack of respect.

They respect and show mature love for one another, as well,
in the difficult and beautiful area of sex. They realize that sex
is a powerful thing, reflective of their deepest attitudes toward
one another, and the power that produces new human life. In
this matter, particularly, the wise couple respects one another's
ideals.

> Premarital chastity is the Christian ideal, not because sexual
> intercourse is something "dirty," but because it is the symbol and
> expression of a permanent union, of a life-long commitment to
> one's partner. There is the type of young man who tries to "get
> what he can" from the girls he dates and who is usually quote
> boastful of his conquests, and there is the girl who clutches at
> whatever affection, she can get, who is starved for true love, who
> wants someone to commit himself to her, and who therefore gives
> herself to almost anyone. These are running from the real-life,
> permanent commitment to another that true love involves; they
> flit from one affair to another, trying to convince themselves that
> they are involved in loving, but actually they are avoiding any
> truly deep or mature human relationships. They usually have been
> rejected to a greater or lesser extent in their childhood attempts
> to love and so ever after they are fearful deep within themselves
> of being wounded by one to whom they would give themselves
> totally. They usually cannot conceive of themselves as truly lov-
> able. Sometimes the mature and persistent love of another for
> them—often together with professional counseling—might bring
> them to overcome most of their fears of commitment.
>
> However, there are those who are capable of loving maturely,
> who are truly in love and intend to enter a permanent union and
> who therefore want to express their love, meaningfully and totally,

by intercourse. Here, too, premarital chastity is the ideal, because the public, life-long communal commitment of the marriage ceremony has not yet been made. God, who surely has been in the relationship before, comes in this ceremony in a special and fuller way, as the couple make their commitment public before the Christian community and the world. In this ceremony they pledge themselves to this community, and to the world, no longer as two, but as one—and this permanently. They are announcing publicly that they belong solely to each other—they are now celebrating this with the community of those who know and love them most. The community, in turn, pledges them its support and strength for the rest of their lives.

Thus the marriage ceremony is far more than a mere giving of a "piece of paper" which says that the couple is legally and sacramentally married. It is a sacred occasion, perhaps the most sacred of the couple's lives. By this ceremony the couple express and celebrate the commitment they have made to give and accept one another totally, for life, taking on all the day-to-day consequences with no longer any possibility of its ending. It is at this point that the total covenant commitment of the couple takes place; here it is that God gives them his special blessing and grace.

The act of intercourse is the fullest possible physical expression of the couple's total giving to each other. The Christian ideal, then, is that it should take place when there has been the public, total and final commitment of one to the other in the marriage ceremony. The partners save for one another, in a sense, their wedding gift to each other—this fullest expression of their love. Many couples have found by experience that it is deeply worth waiting until marriage before engaging in sexual intercourse because it makes the marriage that much more special.

Some couples feel that they have a deep, mature and permanent commitment to one another before the marriage ceremony—and often it has its consummation in the sexual union—and in the judgment of the couples this is not wrong. Their permanent, unconditional commitment (not the instability of trial or companionate marriage) draws them to a fuller expression of their love. Priests who are counselling couples, while they must present the Church's ideal regarding this, also realize that what is a beautiful and attainable ideal for one couple may be deeply frustrating and disruptive for another. Each couple, in dialogue with God, will have to do what they are capable of. Discipline is always necessary, and the realization that there will always be difficulty in attaining any ideal. Yet, we must face the fact that individuals and their moral capacities do differ; while there are objective moral norms to guide us, not everyone can follow these equally.

Sex can be a beautiful experience; it can express and deepen one's growing together with another, the developing, expanding, deepening that are what life is all about. Accepting one's sexuality—being regarded fully as a woman or a man—can be a great experience. It implies commitment and growth together, not something passing or merely fulfilling of one's physical or emotional needs. It means there must be love—enduring, growing daily, experiencing together the grime as well as the glory—in other words a permanent commitment to one another.

Sometimes living together sexually is a stumbling, questing experience in which two people seek to discover one another—and each his or her own identity as well. The couple should bear in mind that this is a powerful thing that brings them together; if it comes to be regarded lightly (as can happen in our "pill"-oriented society), they will have destroyed the meaning of one of the most beautiful and fulfilling experiences in life.

Sinfulness enters into sexuality when one uses it to take advantage of another, or uses another for one's own selfish ends, as an object of one's lust, hostility, or the need to build one's own ego. This exploitation of another through sex is the root meaning of the "adultery" forbidden by the eighth commandment of Judaism and by Christ himself.

There can also be a sinful *mutual* exploitation by a couple engaging in sexual actions; they might use one another as objects, to simply gratify one another's passions, escaping from life's responsibilities in one another's arms, seizing this passing sexual pleasure without reference to the future. They are indulging in the immature and sinful "luxury of suspended commitment." This is a great temptation in today's confused world, to ". . . be merry, for tomorrow we die"—it is sex without hope, choosing death in an act whose meaning is life.

One thing is certain: A truly authentic act of sexual intercourse will be expressive of a love that is totally self-giving, a final, permanent, and exclusive commitment. If it is less, it is a sinful lie, a betrayal of the genuine meaning of the sign of intercourse and a trivialization of the genuine meaning of human sexuality.

The love of a couple, if it is genuine, will be expansive. It will not only stay within themselves but reach out to others. The couple will see beauty everywhere, especially in other people. They will find themselves more concerned with others, more understanding, tolerant, sympathetic. They will want to share the happiness of their love with all.

The couple must realize that they are still part of the human family, and have relationships to others of love, friendship, concern. Their own love should help, should deepen their bonds with others—and in turn, by the mysterious chemistry of charity, their love will be deepened by these other human involvements.

The deep sharing and intimacy of love can involve risks for the couple, but the risks, if the love is genuine, are worth it. A test might be this: Does their relationship make them turn out toward others in understanding and concern—even though they may at times fail—or does their relationship cause them primarily to turn in on themselves, feel sorry for themselves, be disturbed, not at peace, or resentful of others?

HOW TO GET MARRIED

A Catholic is normally married before a priest and two witnesses. Marriage is a sacrament of the Catholic Church. Just as other important religious actions are celebrated by Catholics in the presence of the Catholic community, with a priestly representative presiding—for example, confession or holy communion —so is marriage normally solemnized this way.

> However, for good reason the bishop may allow an interfaith couple to be married before a non-Catholic minister. This might be more deeply meaningful to a couple, or at least to the family of the non-Catholic. In some cases a couple may wish a priest to be present also and offer some prayers or a blessing after the minister has officiated at the exchange of vows. Each couple should work this out for themselves, respecting each other's religious sensibilities.

These are some of the things necessary for a valid Catholic

marriage: A man and woman must be of age, never before
validly married, capable of sexual intercourse, freely intending
to live together until death, and raise a family (if physically
possible), not closely related by blood or marriage, and otherwise legally capable of marrying. The Church, incidentally, sees
no obstacle to marriage in the fact that prospective partners are
of different races.

   What was mentioned above covers most of the impediments or
"blocks" which the Church has set up to safeguard marriage. The
most common of these are grave fear or violence, lack or sufficient age, close blood or marriage relationship, a previous marriage by either party, lack of intention to live together and have
children, certain mental or physical defects, and the common
impediment of one party not being a Catholic. When there is
sufficient reason to do so, the bishop may grant a dispensation
which nullifies certain impediments.

To arrange for a marriage, the couple should see a priest in
the parish of the bride at least a few months before their intended marriage, to fill out the necessary papers and to take part
in whatever instruction he judges necessary. In the case of an
interfaith marriage, the couple should see a priest in the parish
of the Catholic party, and should allow an additional month or
two for instructions. Permission can be obtained to have the
marriage elsewhere than in the parish of the bride, or of the
Catholic party to a mixed marriage.

The "banns" of marriage are usually announced for the marriage of two Catholics on the three Sundays before the marriage, usually at the principal Mass, in the respective parishes
of the bride and groom; sometimes the banns are printed in the
parish announcements. The banns may be dispensed with for
any good reason.

Catholic marriage is normally celebrated at a nuptial Mass,
although a couple could be married outside of Mass. (The
nuptial Mass is briefly described in the section "IN THE
LITURGY"). Interfaith marriages may also take place at a
nuptial Mass if the couple so desires.

There should normally be two Catholic witnesses to the marriage, but one may have a non-Catholic as best man or maid
of honor. Other attendants may also be non-Catholic.

CREATIVE, RESPONSIBLE MARRIED LOVE

True married love shares in the love of God for man, the love of Christ for his Church. By the total giving of one's self to another, asking nothing in return, the married couple participate in the nature of God, which is love. And likewise, each receives the tremendous support that comes with having his love accepted by his spouse. Each can abandon himself in complete trust to the other. Christ's example of love is his death, his abandonment of self, and his resurrection. For the married couple, sexual intercourse is the highest expression of total, unselfish, trusting love, of the giving of body, intellect, and spirit.

Like the love of God for us, true married love is meant to be creative. As the resurrection followed Christ's death, so new life follows the gift of selves between married couples. This life is shown in a deeper love between the couple themselves and the more encompassing love that they extend beyond themselves to include others. The unique extension of total love expressed by sexual intercourse—the living symbol and embodiment of their love—is another human being, their child. Married people, then, have this great privilege: "to be ready with stout hearts to cooperate with the love of the Creator and the Savior who through them will enlarge and enrich his own family day by day." (Church in the Modern World, no. 50).

A couple's sexual expression of their love, therefore, is a wonderful privilege given them by God. The married man and woman celebrate each other's beauty and goodness, with truly creative interaction, sharing intimate knowledge of each other. "With my body I thee worship," runs the mutual pledge in the form used by English Catholics. In an earlier period in the Church, the priest would often bless the wedding bed of the newly married couple; it is for them a sacred place where they find God in each other. Indeed, there is no such thing as immodesty when they are alone together. There is a call to complete trust in the hands of the other. The body of each is sacrament: "This is my body which is for you."

Sexual intimacy is a profound communication of one partner to the other, sometimes revealing God himself. Couples testify to this: in the heights of the sexual union, they soar beyond themselves and experience a sense of belonging to what can only be God. Some compare this to the experience of the mystics in prayer—profound, surpassingly beautiful, indescribable.

This can also be vastly revealing of oneself, and therefore cries out for a fully open and honest commitment. This profound discovery of God and each other in sexual intimacy, this most beautiful experience, means that it must never be abused, but must be used with deep consideration, foresight, honesty, and as God has meant it from the beginning.

The sex power must be used according to reason and God's plan. Man alone among the earth's creatures controls this power by his mind and will simply because it has such deep and lasting consequences. It can be compared to a beautiful lake formed above a dam: properly channeled, the water provides life and beauty, but if the dam breaks down havoc and ruin will follow.

Because this is such a complex power, reflecting the depths of a person's being, it takes time for a couple to adjust sexually to one another—a mistaken modern notion is that sexual compatibility can be achieved almost immediately, or that its near-perfect achievement is necessary to the success of a marriage. There will be intercourse of the mind and heart between a couple a hundred times more often than that of the body. Each couple also has special communications—words, touches, even looks—that can be as meaningful as the act of intercourse, and sometimes more so.

The deliberate abuse of one's sexual powers is seriously wrong, and can often contribute to the destruction of a couple's happiness, if not their marriage. Adultery, abortion, unjustly refusing intercourse to one's partner, and sometimes masturbation are ways by which people abuse their sexual powers.

Abortion is wrong because it takes away an innocent infant's right to life. If it is not killing an innocent person—and today's genetic evidence indicates that the embryo and fetus are a full human person—it is a willingness to kill an innocent person. The "conceptus" has a right to life, and if we take innocent life at its inception because it is judged to be for the good of others, there is nothing to prevent society's one day doing away with anyone judged to be useless, unfit, a burden on society, or simply unwanted.

Adultery (sexual intercourse with someone other than one's marriage partner) is a perversion of the basic meaning of the act of intercourse. It makes of this fullest sexual expression not a giving of oneself to fulfill one's covenant of love and duty, but rather a means of self-gratification or a confused seeking of love. It is a sign that something is seriously wrong in the marriage, and that help should be sought by the couple.

Also it is a sign of something seriously wrong in the marriage when one partner continually refuses intercourse that is reasonably asked for by the other. The practice of unjustly refusing intercourse can lead to frustration, having sexual pleasure alone, or adultery. The sex act is an expression of mutual love, of union, of total giving. Sometimes the expression may be hard, but to our partner it says that we love. Therefore both should be responsive and cooperative. When sex is used as a weapon, or bestowed as a reward for the good behavior of one's partner, the marriage is in trouble. There are times, of course, when love demands that partners restrain themselves. Wise partners are sensitive to each other's feelings and needs.

Also Masturbation has been considered wrong through the centuries as a perversion of the sexual act which of its nature is social, meant to be generative and expressive of love, and not solitary. Priests and others who are counselling with regard to this today find that masturbation is sometimes described as a satisfying release from tension, frustration, etc., and is an almost inevitable experience of adolescent boys—and contemporary studies bear this out. Habitual masturbation in adulthood might also be a symbol of a deeper problem which requires attention. The sin here is in using this as an escape, a stunting of one's heterosexual and interpersonal growth. To be avoided is worrying over masturbation as a great, serious wrong, on the one hand, and on the other, taking it too lightly with little or no attempt at personal discipline.

Homosexuality, too, has been considered through the centuries as a perversion of the natural order of the sexes and often as a threat to human society. Modern studies, however, show that there are types and degrees of homosexuality, some evidently morally culpable and some not, and that many homosexuals have made notable contributions to society. Often homosexuals can do nothing about their condition, but must accept and live with it. The sin in a homosexual relationship, as with all sexuality, comes when it is a stunting process, a lustful or mutually narcissistic escape from the responsibility of human growth. Most confessors today would urge their actively homosexual penitents to do what is possible for them, and to never lose hope, consider themselves pariahs, or give up the eucharist because of this.

Parents should have "human and Christian responsibility" in the raising of their family. (Cf. The Church in the Modern World, no. 50). Procreation involves not only having but also raising children. God does not demand that a couple have as many children as possible. Parents must return to God mature Christian adults, not babies. Responsible parenthood goes on for years and demands the best talents, the fullest response a couple are able to give. Each couple must look conscientiously at themselves and at the generosity of their life service—and generosity is not always measured in numbers, though the sacrifice of couples in raising large families and the wholesome love evident in many of them is beyond question a wonderful thing.

> *How many children a couple should have is something that only they, in dialogue with God and one another, can determine.* This is sometimes not easy to decide. Some couples need to plan their family more than others, and for many it can become a positive obligation. Couples can differ greatly—some have difficulty raising a few children, while others can successfully raise a dozen. Capabilities, temperament, circumstances of finances, health, and ability to live up to the Christian ideal can vary a good deal.

> Let them thoughtfully take into account both their own welfare and that of their children, those already born and those which the future will bring. For this they need to reckon with both the material and the spiritual conditions of the times, as well as of their state in life . . . (and) they should consult the interests of the family group, of temporal society, and of the Church herself. The parents themselves, and no one else, would ultimately make

this judgment in the sight of God. (*Church in the Modern World,* no. 50).

The "Rhythm" method of periodic abstinence is one definitely approved method of family planning. It has always been considered "natural," since nothing mechanical or artificial is used; it depends on periodic discipline. Sometimes this involves great self-sacrifice on the part of those involved, and they should therefore seek God's grace by more frequent prayer and partaking of the eucharist. The couple also should have the guidance of a competent doctor who himself believes in this method and will take the time to work with them.

Contraceptive birth control as a means of preventing the generation of children has been considered wrong in the Church's teaching. The Church has held to this through the centuries because of its regard for marriage and the sacredness of human life. It has pointed out that one of the great purposes of the sex act is to bring into existence new human beings who will live forever; to interfere with this act unnaturally is to prevent life in an act meant to give life. Further, artificial birth control can frustrate the total physical self-surrender which is vital to married love. Pope Pius XI, Pius XII and Paul VI have all condemned artificial birth control.

However, as is generally known, there is much discussion within the Church today about this question. Many point out now that a consideration of what is "natural" involves not only the physical sex act, but its meaning to the human persons involved and the total context in which it is done (the family the couple already have, their physical, mental, and material capabilities, the society in which they live, etc.); as with any action, the circumstances and purpose of the sex act must be considered in determining its morality. The intentions of some couples seem to be purely selfish, while others are trying their best to live a truly Christian marriage. However, this does not mean that each couple can decide the morality of this solely by themselves, however well-intentioned they may be; while their conscience is always their ultimate guide, they must also consider the objective standards of morality given them by the Church (Cf. *Church in the Modern World,* no. 51).

We must recognize that within recent years our understanding of human problems has increased rapidly. New cultural outlooks,

social conditions and pressures are now upon us—the problem of
overpopulation, for example, is becoming crucial. Our understanding of human nature and of marriage is blossoming, as
articulate Catholic laypeople, particularly, give their views. In
this matter, as in anything, the Church has not spoken the final
word, and a development of its teaching in view of changed
modern conditions is quite possible. No question of infallibility is
involved. As is pointed out in the monumental study, *Contraception,* by John Noonan, the Church's moral teaching on usury and
the transplantation of organs has developed over a period of time
from outright rejection to acceptance; this is also true to an extent regarding religious liberty.

Some leading cardinals and bishops on the floor of Vatican
Council II publicly questioned the Church's traditional teaching
on birth control and asked for a new look at the problem. The
Council did not give any concrete solution. Pope John XXIII
and then Pope Paul VI in June, 1964, formed a special commission of bishops, theolgians, medical doctors, psychologists,
sociologists, population experts, married couples, and others to
study the problem and recommend possible solutions. The Commission recommended by a vote of four to one that the Church
liberalize its teaching on contraception. Then, in July, 1968, Pope
Paul VI in the encyclical "Humanae Vitae" reiterated the traditional ban on any form of contraception: He said that the Church
teaches "that each and every marriage act must remain open to
the transmission of life." Reaction to the encyclical was swift:
Many priests and laypeople dissented from the Pope's statement,
including 172 American teaching theologians who asserted that
for grave reasons Catholics may follow their conscience on this
even though the pope had spoken. Others, mostly bishops, backed
the pope and said his teaching was binding on all.

**In practice there are circumstances in which couples feel that
they cannot now comply with the pope's teaching. The standard
the Church proposes is not possible for some. They are rightly
motivated, are trying to lead a good Christian married life, are
willing to practice self-denial; but they feel that their present
situation is such that for grave physical, financial, or psychological reasons they cannot use periodic abstinence. Their conscience tells them that great damage would be done to their
marital love and perhaps to the children they already have,
if a child were to come at this time—or that to bring more
children into a heavily populated world is wrong. In effect,
today many Catholic couples—and certainly the great majority**

of young people—feel justified in conscience in using contraceptives. Vatican Council II recognized their situation:

> This Council realizes that certain conditions often keep couples from arranging their married lives harmoniously, and that they find themselves in circumstances where at least temporarily the size of their families should not be increased. As a result, the faithful exercise of love and the full intimacy of their marriage is hard to maintain. But where the intimacy of married life is broken off, its faithfulness can sometimes be imperiled and its quality of fruitfulness ruined, for then the upbringing of children and the courage to accept new ones are both endangered. (*Church in the Modern World,* no. 51).

As various national conferences of bishops met in 1968 and 1969, they affirmed the pope's right to speak authoritatively in this matter. But many of them recognized the difficulties for couples in adhering to the pope's teaching. The Belgian bishops, for instance, said: "We cannot assume that those who do not see the convincing value of (the pope's) reasons are acting out of selfish or hedonistic motives. . . . We must recognize, according to the traditional teaching, that the ultimate practical norm of action is conscience which has been duly enlightened. . . ."

The German bishops recognized that "no encyclical of the last decades has aroused so much opposition as this one . . . Many priests and laypeople who want to remain loyal to the Church are greatly perplexed. . . ." Recognizing that many cannot accept the encyclical's statement on the methods of regulating births, they add: "Pastors will respect in their work, especially in the administration of sacraments, the decisions of conscience of the believers made in the awareness of their responsibility." The bishops of Austria speak of the "uneasiness which has gripped many of our Catholics" and say that if someone should go against the teaching of this encyclical, "he must not feel cut off from God's love in every case, and may then receive Holy Communion without first going to confession." The U.S. bishops, after affirming the objective evil of artificial contraception, "urge those who have resorted to this never to lose heart but to continue to take full advantage of the strength which comes from the sacrament of Penance and the grace, healing, and peace in the Eucharist."

The Canadian bishops recognized that on this matter "many Catholics face a grave problem of conscience." They quote Vatican II: "In all his activity a man is bound to follow his conscience faithfully . . . according to truly Christian values and principles. . . . They state that "the confessor or counselor must show sympathetic understanding and reverence for the sincere good faith of those who fail in their effort to accept some point of the (pope's) encyclical," and then they say that there are some who, "accepting the teaching of the Holy Father, find that because of particular circumstances they are involved in what seems to them a clear conflict of duties, e.g., the reconciling of conjugal love and responsible parenthood with the education of children already born or with the health of the mother. In accord with the accepted principles of moral theology, if these persons have tried sincerely but without success to pursue a line of conduct in keeping with the given directives, they may be safely assured that whoever honestly chooses that course which seems right to him does so in good conscience."

LIVING A CHRISTIAN MARRIAGE DAY BY DAY

A Christian wedding is a public expression of a deep personal and spiritual commitment—much more than a license from society or an agreement to live together. It is a lifelong commitment of two persons to merge their two lives into one. It is an awesome commitment and an awesome responsibility—possible only because of God's help.

God is the third partner in every successful marriage. A Christian couple will pray each day for their marriage and for their family. Each will spend some "quiet time" periodically in prayerful reflection before God, considering the course of his life and his marriage relationship, the needs and wants of his partner, etc. Some very happy couples pray together regularly, or read the scriptures to one another; awkward at first, this can become a beautiful habit, and then they will do it spontaneously with their children. Some couples come on occasion to make their confessions together to a priest who will sit and discuss with them their failings and hopes.

Success in marriage requires much more than a romantic feeling of loving and being loved. True marital love consists of a fundamental choice made from the depth of one's being, a decision to give oneself totally and unconditionally to one's partner.

"The impulse of feeling is often part of love, but love is always more than that. . . . If a man is honest with himself, his experience shows him that some of his affectionate impulses lead to actions which, in the long run, badly hurt the person he loves. . . . He concludes that these are not impulses of love. He is coming to realize, as most of us human beings do, what we really mean by love. It lies deeper than feeling. It must include the free determination, commitment, of a man or woman to unceasingly further the good of another." (Milhaven, *Toward a New Catholic Morality,* 1970, p. 62.)

A Christian marriage is a commitment of a man and woman to learn to love ever more perfectly. It is a promise to grow in love, including a pledge to cooperate actively in providing nourishment to the budding relationship. Marriage is not an "end" but rather a "means"—and thus only the beginning of an ever-deepening love relationship which will require a great deal of effort, patience, and grace. It requires a strong, total commitment to the basic marriage commitment—and to its permanence. When times of conflict arise, this "commitment to the commitment" can provide the determination necessary to refuse to abandon a troubled marriage and to work together through the difficult times toward a more rewarding marriage relationship.

Christian marriage is a commitment to life—to becoming fully alive. A good marriage provides a secure setting in which each partner has the time and freedom to become more truly himself, more creative, more productive, more loving—nourished by the spouse's love and support, and guided and strengthened by one's Christian faith. Marital love is likely to thrive in an atmosphere of freedom and trust, where each is allowed and encouraged to grow, individually and together. In the absence of such a climate, the marriage commitment can become a stifling bond which hinders rather than aids the partners' development and which eventually suffocates the love relationship. Each partner should be free to develop his own interests, while at the same time being sensitive to the couple's mutual need to share common interests and goals. It is vitally important that basic long-range goals be similar, so that the partners are oriented in the same general direction rather than opposing directions.

A mature Christian married couple will realize that they are

an integral part of the human community which surrounds them in their daily living. They will reach out in love to others who come into their lives, rather than being selfishly absorbed in only their own happiness. They will develop relationships of love, friendship, and concern with those around them. Each of these relationships contributes to the growth of the couple, individually and jointly. Both partners will inevitably have some personal friendships which the other does not share. Even cross-sexual friendships need not be a threat to fidelity, but rather an evidence of genuine fidelity unpoisoned by possessiveness and jealousy.

They will share in the discovery of new ideas through reading, adult education courses, discussion groups, marriage enrichment encounters, retreats, etc. They will try to confront problems intelligently as they arise, and seek outside help and advice when needed.

Partners in a successful marriage will develop their imagination and spontaneity. They will make every effort to be aware of the "little" things which especially bring joy and pleasure to their spouse. They should express their love often in words and actions, and work together to awaken the excitement of real loving, discovering new depths and resources within each other. Often this will require a conscious effort to plan for special times together. The sexual expression of their love will be their most precious gift-of-self to one another. Each will be sensitive to his partner's needs and desires, and will approach their sexual sharing in a spirit of loving cooperation and willingness to learn and discover.

Good communication is an absolutely essential ingredient of a successful marriage. If each partner is able to express himself freely, and if each has learned to listen to what the other is really saying, almost any problem that arises in marriage can be resolved. Truly honest communication can be delightfully satisfying, painfully disrupting, and many variations in between. For real knowledge and understanding of one's partner, however, honest communication is absolutely necessary. To maintain open and intimate emotional contact, it is essential to share verbally one's likes and dislikes, compliments and complaints, hopes and fears. Partners may choose to avoid the discomfort that honest interchange can bring, and wind up with a very superficial, unfulfilling relationship—an expensive price to pay for "comfort."

A wise couple will learn how to handle conflicts. In any relationship between persons, conflicts are bound to arise occasionally—and particularly in a relationship as intimately personal as marriage. Conflicts, in fact, seem to be not only inevitable but necessary at times. Modern psychological insights can give many helpful suggestions for meeting and resolving these personal conflicts (Recommended by many is **The Intimate Enemy,** How to Fight Fair in Love and Marriage, by Bach and Wyden). Each couple will learn through experience habits of handling conflict which work well for them. Constant and serious conflict, however, indicates a need for professional counselling.

Financial difficulties are a cause of many marital problems. Some people allow themselves to be truly enslaved by a craving for material things, or for the status and power that money can bring. One day they may find that they have all they want —but have no marriage—for in their greed they have forgotten how to love. Many couples find that spending more than they can afford will cause much anxiety which in turn affects all the other areas of their marriage. A couple must be truly wise to resist the subtle pressures of modern advertising which makes luxuries seem like necessities, the desire to "keep up with" their neighbors, etc.

Disagreement over the manner of raising children is another frequent problem. Here, as in all other areas, the partners should communicate openly—sharing their most honest feelings and opinions—to arrive at a unified parenthood. Methods of discipline may vary widely from family to family; degrees of firmness or permissiveness will differ; and yet, in the long run, love seems to be the most important factor. Love necessarily entails enforcing some guidelines and restrictions, and yet the most valuable long-range effect of consistent parental love appears not to be obedience to rules, but the child's development of a good self-image. A child who grows up with a genuine belief that he is a worthwhile, valued human person—entitled to his own distinctive opinions and feelings—will become a well-adjusted, contributing, loving member of the human and Christian community.

WHAT OF INTERFAITH MARRIAGES?

The Catholic Church, like most other faiths, wants marriage partners to be of the same religion, but allows interfaith marriages because of the circumstances of our society. A couple who disagree on the basic point of religion usually cannot expect to have the perfect union and total sharing of interests and ideals that those of the same religion should have. Serious differences often arise over prayer, church attendance, the children's education, etc. Religion is often pushed into the background because it is a point of conflict, and both parties and their children can end up with no religion.

However, some interfaith marriages have a greater chance of succeeding than others. There is, first of all, a crucial distinction between a marriage of two Christians, one of whom is a Roman Catholic, and a marriage of a Christian to one who is not. Further, if a couple is compatible in other things, well-adjusted and mature, their interfaith marriage obviously has a better chance of succeeding than one in which there are other major differences as well. If both can genuinely agree on the religious upbringing of the children, they have far more in their favor than if one only reluctantly agrees to raise the children in another faith. If each has a thorough understanding of the other's religious belief, the chances for a successful marriage are greater.

The Catholic in an interfaith marriage is asked to promise: "to do all in my power to share the faith I have received with our children by having them baptized and reared as Catholics." This simply means that the Catholic will do all that, according to his grasp of and degree of faith, he feels is necessary and feasible for the children's religious upbringing. What is able to be done by one parent in one marriage may not be possible for another in another marriage. The couple must respect one another's conscience and religious sensibilities. Catholic upbringing means a pledging of the child to this Christian community in baptism and the other sacraments; it does not necessarily mean attending Catholic schooling, nor that other religious beliefs should not be taught, but that the child's basic orientation is Catholic. It is a choice made for the child, as parents will do in many areas they consider important; later in life he may feel in conscience that he wishes to change his religious commitment.

The Church has asked this promise because it honestly believes it can present the children with the truth that God gives us in Christ and that any good Catholic who knows his faith would want his children to share that faith. Any responsible parent wants his child to have the best training and upbringing possible; in this most important area of all, our relationship with God and attainment of heaven, the Catholic parent normally wants his child to have all the helps he has, to share most completely in God's plan of salvation.

> *The problem which might arise is that the partners may not be able to agree on the religious upbringing of their children.* Couples should definitely discuss this before marriage. Sometimes the inability of a couple to agree beforehand on this is a sign, however painful it is to face, that their marriage might not work out—they are simply too far apart on this fundamental point, and they should have the maturity to break off their relationship. Couples who must face this should realize that their relationship has not been a "total loss," that each has received much from the other, that they both have matured toward even better future relationships—however remote this may seem at present.
>
> There are other cases, however, in which the couple themselves recognize that the non-Catholic is *de facto* a better Christian than the Catholic, and better able to communicate a mature and wholesome faith to the children. This may arise particularly when the woman, the prospective mother, is not Catholic and is very active in her own faith. The Church now allows an appeal to Rome, through the local bishop, if the couple feel that they wish to raise their children in another faith.

The Church's attitude toward interfaith marriages has changed in recent years from grudging approval to recognition; now it tries to give as much spiritual help as possible to the union. The nuptial Mass and blessing may be used to celebrate interfaith marriages, if the couple so desire. Local bishops may allow the couple to ask a minister to say some prayers, give a blessing and exhortation to the couple after the Catholic wedding ceremony. Also the local bishop may allow the couple to have a non-catholic minister perform the whole marriage ceremony—usually with a priest present as the Catholic Church's official witness—if there is some good reason for doing so (e.g., it would ameliorate the feelings of the non-catholic family) and providing there is no scandal by doing it.

With intelligent cooperation and the help of God, an interfaith marriage can enjoy a good deal of success—and sometimes have more of God's love than one between those who have the same faith but are lukewarm in their practice of it and their love. The couple must respect one another's belief, and should try to discuss their religious convictions frankly, calmly, and with a sincere desire to learn.

In some cases, especially after adequate previous instruction, the points of agreement will be found to far outweigh those of disagreement. Above all, religious discussion and practices should never be pushed into the background simply because of differences.

The common religious beliefs of a couple should be sought out and emphasized, particularly in raising the family. Both partners should take an active part in the religious upbringing of the children, for each has insights, ideals and practices to communicate; a situation should never develop where one party feels "left out." Although the children are being raised basically in one belief, the convictions of the other partner should also be honestly and tactfully presented.

Some further suggestions: If both parents are believers, they can pray together and with the children—prayers of any faith, or "made up" by the parents or children. The bible can usually be a common source of religious inspiration, stories and teachings for the children in which both parents can take part. Teachings and stories about God, his love for us, our moral obligations, etc. are things both can share in.

If both parents are Christians they can share even more: They pray to the same Triune God, profess their faith in the same apostles' creed, take their teachings from the bible, believe in Christ as Savior, acknowledge their Christian unity by baptism, know the importance of some sort of confession and forgiveness of sin, share basically the same moral code, celebrate the same feasts, and often follow the same liturgical cycle of scripture readings.

IN THE LITURGY

The Catholic marriage ceremony takes place after the gospel of the nuptial Mass. The priest usually gives them an instruction on what they are about to do. Then he asks the bridegroom and bride to repeat their vows to each other. The wedding rings are then blessed by the priest and exchanged by the couple. After this he asks God's blessing upon them. The Mass continues: the couple offer themselves through Christ, with Christ, and in Christ to the Father. After the Lord's Prayer the priest reads over them the nuptial blessing. At communion they are joined in the most intimate way possible with Christ and through Christ with one another. After communion there is a final blessing over them, and they go forth as husband and wife.

SOME SUGGESTIONS FOR . . .

DISCUSSION

What, for you, are the most essential ingredients for a successful Christian marriage?

Can you understand the place of sex in marriage, and why there can be a development in the Church's teaching on birth control?

What do you think are some of the liabilities and possibilities of an interfaith marriage?

FURTHER READING

* *Together for Life*, Champlin (Ave Maria Press, 1970)—A "must" for a couple about to be married, giving the wedding ceremony, alternative Scripture readings, and excellent practical advice.
* *The Secret of Married Love*, Mow (Lippincott, 1970)— Concerns the giving, Christian love that can overcome all problems; written with understanding and insight.
* *A Time for Love*, Kennedy (Doubleday, 1970)—A perceptive and popular priest-psychologist discusses St. Paul's famous descriptions of love, and gives examples in very

human, insightful, modern terms; this is particularly good
regarding married love and the fact that it takes time to
really love.
** *Contemporary Sexual Morality,* Dedek (Sheed & Ward, 1971)
—A modern moral theologian's presentation of traditional
teaching and modern views on sexual morality—a balanced
view in the midst of today's sexual revolution.
* *Head of the Family,* Barbeau (Regnery, 1970)—Clearly
written, perceptive essays on father's place in the family.
* *Parent and Child,* Trese (Sheed & Ward, 1962)—A well-
written and fairly brief book to prepare parents for their
role.
* *A Girl and Her Teens,* Rohrback (Bruce, 1959) and
* *A Boy and His Teens,* Madden (Bruce, 1963)—Two excellent, interestingly written books for teenagers on the
major problems of their maturing years.
* *The Future of the Family,* Barbeau ed. (Bruce, 1971)—
Perceptive and profitable insights into family life today—
this could be a help to anyone trying to raise a family.
** *The Human Mystery of Sexuality,* Oraison (Sheed & Ward,
1967)—Somewhat lofty but quite readable, this shows the
role of sexuality in the development of children and as it
is lived by men and women, with particular emphasis on
its religious significance.

FURTHER VIEWING

The War of the Eggs (Paulist Productions, 17575 Pacific Coast
Hwy., Pacific Palisades, Calif. 90272)—27 minutes, in color
—An incisive exploration of the anatomy of a modern marriage.
The Party (Paulist Productions)—27 minutes, in color—The diffi-
culty encountered by several teenagers in their search for sexual
maturity.
Nobody Waved Goodbye (Brandon Films, 221 W. 57th St., New
York, N.Y. 10019)—An 80-minute, dramatic appealing pre-
sentation of a teenage couple searching for guidance in a
world of confusing change.

PERSONAL REFLECTION

"The steady fulfillment of the duties of this Christian vocation
demands notable virtue. For this reason, strengthened by grace

for holiness of life, the couple will painstakingly cultivate and pray for constancy of love, largeheartedness, and the spirit of sacrifice" (**The Church in the Modern World,** no. 49).

Christ promises a couple all the graces they need to make their marriage a success—but he will never force himself upon them. The couple must come and receive these graces, especially by prayer and taking part in the Church's sacraments. In confession the couple should concentrate on overcoming the faults that interfere with their union; when taking part in communion they should particularly ask to grow in love for one another in Christ. Each of us should pray daily for our own happy marriage, or for those closest to us.

22

The Family That Is the Church

How can the Church be a meaningful community of love in today's world? What place do laypeople have in the Church? Why are priests and nuns particular groups within the Church, and what are their basic functions? What is the role of the bishop?

GOD'S GIFTED PEOPLE

The Church is a family in which all the members should love and serve one another and all men. We are "one body and one Spirit . . ." We have "one Lord, one faith, one baptism: one God and Father of all, who is above all and throughout all, and in us all" (Ephesians 4, 4-6). What affects one, affects the others. We must love one another and work together for the good of all. Christ tells us clearly, "By this all men will know that you are my disciples, if you have love for one another" (John 13, 35).

Our Christian family love extends to all men, for all have God as their Father and Christ as their brother. Race, creed, color, talents or social status should make no difference. Christ reminds us again, ". . . as you did it to one of the least of these my brethren, you did it to me" (Matthew 25, 40).

No one is essentially holier or better than anyone else in the Church. Christ said to all his followers, "You, therefore, must be perfect, as your heavenly Father is perfect" (Matthew 5, 48). The Church today emphasizes his words: ". . . All the faithful of Christ, of whatever rank or status, are called to the fullness of the Christian life and to the perfection of charity . . ." (**Constitution on the Church,** no. 40). Some seek this holiness as priests, others as nuns or brothers, others in the married state, in the single state, or by their labor.

344

Everyone in the Church, clergy and laity, is to share in its work, each using his particular gifts. We saw how all the members of the Church have particular charisms, or gifts of the Spirit, to be used for the good of all. Vatican Council II reminds bishops and pastors that "the right and duty to exercise the apostolate is common to all the faithful, both clergy and laity, and . . . the laity also have their proper roles in building up the Church . . ." (Decree on the Apostolate of the Laity, no. 25).

The laity are "sometimes even obliged" to express their opinion on what concerns the good of the Church. The Council envisions that this will be done "through the organs erected by the Church for this purpose." Pastors are exhorted to give the laity responsibilities, to allow them freedom of action, and listen to their advice. (Cf. *Constitution on the Church,* no. 37; *Decree on the Apostolate of the Laity,* no. 3).

Let the layman not imagine that his pastors are always such experts that to every problem which arises, however complicated, they can readily give him a concrete solution, or even that such is their mission. Rather, enlightened by Christian wisdom and giving close attention to the teaching authority of the Church, let the layman take on his own distinctive role (*The Church in the Modern World,* no. 33).

. . . Let it be recognized that all the faithful, clerical and lay, possess a lawful freedom of inquiry and of thought, and the freedom to express their minds humbly and courageously about those matters in which they enjoy competence (*The Church in the Modern World,* no. 62).

We saw that every Christian layperson shares in Christ's priesthood and is a special mediator between God and man. Every Christian by the power of baptism, and again by confirmation, can offer Christ at Mass in a special, powerful way, and can bring down grace upon mankind by his prayer and partaking of the sacraments. Reread 1 Peter 2, 9.

Every Christian also teaches and bears witness to his faith as one specially chosen by Christ. "Christ . . . continually fulfills his prophetic office . . . not only through the hierarchy who teach in his name and with his authority, but also through the laity whom . . . he made his witness and instructed by an

understanding of the faith . . . and the grace of the Word . . .
(Constitution on the Church, no. 35). Each person has the
understanding, power, and grace to be an instrument of the
Spirit in bearing witness in his own way. Each should ask the
Spirit to help him fulfill his role.

> *Some suggestions* for Christians who are serious about working
> at the lay apostolate: to unite one's efforts with others, in small
> groups whenever possible, so as to help one another, share with
> one another, and give witness to others by this mutual love; to co-
> operate with other Christians wherever possible, and with "men
> who do not profess Christ's name but acknowledge common hu-
> man values." To help their theological formation there should be
> study sessions, congresses, periods of recollection, spiritual exer-
> cises, frequent meetings, conferences, and use of books and peri-
> odicals (*Decree on the Apostolate of the Laity,* no. 4).

PRIESTS, GOD'S INSTRUMENTS AT THE
SERVICE OF MEN

Men have always had need of mediators, those who can give
assurance, particularly from the witness of their own lives, that
they are "in touch" with the beyond. They are those who struggle
as anyone does, but they show by their example, by the inspiration, learning, discipline and service of their lives that they
know of a power beyond. Men want the testimony of someone
they can trust, particularly if he is learned, not prejudiced or
narrow, in touch with human realities and concerned about
people. People seem to intuit the divine presence behind his
words, that he is the instrument, however poor and stumbling,
of this power.

**There have always been priests among men, mediators be-
tween God and man.** Ancient pagan tribes had priests to offer
sacrifice. In Israel as in other societies the oldest member, or
patriarch, of the family or tribe offered sacrifice and acted as
mediator between God and his people. Then Aaron and his sons
were chosen as priests, to offer sacrifice; they were to be made
"holy to the Lord," specially consecrated, clothed in sacred
vestments and anointed with oil: Read Exodus 40, 12-15.

Jesus Christ is the one priest of the new covenant, the great

and only necessary mediator between God and us. He offered himself in sacrifice, shedding his own blood, to seal the new covenant for all time. "The former priests were many in number, because they were prevented by death from continuing in office; but he holds his priesthood permanently, because he continues forever. Consequently, he is able for all time to save those who draw near to God through him, since he always lives to make intercession for them . . . he has no need . . . to offer sacrifice daily, first for his own sins and then for those of the people; he did this once for all when he offered up himself" (Hebrews 5, 23-27).

Christ made his apostles his first priests. He sent them out early in his ministry to preach the kingdom of God, to exhort the people to conversion, to cast out devils and heal the sick (cf. Mark, 6, 7-13). Then, at the last supper he gave them the central priestly power of continuing his sacrifice: "Do this in remembrance of me" (cf. 1 Corinthians 11, 23-26). When he appeared to them on Easter evening he gave them the power of forgiving sins (John 20, 21-23).

In the New Testament the term "priest" is used almost exclusively of the Jewish preisthood; it is sometimes applied to Christ (in the Epistle to the Hebrews) and to the whole Christian people who are a "royal priesthood" (1 Peter 2, 5 and 9). Yet it is evident that the apostles were specially chosen by Christ to do what ordained priests do: to sacrifice, teach authoritatively, and bring men his saving helps.

From the beginning in the Church certain men were ordained by laying on of hands and prayer, to minister to the spiritual needs of the community. In the account of the ordination of the Seven who would serve at table (undoubtedly often the Lord's supper or eucharist) and who later preached and baptized, we read, "these they set before the apostles, and they prayed and laid their hands upon them" (Acts 6, 1-6).

We saw (chapter 10) that the organization of the early Church was formed only gradually—Christ left it to his followers to work out—and that New Testament terms do not necessarily mean what they do later. But the terms "presbyter" (elder) and "bishop" refer to those who had some office in ruling over the local churches (Acts 14, 23; 20-28, etc.). The ordination ceremony of Timothy, chosen by Paul to lead a local church, is clear: Paul writes, "Do not neglect the gift you have, which was given

you by prophetic utterance when the elders laid their hands upon
you . . . I remind you to rekindle the gift of God that is within
you through the laying on of my hands . . ." (1 Timothy 4, 14; 2
Timothy 6).

While the New Testament stresses the pastoral work of the
apostles and their successors, the bishops, early Christian tradition shows that they also presided over the eucharistic sacrifice-
meal. Clement of Rome writes near the end of the 1st century:
"It will be no small sin for us if we eject men who have irre-
proachably and piously offered the sacrifices proper to the episcopate" (Epistle to the Corinthians, 42, 44). These sacrifices are
"the bread and the cup," the eucharistic sacrifice. In an early
third century Roman liturgy, the newly ordained bishop consecrates the bread and chalice and then addresses God with the
remembrance prayer or "anamneses": "Doing therefore the an-
amnesis of his death and resurrection, we offer to thee the bread
and the cup, making eucharist to thee because thou has bidden
us to stand before thee and minister as priests to thee" (*The Apos.
Trad. of Hippolytus* 4, 11).

From the first century there has been a hierarchy of orders in
the Church—bishops, priests (presbyters), and deacons. (cf.
chapter 10). For the first eight centuries the rite of ordination
to these offices was simply an imposition of the bishop's hands
and an invocation of the Holy Spirit. In the middle ages the
rite was expanded to include an anointing of the hands, be-
stowal of chalice and paten, etc., but the heart of the ceremony
remained what it was from the early centuries.

The earliest detailed rite is given in the *Apostolic Tradition of
Hippolytus* referred to above, a Roman bishop's book compiled
about 215 A.D. In this we find the hierarchy of bishops, presbyters, and deacons, each ordained by a laying on of hands. There
are other, lesser offices, but these are merely appointed, not ordained by a laying on of hands. The bishop is chosen by all the
people, and is ordained by the imposition of hands of his fellow
bishops alone; the presbyter is ordained by an imposition of the
bishop's hands with "the presbyters also touching him."

Men become priests today as always—by the sacrament of holy
orders—the laying on of the bishop's hands and prayer. Through
this sacrament Christ changes the man interiorly, giving him the
powers of the priesthood, a great increase of his grace-presence,

and a promise of all the actual graces and helps he needs to carry out his priesthood.

Holy orders is received only once, like baptism and confirmation. By it a man is changed permanently; he is a priest forever. Even if he stops practicing the priesthood, or is released from his priestly vows, he still is a priest in God's eyes. He is established for all time in this permanent function for God and men.

There are different orders or degrees in the priesthood:

A bishop has the fullness of Christ's priesthood. He is, in a sense, a "super-priest," a succesor of the apostles. He acts as Christ's instrument in giving all the sacraments, is the only one who can administer holy orders, and is normally the one to give confirmation.

A priest has the power of presiding at Mass, leading the people and acting as Christ's special instrument re-presenting his sacrifice. He also acts as Christ's instrument in giving the sacraments (except holy orders and normally confirmation), in preaching and teaching, and in asking God's blessing upon people and things.

A deacon's ministry is to baptize, distribute communion, anoint the sick, read the scriptures and preach, conduct marriages and funerals, give sacramentals, and give himself to works of charity and administration; these works are done to the extent the local hierarchy sees fit. A deacon is also ordained by a bishop. A permanent diaconate has been revived by Vatican Council II, and can include married men "of more mature age" as well as celibate young men.

According to the Apostolic Letter of Pope Paul VI, *Ministeria Quaedam*, the following changes in regard to major and minor orders are to be noted:

1. Minor orders are henceforth called "ministries." They are no longer seen as steps to the priesthood, but they are also open to lay Christians who have no intentions of going on for the priesthood.

2. First tonsure is no longer conferred; entrance into the clerical state is joined to the diaconate.

3. Only the ministries of *reader* and *acolyte* have been retained.

4. The *Subdiaconate* has been suppressed.

A *"monsignor"* (as the term is used in America) is a priest who receives this honorary title from the pope, at the request of his bishop, because of some outstanding work he has done or some position of importance he holds. There is some discussion today about the meaningfulness of such titles in the Church.

"Priests, as co-workers with their bishops, have as their primary duty the proclamation of the gospel of God to all. In this way they fulfill the Lord's command: 'Go into the whole world and preach the gospel to every creature (Mark 16, 15). Thus they establish and build up the people of God" **(Decree on the Ministry and Life of Priests, no. 4).** Preaching the Word leads to faith, to conversion, to holiness. If one is to take part profitably in the sacraments and the Mass he must listen openly to this preaching, allowing faith to grow in him and his heart to be converted. God speaks even through the dullest sermon; his Word always does something to us if we but let it.

The celebration of the eucharist, the Mass, is the high point of a priest's work, ". . . the source and the apex of the whole work of preaching the gospel. . . . The other sacraments, as well as every ministry of the Church and every work of the apostolate, are linked with the holy Eucharist and are directed toward it . . . (as) the very heartbeat of the congregation of the faithful over which the priest presides" **(Decree on the Ministry and Life of Priests, no. 5).**

For a further glimpse into how the Church views the mission of her priests, we have this summary of Vatican Council II:

For the sick and penitents among the faithful, they exercise the ministry of alleviation and reconciliation, and they present the needs and the prayers of the faithful to God the Father. . . . They gather together God's family as a brotherhood, all of one mind, and lead them in the Spirit through Christ to God the Father. In the midst of the flock they adore him in spirit and in truth. . . . They labor in word and doctrine . . . believing what they have read and meditated upon in the law of God, teaching what they have believed, and putting in practice in their own lives what they have taught (*Constitution on the Church*, no. 21).

Two priests write thus of their calling: "The heart of the vocation of the priesthood is to minister to the deepest needs of man: man's need for meaning in life, man's need for encouragement in

despair, for support in crisis, for forgiveness of guilt and return to
God . . ." (Kennedy and D'Arcy *The Genius of the Apostolate,*
Sheed & Ward, 1965, p. 7).

Priests are called "Father" because they give the life of grace
to their spiritual children and teach them God's Word—just as a
natural father gives physical life and instructs his children.
". . . I became your father in Christ Jesus through the gospel,"
says St. Paul (1 Corinthians 4, 15).

**Priests are chosen from among God's people to serve the
people.** They are first of all Christians, and then priests. They
live a special life in order that they may be better instruments
of Christ in serving the whole Church. They are not necessarily
holier, nor are they of a higher class in the Church's structure;
whatever authority they have, or respect they are given, comes
to them only because they visibly represent Christ—as deference
to an ambassador is meant for the country he represents. Laypeople may often be gifted by God to accomplish far more for
the Church and the world.

> Vatican Council II says that while priests are "set apart"
> among God's people, "this is so, not that they may be separated
> from this people or from any man, but that they may be totally
> dedicated to the work for which the lord has raised them up. They
> cannot be ministers of Christ unless they are witnesses and dis-
> pensers of a life other than this earthly one. But they cannot be of
> service to men if they remain strangers to the life and conditions
> of men" (*The Ministry and Life of Priests,* no. 3).
> Today in the Church there is stress on the priesthood of service
> as well as of sacrifice, on the ministerial as well as the cultic
> priesthood. The modern priest sees that he follows one who
> "came not to be served, but to serve" (Mark 10, 45), and who
> gave a striking example of service by washing the feet of his first
> priests, the apostles, when he "ordained" them at the last supper.

Priests also have different charisms or gifts for different works.
One is talented at a certain type of work, while another may be a
failure at it. In today's age of specialization, particularly, it is
almost impossible for priests to be "all things to all men"—and
yet this is required of many, especially parish priests. Catholic
people, however, are usually wonderfully understanding of the
inadequacies of their priests.

To become a priest a man studies from 8 to 10 years after high school. Usually he does his last few years of undergraduate work and at least his graduate work in theology in a seminary with other candidates for the priesthood. He must not only have the continuing and free desire to be a priest, but must be judged suitable (by his bishop or religious superior) in learning, character, health, etc.

Priests of the Latin rite bind themselves to celibacy, not to marry. This custom began to grow from the 4th century and was made a general law of the western Church in the 12th century. Priests of the eastern rites may marry, usually before the diaconate. The basic reason for celibacy is that the priest might better be a living sign or witness to the reality of Christ among us. In giving up the fundamental and deepest human love relationship, marriage, the priest expresses his total attachment to the divine. He is staking all on the reality of God among us. The loneliness that is his gives him a kinship with all who are alone or who are neglected in their pain, and can propel him into a deep intimacy with Christ. Christ alone is at the core of his being, and no one else.

The celibate priest can often have a greater independence, be more totally at the service of others. St. Paul expresses it: "The unmarried man is anxious about the affairs of the Lord, how to please the Lord; but the married man is anxious about worldly affairs, how to please his wife, and his interests are divided" (1 Corinthians 7, 32-34).

As to why they are celibate, however, many today in the priesthood, religious life, or among the laity, would probably echo these perceptive words of one of the influential celibates of our time:

"Today, the Christian who renounces marriage and children for the kingdom's sake seeks no abstract or concrete *reason* for his decision. His choice is pure risk in faith, the result of the intimate and mysterious experience of his heart. He chooses to live *now* the absolute poverty every Christian hopes to experience at the hour of death. His life does not *prove* God's transcendence; rather, his whole being expresses faith in it. His decision to renounce a spouse is as intimate and incommunicable as another's decision to prefer *his* spouse over all others" (*Ivan Illich, in "The Critic," June-July, 1967*).

A modern poet/priest writes: "In love we desire to possess a human body, but the body of the beloved can never be wholly possessed. Only God can be totally possessed. Only God can be truly embraced, because the arms of the human soul were created for the infinite, for nothing more and nothing less. Thus neither the world nor the woman we love can be truly and wholly embraced and possessed, and neither the world nor a woman can fully satisfy human desire, for only God can do that." (Ernesto Cardinal, in *To Live is to Love*.)

However, many in the Church today recognize that there is no necessary connection, historically or pastorally, between the priesthood and celibacy. The pope in his recent encyclical reaffirming celibacy allows for further study of the question. Many today recognize that among priests, as among all Christians, there are different charisms. Some are called to work and witness as celibates, others as married. Many feel that good men are being eliminated from the priesthood because of celibacy. Among Eastern Rite Catholics and among Orthodox Christians both forms of the priestly life have always been recognized. Countless Protestant ministers have effectively served the Lord and their flocks while married, while celibacy too is practiced among them by individuals and by small but significant groups. In southern France is the remarkable monastery of Taize to which are attached almost 100 Protestant monks living in celibacy, poverty, and service to God and the world. In the Church of the future, many predict, religious communities will be celibate, while diocesan priests will embrace either state of life.

There are two general types of priests: diocesan or secular, and religious. While the work of the priesthood is basically the same, these two general types of priests have developed over the centuries to better carry out this work. The diocesan priest works under the bishop of a particular diocese, is bound by the law of celibacy (not to marry, in the Latin rite), and provides for his own support from a small salary, offerings, etc. The average parish priest is a diocesan priest, though these may also specialize in particular works. Bishops are usually chosen from among these.

Religious priests belong to a religious community, and take vows or solemn promises of poverty (in some way restricting their ownership of things), of celibacy or chastity, and of obedience to their religious superior whom they usually elect. Each religious community has a particular spirit and work, and strives to have a "common life," praying and working together as a group and ready to move from diocese to diocese or even to other countries to carry out their particular priestly work.

Priests are human instruments of Christ, often sinful and defective, and in need of the support and prayers of the people. Eleven of the first twelve priests deserted Christ, their leader denied him and one of them betrayed him—so we should expect to find weaknesses among his priests today. People often do not realize how much their priests need the constant support of their prayers. No one realizes his inadequacies, limitations, and sinfulness more than a priest. St. Paul expresses every priest's feelings when he writes: **Read 1 Corinthians 1, 26-31.**

> Vatican Council II also poignantly expresses the mind of every priest: ". . . the ministers of the Church and even, at times, the faithful themselves feel like strangers in the world, anxiously looking for appropriate ways and words with which to communicate with it. . . . The modern obstacles which block faith, the seeming sterility of their past labors, and the bitter loneliness they experience can lead them to the danger of becoming depressed in spirit. . . . Priests should remember that in performing their tasks they are never alone. . . ." (*Decree on the Ministry and Life of Priests,* no. 22).

Christ, then, shows himself among us today in a particular way in his priests. One of Christ's first and greatest priests, St. Paul, describes all priests when he says, ". . . we are ambassadors for Christ, God making his appeal through us" (1 Corinthians 5, 20). Through the priesthood Christ makes himself available to all in a special, organized, human way. The priesthood witnesses to God's loving reality among us by serving all men—making God's love real to people as best we poor humans can.

The priest is there at the high points and critical moments of people's lives: When men come before God in worship, when they come to express repentance, at the moment of their life-long commitment in marriage, in sickness, and when they are facing the conclusion of it all in death—and with advice and guidance in many little ways along the path of life.

> Every priest also has insights like that of the fictional Pope Kiril I, in Morris West's novel, *The Shoes of the Fisherman:*

"Once more I have been brought to see vividly that the real battleground of the Church is not in politics or in diplomacy or finance or material extension. It is the secret landscape of the individual spirit. To enter into this hidden place the pastor needs tact and understanding, and the very particular grace bestowed by the sacrament of holy orders. . . ."

The great modern priest-paleontologist, Teilhard de Chardin, expressed his priestly vocation in this way: "To the full extent of my power, because I am a priest, I wish from now on to be the first to become conscious of all that the world loves, pursues and suffers; I want to be the first to seek, to sympathize and to suffer; the first to unfold and sacrifice myself . . . to become more widely human and more nobly of the earth than any of the world's servants."

Today it is seen more and more that the Church is a community in which different people have different gifts, all of which are necessary and important. The once clear distinction between priestly leaders and people whose role was mainly to follow, is gradually disappearing. We are coming to realize that each member has something to contribute, and often the contribution of a layperson in a particular matter is more vital than that of a priest or religious. We are coming to see that the Spirit speaks and acts through all, particularly where "two or three are gathered together" as a group in his name. It is also becoming clear that the special way of dress, titles, separate living facilities, etc. which are generally part of the priesthood today, while often helpful, need not be necessary to the priest's role in the community, and sometimes may in fact be a hindrance to his work.

There is much discussion about the essence of the priesthood today—particularly when the Church is seen both as a hierarchical community and as one of people with different gifts. One way of viewing the priesthood is to see the priest as the one who particularly shows forth, and brings about, the unity and order of the community—and this especially when he leads the community in liturgy. Though others may have gifts that are more important to a particular community, the priest is the unifier and the one who assures that gifts of all are recognized and used effectively.

Some today also see the priesthood as an office within the community to which one is called by God either for life or for a time—though the role of the priest as the unifier and stabilizer of the community would seem to usually call for a long-term com-

mitment. Some priests see themselves serving the Christian community as priests for the present and foreseeable future, but
perhaps one day leaving the priesthood and serving the Church
in another capacity.

THE ROLE OF RELIGIOUS

**The religious life is that by which priests, nuns, or brothers join
together in a particular religious community, with a particular
spirit and "rule" or way of life, to do particular works in the
Church.** Religious life is found in all the world religions, in Islam,
Buddhism, Hinduism, among Catholics and Orthodox Christians,
and it is a small but growing movement in Protestant Christianity. In the Catholic Church there are several hundred religious
communities, each with its particular spirit and functions.

**"Religious," that is, men and women in religious communities,
have a "common life."** They usually live together, have some daily
pattern of prayer and work, and to a greater or lesser extent share
what they own with one another. Each community has some
distinctive "habit" or garb worn by the members; this might be
thought of as a sort of uniform signifying their profession. Many
religious habits, particularly of nuns, are being modified today to
conform to the realities of life in the modern world. Some religious live in their homes, wear ordinary clothing and may have
regular jobs or professions; these come together periodically for
study and spiritual renewal.

**Religious take vows, or solemn promises, of poverty, chastity,
and obedience.** By these they seek more fully to imitate Christ,
and serve the Christian community. By poverty they restrict
their ownership of things and depend for their support upon their
religious community; this detachment from material things enables them to give themselves more fully to God and to others.
By chastity, they witness to the reality of God among us, and can
give themselves fully to the service of all in the Christian community. Obedience puts them at the service of the Christian community in that they better use their talents in the cooperative
effort of all. In some newer religious groups, nuns write their own
expressions of dedication which retain the essence of the three
vows.

These vows do not mean that religious are in a state of life

higher than the other people of the Church, nor that they are holier. Rather they join together with others in the stable life of a religious community, and bind themselves by vows, to better attain the perfection to which all Christians are called, and by their lives to be "a sign that can and ought to attract all the members of the Church to an effective and prompt fulfillment of the duties of their Christian vocation." (**Constitution on the Church,** no. 45). They should be living reminders to all Christians that Christ is now among us and that shortly we will be with him forever.

A nun or "sister" is a woman who belongs to a particular religious community. Most nuns serve the Church by teaching school, doing hospital and social work, working in the missions, etc. Others live relatively secluded lives of prayer and penance, doing a minimum of outside work, in contemplative orders; these might be compared to unnoticed but vitally necessary power-houses—they bring God's grace and love into all our lives, especially doing penance for the sins of all mankind by their rigorously ascetical lives.

A brother is a man who lives the religious life in a state other than the priesthood. As with nuns, some brothers are teachers, others do hospital, social or missionary work, or any work for which they are judged suitable by their community; some too are in contemplative communities.

To become a nun or brother, as in becoming a priest, one must have a desire for this life, undertake several years of study and training, and be judged suitable in character, health, etc. After taking temporary vows or promises for several years, perpetual vows are taken, committing one for life to this vocation; but even after this one could leave and return to a lay Christian life.

All religious communities today have been in the process of up-dating themselves, changing the rules under which they function, according to the principles of Vatican Council II. The process of change is often painful and stress-filled for all concerned, but it must go forward if the religious communities are not to become ineffective and irrelevant in a changing world. There is much discussion about the role of religious communities themselves in the future Church; some foresee the emergence of many smaller, less structured, more homogeneous groups in which the talents of the individual members will be used more effectively for particular works of service. Laypeople, often married, are becoming "co-members" of some of these new groups.

Religious and priests might be compared to signposts—standing somewhat apart, often lonely, but at the service of men as they point the way to God; others may pass them on the way to holiness, but without them the others would have a much harder time finding their way.

OUR BISHOP AND OUR DIOCESE

A bishop has the highest degree of holy orders, the greatest share in Christ's priesthood. We saw (chapter 10) that the bishops occupy the same place in the Church as the apostles chosen by Christ—that they are ordained, as they have been for 2000 years, by the laying on of hands of another bishop (usually three bishops have this function)—that bishops are chosen by the pope usually upon the recommendation of the other bishops of the area, and that many today favor giving the local clergy and laity once again a voice in the selection of their bishops.

The bishops of the Church are responsible for the welfare of the whole Church. They have a responsibility of teaching and governing all the parts of the Church (cf. chapter 10), and particularly their own region or country—for this latter, regional or national conferences of bishops have been established. Each bishop should especially be concerned to provide clergy, laypeople, and material help to the deprived parts of the Church.

The bishop is the leader of the local church or diocese—in a sense, its spiritual father. If the diocese is large, he may be assisted by auxiliary bishops. Dioceses are grouped into provinces centered around an archdiocese (usually the largest diocese of the area) presided over by an archbishop. Each bishop in his diocese is independent, subject only to the pope and in some matters to the national conference of bishops.

A *"cardinal"* is a bishop who is the leader of a particuarly large archdiocese or has some high administrative position in the Church. This is essentially an honorary function, dating from the middle ages. The cardinals come together when a pope dies to elect a new one, chosen for the last several centuries from their own number—in this they are the successors of the ancient clergy of Rome who from the earliest days came together to elect their bishop, who was therefore the pope. The pope chooses the members of the "college of cardinals" which in recent years has been made a more international and representative group. There is much speculation today as to the future status of this group, since their function of advising the pope and setting Church policy, and perhaps the election of the pope, will probably be more and more taken over by or shared with the synod of bishops.

The bishop is the chief preacher and teacher of his diocese, its chief priest and pastor. He should make Christ's doctrine relevant to the needs of the time, bring forth holiness in men, and should himself give an example of holiness "in charity, humility and simplicity of life." The liturgy celebrated with the bishop is the high point of the worship of the diocese. The bishop is also to "seek out men and both request and promote dialogue with them" and should "deal lovingly with the separated brethren, urging the faithful also to conduct themselves with great kindness and charity in their regard, and fostering ecumenism. . . ." (Cf. Decree on the Pastoral Office of Bishops, nos. 12, 13, 16).

"In exercising his office of father and pastor, a bishop should stand in the midst of his people as one who serves." A bishop is not above the Church, nor is the Church his private domain. He is to be a servant of the people of God, in imitation of the servant of all, Jesus. He should know his people and they should know him. He should be "a true father who excels in the spirit of love and solicitude for all." He should "so gather and mold the whole family of the flock that everyone, conscious of his own duties, may live and work in the communion of love" (Cf. Decree on the Pastoral Office of Bishops, no. 16).

The people of a diocese, in turn, should give respect to their bishop, assisting and working with him in whatever way they can. The people realize that bishops are only human, that in fact the twelve apostles themselves could even betray, deny and desert Christ. They know, too, that only so much can be expected of an older bishop in today's rapidly changing world. They realize that their bishop is given a special gift to guide them. They should remember particularly that he is in need of their prayers because of his great responsibilities.

The priests and people of a diocese should be in continual communication with their bishop, giving him "active cooperation rather than passive obedience." They should try to use their particular gifts for the service of the diocese, realizing that the Holy Spirit also acts through them. Almost all dioceses now have a senate of priests set up as a consultive body to assist the bishop in governing the diocese. This is the result of Vatican Council II:

> To the priests of the diocese, particularly, the bishop should be not only a father but also a brother and friend. He should have special regard for them, and should gladly listen to them and consult them, and should establish a group or "senate" of priests to assist him in governing the diocese. The priests, in turn, should give their bishop a sincere love, obedience and cooperation, recognizing in him the fullness of their common priesthood. (Cf. *Decree on the Pastoral Office of Bishops*, nos. 7 and 28).

All the people of the diocese should be brought to share in the work of the diocese, contributing not only their talents and money but opinions that would be helpful in its administration. Vatican Council II recommends that "in each diocese a pastoral council be established over which the diocesan bishop himself will preside and in which specially chosen clergy, religious, and laypeople will participate . . . to investigate and to weigh matters which bear on pastoral activity, and to formulate practical conclusions regarding them." Some dioceses have had "little councils," and many others are gradually incorporating more clerical and lay representatives into their administrative structures.

Until the regular channels of communication and common effort envisioned by the Council are fully set up, laypeople should write their bishops when they feel they have something to contribute, so the bishops can more easily get to know the views of their people.

> Some suggest today that in our rapidly changing world the Church would be better served if bishops were elected for a certain term of office, long enough to give stability and yet limited enough to make those selected sensitive and responsive to the needs of the times. Some see this as a partial solution to the evident credibility gap that now often exists between hierarchy and people. A few dioceses have begun appointing parish pastors for a limited tenure of office; religious communities have long had this practice in their parishes.

Dioceses are divided into parishes, each of which has a pastor and, if needed, assistant priests. The pastor and priests are to serve the people of the parish, teaching them, leading them in the liturgy and in lives of practical charity. The people should cooperate with them, contributing their talents in whatever way they can. There is usually some parish organization of which one can be an active part. If there is no suitable group in his own parish, he should seek out one in a neighboring parish, or perhaps a diocesan or informal interparochial group.

Vatican Council II recommended regular meetings of the clergy, religious, and laypeople of the parish, and also interparochial meetings. (Decree on the Apostolate of the Laity, no. 26). It is evident today that much of the administrative work of a parish might be taken over by competent laypeople; various types of lay boards are successfully operating in some places. We can learn much from our Protestant brethren about this.

> Where diocesan and parish councils are functioning in the Church, getting them under way and keeping them operating effectively has usually been a difficult and yet deeply rewarding process. Gradually clerical authorities and people come to know and trust one another, and also trust the democratic process, and real progress can emerge. Catholicism is now experiencing what our Protestant brothers have long been struggling with; it is a slow but vitally necessary process, requiring patience, openness, and charity of all involved.

The parish, with the church as its center, is the place where the Christian people gain strength and go forth continually into the world to witness to Christ. From the local Christian community grace goes forth into the whole neighborhood—and the more truly Christian they are, the more their influence will radiate to everyone, to the whole world. The parish priest is the living sign of the unity of those who are a part of their little community; he must do the best he can to represent Christ by his service to all who come to him.

> However, in today's increasingly urban and mobile society, our large city parishes particularly are less and less able to produce an effective contact, or any real sense of community, among the people within their boundaries. Solutions are gradually being

tried: smaller parishes that are not burdened with the upkeep of a large "plant"; "little parishes," ideally with a priest over each, within the structure of the larger unit; or special services given to specialized groups by priests trained for this, using whatever facilities of the "secular city" are available.

In today's changing Church, a number of people, especially those who are younger, are seeking out parishes other than their own where the style of worship and activities are compatible with their religious needs. While we might wish that every parish could be "all things to all men," it is evidently not possible, particularly in this age of change and polarization.

Mutual aid among parishes of a diocese—and of the world—should be practiced more and more, with the wealthier in terms of money, talent, and stable population helping the less well off. Interparochial structures are also being used more today, particularly for effective religious education, social action, etc.

IN THE LITURGY

At Mass in the Prayer of the Faithful we pray particularly for those who are associated with us in the Church—for those who are sick, deceased, or in any need, as well as for our bishop, priests, and religious. During the eucharistic prayer of the Mass we pray for all the types of people in the Church, clergy and lay, living and dead, and ask the intercession of those who have gone on ahead of us into eternity.

DAILY LIVING: THE MATTER OF VOCATION

People are gifted and inspired by God to live a particular form of life. This is their vocation. Most are to be in the married state, others are called to be priests or religious, and yet others are attracted to remain in the single life. An indication of one's vocation is an attraction to that particular state plus the capability of living it. Each person should ask for guidance in choosing or in living the vocation that he feels God wants him to have.

We should recognize also the single life—aside from the priesthood or religious life—as a true vocation, and one that can be fruitful and joyful. Some can be single involuntarily, or have a divided mind about marriage, and their lives might be filled with sadness and frustration. But others accept their single state, try to center their lives on others, and often show great creativity in helping others and the world in general. Some of the best people in the Church are living this sort of life.

If one's son or daughter feels an attraction to the priesthood or religious life, he or she should be encouraged to follow this up freely and intelligently. Good vocational counselling is available today in the Church. No seminary or religious community wants to carry along those who would be misfits in such a life. More and more, too, it is seen that this choice must be made when young people are more mature, if they are to persevere in this life.

On the other hand, there are a number of unhappy people in our midst who were blocked when they were younger by possessive parents from following an attraction to the priesthood or religious life. ". . . One does not take the honor upon himself, but he is called by God, just as Aaron was" (Hebrews 5, 4).

SOME SUGGESTIONS FOR . . .

DISCUSSION

Is it evident to you how the Church is a family, a community in which all should have a part?

How do you think the Church locally, as you know it, might more effectively use the gifts of all to serve all? What do you think are the most notable problems, and possibilities, of the priesthood today? Of the religious life?

FURTHER READING

* *The Priestly Amen,* Rihn (Sheed & Ward, 1965)—An incisive book by a priest on the life of a priest today.
* *The One Bride,* Sr. Mary Jane Klimisch (Sheed & Ward, 1965)—An entertaining, informative, and theologically sound book on the life of the modern man.
** *Priest & Bishop,* Brown (Paulist Press, 1970)—An excellent study of the biblical and historical roots of the episcopacy and priesthood, and their relationship.

FURTHER VIEWING

Fisher of Men (Paulist Productions, 17575 Pacific Coast Hwy.,

Pacific Palisades, Calif. 90272)—A well executed, 30-minute portrayal of a day in the life of a priest in a busy metropolitan parish.

Consider the Zebra (Paulist Productions)—27 minutes, in color —A parish council is torn apart by differing understandings about the meaning of the Church.

PERSONAL REFLECTION

God has given each of us particular talents—gifts to help carry out his plan. I might ask myself how well I am using the gifts I have—particularly in working with others in the Church family, or with other men of good will.

23

The Greater Family to Which We Belong

Why do Catholics pray to saints? Why is such honor particularly paid to Mary, the mother of Christ? Is prayer to Mary or the saints essential for a Catholic? Can these and other dedicated Christians help us to lead better lives?

THE SAINTS: OUR MODELS AND INTERCESSORS

To be a Christian is to realize that we are joined with one another on the way to heaven. One does not go alone, as if sealed by oneself in a sort of space capsule. We must help and be helped by others. Unfortunately the religion of some is narrowly individualistic, a "God-and-me" relationship. The Church, however, is a family in which we are concerned for one another: "If one member suffers, all suffer together; if one member is honored, all rejoice together" (1 Corinthians 12, 26).

Besides our Church family on earth, we belong to a larger family of God, the Communion of Saints. We are united with those who have gone before us—those in heaven and in the preparatory state of purgatory (these latter we will discuss in the last chapter). We call this the Communion of Saints, that is, the union of all who share in the life of Christ, whether on earth or in the next world; this is why the early Christians used the term "saint" for one another. Later the word came to mean primarily a person in heaven.

From the beginning Christians have believed that our love and help for one another could extend beyond death (except, of course, to the damned). Early inscriptions, as in the Roman catacombs, show that the first Christians prayed for those who had died, and also asked their prayers. Those who had died were still part of the Christian family, loving and being loved, only temporarily hidden from the sight of those yet here below.

We honor and imitate the saints—those in heaven—as we would anyone we love, particularly if he or she is outstanding. The saints are the outstanding members of our Christian family, our Christian heroes. They are the truly great lovers of history. Each one shows some particular aspect of Christ, and in imitating them we are trying to imitate Christ; thus St. Paul could tell his converts, "I urge you, then, be imitators of me" (1 Corinthians 4, 16).

There are saints from every class, every occupation, with every type of temperament and background. They show us how Christ can be imitated in anyone's life including our own. As we tend to follow models in medicine, business, science, homemaking, etc., so here. Statues, pictures, relics (things which belonged to the saint) are reminders of them and their holiness; such things have no power of themselves, and to believe such would be superstition.

The Church is careful about who is declared to be a saint. For the past several centuries they have had to undergo the long process of "canonization", a scrupulous investigation for several decades of every aspect of their lives including the scrutiny of a "devil's advocate" whose sworn duty it is to try to disprove their holiness, and usually the requirement of miracles (cures with no known physical or psychic explanation) through their intercession. Despite this, several thousands have been canonized for their heroic sanctity, declared to be with God in heaven.

In earlier centuries saints often became such through popular acclamation or continued veneration. During those more credulous centuries some were venerated as saints about whom little or nothing was known, and others have been shown by modern research to have little claim to our veneration. A group of historical researchers called the Bolandists have been at work for the past few centuries systematically and painstakingly separating fact from fiction about the saints. No claim is made that the canonized saints are more than a tiny fraction of those who are with God in heaven. They are simply the ones that God has brought to our attention in the Church, to spur us on to imitate them. Undoubtedly there are other and holier people in heaven, but the saints are proof that holiness and heaven are attainable, that it *can* be done, and they show us how to do it amidst the same circumstances of life as our own. The great Swedish Lutheran

Bishop Soderblom put it precisely: "The saints make clear to us that God lives."

We ask the saints to pray for us, as we might ask someone here on earth for their prayers. Since we are all one family, if we are attracted to certain saints and ask for their help, their love can help us as it might have if we had known them on earth. This is only natural; if love and interest toward our neighbor sums up the way we should live on earth, we would not expect that those in heaven would suddenly forget us here on earth and have no more interest in us.

For those not used to asking others to pray for them, this practice will seem especially strange. Sometimes Catholics are little help when they speak of "praying to Saint Such-and-Such"— actually a prayer can end only with God, and to believe differently would be idolatry; we should rather speak of asking a saint to pray with us, or for us, to Christ and the Father. The Church's liturgy always asks the saints to pray for us, through Christ to the Father.

> *A patron saint* is chosen at baptism and at confirmation—someone with whom we can feel particularly close. Most churches are named in honor of saints, and there are patrons for various professions, trades, etc., usually from some connection of the saint's life with that work.
>
> *Devotion to the saints is one of the less-important and strictly optional practices of Catholicism.* Often people of a certain temperament or cultural background will find this helpful; it is interesting to note, as was pointed out at Vatican Council II, that some 90% of the saints venerated by the Church to date have come from the three main Latin countries. In the history of Catholicism there has been a good deal of exaggeration in the veneration of the saints; present-day abuses regarding this were reprimanded by Vatican Council II, and significantly at the particular behest of the Latin American bishops.
>
> Reading some well-written, modern life of a saint—or one of the good collections available—can often be a great help and spur to the better practice of one's own faith.

GOD'S MOTHER AND OURS

We particularly honor Mary, the mother of Christ, because of her great role in God's plan of salvation. She was closer to Christ

Christ Among Us

than anyone else, particularly by her virginal conception and sin-lessness—and it was he who chose her for the great honor of being his mother. If she were the mother merely of a great man we would have some reason for honoring her, but not for paying her the honor we do—but if one believes that her son is divine, then it is only natural to honor her greatly. The fact that she is the Mother of God is the basis of our veneration of her.

Mary is God's masterpiece. To honor her is to honor God who made her what she is. Luke depicts her saying this: "For behold, henceforth all generations will call me blessed, for he who is mighty has done great things for me. . . ." (Luke 1, 48-49). If we are sincere in our praise of an artist, for example, we will praise his paintings without hesitation. Mary is God's creature, infinitely distant from him, as are any of us—but she is unique among us in that she was totally centered on God.

Mary shows what God could do with any of us, if we but fully opened ourselves to him. She gave herself wholly to doing God's will—this was the purpose of her Son's mission and therefore of her life. One day a woman cried out to Christ, "Blessed is the womb that bore you, and the breasts that you sucked!" His an-swer shows the real source of Mary's holiness: "Blessed rather are those who hear the word of God and keep it!"

> *Because of Mary's great role she was conceived without sin, remained sinless throughout her life, and was perpetually a virgin.* We saw (chapter 6) the continuous belief of the Church in Mary's sinlessness and lifelong virginity. These privileges of Mary, however, should not obscure the fact that she was totally human, tempted as any of us, sometimes lacking in understanding of her Son's mission and pained by it (Luke 2, 48-49). But she clung to God's will in great faith, as we must often do.

We believe in Mary's assumption, that she was taken into heaven body and soul at the end of her earthly life. Here again Mary imitated her Son who was taken to heaven when his work was finished. What happened to her is meant to encourage us —as she was taken to heaven and glorified, we have the assur-ance that one day we also will be. She was taken in a special way because it was not fitting that the body from which God the Son had taken his human body should undergo corruption.

Mary's assumption is celebrated on August 15th as a holyday in the United States. The assumption was declared solemnly to be an infallible teaching of the Church in 1950, but belief in it goes back to the early Church; a tomb of Mary was venerated, but there were no relics of her body, unlike the apostles and other early Christian heroes; when Christian writers and the liturgy became concerned with Mary's assumption in the 6th and 7th centuries, it was accepted throughout the Church.

Art and popular imagery have been little help in trying to grasp the assumption. We should not think of Mary being taken up through the clouds to some realm in outer space. Our existence after death is not confined by the dimensions of space and time. Mary, like Christ, has disappeared from physical contact with us, and is with God, but in a real sense she is also among us and present to us.

We give special place to Mary's intercession and sometimes consider her our spiritual "mother." Scripture shows her interceding with Christ for a young couple on their wedding day, and despite his seeming reluctance he worked his first miracle to fulfill her request (Cf. John 2, 1-11). Many of the early Church fathers saw a special significance in Christ's giving his mother to John as he was dying on the cross—she was to be a mother to all his followers, by her love and tenderness bringing them to him, as she had once brought him to the world (Cf. John 19, 26-27). So many today, as through the centuries, ask her intercession.

Mary's intercession must not be misunderstood. Vatican Council II tells us: "There is but one mediator as we know from the words of the apostles, 'for there is one God and one mediator of God and men, the man Christ Jesus, who gave himself a redemption for all' (1 Timothy 2, 5-6). The maternal duty of Mary toward men in no way obscures or diminishes this unique mediation of Christ, but rather shows his power. For all the salvific influence of the blessed virgin on men originates, not from some inner necessity, but from divine pleasure and from the superabundance of the merits of Christ. It rests on his mediation, depends entirely on it and draws all its power from it. In no way does it impede, but rather does it foster the immediate union of the faithful with Christ" (*Constitution on the Church*, no. 60).

How, then, can we speak of Mary's intercession or mediation? The more perfectly our will is aligned with God's the more we ask for whatever he wants to give mankind, the more grace and love we can have a share in spreading in the world. Thus St. Paul said, ". . . I complete what is lacking in Christ's afflictions for the sake of his body, that is, the Church. . . ." (Colossians 1, 24).

Mary's will was perfectly open to God's will. She cooperated with Christ's work of salvation as fully as she knew how, more fully than anyone before or since. Not only did she give him birth and lovingly raise him, she watched the progress of his preaching, his final rejection, and then as he hung dying she freely and painfully offered him back to the Father. Her faith and obedience to God's will was total. In heaven now, she continues to totally desire God's will, asking for whatever he wills to give to men.

It is in this light that we must understand such terms as "spiritual mother," "mediatrix," co-redemptrix," and "Queen." By her special closeness to Christ and openness to God's will she does for all what the rest of us do for some. She leads us in our intercession and mediation.

MARY, FIRST AMONG CHRISTIANS

Mary is the model Christian, the preeminent member of the Church. She is a model for us all, particularly in her faith and love. She is the "humble virgin," not noted in scripture for any great deeds, and therefore, one whom we all can imitate. Her life consisted simply in being totally committed to God's will. She is the "fully redeemed one"—she shows how Christ's saving power can transform the entire personal existence of the humblest human being.

Mary is the perfect image and model of the Church itself. She is unique in that no other person has the Church so fully concentrated in herself. From the early Christian centuries the same titles are again and again given to Mary and to the Church: for instance, both are referred to as the Woman who is the enemy of the serpent (Genesis 3, 15), as the Virgin Mother, the Bride of Christ, the great sign that appeared in heaven (Rev., chapter 12), and as the "New Eve" who undid the damage of the first by her cooperation with Christ, the New Adam.

Mary was the embodiment of the Church of the Old Testament, the "daughter of Sion" who personified the people of the promise (Cf. Isaiah 66, 7ff). She was the climax of the Old Covenant, the one who was perfectly faithful, who alone could fully welcome the Messiah and be the dwelling of God among men.

From what Mary is, the Church sees what it should become; by her virginity Mary shows the total dedication to God and to Christ that the Church too must have. As Mary, the Church must be the "handmaid of the Lord" in her trusting faith and love and service. As Mary was the Mother of Christ, so the Church is the mother of Christians—we often speak of "Mother Church." Mary particularly shows the patience, gentleness, and understanding the Church must have to balance its organizational and legalistic aspects.

Mary is particularly the model of our worship. We could say she is in the first pew, leading us by her example, directing us to her Son and our Brother as together we worship the Father. "But standing by the cross of Jesus were his mother. . . ." (John 19, 25) —as she was there on the first Good Friday, so she above all will help us to sacrifice ourselves totally with him at each Mass. Her whole life and purpose are simply to bring us to him.

Mary's influence in the history of the Church has been great. At first little attention was paid to Mary because of the necessary concern with who and what Jesus Christ was. Then she came to the fore particularly as the "Mother of God", a title which was meant to safeguard the true nature of Christ. The medieval veneration of the virgin-mother did much to give woman a dignity which was unthought of in the ancient world.

The devotion of the rosary has had a tremendous influence in helping hundreds of millions of Christians to pray. Among Orthodox Christians an even greater regard for Mary has developed than among Catholics. The shrines of Mary have also had a great influence, particularly places like Lourdes in southern France where each year a few million people come to strengthen their faith in the supernatural—or Czestochowa in Poland which is the center of that nation's resistance to political godlessness.

There have been, and are, exaggerations in the honor paid to Mary. Some, particularly among the less educated, have tended to regard her in isolation from the Church, as one who grants favors in her own right; perhaps much of this is inevitable, particularly among those for whom Christ is more divine than human, who would therefore turn to another whom they could more easily think of as human like themselves.

As we saw (chapter 17) when Christ's divinity was overstressed in the medieval liturgy, the cult of Mary and the saints developed in order to bridge the gap with the divine. Also some prayers and devotions, even of recent times, have been exaggerated, or could easily be misunderstood like the "Salve Regina" which speaks of Mary as "our life, our sweetness, and our hope." On the other hand, we should not expect the language of poetry and popular piety to be theologically exact. An Anglican priest writes of this: "Prayer should always be theological, but not nervously so. Always to be stopping short in praises of the Virgin lest we might overstep the bounds of exact truth is like the man who is terrified lest he might say something extravagant about his mother. A good mother would not mind if he did; still less, if I may use a daring, yet I hope not irreverent, analogy, would a good father overhearing" (*Ways of Worship,* WCC, 1948).

Today many non-Catholics recognize the rightful place of Mary in the Christian Church, just as Catholics recognize a frequent overemphasis on her role. Many theologians in Protestantism are urging that a proper honor be paid to Mary and the saints as a way of bringing us closer to Christ.

IN THE LITURGY

At Mass we commemorate Mary and the saints during the official eucharistic prayers, asking their intercession, that we may be admitted to their eternal fellowship. The various feasts of Mary and the saints during the year are meant to spur us on to imitate Christ's passion and glorification as they did.

The Rosary is the devotion by which we meditate on Christ's life and ask Mary to bring us closer to him. The months of May and October are those in which devotions to Mary are held in some places.

DAILY LIVING: THE SPUR OF SANCTITY

The example of what others have done can often spur us on to do good. Considering how others have overcome their weaknesses can help us overcome self-pity and do something concrete about our faults. Sometimes, when we realize what others have suffered for God and their fellow men, we can be very ashamed of our complaints.

We should read the life of some dedicated Christian, some saint, or some truly committed person—Christian or not.

In asking the help of those who have gone before us, we need not be concerned only with the Christian saints. Perhaps we might feel a kinship with other outstanding and dedicated men of our own era who are in the next life, as Dr. Tom Dooley, the great Indian leader Gandhi, Dag Hammarskjold, or some friend or relative whom we greatly admired during life.

There are many kinds of saints, today as in times past, both canonized and unrecognized. The heroic Dr. Tom Dooley who himself died of cancer while helping the natives of Laos, describes some contemporary Christian martyrs: an old priest there was hung by his heels and beaten throughout the night with stout bamboo rods; another had nails driven into his skull. (*Deliver Us From Evil*, New American Library paperback).

Several years ago 22 young men were canonized as saints and martyrs of the Church in Uganda. They were lay catechists who had been tortured and killed by a fanatical anti-Christian king because they would not renounce their new faith. One had his limbs amputated, first at the ankles and wrists, then at the knees and elbows, strips of flesh were taken from his body and roasted before his eyes, and finally after three days of agony he died. Another was lashed to a tree to be torn apart while alive by savage dogs, while others were burnt alive.

A current candidate for canonization, Father Titus Brandsma, a Dutch Carmelite, defied the Nazi occupation authorities and saved many of their intended victims. He was imprisoned in Holland, and for leading prayers and preaching in the prison barracks was transferred to the infamous Dachau. There he was continually beaten, though broken in health—and finally a beating by a guard killed him.

Several years ago in Hayneville, Alabama an Episcopal seminarian was killed by a shotgun blast outside a grocery store, and a Catholic priest was seriously wounded with him. A girl civil rights worker testified that she was pushed to the ground by the seminarian just before the shooting, thus saving her life.

There are also those who are living daily lives of heroic sanctity, like the slum mother abandoned by her husband who works twelve hours daily to keep together her family of three children; the possibility of giving up, of turning her children over to the welfare authorities has never occurred to her; she has a face worn beyond her years, but her tough, bright spirit shines through.

SOME SUGGESTIONS FOR . . .

DISCUSSION

Does it seem logical that our love for one another should extend beyond the grave?
Does the notion of Mary as the model Christian have meaning for you?
Is there some outstanding person now dead, Christian or non-Christian, for whom you feel a particular attachment, and whose example is of help to you?

FURTHER READING

* *Mystics of Our Times,* Graef (Paulist Deus Book, 1963)— An excellent collection of the lives of outstanding Christians of recent times, who have in common a deep spiritual life.
* *Give Joy To My Youth,* Gallagher (Farrar, Straus and Giroux, 1965)—An interestingly-written biography of the late Dr. Tom Dooley, the heroic medic whom many consider a model of modern, serving, uncanonized sanctity.

PERSONAL REFLECTION

I might try asking for the help of someone I believe is now with God in heaven. Perhaps it will help me to better imitate Christ.

24

Christ's Church in the World Today

What does Christ's Church have to offer the world today? How does one know whether or not to join the Church? What of the scandals and weaknesses within the Church? What of the scandal of disunity among Christians?

CHRIST'S CHURCH IS DIVINE

Vatican Council II "yearns to explain" to all men the Church's work in the world today. The Church is at the service of mankind, particularly to make all men brothers. "Inspired by no earthly ambition, the Church seeks but a solitary goal: to carry forward the work of Christ . . . (who) entered this world to give witness to the truth, to rescue and not to sit in judgment, to serve and not to be served" (The Church in the Modern World, nos. 2 and 3).

Christ's Church is himself and us—divine and holy, and yet human and imperfect. We have seen how Christ is among us in the Church, uniting us with himself, using human instruments to bring us to heaven. He teaches us with authority and certainty through the pope and bishops. He communicates his grace primarily through men chosen by him as his instruments.

The Church is divine and holy because she has Christ as her head, is guided by the Holy Spirit, and has all the helps necessary for us to live a holy life. Obviously not all Christians are holy, but the Church has all the means to make them so. These we have seen: the Mass and the sacraments, the great ways we meet Christ at the critical moments of life, and by which we can be certain of making contact with God; and all sorts of devotions and sacramentals to bring God into our daily life. The Church's laws provide that we perform regular acts of worship and reparation for our sins. It has many groups to help us and millions of people whose lives are totally dedicated to God and others.

The Church has produced thousands of saints, extraordinarily holy people. It is hard to find any group in history that compares with them. The Anglican author Evelyn Underhill says in her classic on mysticism, that it is an historical fact that mysticism is at its best in Christianity, and the greatest mystics have been the Catholic saints. (*Mysticism*, Meridian Books, 1955, pp. 104-05).

The Church throughout her history has worked to take care of the poor, uneducated, and underprivileged, laying the foundations for the education and philanthropy of our western civilization, and influencing other cultures as well. The hospitals, old age homes, orphanages, schools, etc. that have become a part of our way of life were originally sponsored by the Church. The Church civilized and christianized the pagans, brought to the world a new respect for women, marriage, and virginity, and taught men to take care of the poor, the sick, and the aged, all the while continually upholding the dignity of the individual person.

Today many have noted that the Catholic Church has a particularly universal appeal while yet maintaining a striking unity— that it seems to have more to offer for more people of diverse cultures and social classes. In this it is trying to earn its title of "catholic." Vance Packard has remarked in **The Status Seekers** that religion in America tends to stratify according to social status and wealth—certain groups gravitating toward certain churches —with but two notable exceptions: in the area of desegregation, the Congregational Church, and in general, the Roman Catholic Church.

The survival and influence of the Church after almost twenty centuries of opposition and persecution and scandal seems to Catholics to show that it is uniquely guided by God. The Church began with a dozen simple men—one a traitor, another a perjurer, and the rest cowards—and the wildly improbable story that a man put to death by his own people as a criminal was God himself. They started out preaching a way of life that challenged almost every standard of the world around them. Christ had predicted, "They have persecuted me, they will persecute you also . . ." (John 15, 20)—and so they were. First by the leaders of the Jews, their own people; then under the Roman emperors the Church endured three centuries of persistent harassment, torture, imprisonment, and death.

The official attitude was, "Non licet esse vos!"—"It is not permitted you to exist!" The Roman emperor Diocletian confidently built himself a column bearing the inscription: "To Diocletian, who destroyed the very name Christian." Yet the Church did not change its principles in the face of this. Unlike other kingdoms and empires of history, it spread simply by sanctity and suffering.

Scarcely had the Church gained recognition in the Empire, when there came the barbarian invasions and the gradual collapse of civilization. The Church converted and civilized the barbarians, and became the center of stability and learning, the heart of western civilization in the middle ages. But then scandals, quarrels, and apostasies disrupted her from within. Often those within the Church who paid her lip-service—Catholic princes, her own officials—were her greatest enemies because of their greed and corruption.

By all human rules, the Church should have died many times. There were scandals in high places, even in the highest—Dante put two popes in his Inferno. Then came the Reformation which rent the Church, the "Enlightenment" with its apostasy from religion, the age of reason, and the modern "isms." There has been no period, except briefly in the middle ages, when the Church was in tune with the prevailing intellectual atmosphere. Yet today those who called the Church "backward" are dead and largely forgotten, and the Church continues to influence hundreds of millions.

The Church has been persecuted in almost every modern nation. It has survived the oppression of recent dictators, and Communism has waged against it a relentless war of suppression, closing churches and schools, harassing, imprisoning, and killing believers. Yet the Church goes on guiding and influencing millions. For many millions, then, the only possible explanation for the survival and influence of the Catholic Church is that it is uniquely guided by God.

Catholics conclude that it is in their Church that Christ gives men the fullness of his truth and grace. It can trace itself back to Christ and the apostles, under the authority of the pope and bishops, with the same basic doctrine of the apostles. It is united

all over the world in its doctrines, moral code, and liturgy, with
the same authority over all. It embraces all types of people, of
every race and nation. Its holiness, its survival and influence
shows it to be unique. For Catholics then, it is the Church
founded by Jesus Christ to give the fullness of his teaching and
grace to the world.

> *Catholics have maintained their own schools because they wish
> to communicate their faith as well as possible to their children,* as
> a day-by-day part of their lives. Parochial schools came into
> being to preserve and develop the religion of a largely immigrant
> people in an often anti-Catholic atmosphere, and over the years
> they have done a remarkable job. Catholics have sacrificed billions
> of dollars to maintain these schools, and many think it patently
> unfair that their tax dollars cannot go to maintaining their own
> schools as is done in some other countries.
>
> *Today, however, there is much discussion regarding the effec-
> tiveness of Catholic schools.* Some wonder if they have not often
> failed to develop a social conscience. Others ask whether many of
> their teachers could not better be used to teach religion full-time
> to young people who are now obtaining a good public education,
> while most children—to say nothing of adults—are either ne-
> glected or inadequately cared for in their religious training. The
> schools are becoming more and more difficult to maintain as edu-
> cational expenses mount and religious vocations decrease. Some
> see catechetical centers as a possible answer, together with more
> attention to adult education so that parents might truly fulfill their
> role as the primary religious educators of their children.

**The Church, however, is not a privileged, exclusive club for
those who have a sure way to salvation, as opposed to those
who have not.** The attitude of a Catholic can never be one of
smugness or pride. It is only through God's goodness that he
possesses what he does. If he does not live up to his belief, he,
too, can be lost. If he knows more of the truth, he also has a
greater responsibility for living up to it. Often those who are not
Catholics put us to shame by their holiness and love.

> *To say that the Church has the fullness of Christ's truth is not
> to imply that we have all the truth and no one else has any.* Nor
> is it to say that there have been no theological errors held by
> those even in high position within the Church; the Church's
> infallibility, as we said earlier, is quite limited. Nor can the

Church give us the truth in the sense of answering our every question or solving every moral problem. "The teaching office of the Church is not commissioned to tell people what to do, but to make it possible for people do decide what to do." (Father John McKenzie, in *The Catholic World*).

While in the Catholic view there is available in Catholicism all that God has revealed to man, the fullness of his grace and truth, yet the expression of this truth may not be the best, and the communication of grace might be hindered by human weakness. For various reasons Catholics might not use, or might be unable to use, what is available. The Church known by an individual Catholic might be much more human than divine. Then, too, a Catholic might deliberately turn away from the Church's truth and grace. Others who are not Catholic, might use better the truth and grace they have—and many have a great deal—and thus be closer in faith and love to God and their fellow man.

God is present through all of creation, and uses many ways to communicate his truth and grace. He works especially through those who are baptized—"Where two or three are gathered in my name, there am I in the midst of them" (Matthew 18, 20). All men, however, can have access to his truth and grace. To be saved we must be united with Christ, but most of mankind does not realize their union with him. Other leaders, prophets, "gurus," have been God's instruments to bring them truth and grace. Christ is humanity's unique, divine savior and teacher, but others too show forth aspects of God.

The Church's purpose in the world is to bear witness in a special way to God's love among men. By its beliefs it wants to tell men that God has come among us and saved us, that he loves us infinitely and wants us to love one another. It is the way of salvation not for all of humanity, but for those chosen to work more closely in a visible, communal way for the salvation of all— the minority whose purpose is to serve the majority by trying to show God's love in the world. Its members are to proclaim— however inadequately—that the world has been saved and is filled with God's love.

The Church, therefore, is a sign set among the world's people to give them hope, to assure them that God and his love are ever with us, so that all in the world will continue to strive together to grow in love, and not resort to unloving ways. The Church is there to tell us that none of our efforts—even the slightest—is ever in vain, but is helping to bring about an eternal, perfect universe.

WHETHER OR NOT TO JOIN THE CHURCH

If one comes to know and believe in the Catholic Church, he should become a Catholic. If he comes to believe that this is the Church founded by Jesus Christ with his complete truth for the salvation of men, and refuses to join it, he would be refusing to follow what his conscience tells him is true. Christ said of a person like this. " . . He who does not believe will be condemned" (Mark 16, 17).

But if one has doubts about the truth of one or another of the Church's basic doctrines, or if he is satisfied with his present belief, he should not become a Catholic. Some are able to accept the Church's teachings, and others of equally good faith are not. The ability to believe, as we said earlier, comes ultimately from God. All one can, and must do is try to live up to his conscience.

Our belief must always be a free response to God, with our conscience our supreme guide. If we have tried to inform ourselves about what God wants, and sincerely try to live up to our conscience, we can rest content. In finding God's will for us, we must "enjoy immunity from external coercion, as well as psychological freedom" (**Declaration on Religious Freedom, no. 2**).

. . . Every man has the duty, and therefore the right, to seek the truth in religious matters, in order that he may with prudence form for himself right and true judgments of consciences . . . However . . . the inquiry is to be free . . . In all his activity a man is bound to follow his conscience faithfully . . . he is not to be forced to act in a manner contrary to his conscience. Nor, on the other hand, is he to be restrained from acting in accordance with his conscience, especially in matters religious. (*Declaration on Religious Freedom*, no. 3).

One should never become a Catholic solely to have the same religion in a marriage, or to please someone else. He may have come to investigate the Church because he intended marrying a Catholic (as most do), and he sees that sharing the same faith will be a great thing for the marriage and for the children—but now, to become a Catholic, he must believe on his own. He must now feel that there is something more in Catholicism than what he already believes, something that he wants and feels he should have in his life—that Catholicism has become one's spiritual home. He may know that the help of a Catholic spouse will be needed to live his new belief, but he can sincerely say that he is not becoming a Catholic for the other but rather on his own.

If one is undecided, it is good to consider whether he has true doubts or only difficulties. If one doubts the truth of one or another of the Church's basic doctrines, or if one is simply not sure, he or she should not become a Catholic. One should remember, however, that one does not have to accept, or practice, every Catholic belief with equal attention or enthusiasm. One might, for example, accept the Church's Marian doctrines, but realize that they probably will never be very meaningful in one's life. This would be a difficulty—something hard to accept. Or it might be something one is not able to understand, for example, how Christ's presence can be in the wafer of the eucharist, or how three Persons are one God, or something intellectually or emotionally repugnant—such as some Catholic devotions or some clerical attitudes.

There may be family opposition to one's becoming a Catholic (read Luke 12, 51-53, and Matthew 23, 34). This can be particularly difficult. Usually later, when the family sees the convert is happy in his new faith, opposition is replaced by acceptance. Then, too, one should realize that after twenty or thirty years in another religious background, or with perhaps no religious background, it is only natural that he should take time to adjust to Catholicism. There many be little or no emotional enthusiasm about this step. The famous English convert, Cardinal Newman, summed up such feelings: "A thousand difficulties do not make a single doubt."

If one wonders whether there are doubts or only difficulties, he might consider whether or not he wants to live the life of a good Catholic. Despite the fact that some of the teachings may not yet be fully accepted intellectually, or he is simply not sure, is there the interior desire to live a Catholic life? One might also ask himself: Do I feel at home, comfortable at worship here in this Catholic community—Do I feel that Catholicism is helping me find God and do his Will—Do I think that I am a better person because of my Catholic experience? Obviously, too, one who is thinking about this should consult a priest.

Finally, the way to the Catholic Church for any individual is a two-way street. One usually brings to it as much as he receives. The Church needs and profits by the things the convert has acquired from a background in another religion, from his or her own religious insights and moral strivings. The convert must try to be aware of what he or she can contribute, and patiently but perseveringly try to use one's special gifts within the Church. Many of the Church's best people are those who found their way to it as adults.

CHRIST'S CHURCH IS HUMAN

The human beings Christ uses in his Church remain truly human, weak, and subject to sin. This is why he guides his Church through infallibility, to make sure it will never teach error because of human weakness. There have been bad popes, bishops, priests, and people throughout the Church's history. Christ warned us that this would happen. He compared the kingdom to a net containing good and bad fishes, a flock from which some sheep stray, a field containing both good and bad growths: Read Matthew 13, 24-30.

Of Christ's chosen apostles, Peter denied him, Judas betrayed him, and all but one deserted him in his most crucial hour. If these who were close to him could act so scandalously, we should expect scandals among their successors centuries later—". . . it must be that scandals come, but woe to the man through whom scandal does come!" (Matthew 18, 7). It is significant that the gospels tie in a personal reprimand of Peter with each conferral of power on him; this clearly shows the distinction between the man, who would be weak and sinful, and the office which would be divinely protected. Unworthy men are then to be expected in Christ's Church in all ages; they should not cause us to have doubts about the truth of the Church, any more than one would have doubts about mathematics because some professors are poor teachers.

The Church is "very well aware that among her members, both clerical and lay, some have been unfaithful to the Spirit of God during the course of many centuries; in the present age, too, it does not escape the Church how great a distance lies between the message she offers and the human failings of those to whom the gospel is entrusted . . . The Church also realizes that in working out her relationship with the world she always has great need of the ripening which comes with the experience of the centuries. Led by the Holy Spirit, Mother Church unceasingly exhorts her sons to purify and renew themselves so that the sign of Christ can shine more brightly on the face of the Church" (*The Church in the Modern World*, no. 43).

Many of the institutional elements of the Church particularly scandalize people, and must be unrelentingly reformed. There are many things in the Church's human organization which cause the best people both within and without the Church to draw back from it. The best people within the Church are facing these realistically, and are determinedly working to improve them:

The panoply and pomp of the Church's ceremonial, the formalities, medieval garb and monarchical titles, especially surrounding the papacy and the hierarchy. The Church, however, is an ancient institution and much of its ceremonial expresses its tie with the past, like that of many European governments, our own governmental and military ceremonies, fraternal rituals, etc. Today, however, there is under way a promising movement of simplification, spurred by Pope Paul's simplification of Vatican ceremonies and practices, and the Council's decrees on the liturgy, the stress on a hierarchy of service, etc.

The bureaucracy, over-centralization, and legalism of many of the Church's structures and procedures. Some wonder why the Church's cannot have the gospel simplicity of Christ's band of followers—but any human organization must grow in complexity as it grows in size. Yet it is all too true that churchmen often have become "frozen" in bureaucratic methods, that there is too much legalism in the Church's procedures. But here again the Council has spurred a movement of adaptibility, decentralization and simplification that hopefully will continue to gain momentum. Many scandalous procedures—silencing of scholars, arbitrary censorship, political involvements, excessive secrecy—are slowly being reformed as a result of stinging conciliar and lay criticism.

The lack of Church leadership especially in the great social issues of our time. In Nazi Germany, though the Church was persecuted, the "sin of silence" was committed by Christian prelates and people alike; the German hierarchy has since made many calls for repentance and restitution and spurred the Council's declaration condemning anti-semitism. Today, unfortunately, the Church's hierarchy has sometimes been divided, silent or trivial on relevant moral and social issues—many of them

wanting to keep intact the institutional structure at the cost of
human rights. This is the recurring temptation of any institution,
even one with a divine aspect. The struggle for a truly free
and prophetic Church that will make itself heard when grave
questions are presented to a nation's conscience is one that must
always go on with persistence and patience.

In all this Catholics remember that the twelve apostles chosen
by Christ himself were far from outstanding. They realize, too,
that many of today's issues are complex, and that bishops trained
and skilled in administration cannot usually be expected to speak
expertly on these things. They look for improvement to the imple-
mentation of the Council's recommendation that bishops regularly
consult with their clergy and people, and with one another, in a
more organized way, and they look also to a more representative
way of selecting bishops in the future. The potentially articulate
voice of a better-and-better educated laity will, hopefully, help im-
mensely in forming the Church of the future.

**The Church, then, is in need of continual reformation and
renewal.** "While Christ, holy, innocent and undefiled, knew nothing of sin . . . the Church, embracing sinners in her bosom, at the
same time holy and always in need of being purified, follows the
endless way of penance and renewal. Christ summons the Church
to continual reformation as she goes her pilgrim way . . ." (**Constitution on the Church,** no. 8; **Decree on Ecumenism,** no. 6). God
afflicts the Church so that it will never forget it is a pilgrim here
below; he hammers and chisels at it so that it will remain a useful tool.

**As a member of the Church one is a part of its structure, with
its strengths and its weaknesses,** its certitude and formalism, its
love and legalism. Many have suffered much in remaining loyal to
the Church. When the French worker priests, for instance, were
suppressed by insensitive Roman authorities, one of them, Father
de Lorgeril, literally died of sorrow. The great Teilhard de Chardin also suffered much from the same narrowness and short sight-
edness, yet he wrote.

Blessed are they who suffer at not seeing the Church so fair as
they would wish, and are only the more submissive and prayerful
for it. It is a profound grief, but of high spiritual value. It can
never be repeated too often: the Catholic is the man who is sure
of the existence of Jesus-Christ-God, for a number of reasons and
in spite of many stumbling-blocks. Why is it that so many minds

see nothing but the stumbling-blocks and wait until they are removed before they look at the reasons? (Teilhard de Chardin, *Making of a Mind,* Harper and Row, 1965, p. 59).

Franz Jagerstatter was an Austrian peasant who was beheaded in 1943 because he refused to serve in Hitler's army. A loyal Catholic to the end, he went against the advice of his compromising bishop, priest-friends, and family, and died like St. Thomas More. *"In Solitary Witness"* is the title of the inspiring book about his life and martyr's death. Like Joan of Arc he is now being proposed for canonization by some of the very churchmen who acquiesced in his death. Countless others have helped fulfill the Church's mission of redemption while yet suffering deeply from her inadequacies.

Our current age particularly is a time of crisis and change in which the Church is becoming less an institution and more a community—less a structure and more a place where truly human persons encounter Christ and one another—less a judge of the world and more in love with the world. The work of renewal begun by Pope John and Vatican Council II is continuing, and this means critical re-examination, development, creativity— and also confusion, reaction, uncertainty.

Today, since Vatican Council II, the Church has come into difficult times, in the opinion of many. The hopeful, halcyon days that followed Vatican II are over, and the Church in many places is divided and confused. Conservative Catholics are unhappy with many of the changes that have taken place; it has been very difficult for many to see cherished practices discarded and old certitudes universally questioned. Progressives, on the other hand, feel that the brakes have been put on the reforms begun by the Council, by a frightened, tired, and conservative hierarchy which is very often incapable of real leadership. Young people are clearly not taking the Church as seriously as they once did, and uncounted numbers of them have abandoned it altogether, "turned off" by irrelevant liturgies, negative sermons, by proscriptions against birth control, divorce and remarriage, etc., and by a general dissatisfaction with the inadequacies of institutional religion.

Many of the Church's current difficulties are due to the era of rapid change in every field, and the consequent confusion and conflict, through which we are now living. It was inevitable that the Church should suffer from the same stresses as the other institutions of our society. The Church particularly, as the great stabilizing influence of Western civilization for almost two thousand years, could not be expected to cope with the change that is all about us to everyone's satisfaction. It was inevitable that many people in the Church would be hurt and alienated.

But there are hopeful signs as well: In many, many places the reforms of Vatican II are slowly and quietly going forward; aging obstructionists are gradually disappearing from the scene, and in many parish councils, for example, conservatives and progressives are learning to dialogue and to work together. Many people are learning a new tolerance, an appreciation of other world religions, the fact that there are many theologies within the Church, that one can submit to the Church's guidance without giving up the inviolability of his conscience. Many detect an increased moral awareness and sensitivity today, particularly in social matters, by comparison with only a few decades ago. In many places, new, imaginative liturgical forms are slowly emerging and often stir young and old alike. The "people of God" are more and more realizing that the Spirit is stirring among them, and that they need not wait for official leadership to act. Change usually begins from below and then is gradually accepted above—the "peace movement" within the Church comes immediately to mind. A new and deep interest in spirituality (Pentecostal, private, or otherwise) is manifesting itself. New theological insights, often upsetting at first sight, are bit by bit revealing a profound and staggering vision of God, man, and the universe undreamed of before. Today the Church can no longer be triumphalistic—it must be humbler, poorer, simpler, and more honest—more like the way Jesus Christ himself envisioned it.

Today particularly it seems to take maturity to be an active member of the Church. It is no longer as simple and unchallenging as it once was. Each of us is challenged to examine his faith and find God for ourselves within the Church, instead of having him spoonfed to us. The most authentic religious act of some will be to reject the caricatured God of the institution, the comfortable, narrow God that was once given them.

In all this we recognize that the structures of the institutional Church, however inadequate and in need of continual reform, are

necessary. Those who know the Church realize that Christ's message would have been lost to history had the institution not been there—however it obscured his message at times. They know that the institution is basically meant to be a ministry to serve the Christian people, that it can never do this adequately, and that even when it fails Christ goes on accomplishing his work in mankind. He brings success out of our human failures. This should not surprise us, for it is ultimately Christ who is working among us.

The Church reproduces the weakness and humiliation of Christ. Christ was sinless but accounted a sinner and traitor to his people. The Church is sinners who are trying to bring Christ to all people. The Church must reproduce in itself the whole mystery of Christ, especially that of his cross—and no cross is greater for those who love Christ than the weaknesses of his Church. "Christ lives on in the Church, but he lives as crucified. . . . The imperfections of the Church are the cross of Christ. (Guardini)

A modern theologian writes perceptively:

. . . *Let us love the Church of weakness* . . . We are not ashamed of her because there are so many shameful things about her. We take it for one of the most overwhelming proofs of her unity and holiness that she has always had to suffer from the disdain of human refinement . . . We tremble for her when we see her excessively honored by the world. Rather—wherever in the world it is a disgrace or a ridiculously old-fashioned thing to be a Catholic, there we know in the pure joy of our faith: the kingdom is near . . .We must cherish the Church as Christ does. We must fill her with warm love. We must console her and embrace her. We must intercede for her with the jealously of God. In a word, we must love her in her totality and without conditions. And behold, precisely in this love, the transformation of the Church from weakness to power, from crippled ugliness to immortal beauty, is taking place, silently and irresistibly until the end of time . . . (Hugo Rahner, in *The Church: Readings in Theology* (Kenedy, 1963), Vol. 1, pp. 12-13).

RECONCILING THE DIVIDED CHURCH

Due to human weakness through the centuries the unity of Christ's Church has been upset by individuals and groups. These splits within the Church have usually been caused, on the one hand, by the shortsightedness and sinfulness of the Church's members, and particularly those in authority, and on the other, by the impatience of those who wanted to reform the Church.

Among those who split from the Church, a heresy is a denial of an infallible teaching of the Church, while a schism is a denial of the Church's authority. Both have existed from the beginning in the Church. John wrote the fourth gospel with those in mind who were even then denying the true nature of Christ. St. Paul was constantly harassed by those he calls "deceitful workers, disguising themselves as apostles of Christ" (2 Corinthians 11, 13). 1 John 2, 19 and 2, Peter 2 also refer to those who broke away from teaching of the apostles. In the early centuries and into the middle ages there were many heresies, great and small; most of them have long since passed into history and a few continue today in a weak form.

The Eastern Orthodox Churches came about when certain ancient Churches, mostly of the Middle East, separated themselves in the 11th century from the authority of the pope. The background of this split (touched on briefly in chapter 10 in the discussion of the papacy) shows that the causes were more cultural and political than religious.

As the Christian Church developed, the four great patriarchates, particularly Rome and Constantinople, became the leading churches and centers of unity. In the East, the local churches gradually found a common unity—geographical, political, social, and cultural—under the same emperor, who came to consider himself the ultimate representative of Christ on earth. In the West, however, the unity of the Church was to be independent of all secular power, including that of the emperor. We saw that while the Eastern Churches had little recourse to Rome during the first four centuries, their recognition of Rome's teaching as the criterion of orthodoxy became more frequent from the 5th century on; they were thus originally united with the Roman Church.

However, with the rising political power of Constantinople, an inevitable rivalry developed between it and Rome. The pope assumed a central role in uniting the western world that was becoming more and more opposed to the Byzantine Empire. The eastern emperors tried to browbeat the popes and sometimes imprisoned them, and the popes in turn showed a disdain for the legitimate leadership among the Eastern Churches of the patriarch of Constantinople. Then a 9th century pope, who was particularly insensitive to the eastern tradition of autonomy among the patriarchates, tried to impose upon them a strongly centralized papal authority. They reacted and eventually, in 1054, split with Rome.

A few times during the succeeding centuries these Churches were again united with Rome, but the positions against one another gradually hardened: the Latins would not recognize the legitimate basis of the powers of the oriental bishops and saw the uniformity of western Catholicism as the only ideal (positions reversed by Vatican Council II, incidentally). On the other hand, the Orthodox came to look on every development of dogma in the Western Church as a betrayal of apostolic tradition, and the Churches often became isolated nationalistic enclaves.

The causes of this schism were as much political and cultural as doctrinal—the Greek mentality versus the Roman, the isolation caused by Islam, etc.—furthered by a good deal of pride and lack of understanding on both sides. Today an ecumenical "thaw" has been developing between the Churches, culminating in the moving meetings of Pope Paul and Patriarch Athenagoras of Constantinople in the Holy Land in 1964 and recently in Istanbul, from which have come regular theological discussions with the hopeful ultimate goal of unity. The recent Rhodes Conference of the Orthodox Churches also attempted to achieve more unity for this dialogue with the West.

The Orthodox Churches have the same basic doctrines, moral code, Mass, sacraments, devotion to Mary and the saints, etc., as the Roman Catholic Church. They are the same as the Eastern Rites of the Roman Catholic Church in almost every respect, except that they do not recognize the universal authority and infallibility of the pope. They have suffered heroically for their Christianity, especially from the Turks, and in recent years from atheistic Communism. They are gradually attaining a closer working unity among themselves, and their titular leader ("first among equals"), Athenagoras, is a holy and heroic man who has been harassed by the Turkish authorities—as many of his confreres have been by the Communists.

The Eastern Rites of the Catholic Church are the groups among the Eastern Churches that are united with Rome. A "rite" is not just a particular way of worship, but a whole unique, yet Catholic tradition, including schools of theology, devotions, spirituality, church discipline, art, architecture, music, etc.—in other words, a particular Catholic culture. We of the West must remember that the Christian Church was born in the East and that her life during the early centuries was centered in the East. From there originally came her theology, monasticism, liturgy, and her greatest Fathers and Doctors.

The Eastern Christians' point of view is as truly catholic as that of Latin Catholics, but the emphasis is different. Eastern Christians emphasize the autonomy of the local church, collegiality among the hierarchy, and the mystery of the Church, rather than organizational uniformity and discipline. Their liturgies have many local differences, but this is what largely preserved their cultures and national unity during centuries of oppression. While the West developed an "incarnational" spirit, involved in the present problems of Christian life on earth, Eastern Christianity expressed itself in a more mystical, "otherworldly" point of view; the institutional and juridical aspects of the Church were relegated to the emperor. The extreme autonomy of the Eastern Churches and their attitude of detachment from institutional concerns have obviously had both good and bad effects, as history shows. The same, of course, can be said of the West's more pragmatic approach.

Most people notice the obvious differences of the Eastern Churches from the West in discipline and ceremonial. They baptize by immersion, confirm immediately after baptism, give the eucharist under both forms, have a more elaborate Mass ritual, make greater use of images (ikons), incense, etc.—and their priests normally can marry. Eastern liturgies have a great sense of sacredness and mystery, and they emphasize man's openness in worship to God's majestic action, rather than our own action; they are less simple and orderly than those of the West, but are usually participated in more fully and continually by the whole congregation. More and more, their liturgies are gradually undergoing a needed simplification.

For a further appreciation of the riches of the Eastern Churches and the possibilities of reunion, cf. Vatican Council II's Decree on Ecumenism, nos. 14-18).

The Protestant Reformation was the split in the Western Church in the 16th century. It is seen today that its effects were both bad and good. It was inevitable, we realize now, so many and so deep were its causes.

By the 16th century there had been for some time widespread evils in the Church. There was corruption and scandal in the lives of many churchmen. The prestige of the popes was seriously impaired by scandals and political maneuverings; during the Great Schism, two and even three men claimed to be pope. In many places, there was a superstitious over-emphasis on externals and neglect of an inner religious spirit. At this time also the spirit of nationalism was growing and with it a spirit of rebellion against any authority higher than a local one. A pagan spirit from the Renaissance and a breakdown of the Church's scholastic scholarship contributed to the immorality and confusion.

However, the evils within the Church, bad as they were, should not be exaggerated. The basic doctrines of the Church were still there, though some churchmen were greatly distorting some of them. Historians today testify that there was no general breakdown in the Church's works of charity and mercy and in her care for souls; there were many holy men and women all over the Catholic world who had been working and praying for reform. Much of what happened was due to the fact that this period was a transitional one in history, much like our own, but the church leaders then were too blind, too ensconced in their positions, to see this and change their ways.

Martin Luther, a Catholic priest, joined others in protesting against some of the more flagrant abuses. He did not intend to rebel against the Church itself. His early teaching is a return to genuinely Catholic beliefs that were being largely overlooked. But, caught up in this crucial period of history, faced with the intransigence of the papal court, and encouraged by some of the German princes for their own purposes, he was pushed to some extreme views of his own. Today we recognize that he had genuine insights into the nature of Christianity and that his views were generally not as uncatholic as was once thought.

But anathemas and counter-anathemas had been hurled by both sides, and the split became an irreparable fact. Martin Luther was the first of the reformers. After Luther, others broke away— John Calvin in Switzerland, Henry VIII in England, John Knox in Scotland, etc. Generally, as in Scandinavia, most people did not realize what was happening, but simply followed their rulers, whether Catholic or Protestant.

The result of the Reformation was that Christ's Church was split, dividing millions of Christians as the Eastern Schism had done

earlier Within a short time numerous rival Christian groups sprang up. It was responsible for much religious anarchy, as even Luther testified in his day. It caused much of the confusion we find in Christianity today, with rival Christian Churches disputing among themselves. Only today, four hundred years later, is the movement for unity finally coming to the fore.

The splitting of the Church at the Reformation was the fault of both "sides," as Popes John and Paul and many at Vatican Council II have declared. If the reformers were sometimes extreme, Catholic leaders on the other hand had blinded themselves to how bad things were. As Cardinal Pole, the pope's representative at the reform Council of Trent, admitted:

"Before the tribunal of God's mercy we, the shepherds, should make ourselves responsible for all the evils now burdening the flock of Christ. The sins of all we should take upon ourselves, not in generosity but in justice; because the truth is that of these evils we are in great part the cause, and therefore we should implore the divine mercy through Jesus Christ." (Henry S. John, *Essays on Christian Unity*, p. 12).

One crucial question posed by the Reformation is that of the nature of Christ's Church. The Reformers rightly emphasized the inner nature of the Church as against an exaggerated external authoritarian structure. But by emphasizing the spiritual union of the Church at the expense of the united, visible organization, they went too far in the opposite direction. This was natural, in view of the circumstances of the time—and, as Pope John XXIII said, "We do not intend to conduct a trial of the past, we do not want to prove who was right and who was wrong." But the succession of an hierarchical authority from the apostles had been broken.

Today more and more thinking Christians agree that there must be some external, unified organization in Christ's Church. Unless there is some final institutionalized authority which all will recognize, we shall never have unity—this would certainly seem to be the lesson of 2000 years of Christian history.

The Reformation, however, spurred the Catholic Church to reform itself. History has shown that it was de facto necessary that certain insights and aspects of the Church might emerge, and that abuses be shunted aside. While we feel that some teachings of Christianity have been neglected by our separated brethren, other aspects of Christ's teaching have been well developed and many new insights gained among them. They have "many elements of sanctification and truth" (**Constitution on the Church,** no. 8). We can learn much from each other, as we seek together to know Christ's will more fully and follow it.

> . . . the Catholic Church looks upon them as brothers, with respect and affection . . . in real communion with the Catholic Church even though this communion is imperfect . . . Some, and even most of the significant elements and endowments which together go to build up and give life to the Church itself can exist outside the visible boundaries of the Catholic Church: the written word of God; the life of grace; faith, hope, and charity, with the other interior gifts of the Holy Spirit . . . and also many liturgical actions of the Christian religion (which) most certainly can truly engender a life of grace . . .(*Decree on Ecumenism,* no. 3).

(For a further description of the good things held by our Protestant brethren, cf. Vatican Council II's **Decree on Ecumenism,** nos. 19-23).

We cannot see clearly why God has permitted divisions among Christians. But one thing seems obvious: they were brought about originally by the evil lives of Christians. When God's people of the Old Testament were unfaithful to him, Israel was split. So too among us. Perhaps the confusion and pain of division will make us realize that unity must be earned by the good lives of us all.

Today we see that we deeply need one another. To Catholics, other Christians are our brothers who come from the same family as ourselves. There was a tragic "family quarrel" and we have split up. Today we see once again that our family, the Christian religion, is not what it should be because of our separateness. While, therefore, avoiding a "false irenicism" which pretends that there are no real differences between us, we should try to patiently explain our teachings to one another, discuss our differences, and work to understand and share one another's insights. We should cooperate wherever we can, trying never to do separately what we can do together. Even though our communion is imperfect we are united in the most important things.

Vatican Council II stresses particularly our cooperation in social action:

> "Cooperation among Christians vividly expressess the relationship which in fact already unites them, and sets in clearer relief the features of Christ the Servant. Such cooperation . . . should be developed more and more, particularly . . . where a social and technical evolution is taking place. It should contribute to a just evaluation of the dignity of the human person, to peace, the application of the gospel principles to social life, and the advancement of the arts and sciences in a truly Christian spirit. It should also be intensified in the use of every possible means to relieve the afflictions of our times, such as famine and natural disasters, illiteracy and poverty, lack of housing and the unequal distribution of wealth . . ." (*Decree on Ecumenism*, no. 12).

Today the great movement for Christian unity, the ecumenical movement, is well under way among almost all Christian Churches. The "siege mentality" that had developed during the centuries after the Reformation has finally been almost wholly dissipated, and a new appreciation of Christian Churches for one another has been growing—more fruitfully, as has been remarked, in the past four years than in the previous four hundred. This movement is not man-made, and so we should not expect facile, man-made solutions. It is the merciful God who "has begun to bestow more generously upon divided Christians remorse over their divisions and longing for unity." (**Decree on Ecumenism no. 1**).

To contribute in a practical way to Christian unity, Catholics must first of all take part fully in their own renewal, to which the Council has given such an impetus. ". . . Their primary duty is to make a careful and honest appraisal of whatever needs to be renewed and done in the Catholic household itself, in order that its life may bear witness more clearly and faithfully to the teachings and institutions which have been handed down from Christ through the apostles." (**Decree on Ecumenism, no. 4**).

We must above all pray for unity, among ourselves, and particularly with our fellow Christians. There is simply no substitute for praying together to make us realize the unity we have, and to spur us to work for further closeness. Pope Paul showed the way when he took part in an interdenominational bible service at the close of Vatican Council II. (We saw in chapter 17 the principles that must guide our common worship.)

We must change our attitude, and ask for a humble, open appreciation and love of our brethren. "There can be no ecumenism worthy of the name without interior conversion. For it is from newness of attitudes of mind (Cf. Ephesians 4, 23), from self-denial and unstinted love, that desires of unity take their rise and develop in a mature way. We should therefore pray to the Holy Spirit for the grace to be genuinely self-denying, humble, and gentle in the service of others, and to have an attitude of brotherly generosity toward them. The Apostle of the Gentiles says: **Read Ephesians 4, 1-6.** "This change of heart and holiness of life, along with public and private prayer for the unity of Christians, should be regarded as the soul of the whole ecumenical movement . . ." (**Decree on Ecumenism,** nos. 7 and 8).

Prayer and a gradual, interior change of heart will cause us to be genuinely pained at our division, which "openly contradicts the will of Christ, scandalizes the world, and damages that most holy cause, the preaching of the gospel to every creature." (**Decree on Ecumenism,** no. 1). In many places, unfortunately, people have come to accept the presence of different Christian religions as they accept competing grocery chains or gas stations. Often it is only when one becomes personally involved, as for example when facing a possible interfaith marriage, that one realizes the true pain of division. Division hurts us all. It makes the faith and Christian life of all of us that much poorer, that much less truly catholic.

"We must get to know the outlook of our separated brethren. Study is absolutely required for this . . . Catholics, who already have a proper grounding, need to acquire a more adequate understanding of the respective doctrines of our separated brethren, their history, their spiritual and liturgical life, their religious psychology, and cultural background." (**Decree on Ecumenism,** no. 9). More and more Christians are experiencing the riches of dialogue—getting to know one another, respecting one another, listening, communicating, and mutually growing through one another's insights and our common ministry.

Dialogue with one another, however, can be a difficult and painstaking task. We must go through "the agony of communica-tion." Gradually we learn what is meant by each other's theological terms. Different and seemingly contradictory theological formulations can mask actual agreement, or at least views that are "complementary rather than conflicting"—this because of our "different methods and approaches in understanding and confessing divine things," especially between the Eastern and Western tradition. (Cf. *Decree on Ecumenism,* no. 17.) Pope John XXIII said, "the substance of the old doctrine of the deposit of faith is one thing, the formulation of its presentation another."

We should remember especially that the Church's dogmas, while infallible and therefore irrevocable, can never express everything about their subjects, nor even begin to exhaust the fullness of truth that is in the mystery of Christianity. No formulation can ever adequately express the reality that we come to know in Christ. There is a wide and ever-open field for discussion, explanation, and development in clarifying even infallible definitions. We should also keep in mind that there is a "hierarchy of truths" in Catholic doctrine, that beliefs vary in their relationship to the foundation of the Christian faith, and therefore in their importance in the lives of Catholics.

Appreciation, cooperation and love must also be shown to those of non-Christian religions, and of no formal religion, who so often have good will and seek to carry out their humanitarian ideals. Sometimes non-Christians and secular humanists shame us by the goodness and dedication of their lives; as St. Augustine said, "There are many outside who seem to be inside, and many inside who seem to be outside." There are aspects of truth and love which we can learn from one another; the Church has set up at Rome a Secretariat for non-Christians and also one to dialogue with atheists.

Vatican Council II exhorts us:

Prudently and lovingly, through dialogue and collaboration with the followers of other religions and in witness of Christian faith and life (we should) acknowledge, preserve and promote the spiritual and moral goods found among these men, as well as the values in their society and culture (*Declaration on Non-Christian Religions,* no. 2).

While rejecting atheism, root and branch, the Church sincerely professes that all men, believers and unbelievers alike, ought to work for the rightful betterment of this world in which all alike live; such an ideal cannot be realized, however, apart from sincere and prudent dialogue. . . . Respect and love ought to be extended also to those who think or act differently than we do in social, political, and even religious matters . . . to understand their ways of thinking through courtesy and love. . . . (*The Church in the Modern World*, nos. 21 and 28).

Finally we must remember that the Church is a mystery—it is continually developing, unfolding, growing in its understanding of itself. It is not just a static institution. It is a love relationship with Christ, the Trinity and one another—and like any love relationship it is continually growing, sometimes painfully, revealing new depths and richness. This relationship, however, is unique because it is the mystery of Christ, God communicating himself to men—and this has no bounds whatever.

This is why there will always be change in the Church, new insights, new ways of bringing God to men. The content of our faith remains the same, but what we understand of it grows. The Spirit gives us new understanding, particularly when we are gathered together to hear God's Word and share the eucharist.

Growth, however, comes not only from those within the visible structure of the Church, but from the insights of other Christians, and also from non-believers. The Church must judge these, but must be truly and always open to the Spirit who breathes where he will, and can use anyone as his prophet. At different periods in the Church's history, in answer to the needs of the time, he may bring to light hitherto latent or unnoticed aspects of Christian revelation. Thus there must be among Christians especially a common and continual searching into the "unfathomable riches of Christ."

Changes in the Church call for openness, patience and charity among all. They also call for a deep faith. Some will tend to resist almost any change, others will want everything changed almost at once. The change that is growth is always painful and confusing, but to refuse to suffer this pain is to remain underdeveloped, immature. The willingness to endure uncertainty is a sign of maturity.

The Council recognized the problems involved, that Church members will disagree with one another—but ". . . they should always try to enlighten one another through honest discussion, preserving mutual charity and caring above all for the common good." (**The Church in the Modern World**, no. 43).

> In Morris West's famous novel of the papacy, the hero, Pope Kiril I, comments: "The Church is a family. Like every family, it has its homebodies and its adventurers. It has its critics and its conformists; those who are jealous of its least important traditions; those who wish to thrust it forward, a bright lamp into a glorious future." (*The Shoes of the Fisherman*).

THE CHURCH AND THE WORLD TODAY

The Church rejoices in the world's accomplishments, not only in its own small successes. Every achievement toward making this a better world helps carry out the plan of God, and the Church encourages its members to be a part of this.

> Christians, on pilgrimage toward the heavenly city, should seek and think of the things which are above. But this duty in no way decreases, rather it increases, the importance of their obligation to work with all men in the building of a more human world. Indeed the mystery of the Christian faith furnishes them with an excellent stimulant and aid to fulfill this duty more courageously and especially to uncover the full meaning of this activity. . . . When man develops the earth by the work of his hands or with the aid of technology . . . he carries out the design of God manifested at the beginning of time, that he should subdue the earth, perfect creation and develop himself. At the same time he obeys the commandment of Christ that he place himself at the service of his brethren. (*The Church in the Modern World*, no. 57).

When we work we are carrying out God's plan, as surely as when we pray. There should be no dichotomy though there will always be a "tension" between one's spiritual life and his human accomplishments. Usually an integration is difficult to achieve, but as long as we try, whatever we do is used by God to fulfill his plan for the world's salvation:

> . . . Whoever labors to penetrate the secrets of reality with a humble and steady mind, even though he is unaware of the fact, is nevertheless being led by the hand of God. . . . By his labor a man ordinarily supports himself and his family, is joined to his fellow men and serves them, can exercise genuine charity, and be a partner in the work of bringing divine creation to perfection.

Indeed, we hold that through labor offered to God, many are associated with the redemptive work of Jesus Christ, who conferred an eminent dignity on labor when at Nazareth he worked with his own hands. (*The Church in the Modern World*, nos. 36 and 67).

The Church wants to work with all mankind to make our world a better place, to end war, poverty, and discrimination, to develop the resources of the earth and give all men a share in them. ". . . The world is becoming unified and . . . we have a duty to build a better world based upon truth and justice. . . . We are witnesses of the birth of a new humanism" (**The Church in the Modern World**, no. 55).

One great and pressing need of our world is that of peace. The Church's concern was epitomized by Pope Paul's trip to the United Nations in late 1965 when he pleaded: "No more war— war never again!" Almost everyone knows of the Vatican's constant attempts to bring about a ceasefire, negotiations, and a just peace.

Vatican Council II said this, in part, about war and the arms race:

Any act of war aimed indiscriminately at the destruction of entire cities or extensive areas along with their population is a crime against God and man himself. It merits unequivocal and unhesitating condemnation. . . . The arms race is an utterly treacherous trap for humanity, and one which injures the poor to an intolerable degree. It is much to be feared that if this race persists, it will eventually spawn all the lethal ruin whose path it is now making ready. . . . *It is our clear duty, then, to strain every muscle as we work for the time when all war can be completely outlawed* by international consent. This goal undoubtedly requires the establishment of some universal public authority acknowledged as such by all. . . . The highest existing international centers must devote themselves vigorously to the pursuit of better means for obtaining common security . . . to put aside national selfishness and ambition to dominate other nations. . . . International meetings . . . (and) studies . . . should be promoted with even greater urgency. . . . Those who are dedicated to the work of education, particularly of the young, or who mold public opinion, should regard as their most weighty task the effort to instruct all in fresh sentiments of peace. Indeed, everyone of us should have a change of heart. . . ." (*The Church in the Modern World*, nos. 80-82).

The Church is willing to work with anyone of good will to achieve peace and to better our world. ". . . All men, believers and unbelievers alike, ought to work for the rightful betterment of this world in which all alike live. . . ." Sincere men will disagree on the best means to peace, and it often seems that we have no choice but the lesser of two evils. Unsatisfactory and often agonizing as this may be, it is better than "opting out" and doing nothing to bring about peace. Here again, in our modern world, we must learn to live with uncertainty and doubt, to do what little we can rather than nothing at all.

If Christians must take part in war, they should assure themselves that it is a just war, that is, a last resort, an act of defense against unjust demands backed by aggressive force, with a reasonable hope of victory without doing more harm than good to the people involved—and the military tactics and objectives of the war must discriminate between soldiers and civilians. Some question whether in today's atomic age it is possible to have a just war. Perhaps one's conscience will lead him to be a conscientious objector—providing he serves the human community in some other way. He deserves the support of the Christian community. On the other hand, Christians realize also that they must do what they can to deter unjust aggression and secure peace with justice for all men.

Certain means of warfare are plainly unchristian and immoral. The fact that so-called Christian nations have used them in the past is all the more reason for plainly repudiating them now: attempted destruction of entire cities or of extensive areas along with their population, indiscriminate bombing of populated areas, bombing or terrorist tactics aimed at civilians to weaken the morale of the enemy, torture of prisoners, use of chemical or biological weapons excluded by international agreement, indiscriminate use of napalm, acts of reprisal against prisoners of war or civilians, depriving large numbers of the civilian population of food through crop destruction, demands of unconditional surrender which kill reasonable hopes of a negotiated settlement, and the use of nuclear weapons designed for "overkill" which would very probably lead to nuclear war.

If an enemy uses these or other immoral means, it gives us no right to retaliate in kind. The test of a Christian is his willingness to act as one when others do not.

The role of women in the Church is rapidly and rightly developing today. There is no doubt that, despite the dignity given women in Christianity (in part due to the cult of the Virgin Mother), women have often been exploited and reduced to an inferior status by male celibates who were often unconsciously anti-feminist. This is changing, as woman's role in all of society is changing. Archbishop Byrne of St. Paul summed up the thoughts of many in the Church today at the 1971 Synod in Rome: "No argument should be used to exclude women from any service to the Church if it stems from male prejudice, blind adherence to merely human traditions that may have been rooted in the social position of women in other times, or questionable interpretations of Scripture."

DAILY LIVING: THE COMPASSIONATE CHURCH

The Church's mission, and that of every Christian, must first of all be to the poor, underprivileged, and oppressed. We must desire for all men what we desire for ourselves: civil rights, health, adequate education, development, civilization, and culture. Over half the world is deprived of some major need. Yet our American contribution, to the economies of backward and starving nations is one-half of one percent—less than what we spend annually on cigarettes and chewing gum.

In our own country forty million people are poor or deprived. 12,000 of the world's people die each day from some form of starvation. In India six million babies die each year because of malnutrition. Half the children in the Middle East will not live into adolescence. Several million families in Latin America must survive on the equivalent of a dollar a week. As we consider these facts we should also consider Christ's clear words about how we will be judged at the end: **Reread Matthew 25, 34-40.**

Vatican Council II speaks plainly of the scandal of so-called Christians who are unconcerned with the poor and deprived of the world: "Some nations with a majority of citizens who are counted as Christians have an abundance of this world's goods, while others are deprived of the necessities of life and are tormented with hunger, disease, and every kind of misery. This situation must not be allowed to continue, to the scandal of humanity. For the spirit of poverty and of charity are the glory and authentication of the Church of Christ." **(The Church in the Modern World, no. 88).**

The Council reiterates that the Church must above all imitate the poor and persecuted Christ in carrying out its mission:
"Just as Christ carried out the work of redemption in poverty and oppression, so the Church is called to follow the same route. . . . Christ Jesus though he was by nature God . . . emptied himself, taking the nature of a slave, and 'being rich became poor' for our sakes. Thus the Church, although it needs human resources to carry out its mission, is not set up to seek earthly glory but to proclaim, even by its own example, humility and self-sacrifice.

Christ was sent by the Father 'to bring good news to the poor, to heal the contrite of heart' and 'to seek and to save what was lost'. . . . Similarly, the Church encompasses with love all those who are poor and who suffer in the image of its poor and suffering founder. It does all it can to relieve their need and in them it strives to serve Christ." (*Constitution on the Church*, no. 8).

Those who are poor, underprivileged, persecuted, and wayward are the truly special members of the Church. They are "united with the suffering Christ in a special way for the salvation of the world." **(Constitution on the Church, no. 41).** They are the Church's real power—not its great universities or soaring cathedrals or well-scrubbed suburban multitudes.

Pope John once scandalized his entourage by insisting on visiting the worst prisoners in one of Rome's prisons, among them two murderers. After listening to the pope's brief talk, one of them said, "These words of hope that you have just given us—do they also apply to me, such a great sinner?" Pope John's only answer was to open his arms and clasp him to his heart.

SOME SUGGESTIONS FOR . . .

DISCUSSION

Can you understand how there must be both divine and human elements in the Church?

Can you see evidences of renewal—or lack of it—in the Church today?

What, in your experience, has been most helpful to unite Christians?

Christ's Church in the World Today 403

How do you think Christians might best contribute to making the world a better place?

FURTHER READING

* *The Pillar of Fire*, Stern (Harcourt, Brace, 1951)—A Jewish psychiatrist's journey to the Catholic Church, set against the persecutions of Nazi Germany.
** *How The Reformation Came*, Lortz (Herder and Herder, 1964)—A brief but thorough presentation praised by scholars of all faiths.
** *The Spirit of Protestantism*, McAfee Brown (Oxford University Press paperback, 1961)—A readable, informative, ecumenically-minded presentation of the Protestant contribution to Christianity.
* *Catholic Pentecostals*, Ranaghan (Paulist Press)—The action of the Spirit in our age.
* *Belief in Human Life*, Padovano (Pastoral Education Services, NCRD, 1969)—Basic themes of human life (Loving, Laughter, Tears, etc.) and how they are encounters with God.
* *Renewal and the Middle Catholic*, Bausch (Fides, 1971)—Facts based on history to help assess changes; the good and bad points of renewal.
* *Something Beautiful for God*, Muggeridge (Harper & Row, 1971)—The inspiring story of sanctity today—Mother Teresa of Calcutta, and her Missionaries of Charity who work for the poorest of the poor.
* *Doctrines Do Grow*, McGinn ed. (Paulist Press, 1972)—A good collection of essays on questions that are bothering contemporary Catholic believers.
* *In The Spirit, In The Flesh*, Kennedy (Doubleday, 1971)—Excellent essays by the perceptive priest-psychologist on the way a modern Christian may live and grow in the Spirit in a changing Church in a changing world; Father Kennedy calls for the discarding of many useless religious myths and the fashioning of a new, mature Christian vision—including an excellent chapter on "Leaderless Christianity."
* *They Call Us Dead Men*, and * *No Bars to Manhood*, Daniel Berrigan (Macmillan, 1968, and Doubleday, 1970)—Two excellent books by the famous pacifist/protestor/priest/poet, giving the prodding insights of a modern American prophet.

FURTHER VIEWING

The Death of Simon Jackson(Paulist Productions, 17575 Pacific Coast Hwy., Pacific Palisades, Calif. 90272)—27 minutes,

in color—A contemporary story of a black man's fight for
dignity and freedom.

Some Talk About Pool Rooms and Gin Mills (Paulist Productions)
—27 minutes, in color—A white criminal and a black "loser"
discover their common brotherhood at gunpoint.

The Eye of the Camel, (Paulist Productions, 17575 Pacific Coast
Highway, Pacific Palisades, Calif. 90272)—In a Latin American
barrio the Church struggles to become the Church of the poor.
28 minutes.

The Dangerous Airs of Amy Clark, (Paulist Productions)—The moral
aspects of the ecology crisis are explored in this futuristic drama.
28 minutes.

Something Beautiful for God—A B.B.C. documentary on the work of
Mother Theresa of Calcutta. 55 minutes.

Trial by Fire (Paulist Productions)—A half-hour film on morality
and modern warfare, this shows forcefully the struggle
of an American combat pilot as he obeys his conscience
rather than the commands of his superior officers.

A Raisin in the Sun (Brandon Films, 221 W. 57th St., New York,
N.Y. 10019)—128-minute film that is a deeply moving, truly
outstanding presentation of the ambitions and frustrations of
a Negro family in Chicago's South Side.

PERSONAL REFLECTION

As a Christian, a human being, I must ask myself honestly: Do
I desire for all men all that I have and enjoy? Am I doing something to bring what I have to at least one who is deprived?

I might renew my resolution to help some individual poor person or family, someone retarded, forgotten, discriminated against,
or underprivileged. I might join a group that is combatting poverty or discrimination or working for peace—or I might regularly
send help to some charity, mission, or peace project of which I
know.

25
Living Daily the Christian Life

What should motivate a Christian to be "different" in his daily life? Should one do things out of fear, because he is forced to? What are some practical guidelines by which one can live daily a Christian life?

HOW DO WE KNOW HOW TO LIVE?

The way a Christian lives begins with a loving call from the Father. He invites us to share in a special way in his plan. We are free to respond or not. He reminds us, as he did the Israelites at Sinai, what he has done for us—and then he gives us commandments by which we can give him our response of love.

If we choose to accept the Father's loving invitation, we respond in and through Christ. The Christian life is an imitation of Christ, but it is more. It is being transformed into Christ, sharing his life, being here and now his hands and feet and eyes and ears. He lives in us and uses us to do now among men the things he did 2,000 years ago. ". . . It is no longer I who live, but Christ who lives in me" (Galatians 2, 20).

Each Christian, then, is Christ among us. Each is a new, special manifestation of Christ that will never exist again. Each of us in his own way must expect to undergo his "passover," his death and resurrection. We must struggle and suffer and die in order to be raised up to eternal happiness. It is not easy to live a life with Christ and in Christ. But once one tastes this life, nothing else can satisfy.

Christ guides us in living his life through his Spirit who is within us. It is the Spirit who conforms us to Christ, who shows us what to do and who inspires and strengthens us to do it. The Holy Spirit, we recall, is the Person who is love—and in guiding

405

us to live the Christian life he is simply showing us how to love—
or rather, how to let ourselves be loved by God, and then love in
return.

**The Spirit has been sent by Christ to form us into a commu-
nity, his Church, to** show us how to love one another and be
loved. The Church is Christ among us as he works through his
Spirit to unite and guide us, so we can witness to his love among
men. The Church is Christ among us doing the things he came to
do 2,000 years ago. The Church's role in the world is not to build
itself as an institution of salvation, nor to enforce a series of moral
laws, but always and only to help God's revelation of love reach
the souls of men.

The Church has laws by which we live. (It should be evident
by now that they are not nearly as numerous or as restrictive as
might have been thought.) The purpose of the Church's laws is
simply to show us how to let ourselves be loved by God, and how
to love him in return, particularly through our neighbor. All of
the Church's rules, and its every exercise of authority, are meant
only to help us open ourselves to God's love.

**A mature love recognizes that it must have some rules, restric-
tions, and sanctions within which it expresses itself.** A man in love
wants to know, often in detail, what will please his beloved. He
wants to be told how to avoid upsetting their love relationship,
and what to do to grow in love day by day. He fears, with the
wholesome fear of a lover, to offend the one he loves. And because he is mature, he knows that if he offends his beloved, if he
upsets their love relationship, he will only bring unhappiness
upon himself. His love will punish him for what he has done, and
he cannot be happy until he has righted the wrong he has done to
his beloved.

**He knows, too, that because he is human he will sometimes be
blinded—by emotion, greed, pride—or sometimes he is simply
bored with the whole process.** He then may not want to show his
love at all—he is faithful only from a sheer sense of duty—but he
realizes that faithfulness now is the real test of his love. To obey,
to give up one's own way, to show one's love when it is hard,
even very painful to do so, is the test of true love. So it is with our
obedience to Christ in his Church. We know our weakness, that
we will at times obey only reluctantly, but this can be the truest

test of our love of God.

Of course, there is the ever-present temptation to legalism: to equate keeping the letter of the law with pleasing God. A servile fear or a comfortable, rationalized rule-keeping can take over our moral life. This is precisely what Christ came to dispel. He said, "Beware of the leaven of the Pharisees and Sadducees" (Matthew 16, 6); these had stressed the exact keeping of many observances to the deteriment of the heart and spirit of the law which is love. Some Christians, unfortunately, cannot yet realize that "perfect love casts out fear" (1 John 4, 18).

As one progresses in the Christian life there is less and less need to consult the "rules." One gradually develops a Christian moral sense, comes to "think with the Church." He does not expect of the Church detailed answers which solve his moral dilemmas for him (although such may be necessary, on occasion). Rather he tries to grasp the Church's basic principles of morality, and with the guidance of the Spirit, apply them to his daily life. He takes seriously the guidance of the Church in the formation of his conscience, but realizes it is always subordinate to his own judgment regarding good or evil. He realizes that many moral situations are not clearly black and white, that sometimes all one can do is choose what seems to be the lesser of two evils—but this is maturity. As a child must be given continual, explicit instructions when it is young, but has less and less need of guidance as it matures, so with the maturing Christian in his moral development.

Here, then, are proposed not detailed rules of Christian morality, but some general principles for daily living, suggestions as to how to follow the Spirit's guidance in everyday life. Four main areas of life are considered, those that seem relevant to most peoples' lives: Our homelife, our work or school, our social life, and our religious activities:

OUR HOMELIFE

— At home upon arising, the Christian thanks God for another day in which to live and to love, and asks his help, especially for some particular thing that he will have special need of that day. Realistically, some Christians, like a good proportion of humanity, will hardly feel alive, much less prayerful, when they arise; they would better delay their attempt at prayer until they are on the way to work, or later.

— **Our meals** have always been associated in human custom with an awareness that it is ultimately God who gives us "our daily bread." Hence we precede our meals—and if possible, conclude them—with some sort of brief prayer. Though it is usually the father's role to lead this "grace", others in the family should also take turns doing it. And we should remember that the best prayers are usually those we compose ourselves.

— **Parents remember that they are God's representatives in the home.** They give much love and affection to their children, and particularly good example by their love of one another. They are "by their word and example . . . the first preachers of the faith to their children" (**Constitution on the Church**). They try to make God real to their children, teaching their children simple prayers, talking to them according to their capacity. They pray with their children to the extent that they can, and read with them the bible or other spiritual books; many good ones are available today for children.

— **They try too give their children the vital sense of security that can come only from unqualified love and kindness.** They try to give their children the "why" of anything they ask them to do. They should always know where their children are and should try to make their home the center of the child's social life, a welcome place to come. They should try to do things together with their children, as a family, alert to prepare them in practical ways for maturity and their own marriage—and they also are alert not to "push" but to encourage budding priestly or religious vocations. They correct their children's faults unhesitatingly, with firm but loving discipline, and inculcate a respect for authority. As their children enter the "terrible teens" parents must be especially patient, firm, and loving, always ready to consult together and seek competent advice, and never yielding to the temptation to give up and let the teenagers run their own lives. As the children grow, good parents do not hesitate to teach them, according to their capacity, the wonderful story of sex. There are many good books and programs available to help parents in this.

— Christian parents should remember that they are the "primary and principal educators" of their children. "Parents moreover have the right to determine in accordance with their own religious beliefs, the kind of religious education that their children are to receive." (Declaration on Christian Education, no. 3; Decree on Religious Liberty, no. 5). Theirs, then, is the primary duty of teaching their children religion, and the Catholic school, catechetical programs, etc. are only meant to help them do it more effectively. There is no duty, of both parents, more serious than this.

— The Christian family will look beyond their immediate circle and try to be aware of the needs of others: the needs of their neighborhood, particularly people with few friends, children whose parents neglect them, the poor and underprivileged of their area—and of the world. Wise parents try to direct their children beyond the selfish and suffocating mediocrity that is often a danger of suburbia, to give them a Christian world view.

OUR WORK AND/OR STUDY

— The Christian goes to his job or profession with the knowledge that his work is helping to carry out God's plan for the universe. No act, however boring or seemingly fruitless, is ever wasted. He tries to do his best because by his work he is spreading love and helping to bring the world to perfection.

— The Christian looks for opportunities to help others in his office, factory, or classroom. He expects friction and conflicts, and tries to "see the beam in his own eye before the mote in his brother's." He tries to be genuinely interested in even one other person.

— The Christian gives a full day's work for a full day's pay, and tries to take a constructive interest in his job. If he is an employer, he tries to provide safe and decent working conditions, to give a family living wage, and share profits with his employees to the extent that he can.

— The Christian in his business dealings practices honesty and justice. He realizes that some things are fundamentally wrong: cheating, false advertising, dishonest business agreements, avoiding one's just taxes, bribery, avoiding payment of one's debts, etc. He realizes that if he has been dishonest he owes restitution; if this cannot be made to the one from whom it was stolen, it can be given to charity.

— **The Christian gives regularly to the poor and underprivileged, of his money, and if possible, of his time.** He realizes that he can become caught up in the accumulation of material things that are not really necessary—while more than half the world is underfed, without decent clothing or housing, and with little or no education. The Christian desires for all men the good things he himself enjoys. He may come to realize that if he never refuses an appeal for help, he will himself never be in want of anything essential.

— **The Christian who is a student** is grateful for the opportunities he has for an education. He tries to develop his God-given talents. If he does not succeed in one field, he tries another; he realizes that he has something to contribute, in God's plan, to the world's development. He is honest, avoids cheating or taking advantage of those who are helping him attain an education. He steadily seeks the truth, realizing that this will sometimes cause him problems of faith, but he knows that doubts are usually necessary as he forms a mature faith.

OUR SOCIAL LIFE

— **Here again the Christian's basic attitude is one of universal love:** ". . . As you did it to one of the least of these my brethren you did it to me" (Matthew 25, 40). He tries to reach out as Christ would to all men. He chooses his friends and acquaintances not only from among those who are pleasant and personable, but also among those who are lonely, defensive, embittered.

— **He tries to contribute to his country, his state, and his city,** by being a good neighbor, joining some civic group and by voting for good candidates; perhaps he may feel qualified to run for office himself. He realizes that patriotism is a virtue, and he supports his country when it needs him. If he feels that he must witness by being a conscientious objector in time of war, he knows that he must "agree to serve the human community in some other way." (**The Church in the Modern World,** no. 79).

— He tries to take seriously the admonition of the Council that he "strain every muscle" in working for world peace, realizing that it is the crucial need of our time. He realizes that he is a Christian citizen of the world and he tries to learn about and help those of other countries, particularly the needy emerging nations.

— The Christian appreciates his leisure time, but also realizes that there are many things he can do to help others in his spare moments: he might visit the sick, particularly someone old, neglected, or mentally ill. He might be capable of giving time to a social or civic group working to obtain neighborhood improvements, better and fairer housing, etc. He is alert to speak out against immoral policies of government, entertainment, etc.—but better yet, he looks for achievements for good so that he can compliment others upon them, even if only dropping them a postcard of praise.

— The Christian respects the person and dignity of his neighbor, and his right to his good reputation. He avoids injuring another in any way, except in self-defense, and he keeps to himself information that, however true, would harm another's reputation. He realizes that hatred, carrying a grudge, or injuring another's good name are usually seriously wrong. He recognizes his neighbor's right to the truth, and particularly avoids lying that would do serious harm. He knows, too, that he has an obligation in conscience to drive safely and keep his car in proper repair.

— The Christian remembers his own dignity, and avoids injuring himself and giving scandal by drunkenness, taking drugs, or by excessive smoking that would harm his health. He realizes that alcoholism particularly can get a hold on one without his realizing it, and he is humble and realistic enough to recognize its warning signs.

— The Christian respects his own dignity and that of the one he professes to love by controlling his power of sex. He recognizes that he lives in a sexually over-stimulated society, and realistically takes safeguards to avoid what he knows are occasions of sin. If he fails, no matter how often, he returns to

seek forgiveness and start over again, realizing that he is
thereby building a disciplined and fruitful love.
— The Christian realizes that race relations are often today's test
of the genuineness of his Christianity. He recognizes that an
attitude of discrimination or segregation on the basis of race
is seriously wrong, and he is resolved to do whatever he can
to help bring integration and acceptance of all. He does not
patronize places, or live in housing, which exclude those of
another race; he does what he can to obtain fair housing, education and job opportunities for all. He does not let apathy,
fear, or disillusionment take over. He recognizes that prejudices are deep within us all, and that solving this problem
will require great perseverance and often great sacrifice. He
tries to look on all men and women as individuals, to get to
know them and appreciate them as human beings with
strengths and weaknesses like himself. He recognizes our
past failings in this, but now tries to make his own the statement of Vatican Council II: ". . . Every type of discrimination, whether social or cultural, whether based on sex, race,
color, social condition, language or religion, is to be overcome and eradicated as contrary to God's intent." (**The Church
in the Modern World,** no. 29).
— The Christian expects that he will be mocked and sometimes
harassed for living up to his beliefs. He remembers Christ's
words, "Behold, I send you as sheep in the midst of wolves . . .
If the world hates you, know that it has hated me before it
hated you . . ." (Matthew 10, 16; John 15, 18).

OUR RELIGIOUS LIFE

— The Christian believes that he finds God daily in his fellow
man, that in his work to make this world even a bit better
he is working hand in hand with God. But he knows, too, that
he must pause periodically, to try to be aware of God's
presence, to recollect and re-motivate himself. He knows that
this is particularly necessary in our modern secularistic world,
when religion is so easily forgotten.
— The Christian also pauses to pray whenever he can, though it
may be only once or twice during the day. He prays with

confidence, no matter how sinful he has been, for he knows that his poor prayer is joined with that of Christ and that it is the Spirit who is praying within him. He realizes that some sort of spiritual reading, particularly brief passages from the bible, can be the "food" that makes meaningful these brief prayer-pauses. He may get help from dropping into church periodically for a "visit" with Christ in the eucharist.

— The Christian who is growing in God's love knows that he must set aside a time to spiritually "take inventory," if possible for a few days or more at least once during the year. He might make a weekend retreat, take part in a cursillo or parish mission or at least a day or afternoon of recollection.

— The Christian also realizes that he must join together with others in order to grow spiritually and help others grow. He knows that family prayer and religious discussion are only a start. He looks for some group that he can join, whether a parish group or some informal one to learn more about his faith, perhaps to do some apostolic work; some people particularly need this, and groups of this sort are springing up today more than ever.

— The Christian remembers that a self-centered Christian is no Christian at all, and he tries to take every opportunity to tactfully share his religious convictions with others, especially those who need something in which to believe.

— The Christian has respect for God's name, for the church which is God's house, and for the sacred things associated with his religion. He tries to be an active member of his parish, contributing his talents and suggestions, and financial support according to his means. He is humbly aware of the prevalent Christian sins: passivity, not wanting to get involved—and greed in not wanting to share one's talents and material things.

— The weekly eucharistic family meal of his parish, the Mass, is the big spiritual event of his week. He knows that if he deliberately neglects it he must ask himself how seriously he loves Christ, or whether he appreciates what the Mass is. He should look forward to Mass and perhaps prepare a bit by reading at home beforehand. He tries to get at least one practical point out of the sermon, and above all takes part in communion as the great source of strength and ability to love during the coming week. He recalls that as long as he is not sure of being alienated by a state of serious sin, he should never hesitate to take part in communion.

— The Christian periodically feels the need of seeking God's forgiveness, of making up for what he has done to his fellow man, of making a new start. He realizes that his life will be one of continually failing and starting again—a constant conversion—and is not discouraged because he is always confessing the "same old sins". He comes to confession, then, to meet Christ and get his personal assurance that he is reconciled with God and his fellow men and on the way to heaven.

— The Christian realizes his weakness and takes advantage of the Church's reminders to do penance. He tries to make Lent a time when he can do some positive good, particularly by way of self discipline and mortification; he abstains willingly and fasts if he can, but he tries particularly to make up for his sins by acts of kindness, patience, and interest in others.

— The Christian knows that sometimes doubts will come, or the spiritual ennui in which he no longer seems to get anything out of his religion. He tries to remember that God is always a hidden God, that he never forces himself upon us, but rather solicits our love, and that his ways are not our ways.

— Finally, the Christian knows that he must suffer and die with Christ in order to rise with him. He expects pain, frustration, hardships during the day. But he tries to offer them up with Christ's sufferings, realizing that this may ultimately be his greatest contribution to spreading love in the world.

SOME SUGGESTIONS FOR . . .

DISCUSSION

What should motivate a Christian's daily life?
Can you understand why one needs some "rules" and what part they should play in his daily life?
What do you think is your greatest need in living Christ's life daily?

FURTHER READING

* *In the Spirit, In the Flesh,* Kennedy (Doubleday, 1971)—

How modern man, through maturity and the Spirit, can live
out his Christian faith.

* *How to be REALLY With It,* Basset (Doubleday, 1971)—
A realistic guide to a truly good life rooted in fulfillment on
the deepest level.

* *Christ Is Alive!,* Quoist (Doubleday, 1971)—A very popular
author presents a new spirituality for our time, emphasizing
Christian charity.

* *Blessed Are You,* Murphy (Herder & Herder, 1971) Beatitudes for modern man; a summons and challenge to the
Christian life.

* *Markings,* Hammarskjold (Knopf, 1964)—Penetrating, somewhat mystical reflections on life by the great former Secretary
General of the United Nations.

** *Christian Morality Today,* Curran (Fides, 1966)—Well-
written yet penetrating discussions of some very relevant
questions on moral teaching in light of Vatican II.

* *An Offering of Uncles: The Priesthood of Adam and the
Shape of the World,* Capon (Sheed & Ward, 1966)—A clever,
sparkling book by an Episcopal priest and father of six, showing how to shape and offer to God the dull as well as the ex-
citing moments of life.

PERSONAL REFLECTION

If I believe in Christ I am tremendously privileged. I can consciously live with him and in him each day, doing the things he
did 2,000 years ago. The Spirit within me will help my poor
weakness and gradually form me into another Christ.

I might pick one or two areas in which I am particularly
unlike Christ and ask the Spirit's daily help with these.

26
Fulfillment Forever

Why do we say that death is the climax of a Christian life? What will happen to us after death? What is the meaning of purgatory? What do we mean by saying that Christians expect a new heaven and a new earth forever? What, ultimately, is the difference in being a Christian?

OUR MEETING WITH CHRIST AT DEATH

Death is the climatic experience of our life. It is more than just a moment of time; it is an experience. We awaken to full consciousness and full freedom, and encounter God himself. All our life has been lived for just this. Death has a fearfulness attached to it because of original sin—men, even strong men, shrink from it.

Christ by his death has changed the nature of our death. The Christian knows this: death is now our most meaningful act, the one to which we look forward as the climax and summation of our life. Someone has said, "The moment a man is born he begins to die." None of us can avoid death, but the committed Christian tries to look forward to it.

Some scholars today hold that in the experience of death (after death, as we humans look at it) a man makes his first completely personal, totally free act—his final decision about his eternal destiny. During life he has been too distracted to make this all-important choice. Now after death, with full freedom and his whole being he chooses for God or against him. This, however, does not mean that one gets a "second chance" after death; all the free actions of his life have been preparing him for and pointing him toward this choice. (Cf. Laudislaus Boros, *The Mystery of Death*, Herder & Herder, 1965.)

It is Christ whom we encounter after death face to face, in the clearest, most intimate way possible. He whom we have been reaching for in our prayers, whom we have dimly encountered in the sacraments, is now before us in the overwhelming fullness of his light and love and power. Our whole life is present, summed up, in this experience. People sometimes testify how their life flashed before them as they faced death—this is but a taste of what will happen when we meet Christ.

We should often think of this moment. We know how we long to see someone whom we love and from whom we have been separated for some time—and on the other hand, how ashamed we are at meeting someone whom we have deeply offended. In these first moments of eternity, we shall be face to face with Christ whose love has always been with us, and for whom we should have been reaching all our life.

In this final moment there is no in-between. The time of probation is over; there are no more chances. We are either saved or damned. This is the ultimate and only important distinction between men: either they have God's grace-presence with them or they do not—either they choose him or they turn away. And we never know when this moment will come for us.

To prepare for death, the Church gives a seriously ill person the last rites:

> **The Sacrament of Penance** (or "conditional absolution" if the person is unconscious).
>
> **The Anointing of the Sick.**
>
> **Holy Communion, here called "Holy Viaticum"**—The Church's sacrament for the dying. This is followed by a special blessing for the dying.

During these rites those who are present should join in the prayers to the extent that they can.

A priest should be called as soon as it becomes apparent that an illness is serious. We mentioned before the mistaken charity of not calling the priest for fear of "frightening" the patient. The sooner in a serious illness one receives the anointing of the sick, the better are his chances of recovery, or at least the better he can prepare himself for this final, all-important meeting with Christ at death.

It should be remembered, too, that if someone dies suddenly or is fatally injured, the priest should be called immediately—even though to all appearances death has already taken place.

The Christian's attitude toward death should be one of confidence and expectation. We know that God wants all men to be saved, that he has surrounded us through life with the constant helps of his love. He will surely be with us at death. No matter what sins we have committed, if we are sorry he forgives them all.

As Jesus faced death confident that the Father would raise him to life, so should we. Jesus assures each of us: ". . . I go to prepare a place for you. I will come again and will take you to myself, that where I am you may be also" (John 14, 2-4).

PURGATION

Purgatory is the painful state or experience of encountering God after death, when we see him as he really is, "face to face," and by contrast, ourselves as we really are. An encounter with the living God must always be painful, totally upsetting. God's manifestations of himself in scripture show this:

> Moses veiled his face when he beheld the burning bush, for he was afraid to look on God (Exodus 3, 6). Elijah performed the same symbolic gesture of veiling his face on Mount Sinai (1 Kings 19, 13). In the vision in which God called Isaiah, even the seraphim veil their faces and the prophet exclaims with the terror of any creature menaced by the divine: "Woe is me! For I am lost: . . . for my eyes have seen the King, the Lord of Hosts" (Isaiah 6, 5). Daniel saw God in a vision of fire and the proximity of God caused him to enter something like a mystical agony (Daniel 7, 9-10; 8, 17, 18, 27). Ezechiel fell down before God, striken with a strange paralysis and with dumbness (Ezechiel 3, 23-26). At the transfiguration the disciples fell on their faces and were filled with awe (Matthew 17, 1-6). And John says in Revelation, "When I saw him, I fell at his feet as though dead" (Rev. 1, 17). (Cf. Boros, *op. cit.* pp. 137-38.)

> To encounter God in Christ's eyes of fire is the highest fulfillment of our capacity for love and also the most fearful suffering our nature has to bear. Seen in this way, purgatory would be the passage which we effect in passing through the purifying fires of divine love. The encounter with Christ would be our purgatory. (Boros, *op. cit.* p. 139).

In this state of purgation we make up for our sins by growing in love. While Christ has made up for our sins, we yet have the need of doing something about them ourselves, as when we offend anyone we love. We experience this painful purgation because we have not loved enough on earth. This is only reasonable. Most people realize that they have not made up for all their sins, that they still are clinging to some faults, and therefore could not expect to be perfectly happy immediately after death with the all-perfect God ("But nothing unclean shall enter . . ." —Revelation 21, 27). On the other hand, they know that they are not evil enough to be damned forever. It is only logical, then, to believe in this state of purgation.

> *The Christian Church from the beginning has believed in a state of purgation after death* where the dead could not help themselves but could be helped by the prayers of those on earth. God's people of the Old Testament had only a vague notion of this, but a widespread Jewish tradition of the century before Christ held that it was "a holy and wholesome thought to pray for the dead that they may be loosed from their sins" (2 Maccabees 12, 46).
>
> The word "purgatory" has been prevalent only since the 13th century. Archeology, however, shows that the earliest Christians prayed for their dead who were sometimes said to be in a "place of tears" or a "place of darkness." The ancient liturgies of both East and West contain prayers for the dead, as in our Mass today. Many early Christian writers mention prayers for the dead: Cyprian, for instance, says (c. 245 A.D.) that such had been said in all churches since the time of the apostles. Tertullian also witnesses to the ancient practice of the Church: "The faithful wife will pray for the soul of her deceased husband, particularly on the anniversary of his falling asleep. And if she fails to do so, she has repudiated her husband as far as in her lies." (*De Monag.*, 10).
>
> In a touching passage of his *Confessions,* St. Augustine tells of his mother's dying request: "Lay this body anywhere at all; the care of it must not trouble you. This only I ask of you, that you remember me at the altar of the Lord wherever you are." (IX, chapter XI).

Those passing through this purgatory state know clearly that they are saved, God's love overwhelms them, and they have a joy more intense than anything on earth. Purgatory has been described as a "place" where we would go for a certain "time" to be purified by "fire." We must not misunderstand this—purgatory is certainly not hell for a short time, nor a vast torture chamber where God revenges himself upon trapped souls nor is there time in our sense in this purgatory state. These metaphors attempt to describe the paradox of purgatory—a state of joy and yet of suffering.

In this purgation what we are doing is growing in love, by submitting ourselves to the burning, penetrating, purifying power of God's love. We realize clearly our immature self-love, our ingratitude, sloth, and attachments to sin. We "grow up" in love, break away from our childish self-centeredness. Our real self then emerges, perfected, totally absorbed in God, totally in love.

All our wayward habits and affections must be directed toward this one, true love. One person at death may still cling to material possessions, another has an overly-sensitive pride, and another has never really disciplined his sex power—all these must be purified, "burnt up" in an all-absorbing divine love. God wants nothing to interfere with his love of us.

There is pain in this purgatory-state. Any deep personality change is painful—and this is our final, perfect change for eternity. Growing in love can be particularly painful, especially when we contrast our imperfections with our beloved. A man with a bad habit—alcoholism, a violent temper—might meet a wonderful girl. He realizes he must conquer this habit if there is to be any permanent love between them; if he loves enough, he will strive painfully until he overcomes it. In this purgation we come to love perfectly the Perfect Lover.

One in this purgatory-state, therefore, wants to be with God, and yet does not want to be with him the way he is. He sees clearly God's infinite goodness and his own faults by contrast—like a piercing ray penetrating and revealing the depths of our being. Seeing his miserable state, he wants to be in purgatory, wants to be purified, and yet he aches and burns with desire to be with God. The pain is simply that he cannot be with him quickly enough. "Athirst is my soul for God, the living God. When shall I go and behold the face of God?" (Psalm 41, 3).

Those in the state of purgation cannot help themselves, but we can help them attain heaven more quickly by praying for them, offering Mass for them, offering our sufferings, good actions, etc. The power of love within the Mystical Body goes on after death. We can help others, even as we will be helped. Sometimes people feel helpless at the death of a loved one, wishing there was more they could do for their beloved; the Catholic knows that the power of his love can help even after death.

We should remember that we need not go through this purgatory-state after death if we have loved sufficiently in this life. Some people by their great sufferings seem to be going through their purgatory here.

IN THE LITURGY

The Church treats the dead body with reverence, a sign of our belief that we will rise to eternal life. The body is brought to the church where a Funeral Mass is offered; afterward, it is incensed, blessed with holy water, and brought to the cemetery where after some final prayers it is buried, often in blessed ground.

The new liturgy for the dead emphasizes our confident hope of resurrection and eternal life. The prayers and songs speak of the fulfillment of life and eternal joy. At the weekly parish eucharist the priest usually leads the parish family during the Prayer of the Faithful in praying for the deceased of the parish. At Mass, during some of the official eucharistic prayers after the consecration there is a commemoration of our dead: the priest may pause with his hands joined before him as we pray for our dead. Black vestments used to indicate that the priest was offering a Mass for the dead (formerly called a Requiem Mass). Violet, green or white are now used—the latter, particularly, as a sign of confident hope in our resurrection.

During the month of November we particularly pray for the "holy souls" in purgatory. November 2nd is the Feast of All Souls, "All Souls Day," on which Catholics usually take part in Mass for their dead.

People sometimes have Masses celebrated for deceased relatives and friends: they usually give an offering, not to pay for the Mass, but to help the works of the Church in the deceased person's name. When done with faith and love, this can help the dead person and console his relatives.

Catholics often say this brief, expressive prayer for their dead: "May all the souls of the faithful departed, through the mercy of God, rest in peace. Amen."

AT THE END

When we speak of the end of the world we mean its completion, its consummation and transformation, not its destruction. Then the limitations of time and space, of disharmony and waste, will be over. A new order of things will begin.

We do not know when the end of the world is coming and we know little about how it will take place. Christ says ". . . of that, day or that hour no one knows . . . only the Father" (Matthew 13, 32). The knowledge of this was not part of Christ's earthly mission, and we need not waste time uselessly speculating about it. There is too much to do with the wonderful world we have here and now.

There will be for all of us the "resurrection of the body," that is, we will be alive as full human beings and not just as spirits. In some sense, our world will be there too, only it will be transformed (Cf. the next section).

Christ will appear in judgment and all mankind before him: Read John 5, 25-30.

The sermon of Christ which is often taken as giving a detailed picture of the end uses images from Jewish apocalyptic literature. Many think that it is primarily concerned with the beginning of the messianic era, the "last days" (Cf. Mark 13, 3ff; Matthew 24, 3ff; Luke 21, 7ff; also Revelation 20, 11-13). At any rate, the Old Testament concept of the "Day of Yahweh," reflected in the New Testament in the above sermon and particularly in Revelation (the Apocalypse), is this apocalyptic style of writing. It dates back to the Maccabean persecution and is a kind of "religious underground resistance" literature; it has striking and mysterious visions, symbolic numbers, explanations given by an angel, etc. —all centering on the fact that though the powers hostile to God are triumphing for the moment, a new era will dawn and God and his people will strikingly triumph.

Christ will somehow be revealed as the Lord and Savior of all creation. All the universe will acknowledge him. He will lead those in his kingdom of love to his Father and eternal happiness.

> Many today do not expect Christ's second coming (the parousia) to be an apocalyptic event in the future, but consider that it has already begun, that Christ's presence is gradually being realized in human history. The end of the world, rather than being passively awaited, is actively being brought about by the love and labor of man. Christ who is among us will be revealed at the end, at the culmination of this unfolding, for all to see in power and glory.
>
> . . . Christ is now at work in the hearts of men through the energy of his Spirit, arousing not only a desire for the age to come, but by that very fact animating, purifying and strengthening those noble longings by which the human family makes its life more human, and strives to render the whole earth submissive to his goal. (*The Church in the Modern World,* no. 38).

When Christ comes to us in judgment the whole of human history will be revealed. Then we will understand the "why" of everything, that all has worked out for God's glory and man's happiness—even the crimes, wars, and countless cruelties throughout history. At present we are like someone with a few pieces of a jig-saw puzzle. Then we shall see the whole puzzle of history put together—and our faith tells us that it will be a picture of immense beauty and love.

Our existence immediately after death could already be something like that of the resurrected man. We will then be beyond time as we know it now. So we should not think of ourselves as separated spirits, having to "wait" until events on this earth have been completed before we begin our full human existence in eternity. There are unanswered questions, of course, about this new existence; however, "a biology of our future life is impossible; at the most only a very restrained anthropology can be outlined." (Schoonenberg, *op. cit.*, p. 199).

THE NEW UNIVERSE TOWARD WHICH WE WORK

After the end there will be a new universe—a new heaven and a new earth. "But according to his promise we wait for a new heaven and a new earth in which righteousness dwells" (2 Peter 3, 13). Since the material world has suffered from the disorder that has come from man's sin, it is only fitting that it should share in man's final glory. The universe is now "in labor" toward this better state (Cf. Romans 8, 20-22).

The new universe will be beautiful and perfect beyond imagining. We do not know the exact nature of this perfect universe, but we do know that nature will be in harmony with itself and with man; there will be no more devastating storms, tornadoes, earthquakes, etc., and the immense power we have begun to discover in the subatomic world and throughout the universe will then be put to full use. There will be a vast cosmic renewal and glorification, and God will be revealed in all things, present among us in undreamed of ways.

It is up to us now to bring about this new universe. We said before that God has placed in our hands an unfinished universe, has entrusted to us the privilege of perfecting his work. Every step we take toward harnessing nature, toward using the power of the universe, continues creation and carries out God's plan of love. We are "co-creators" with God—and the more conscious we are of this the more we can contribute. Particularly whenever we spread truth or expend pain and love for others, we help to bring about the perfection of all things.

Christians and all men who realize this have an especially great responsibility and privilege toward helping perfect the universe. We can never be satisfied with things as they are in their present state. We must be driven on to advance truth and love—for every conquest of the universe which does not help to spread love serves to strengthen tyranny and holds back the perfection of all things.

Who then but the Christian—I mean the man authentically inspired by the love of Christ (for there is no other, whether he bears officially the name of Christian or whether he is one in fact without knowing it)—who then but such a man is capable of placing the universe at the service of love and thus contributing, modestly but efficaciously, to the redemption of the universe, the object of his hope? (Lyonnet, in *The Church*).

By their labor they are unfolding the Creator's work . . . and are contributing by their personal industry to the realization in history of the divine plan. . . . Therefore while we are warned that it profits a man nothing if he gain the whole world and lose himself, the expectation of a new earth must not weaken but rather stimulate our concern for cultivating this one. For here grows the body of a new human family, a body which even now is able to give some kind of foreshadowing of the new age. . . . (*The Church in the Modern World,* nos 34 and 39).

The thought of Teilhard de Chardin particularly stresses that to do the work of the world is to contribute to the fulfillment and completion of Christ's redemption of the universe. The world of matter with which men work is "the divine milieu, charged with creative power . . . the ocean stirred by the Spirit, . . . the clay molded and infused with life by the incarnate Word." As we work and love to perfect the world, we are helping to bring about the clear and full revelation of Christ as the center of all things. Then "the presence of Christ, which has been silently accruing in things, will suddenly be revealed—like a flash of light from pole to pole. Breaking through all the barriers with which the veil of matter and the water-tightness of souls have seemingly kept it confined, it will invade the face of the earth . . . (and) the attraction exerted by the Son of Man will lay hold of all the whirling elements in the universe so as to reunite them or subject them to his body. . . . Such will be the consummation of the divine milieu." (*The Divine Milieu,* pp. 7, 133-34).

HEAVEN, OUR DESTINY

Heaven is perfect union with God forever. It is not a place, not "here" or "there," but a state in which, while yet retaining our individuality, we will be caught up into the infinite God. We will love and be loved with an unimaginable, ever-increasing love. We will be fully possessed, continually overwhelmed by God's beauty and goodness, and yet we will go on thirsting for more— even as we are filled to perfect contentment—and yet seek and find still more, and more.

God will give himself to us. No longer shall we have to reason to him from his works, speculate about him, or catch fleeting, unsatisfying glimpses. We shall see him as he is, his very self, "face to face" (1 Corinthians 13, 12). Each of us will know God and be loved in the most intimate way possible, in a way no one or nothing in creation is or ever will be.

This will be incredible, unimaginable happiness. One cannot

now begin to describe it. St. Paul who was caught up into its "outer fringes" was helpless to describe it; he could only quote Isaiah who had also glimpsed it: "What no eye has seen, nor ear heard, nor the heart of man conceived, (this is) what God has prepared for those who love him. . . ." (1 Corinthians 2, 9).

In this heaven-state there will be no sorrow, no pain, no hardship, no struggle or temptation of any kind. We will understand everything we have ever wanted to—the secrets of the universe, the mysteries of our faith. We will have everything we want. And we will be secure in this eternal happiness, knowing that there is no possibility of ever losing it.

> He will dwell with them, and they shall be his people, and God himself will be with them; he will wipe away every tear from their eyes, and death shall be no more, neither shall there be mourning nor crying nor pain any more, for the former things have passed away (Revelation 21, 3-4).

The liturgy calls this "eternal rest" to try to communicate to us its perfect peace and contentment. Yet heaven is really living at last—looking back, our present life will seem by comparison like a dream.

> The bible represents eternal life by images of activity: the celebration of feasts, worship, the service of God; we are to be the servants who because we have been faithful in little things during this life will enjoy not only the Lord's joy but all his goods (Luke 19, 17 and 19). The activity that is touched with anxiety and struggle will cease, but joyous celebration will go on forever. One author says of this, "If this sounds to us monotonous, it is because we need to rid ourselves of a neurotic over-esteem of productive work, and of a use not yet integrated and personalized of our free time." (Schoonenberg, *God's World in the Making*, Duquesne, 1964, p. 204).

We will be continually growing in love and happiness, fulfilling our every power in the most intense activity imaginable. Even now we know how our consciousness can be expanded. Then we will have our full personality, alive to the depths of our being, fully ourselves, and have perfect love and friendship with others. We will be beyond time and space, able to transcend the whole universe in an instant, be wherever we want and do whatever we want. We will be glorified like the resurrected Christ who is "the first-fruits of those who have fallen asleep" (1 Cor. 15, 20).

In our heavenly state we will also know all those we have known and loved in this world, the saints and all the great people of history—in fact we will be strangers to no one, and we will delight in one another's perfections and in our mutual love. There will be no distracted turning away from God to others, or vice-versa—the problem that so often disturbs us now—but rather we will then clearly see God in them, acting through them, giving himself and revealing himself through them. Everything will then be sacred, for God will be "all in all."

There will be degrees of love and happiness in heaven: the more we have loved in this life, the more of God's grace-presence we have with us now, the greater will be our love and happiness forever. The great 16th century mystic, Teresa of Avila, said that she would remain on earth till the end of the world, suffering terribly, if she would love God just a bit more in heaven.

Christ's teaching assures us that heaven goes on forever (Cf. Matthew 25, 46; 1 Corinthians 15, 52). This, of course, we cannot imagine. But we can try to appreciate its astounding privilege: in return for a lifetime of faithfulness on earth, God might have given us a thousand years of happiness in heaven, and this would be a wonderful reward; or he might have given us ten thousand, a million or a billion years of happiness. But he does infinitely more, so great is his love: he gives us eternity, forever and ever and ever, with himself.

The only thing that can keep us from heaven is deliberately turning away from God. If we fully reject God by choosing a condition of mortal sin, and die hardened in our sin, we have cut ourself off from him, from love, from happiness, and have isolated ourself forever in hell. However remote this possibility, it should make us better appreciate how much we need God's love, should make us work now with all our heart and strength to love him and our fellow human beings.

Above all, we should think often of being with God and Christ and one another in heaven, and have a great longing for this. The early Christians lived in constant expectation of Christ's reappearance, and were spurred to astounding deeds of love and sacrifice. This present life is but a brief bridge between nothingness and eternity; when the crossing becomes too difficult, we should think of our real destiny on the other side. We should not hesitate to cry out with St. Paul, "Here indeed we groan and long to put on our heavenly dwelling" (2 Corinthians 5, 2). Or with John as he finished the last book of scripture, "Amen—Come, Lord Jesus!"

DAILY LIVING: THE DIFFERENCE IN BEING A CHRISTIAN

A special view of human history is what makes a Christian different. He believes that it has an author and a plot and a meaningful end. He believes that all things will one day be perfected in Christ. The Christian works and loves with confidence that nothing ultimately is wasted, that he is carrying out God's plan, that the world can and will be perfected. He can fail, hurt his fellow man, neglect to alleviate some of the pain of our existence, but he knows that the victory is on its way. He is convinced of what Christ said: ". . . He who hears my word and believes him who sent me, has eternal life . . . (and) has passed from death to life" (John 5, 24).

The Christian knows that his life is often no better than that of the unbeliever (and sometimes it is worse), that he is weak, a sinner, often confused, and even capable of monstrous misdeeds. He knows that only some Christians grasp and live their life with Christ at all fully. But he believes that somehow God uses his poor efforts, takes them and transfigures them into love that is changing the world. He believes that "he who has begun his work in you will complete it" (Philippians 1, 6). This is because he knows that God has come among men in Jesus Christ, that he himself is now joined to Christ, and that this gives even his poorest efforts a new power.

By his life the Christian tries to radiate Christ's love to the world. He tries to show, especially in the union with his fellow Christians that is the Church, the love that animates them all. He knows that he needs the Church—its Word and its sacraments, particularly the eucharist—as his daily strength. He tries not to expect visible results from his acts of love, and realizes that he must often live in a "dark night" where faith seems to be dead and God vanished.

He knows that he must suffer and die with Christ in order to rise with him—that he also has to undergo much mortification and suffering to make up for his sins and to open himself perfectly to the love God has in store for him. He knows that love must be more than a humanitarian service to one's fellows, that it must also express itself in humbly asking God's help, crying out in worship, in pure, human weakness, asking to know, to be able to do God's will—and not merely his own.

The committed Christian occasionally catches a glimpse of God, even in this age when God is usually considered to have disappeared. He looks at his fellow man, and sometimes, perhaps only for an instant, sees in him something divine. He looks at nature, and on occasion it may cry out to him that there is a Creator. He occasionally has an insight, realizes in retrospect how providence has watched over him, catches a bit of meaning behind it all—and perhaps he once may have personally experienced the great, shattering peace and joy that could only be God.

He holds the conviction, sometimes only mutely and obscurely, but with deep faith, "that neither death, nor life, nor angels, nor principalities, nor things present, nor things to come, nor powers, nor height nor depth, nor anything else in all creation, will be able to separate us from the love of God in Christ Jesus our Lord" (Romans 8, 38-39).

SOME SUGGESTIONS FOR . . .

DISCUSSION

> Why should the Christian, however much he may naturally fear it, and however full life may be here and now, nevertheless have an attitude of expectation toward death?
>
> Can you understand something of what heaven must be like?
>
> What do you think sums up the way a Christian should live?

FURTHER READING

°° *Transformation of Man*, Haughton (Paulist Press)—Building

Christ Among Us

** *God, the Future of Man,* Schillebeeckx (Sheed & Ward, 1968)—Essays on the impact of Christianity for the future of man.

** *The Problem of Eschatology* (Concilium Volume)—Reinterpretation of eschatology from a biblical and historical standpoint.

* *We Are Future,* Boros (Herder & Herder, 1970)—The Christian life of hope as a transcendent creation of the future.

* *Death and Its Mysteries,* Lepp (Macmillan, 1968)—A penetrating look at the problem and mystery of the ultimate act of human existence.

* *The Other Kingdom,* Van Zeller (Templegate)—A practical book of comfort for those who mourn and don't know how to help themselves.

** *On the Theology of Death,* Rahner (Herder & Herder, Questiones Disputatae Series)—Here one of the Church's greatest theologians speaks of the peak experience of death, the epitome of our human condition, and how we are identified with Christ in it.

* *The World to Come,* Gleason (Sheed & Ward, 1958)—Though escatology has advanced quite a bit since this book was written, it yet has some highly readable, profitable reflections on life after death.

A FINAL REFLECTION

The story of Christ among us is now concluded. If you have been using this book regularly, during the past weeks you have been drawing closer to God, to Christ. In the gospels those who drew close to Christ were always changed—deeply changed.

Peter was an ordinary, simple fisherman—and he became the first leader of God's Church on earth. Mary Magdalene was a prostitute known far and wide—and she became a great saint. Judas was an ordinary businessman, and became the prototype of all traitors.

If you have been following this story faithfully, you too are changed. You have had an open mind and heart, and have been willing to risk this encounter with God. Whether you now classify yourself as a believer, an unbeliever, or one wavering between, you can be sure that you have been profoundly changed for the better—and the world has also, because of you.

May you be blessed for your generous effort!

Index

A

Abortion, wrongness of, 328-329

Abraham (or Abram), God's covenant with, 44-45; outstanding faith of, 44

Absolution, Christ's forgiveness in Penance, 303-304

Acts of the Apostles, 172

Adultery, wrongness of, 329

Advent, season of, 62

"Agape," or eucharist, 258-259

"All Souls Day," November 2, 421

Amos, prophet, 58

Angels, as traditionally conceived, 27; relevance of today, 27

Annulment, of marriage, 320-321

Anointing of the sick, as part of last rites, 417; sacrament of, 310-313

Anti-Semitism, cf. "Jews"

Apocrypha or deutero-canonical books, 164-166

Apostles, appointed leaders of Christ's Church, 135-137; original Twelve, 121-124, 135-136

Apostles Creed, ancient Christian profession of faith, 154

Ascension Thursday, 116

Ash Wednesday, 25-26

Atheists, dialogue with, 396-397; salvation of, 200

Authority, and primacy of one's conscience, 152; of apostles in Church 136-137; of bishops, 150; of pope in Church, 142-143, 150; of service within Christ's Church, 145; our attitude toward, 151-153

B

Babylon, captivity in, 58

Baptism, infants, 194-195; renewal of baptismal conversion, 201-202; sacrament of, 190-199; the majority who are not baptized, 199-201

Belief, doubts inevitable, 12-13; need to grow and deepen, 210-211

Benediction, service of, 278

Bible, aids for study of, 174; and interpreted by tradition, 166-169; and Vatican Council II, 156-157; basis of Church's teachings, 156-157; biblical story of creation, 22-23; canon of, 162; daily use of, 175; great force for Christian unity, 163; historical reliability of basic story, 21, 158-159; inspired record, 157-158; meditative reading of, 173-174; New Testament, 21; Old Testament, 21; origin and development of, 160-162; outline of, 169-172; particular type of book, 20-21; relation to sacraments, 187-188; use by Catholic Church, 162-163; use in liturgy, 172-173; various translations, 163-164; "Word" of God, 157; work of men, 157

Birth control, morality of, 330-334

Bishops, at service of Christian Community, 145; College of, 140, 143-144; leaders of local churches, 139-141; ordinary ministers of confirmation, 238; responsibility of toward whole Church, 140-141; synod of, 144; within the Church and the diocese, 140, 358-359

Blessed Trinity, indwelling presence, 97; and respect for our body, 97-98; in our liturgy, 96; mystery of, 93-96; our relationship to, 94-96

431

Body, Christ's among us in glory, 111-112; dignity of, 97-90, meaning of resurrection of, 422
Brotherhood, of all humanity, 26
Brothers, men religious, 356-357
Business dealings, Christian attitude toward, 409-410

C

Canon, of the Mass, or eucharistic prayer, 253-257
"Canonization," of saints, 366
Cardinals, 358-359
Catholic, whether or not to become, 380-381
Catholic or universal, Church of Christ, 126-128
Catholicity, of Christ's Church, 126-128; still an ideal, 128
Celibacy, of Latin rite priests, 352-353
Charisms, "Charismatic Renewal" within today's Church, 240-241; early charismatic organization of Church, 139; gifts for the service of all, 146-147; of different priests, 351; use by people of particular gifts, 235, 345-346
Charity, cf. "Love," virtue of
Chastity, vow of, 356
Children, parents primary educators of, 408-409; parents' responsibilities toward, 408
Christ, the anointed one, 59; cf. "Jesus Christ"
"Christening," baptism, 190
Christian life, and that of unbeliever, 428; as lived in marriage, 334-338; as lived in single life, 362-363; living daily of, 405-415
Christians, and scandal of poor, 401-402; concern with world's problems, 227-231; dignity of, 133, 411; divisions among, 387-397; each is special manifestation of Christ among us, 405; involvement in political and social affairs, 230-231; responsibility and privilege to bring about new universe, 424-425; the difference in being a Christian, 428-429

Christmas Day, 69; liturgy of the Christmas season, 271
Church, and the world today, 398-402; and work for world peace, 399-400; as Christ among us, 130-131, 375, 406; catholicity or universality of, 126-128; catholicity, missionary aspect, 126-128; changes within always necessary, 397-398; Christ's body, 128-132; community of people with different gifts for service of all, 146-147, 355; criteria for joining, 380-382; divineness and holiness of, 375-380; divisions among Christians, 387-398; Eastern Orthodox Churches, history of and relation to Roman Catholicism, 388-390; Ecumenical movement for unity among Christians, 393-398; frequent rejection of structures, 210; God's gifted people, 344-346; humanness of, need of continual reformation and renewal, 382-387; members help one another, 130-132; not exclusive club, 378-379; of the Old Testament, 48; organization of early Christian Church, 139-140; purpose is to serve God and world, 147; purpose of laws within, 406-407; scriptural descriptions of, 129-130; sign of hope, 379-380; some teachings more important than others, 150-151; survival and influence of, 376-377; the compassionate Church, 401-402; today's disillusionment with, 385-386; unfolding mystery of, 397; unity of, 124-126
Circumcision, sign of the covenant, 45
Collegiality, or co-responsibility of bishops and pope, 143-144
Communion, cf. "Holy Communion" at Mass
Communion of Saints, 365
Community life of Religious, 356-357
"Confession," cf. "Penance"
Confirmation, coming of Holy Spirit, 231-236; sign or ceremony of, 231-232